OLIVIER

Also by Philip Ziegler

The Duchess of Dino (1962)

Addington: A Life of Henry Addington, First Viscount Sidmouth (1965)

The Black Death (1969)

King William IV (1971)

Omdurman (1973)

*Melbourne: A Biography of William Lamb,
2nd Viscount Melbourne* (1976)

Crown and People (1978)

Diana Cooper (1981)

Mountbatten: The Official Biography (1985)

Elizabeth's Britain 1926 to 1986 (1986)

*The Diaries of Lord Louis Mountbatten 1920–1922:
Tours with the Prince of Wales* (1987) (ed.)

*Personal Diary of Admiral the Lord Louis Mountbatten, Supreme
Allied Commander South-East Asia, 1943–1946* (1988) (ed.)

The Sixth Great Power: Barings 1762–1929 (1988)

*From Shore to Shore—The Final Years: The Diaries
of Earl Mountbatten of Burma, 1953–1979* (1989) (ed.)

King Edward VIII: The Official Biography (1990)

Brooks's: A Social History (1991) (ed. with Desmond Seward)

Wilson: The Authorized Life of Lord Wilson of Rievaulx (1993)

London at War 1939–1945 (1995)

Osbert Sitwell (1998)

Britain Then and Now: The Francis Frith Collection (1999)

Soldiers: Fighting Men's Lives, 1901–2001 (2001)

*Man Of Letters: The Extraordinary Life and Times
of Literary Impresario Rupert Hart-Davis* (2005)

Edward Heath: The Authorized Biography (2010)

OLIVIER

Philip Ziegler

MacLehose Press
New York • London

MacLehose Press
An imprint of Quercus
New York • London

ISBN 978-1-62365-042-1

Library of Congress Control Number: 2013913477

Distributed in the United States and Canada by Random House Publisher Services
c/o Random House, 1745 Broadway
New York, NY 10019

Manufactured in the United States

10 9 8 7 6 5 4 3 2

www.quercus.com

To Sophie, Colin and Toby with love
and to Clare with love and gratitude

"I can add colors to the chameleon;
Change shapes with Proteus for advantages;
And set the murderous Machiavel to school"

—Henry VI, Part Three

"Rot them for a couple of rogues.
They have everyone's face but their own"

—THOMAS GAINSBOROUGH
on David Garrick and Samuel Foote

Contents

List of Illustrations

1. Olivier in 1914
2. Olivier's mother, Agnes
3. Gerard Olivier, his father
4. As Katherina in *The Taming of the Shrew*
5. Olivier at eighteen
6. As Uncle Vanya in 1927
7. With Noël Coward, Gertrude Lawrence
   and Adrianne Allen in *Private Lives*
8. Working out in 1931
9. Arriving in New York in 1933 with Jill Esmond
10. With John Gielgud and Edith Evans in *Romeo and Juliet*
11. And with Peggy Ashcroft in the same production
12. With Tarquin Olivier, his son by Jill Esmond
13. With Cherry Cottrell in *Hamlet*
14. As Sir Toby Belch in *Twelfth Night*
15. As Henry V at the Old Vic
16. As Macbeth, conceived by Michel Saint-Denis
17. With Vivien Leigh in *Romeo and Juliet*
18. With Sybil Thorndike in *Coriolanus*
19. As Heathcliff in *Wuthering Heights*
20. With Greer Garson in *Pride and Prejudice*

OLIVIER

CHAPTER ONE

BEGINNINGS

The London theater in the late spring of 1907 was not at its most refulgent. The dramatic big guns were conspicuously silent: there was no play by Shaw, no Ibsen, no Chekhov; not even a Pinero or a Maugham. The nearest approach to a modern play of serious import was Galsworthy's respectable but uninspiring *The Silver Box*. Even *The Mikado* had been banned by the Lord Chamberlain, who feared it might offend the visiting Japanese Crown Prince. Among the leading actors and actresses: Irving had died two years before, Ellen Terry was in New York, Viola Tree in Germany, Gerald du Maurier was to be seen, but in a play that *The Times* dismissed as "noisy, rackety, rubbishy tomfoolery." Marie Tempest was the only superstar doing work that enhanced her reputation.

But it was not just the paucity of great plays and players that menaced the London scene. There was a more remote but, viewed in the longer term, more ominous threat to the future of the theater. Several London theaters were interspersing plays with films; even the Old Vic showed every Saturday night "moving landscapes and seascapes" to enraptured audiences. The first theater entirely devoted to films, the Balham Empire, opened in the summer of 1907. Many more were planned: by 1914 there would be more than one hundred cinemas in Manchester alone. Could the traditional theater resist this competition? Some thought not. Within twenty-five, at the most thirty years, prophesied one pessimist, there would be no live acting on the stage in London.

Ralph Richardson had been born in 1902; John Gielgud in 1904; Laurence Kerr Olivier was born on May 22, 1907.

There was nothing in his ancestry to suggest he would take to the stage. The Oliviers were French Huguenots who had settled in Britain early in the eighteenth century. They fitted comfortably into the minor gentry or professional classes; soldiers and clergymen predominating. Laurence Olivier's uncles were a talented lot, among them a colonial governor, who became a lord, and a successful society portrait painter. Laurence saw little of them, however; his father, Gerard—"Fahv," as he was usually known in the family— was far the youngest of the siblings and also the least successful. He was expelled from Oxford, got a dismally bad degree at Durham, became a preparatory schoolmaster, opened his own school, failed to make a success of it, then switched course, was ordained and in 1904 became curate at St. Martin's, Dorking. Some years before, he had married the sister-in-law of his headmaster, Agnes Crookenden, who had hoped for a life of modest comfort as a schoolmaster's wife and instead found herself living in penury on the exiguous stipend earned by a run-of-the-mill Anglican priest.

She accepted her fate bravely. Where her husband was strident, bad-tempered and somewhat stupid, Agnes was quiet, resolute and long-suffering. She bore without complaint the burdens that life and the Rev. Mr. Olivier imposed on her and settled down to give her family as comfortable and secure a life as possible. Her eldest daughter, Sybille, was born in 1901 and a son, christened Gerard after his father but for most of his life known as Dickie, followed in 1904. Laurence was therefore much younger than his siblings, unplanned and, by his father at least, unwanted. Gerard, in the opinion of his younger son at any rate, considered Laurence a bothersome addition to a family that was satisfactorily complete without him. Sybille, whose recollections of their childhood are generally somewhat rosier than those of her younger brother, confirmed that Gerard seemed resentful of Laurence's existence. There was something about the child's seeming stolidity and baby plumpness that drove him almost to frenzy, she remembered. If Laurence was eating too slowly or too much his father would erupt: "Baby or not, he bores me and I've had enough!" He would turn on the terrified child and shout: "You! Have you finished at last? Get out!"[1]

It is only fair to the Rev. Mr. Olivier to say that Laurence, or Paddy, as he came to be called because of his explosive temper, does not seem to have been a prepossessing child. He realized that his mother would be on his side in any confrontation with his father and, according to one family friend, "learned deliberately to provoke his father's wrath in order to produce more love and attention from his mother." Perhaps in response to his father's hostility he felt an urgent need to ingratiate himself with all around him. Everyone likes to be liked, but Olivier's craving for popularity was both exaggerated and enduring. "He's coy, he's vain, he has tantrums, he needs to be wooed," said his friend and admirer Elia Kazan many years later. Still more, he needed to woo. "I had by nature a very unfortunate gift of flirtatiousness," he told Mark Amory, whose many hours of taped interviews with Olivier provide an important element of this book. He cited this as proof that he was a born actor: so he was, but it is equally possible to see it as a defense mechanism, strengthened if not created by the realization that he was being rejected by the one man from whom he had the right to expect support.[2]

He had other traits that gave his father reason to disapprove of if not dislike him, as he admitted in his autobiography. As a child, he was a compulsive liar. To conceal the truth was almost an automatic reflex. Once he touched the scorchingly hot handle of the bread-making machine, causing the dough to sink and burning himself severely. He must have known that, if he had explained what had happened, he would have received sympathy for the pain he was suffering rather than a scolding; nevertheless he clung to his story that he had never touched the machine and tried to conceal his burn. He never hesitated to lie if he thought it would bring him some advantage and showed considerable skill in practicing his mendacity. He

found it easy to convince his nursery schoolmistress that his presence was needed at home and that therefore he must leave early.[3]

The habit of lying he shed quickly, though throughout his life
he allowed himself to embroider the truth with picturesque but
invented detail. The temper that had earned him his nickname,
however, stayed with him all his life. His roar, "reminiscent of a
Bull of Bashan," which his sister remembered from his infancy, was
to reverberate for seventy years or more. His explosions were all
the more terrifying for being unpredictable. Once, dining with the
actor Laurence Harvey, he had been notably dulcet throughout the
evening. Then Harvey ridiculed in turn Ralph Richardson, John
Gielgud and Paul Scofield. Olivier erupted, "How dare you! Call
yourself an actor? You're not even a *bad* actor. You can't act at all,
you fucking, stupid, hopeless, sniveling little cunt-faced asshole!"
He then stormed out: it was as true to his character that next day
he repented and sent Harvey a bouquet of twenty-four red roses.[4]

There were other, more estimable traits that were evident in
his infancy. If he started on some enterprise he would not stop,
he would plug away at a childish puzzle until he had resolved it—
even though it was in theory intended for someone of twice his age.
Nothing would deter him. It was said that Edmund Kean, opening
in the first night of *The Merchant of Venice* in the early nineteenth
century, found himself the wrong side of the Thames without the
money for the toll and swam the river so as to get to the theater in
time. "Even if he didn't do it I'm sure, if it had been necessary, he
would have done," wrote Olivier approvingly. "As, indeed, I would.
Determination." "He was the most disciplined man I've ever met,"
said the director Franco Zeffirelli. "His discipline is the first secret
of his success . . . Steel discipline, and merciless with himself and
others—no excuses, no weakness." Translate this to life in the nursery, allow for a few childish tantrums, and the picture emerges of an
alarmingly resolute child, one who might take some time to decide
upon his course of action but who, once committed, could only
with the greatest difficulty be diverted. Looked at another way, of
course, tenacity became obstinacy. He could be infuriating, his sister

remembered: "He had a habit of saying 'No' slowly and loudly and, however much one might coax or threaten, he remained unshakeable." The Olivier "No," final and unchallengeable, would break the nerve of many an actor or director before his career was done.[5]

His mother, who seems to have been in charge of his early education, was determined that he should go to the choir school of All Saints, Margaret Street. All Saints was an Anglican church so high as to seem to its more austere neighbors dangerously tainted with the odor of Rome. It had one of the best, if not *the* best choir in London and this, coupled with the excellent reputation of the schooling, meant that there was stiff competition for places. Olivier's brother was already there, and for two years Mrs. Olivier battled to secure a place for her younger son. In the meantime the boy was subjected to a series of indifferent preparatory schools—an experience that he much disliked. The first was a boarding school in Blackheath, predominantly for girls, to which Olivier was dispatched at the age of six. He was so miserable that a kindly aunt who lived nearby had to be persuaded by the school to take him in "in case my perpetual crying should do me an injury." The tears were certainly genuine: no doubt, too, they were enhanced by that instinct toward the histrionic that so often led Olivier to turn into a performance something that otherwise might have been unexcitingly run of the mill.[6]

Finally, in 1916, at the age of nine, he was admitted to the All Saints choir school. It was soon evident that he was not going to shine as a scholar: "Handwriting poor. Spelling careless. Composition slovenly. Arithmetic disgraceful," was the harsh judgment at the end of one of his earlier terms. Things improved, but not to any great extent; the fact was that the work did not interest him and he was therefore not disposed to go to much trouble over it. The same was not true of games, where he longed to excel but lacked the talent. He was "totally inept," wrote his brother with some brutality: "Even at the tender age of twelve I had protective qualms about him coming to the school. Not only qualms on his behalf, but on my own, since I didn't fancy being embarrassed by a younger brother who didn't fit in."[7]

Where he did fit in was in the choir. Not everyone agreed. "Larry hath an ugly voice," lisped the organist. "Enormouth, yeth, my goodness yeth. But Dickie ith the really muthical one." Others were less censorious. "He has a fine voice and much ability," was the more usual verdict, and though he rarely featured as a soloist he was one of the elite who were regularly considered for the role. He had become used to ceremony in his father's church and relished the smells, bells and rich flummery at All Saints. At home, he and his brother had used to drape eiderdowns around themselves and indulge in orgies of bowing and intoning; he would have liked to do the same things at All Saints but made do with watching others perform the rituals. The music, too, he found fulfilling. The musical education was as ambitious and as rigorous as any in the country and Olivier acquired a knowledge of religious music that enriched his life. The aura of sanctity hung over All Saints. If Olivier, at this point of his life, had been asked what he proposed to do when his education was behind him he would almost certainly have replied that he intended to become a priest. He would have taken it for granted that his father held the same view. If anything this would have been a disincentive, but Olivier was not so perverse that he would have gone against his own strong inclinations just for the satisfaction of frustrating his father.[8]

But the choir school made a still more significant contribution to Olivier's future. The vicar of All Saints, Father Henry Mackay, was an energetic theatergoer and he had recruited as a master Father Geoffrey Heald. Heald was an amateur actor of distinction, both he and Mackay had friends in the theater world, and the result was that All Saints enjoyed a reputation for its acting far beyond that of most comparable schools. Heald identified Olivier as being a boy with both potential as an actor and an eagerness to perform, and Olivier responded to his encouragement with rapturous enthusiasm. "I had complete faith in this man," Olivier said many years later. "I was devoted to him, and I think he was very fond of me." Too fond, in the opinion of one of Olivier's biographers, Michael Munn, who suggested that Heald had physically molested his young pupil and left a permanent psychological scar. There is no evidence to support this and Olivier's words suggest the contrary. Far from pursuing small boys it seems that Heald's tastes were robustly heterosexual. He made something of a fool of himself a few years later when he fell in love with the actress Edna Best, star of the successful *The Constant Nymph*, and pursued her with conspicuous but unrequited zest.[9]

Heald gave Olivier his first chance to shine on the stage when he produced *Julius Caesar* in 1917. Olivier, who was only in his second year, was originally assigned the humble part of First Citizen but, in a general shuffle, was recast in the more important role of Brutus. Few nine-year-old boys can have been more acclaimed on their debut. As usual, the school had drawn a distinguished audience. The Duke of Newcastle, a prominent benefactor of All Saints, presented Olivier with a copy of *Julius Caesar* taken from his own library and inscribed "As a souvenir of the splendid performance." Johnston Forbes-Robertson, renowned actor-manager and the foremost Hamlet of his generation, wrote to Heald praising Olivier's "pathetic air of fatalism that was poignantly suggestive—remarkable in one so young." Most striking of all, Ellen Terry—in most people's view the leading actress of the age—noted in her diary that the boy who had played Brutus was "already a great actor." A year later she was still remembering his "wonderful" performance.[10]

More successful still was Olivier's last appearance at All Saints, as Katherina in *The Taming of the Shrew*. The role of the heroine in this detestable play is one of the most difficult in the Shakespearean repertoire. Olivier handled it with astonishing aplomb. Ellen Terry was there again and wrote that she had "never seen the part played as well by any woman," while the enormously influential Russian director Theodore Komisarjevsky—surely a most improbable spectator at a schoolboy performance in London?—praised "the sincerity, the seriousness and the simplicity of the acting" and in particular acclaimed the "especially impressive Katherina."

He was "wonderful—a bad-tempered little bitch," remembered
Sybil Thorndike, who was then in the early stages of her resplen-
dent theatrical career, "and he looked just like his mother in the
part—gypsy-like." Sybille too remarked how closely he modeled
Katherina on their mother—not in personality, because there had
been nothing shrewish about Agnes Olivier, but in her manner of
speech and her movements. Their father came to one of the performances, "and he had to get up and leave, so shaken was he to see
Larry recreating Mother down to the last detail."[11]

It was recreation because, after a brief illness, Agnes Olivier had
died in 1920. For any twelve-year-old boy the death of a mother
must be a fearful blow; for Olivier, frightened and remote from his
father and, as a result, cherished with particular determination by
the warm-hearted and affectionate Agnes, it seemed that his world
had been obliterated. He was given the news by Father Heald, wept
briefly, then remained dry-eyed. Throughout his life he was given to
extravagant displays of grief or joy; this was one of the few occasions
in which he did not externalize his emotions. "I've been looking for
her ever since," he remembered many years later. "I can't think I've
ever loved anybody quite as much . . . My mother was my life really,
she was my entire world." Olivier believed that, dreadful though it
was, the experience fortified him for the future; others might feel
that it extinguished in him the capacity for unequivocal love, the
lack of which impoverished his emotional existence. The biographer is well advised to avoid glib psychological pronouncements,
but it is difficult not to feel that the loss of his mother when he was
at his most vulnerable did do him lasting damage. His personal loss
may, of course, have been the world's gain. The deprivation that he
endured may in itself have been an important factor in shaping the
personality of that most complete of actors.[12]

He was sustained by the support of his brother and sister. Fifty
years later he was to reproach his own children for their perpetual
bickering. "It's so hard for me to understand you three," he said. "My
family was the happiest family ever in the world. We all absolutely
adored and worshipped each other." Things can hardly have been

as rapturous as that, but Sybille and Dickie stood by their younger brother and restored to him some of the sense of intimacy and belonging of which his mother's death had deprived him. Sybille in particular assumed many of the responsibilities of a mother. Agnes Olivier's last words had been "Be kind to Larry." Her husband paid them scant attention; Sybille took them to heart and did her best to obey them.[13]

By now Olivier's time at All Saints was almost finished. "His work has improved and he is taking more pains," the report for the Lent term 1921 noted approvingly. He had been made a monitor, "which will, I hope, help to develop a stronger sense of responsibility." Evidently it did. "A most satisfactory term," recorded his final report. "He has proved quite efficient as a monitor and has developed considerably. He is a very nice boy and we shall miss him greatly." The boys were not all as enthusiastic. "He was not altogether a nice boy . . ." one contemporary remembered, "a bit of a bully." "No one could trust him to be constant," another complained. "He would be your great pal one day, and then turn round and try to humiliate you the next." Physically, he had a long way to go. "He was thin and bony with knobbly matchsticks for legs," remembered one boy of his generation. His hair grew low out of his forehead that, combined with his thick eyebrows, "gave him a decidedly mole-like appearance." Such photographs of him as survive are less unflattering: he seems an obviously good-looking child. But he was naturally ungainly: when he played games he was "as awkward as a cow trying to balance on a wire," the future actor Laurence Naismith remembered. Olivier himself was dissatisfied by his appearance and uneasy about his standing with the other boys. He was inclined to slink furtively around the edge of groups, reluctant to draw attention to himself yet wishing to be close to the heart of things.[14]

On the whole, though, he had enjoyed his time at All Saints. His elder brother had moved on to Rugby and it had been his mother's hope that Larry would follow him. Perhaps, if she had lived, he would have done so—her small private income made a substantial contribution to the family's financial situation—but left to himself the Rev. Gerard concluded that he could not afford it. Instead he settled for St. Edward's, Oxford, a school that admitted clergymen's sons at a preferential rate of £60 a year and, as a result, boasted a disproportionate number of clerical offspring among its 230 pupils. The high moral tone that one might have hoped this would produce was sadly lacking: all minor public schools have their ups and downs and St. Edward's in 1921 was not at its best. Kenneth Grahame, author of *The Wind in the Willows*, was one of the few old boys of distinction. No dispassionate observer surveying the school at that period would have been likely to predict that many of the current vintage would join him in the halls of fame. In fact, as well as Olivier, the school boasted the future fighter-pilot hero Douglas Bader. Bader, who was two years younger, was imprudent enough to push Olivier under the water in the school swimming pool. Olivier complained to the President of his form room that Bader had been "intolerably saucy." Bader was beaten and Olivier was allowed to administer two of the strokes. "I simply loathed myself," he remembered. "I didn't hurt him at all, of course; he just got up, grinned and left." Bader bore no grudge but soon afterward got his own back by bowling Olivier for a duck in a cricket match where four runs were needed for victory and the last man was in. It was an incident typical of an undistinguished athletic career. Olivier longed to be good at cricket, but never rose above the Fifth XI. In his last year he took to rowing, but had left it too late to make any real mark. "I wish to God that I'd been a wet bob. I adored it," he maintained, but though his eldest son was one day to be successful as an oarsman it does not seem likely that Olivier's own failure to take it up deprived British rowing of any significant talent.[15]

According to Olivier at least, discipline at St. Edward's had been neglected and the boys, in effect, were left to their own devices. Those devices were often mischievous. "It was a terrible school," recalled a contemporary of Olivier's whose father had been a master there. "The boys ran the school and it was quite horrific." The Rugby of *Tom Brown's School Days* may have been a little turbulent, but, at least in Olivier's view, it was a proper public school. At St. Edward's: "I felt unhappy and awkward and misplaced . . . I hated it all the time." He convinced himself that he was disliked by the other boys and, by behaving as if he were, succeeded at least in part in making it true. Probably he exaggerated his misery. In Bader's view he was not in the least unpopular: "He was perhaps introspective, lived within himself, and he had the sort of artistic makeup that might have made him *think* he was unpopular." In his own eyes, however, his period at St. Edward's was both unpleasant and a waste of time. The sooner he could escape from it the better.[16]

In fact the schooling cannot have been as bad as all that. It was at St. Edward's that Olivier learned the value and satisfaction of hard work. "A man's prime interest in life must be his work," he told his first wife many years later. He did not find the work at St. Edward's congenial, nor was he well suited to it, but he buckled down. He was not a notably clever boy but was endowed by nature with an extraordinarily retentive memory that, for a schoolboy faced with examinations, is quite as valuable as intellectual powers. To his mild surprise he won the Senior History Prize and was rewarded with a handsome copy of Kipling's *Kim*; nothing sensational as academic achievements go but proving that he could more than hold his own.[17]

It was curious that he tried to avoid featuring in the one field in which he felt confident he could excel. When it was suggested that he might act in the school play, he refused. He believed it would make him still more unpopular; already, he complained, he was known as "that sidey little shit Olivier"; if he seized the limelight on the stage his reputation would be still worse. This may not have been the whole story: the master in charge of the school plays had taken against him and it seems that the antipathy was mutual. Whatever the explanation, his resistance was overcome. He agreed that he would act in *A Midsummer Night's Dream* and was assigned the role of Puck. It was typical of him that, having finally accepted that he must play, he at once began to deplore the inadequacy of his role. "This dismally wretched part, this utterly hopeless, so-called opportunity," he stormed. It was as typical that he resolved to make something special of it. He flung himself into the role and, in a way that was going to become maddeningly familiar to fellow performers over the next sixty years, attracted attention far greater than his part would have been expected to command. "By far the most notable performance," judged the school magazine. "He seemed to put more 'go' into it than the others." "He was the only one in the cast who was really exciting—a born actor," a fellow schoolboy recalled. Contrary to his fears his success earned him popularity; his last months at St. Edward's were relatively happy.[18]

They had need to be, for his life at home, such as it was, was fast disintegrating. His sister Sybille had gone on the stage. It soon became clear that her talents were limited and that she would never make a successful actress. Her father deplored her failure and was still more disapproving when, without his blessing, she married a man whom he felt unsuitable. Laurence Olivier became involved in her disgrace; his father discovered that he had known of the affair, but had failed to report it. Dickie was not there to share the blame since he had left home to plant tea in India. To cap it all, the Rev. Gerard remarried. "I didn't feel sore on my mother's behalf," Olivier recalled many years later, "because I knew my mother was saint enough to wish him to be happy. He was very miserable and dreadfully lonely." It seems that at the time Olivier was rather less accepting. Sybille wrote that her brother resented the affection that their father lavished on his new wife. "Really, the old man is impossible," Olivier would grumble. "Why can't he think of *our* feelings sometimes?" Fortunately his new stepmother, Isabel or "Ibo" as she was generally known, was a woman of generosity and perception who understood Olivier's feelings and sympathized with them. Thanks to her, the atmosphere at home was not insufferable, but Olivier was still anxious to escape from it as soon as possible. He was now seventeen. It was time to decide the pattern of his future life.[19]

Up till then he had assumed, without thinking very much about it, that he would follow his father into the church. He was still a firm believer and attached great importance to regular attendance, but he had by now concluded that he did not have a sufficiently strong vocation to take the plunge. In one account of his feelings at the time he says that he contemplated following his brother to India; elsewhere, he says that he considered the possibility of an Asian exile but rejected it. Whichever may have been true, it seems to have come as a complete surprise to him when one evening the question of his future life came up and he mentioned the possibility of a career abroad. "Don't be such a fool," said his father: "You're going on the stage!" "Am I?" stammered Olivier. "Well, of course you are."[20]

His father had decided not only on Olivier's career, but also on how he was to equip himself for it. Olivier was to go to the Central School of Speech Training and Dramatic Art, an institution where his sister Sybille had studied some years before and which was run by a formidable lady called Elsie Fogerty. There was a snag, however. No money was available to cover the cost of his tuition. Olivier would have to secure not only a scholarship but an additional bursary as well, so as to pay for his upkeep. He trailed off to the Albert Hall where Miss Fogerty was selecting her future scholars. In the innumerable auditions that he was to endure through his acting life Olivier almost always chose Mark Antony's speech over the corpse of Julius Caesar, but for this first effort he offered Jacques's "All the world's a stage" from *As You Like It*. He rendered this with immense fervor and much gesticulation—too much so in Miss Fogerty's view. It was not necessary, she observed, to make fencing passes when delivering the words "sudden and quick in quarrel." Nevertheless she liked what she heard: the scholarship was Olivier's and, after some debate, an additional bursary was thrown in as well.[21]

The emphasis in the Central School was much more on Speech Training than Dramatic Art. Peggy Ashcroft, who joined the same term as Olivier (rarely can any drama school have welcomed two such talented recruits at the same time), went so far as to say that the teaching of acting was virtually nonexistent. So far as speech went, however, Miss Fogerty's training proved invaluable. It provided the foundation for a lifetime's achievement. Olivier throughout his career was famed for his breath control. "Larry has a longer breath than anybody I know," said Sybil Thorndike. "He could do the Matins exhortation 'Dearly Beloved Brethren' twice through in one breath. Lewis [her husband, Sir Lewis Casson] could do it in one and a half." To be able fully to control one's voice is not necessarily the most important element in acting, but without it all the other elements will be irreparably diminished. Olivier's powers were phenomenal. His ability was innate, but it was Miss Fogerty's early training that developed it.[22]

Not everyone was as perceptive as Miss Fogerty. One teacher is said to have written to Olivier's father urging him to withdraw his son: "He's no good. He looks like a farm boy." His appearance, indeed, still verged on the uncouth. His hair grew down to his brow, he had buck teeth. Miss Fogerty disconcerted him by putting the tip of her finger at the base of his hairline and running it down to the top of his nose. "You have a weakness *here*," she pronounced. Olivier attributes to this gnomic utterance his passion for disguise: for many years at least, he was ill at ease with his own appearance and sought to conceal it with false noses or other such devices.[23]

Uncouth or not, his talent was obvious. Together with Peggy Ashcroft he won the gold medal for best actor of the year. They performed a scene from *The Merchant of Venice* for the benefit of Athene Seyler, the celebrity imported for the occasion to award the prizes. According to Olivier, Ashcroft played Portia. Miss Seyler remembered it rather differently. Olivier was growing a beard for the part of Shylock "and Peggy, who was also playing a man, put on a false beard—so these two young people both looked idiotic. I couldn't tell, of course, how good they were." At all events, Olivier graduated with a First Class Dramatic Certificate adorned by a star.

It was a satisfactory end to his education. Now it remained to put that education to good use. He had no doubts or inhibitions. Whether or not he had been taken by surprise by his father's announcement that he was to go on the stage, he had, he told Peter Hall many years later, wanted to be an actor from the age of nine. Now the dream had become reality. From that moment his ambitions were boundless. "Don't you realize?" he blurted out to a friend. "I want to be the greatest actor in the world."[24]

CHAPTER TWO

APPRENTICE DAYS

In 1977 Olivier received a letter from an American admirer asking for advice on how to become an actor. Before going any further, he replied, "please inquire the employment rate against total membership of Equity in your country. In my country it is about 2 percent, or 800 out of 25,000." With gloomy relish he passed on the same message to any of his children who contemplated taking to the stage: going on to say that even of those who got a job only a handful could make a decent living from their activities.[1]

His own career was very different, but even he had some tough years at the start. He had been lucky enough to find employment of a sort during the holidays from the Central School at a playhouse in Letchworth Garden City. Most of his work was behind the scenes as second assistant stage manager—when you hear the bell ring at the end of the intermission, he proudly told the family's old cook, "you will know, *my finger will be on it!*" In his second spell at Letchworth he did manage to sneak onto the stage in the inconsiderable role of Lennox in *Macbeth*, but though he extolled the significance of this experience when he began to haunt the offices of theatrical agents, it did not seem unduly to impress potential employers. Olivier recalled those first two years with horror, blended with profound relief that they were well behind him: "They were awful, awful, awful," he remembered, and he was "hungry, hungry, hungry, a glass of milk for lunch, sandwich at a coffee stall for dinner." His father rather grudgingly allowed him a few pounds a week, so starvation was averted, but at times even *his* ebullient self-confidence burned low. His first job as a fully-fledged professional was at the Brighton Hippodrome in the summer of 1925. Suffused by the excitement of the occasion he ignored the warnings of stage hands and fellow actors that he should take great care when emerging from the wings, strode onto the stage, tripped over the concealed sill and fell flat on his face. He prided himself on being able to exploit any situation for as much humor as it could contain, but never, he recorded, "have I heard a sound so explosively loud as the joyous clamor made by that audience."[2]

A few months later Olivier secured a job playing small parts in a touring company called the Lena Ashwell Players. They tended to end up in dismal venues around the outer London suburbs, sometimes performing in boarded-over swimming pools and changing in the lavatories, but Miss Ashwell took her work with great seriousness. Unfortunately Olivier did not or rather, though he pursued his career with dedication, he had a strong inclination to clown. Throughout his life he found almost irresistible the impulse to raise a laugh. With experience he learned to indulge this weakness only when no mischief would thereby be done; in his early days on the stage he felt no such inhibitions. After all, he told himself, Edmund Kean when young had been notorious for his delight in tripping up his fellow actors; what was good enough for Kean was good enough for Olivier. Alan Webb, a fellow sufferer in the company, remembered saying to him one night: "Larry, if you don't take your work more seriously, you'll never get on." He never took his work lightly, but it was fun to play the fool. He cut a hole in the back-cloth so as to expose the naked bottoms of the female members of the cast changing behind the scenes; helpless with laughter, he abandoned one of his colleagues on the stage when the actor's underpants fell down beneath his toga. Twenty years later, his wrath would have been terrible if some small-part actor at the Old Vic had behaved so irresponsibly; in 1925 he felt aggrieved when Miss Ashwell expelled him from her company.[3]

Once again he was looking for a job. He was offered the chance of joining a Shakespearean company touring the provinces, run by a "well-known queer." Though in later life he was considered by some to be first and foremost a Shakespearean actor, at the time he felt no particular calling in that direction: "I just wanted to get on and I didn't care what in." He had no objection to the idea, however, and the sexual proclivities of the director mattered nothing to him. He had no urge to indulge in homosexuality himself, but he never saw anything reprehensible in the practice and was always ready to work with those who had other tastes. He consulted Lewis Casson about the proposition. Whether it was Shakespeare, the provinces or the queerness that displeased him, Casson dismissed the idea out of hand. "I think you'd better come to us," he said.[4]

"Us" was a company run by Casson and Sybil Thorndike that the previous year had enjoyed a triumph with Thorndike's rendering of Shaw's *Saint Joan*. It was a splendid opportunity, and Olivier seized it with gratitude and alacrity. He played no role of any importance while he was with the company; indeed, he was involved as much in stage management as in acting, but he was associating with actors of the first rank and learning all the time. One of his two roles was that of a serving man in *Henry VIII*. Together with Carol Reed, the future film director, he had to hold up the train of Queen Katharine, played by Sybil Thorndike. Both men were in love with the already successful actress Angela Baddeley and their devotion sometimes interfered with their performance. "Calf love," wrote Thorndike dismissively. "They used to quarrel like mad. I used to say: 'You shut up, you two, and attend to what you're doing.'" But she was struck by Olivier's abilities and was convinced that he had a considerable future. It was the quality and range of his voice that most impressed her: "Larry didn't have any formal musical education, but his family background was musical, and that must have helped."[5]

The Cassons knew that there was not much opportunity for Olivier to forward his career within their company and they encouraged him to look elsewhere. In particular they urged him to try his luck with the Birmingham Repertory Company. This was the leading provincial theater of the country. It was run by Barry Jackson, a rich man, devoted to the theater, adventurous in his tastes, ready to

put on plays by Pirandello and Ibsen at a time when such dramatists were viewed nervously by London managements. Jackson had
fostered the careers of Cedric Hardwicke, Gwen Ffrangcon-Davies,
Felix Aylmer, Leslie Banks; it was, said Bernard Shaw, "a place where
all genuine artists have found themselves happily at home." Olivier
knew that to secure a job there would be an important step forward
in his career. On March 8, 1926, shortly after the closing of *Henry
VIII*, he secured an interview with Jackson. It went well. He was
not immediately offered a permanent place at Birmingham but was
invited to play a small but significant role in a play by the fashionable French dramatist, Henri Ghéon. His foot was in the door.[6]

The two years or so that Olivier spent with the Birmingham Rep.
changed the whole course of his career and, more immediately evident, his physical appearance. Olivier had gone to Birmingham as
a gangling young man, almost uncouth, with too much hair in the
wrong place and spindly, inadequate legs. "My mouth is like a tortoise's ass," he once complained. "It's an absolute slit. I have a very,
very mean mouth." He exaggerated his physical deficiencies, if only
to point up the improvement that he had later brought about, but in
1926 he had a long way to go. One of his closest friends was Denys
Blakelock, whose mother once referred to the young Olivier as "very
plain." She was right, commented Blakelock, "he had teeth that were
set too far apart and eyebrows that grew thickly and without shape
across his nose. He had a thatch of unmanageable hair that came
far forward in a kind of widow's peak, and his nose was a broad
one." Not much could be done about the shape of the nose and the
mouth but the hair was refashioned and, at some expense and with
a lot of pain, the teeth were fixed. No longer would a director say
that his hair made him look "bad-tempered, almost Neanderthal";
by the time he left Birmingham it had been groomed into the glossy
splendor that was to be the delight of several generations of wor-
shippers. More significantly, and with far greater effort, he recreated
his body. By a grueling program of exercises, much long-distance
running and rigid dieting, he built up his strength and acquired the

muscular arms and legs for which he was striving. He never wholly satisfied himself. "He always said his legs were a problem," remarked his dresser many years later. "I thought they were very good legs, a bit on the thin side but well shaped." Olivier would have accepted that they were better than they used to be, but that was not enough. William Gaskill, the director, said he had never met an actor so concerned about his physical appearance. No man so obsessed with his own appearance can be acquitted on a charge of vanity, but Olivier was not seeking beauty just for beauty's sake. If he was going to be the greatest actor in the world then everything must be subordinated to that quest: perfection was the aim and the perfecting of his appearance was an essential element in the crusade.[7]

It was while he was at Birmingham that any last doubts about his destined career were put to rest. He suspected already that it was only in acting that he would find complete fulfillment, but the fact remained that he had been offered few opportunities to show off his talents and that such success as he had achieved had been in the role of stage manager. He enjoyed that work and took pride in doing it well. Was it possible, he wondered, that this was to be his destiny? "It staggers me a little," he wrote in his autobiography, "that I could ever have nursed such thoughts." They were soon put behind him. It took only a handful of performances with the Birmingham Rep. to convince him that there could be no second best; he must be an actor, nothing else would be acceptable. Quite why he felt so certain he never knew. Something irresistible was driving him forward. "I've got an awful feeling," he confessed, "that that thing is a little voice saying 'Look at me! Look at me! Don't look at anybody else, look at me!'"[8]

It was a perceptive and revealing comment. A craving to be at the center of attention was indeed a prominent element in Olivier's personality. But this was not the whole story. He wanted to be admired in the part he was playing, not for being Laurence Olivier. Some actors, whatever their role, remain always themselves. Olivier longed never to be himself. "I had a silly little ambition when I was at the Birmingham Rep. not to be recognizable from one part to another, either in looks, voice, walk, behavior, anything." He wanted people to say: "That can't be the young man we saw last night." He would not admit that there was any part he could not play yet did not want there to be any one part for which he was obviously destined. He disliked being compared with other actors, however flattering the analogy. When he was young he had kept a photograph of Henry Irving in his bedroom: admiring not so much Irving's acting as the way that he had become the figurehead of his profession and had enhanced the standing of the theater in British life. But he did not wish to be compared with Irving. He was irritated when he heard a fellow actor's rendering of Lear praised by a gushing admirer, "You were just like the Old Man"—as Irving was known to his fans. "I came to a decision. I vowed to eradicate all knowledge of the Old Man from the public's memory forever. I was determined to become the Old Man myself." But he did not suppose that this would come easily. Work, more work, and yet more work, would be essential. He compared himself with Margaret Leighton. "She does everything quite naturally. It took me two years to walk around a chair with ease; it took me another two years to learn how to laugh on stage— and I had to learn everything. What to do with my hands, how to cry . . ." By the time he went to Birmingham he had already learned a lot; into the next two years he crowded what, for most people, would have been the experience of a lifetime.[9]

It was an indication of the Birmingham Rep's importance to the British theater that both Peggy Ashcroft and Ralph Richardson were there at the same time as Olivier. Richardson was some five years older than Olivier and felt himself immeasurably superior; he considered Olivier gauche, cocky and inclined to overrate his talents. Olivier for his part thought Richardson ponderous and smug. For several months they coexisted frostily, then came the thaw. It was mainly Olivier's doing. Once he had decided that he wanted to be friendly with somebody he was difficult to resist. He was most excellent company; an accomplished raconteur, a brilliant mimic, not a sophisticated wit like Noël Coward but bursting with exuberant vitality. He was the greatest fun to be with. He was at his happiest when holding the floor but was wise enough to realize that, if one wanted to retain an audience, one had to be prepared to listen too. The fact that he was absorbed by his own activities did not prevent him from being fascinated by other people and their preoccupations. He wanted to know how the men and women he met in his daily life had got where they were and in what direction they were hoping to progress. In a way they were all raw material on which he would draw for his own performances, but he was curious about them for their own sake too. Once he spent more than twenty minutes in the cloakroom of the Savoy. His surprised companion asked what he had been doing. He had, said Olivier, discovered that the attendant was a Hungarian refugee and had been talking to him about the problems involved in a life of exile.

Once the ice was broken between Olivier and Richardson they became the closest of friends. Richardson, said his biographer, found Olivier "warm and affectionate, a wonderful companion, blessed with a gaiety of heart." "I have never ceased to laugh my head off with him," Richardson himself remarked. Their mutual affection endured: "It was heart-warming to see Ralph so content in your company," wrote Richardson's wife, Meriel Forbes, after the two men had spent an evening together sometime in the late 1970s. Olivier, who searched always for an affectionate diminutive, called Richardson "Ralphie"; Richardson, who deplored informality, was one of the few people to address Olivier as "Laurence"; the two men were admirably matched. There was mutual admiration, too. "Larry had a lot of time for Ralphie," wrote Olivier's occasional mistress, Sarah Miles. "I had the impression he respected him more than any other actor." It was said that Olivier begrudged giving praise to any- one whom he deemed a serious rival. There are many instances to the contrary. Of Richardson in particular Olivier said that he was "marvelous. . . . He was a thoroughly excellent actor, exemplary to other actors. We all used to worship at his shrine." Of *Henry IV* Olivier wrote that he was thrilled by "Ralphie's really heavenly and superb performance. This is the Falstaff that I have always dreamed about." Over the years there were plenty of less laudatory comments as well, but that Olivier rated Richardson high in the pantheon of twentieth-century acting cannot be questioned.[10]

Richardson was not the only member of the Birmingham Rep. to take immediate exception to Olivier. Eileen Beldon, six years older than Olivier and reasonably well established, found him "obnoxious. He was slovenly and high falutin'. Of course I realize now," she added forgivingly, "that he was just a young boy trying to prove himself." Most of the other women in the company seem to have found his failings endearing rather than repulsive. Another actress, Jane Welsh, concluded that he was "an astonishing mix of boy and man. Many of us wanted to both love him and mother him." He was brash, he was noisy, he was patently ambitious, he could be alarmingly insensitive, but there was no malice in him and his eagerness to please and to make friends with all the world was disarmingly evident to all except the most embittered.[11]

However great his ambitions, he was still insignificant. In the program for the first production in which he appeared under the flag of the Birmingham Rep. "Olivier" is spelled incorrectly— a bit better than in his first appearance in Brighton, where he featured as "Lawrence Oliver," but still not suggesting he was a household name. The play was *The Marvelous History of Saint Bernard*. He somewhat euphemistically described his role in it as "small but fairly telling." It was certainly small. Nor did the play's course run smooth. His diary entry for May 3, 1926, read "STRIKE ??!" The General Strike closed the theaters. Olivier put on his most country-gentleman plus-fours and sallied out to do his bit. "The luck of it!" he observed. "The show shuts with a bang and I have a gorgeous time helping run Underground trains . . . and the loveliest debs in all London giving you food at the canteens. Then, just when I've had everything possible out of banging doors on trains . . . the strike ends, the show goes on again, and back I go fresh as a daisy!" On the whole those in the theatrical world tend to be at least mildly left-wing in their political views. In his autobiography Olivier mentioned that he was frequently told he had backed the wrong side in the General Strike; he should have been supporting the workers, not helping to break their strike. No doubt he listened with courtesy to such comments and may even have given the impression that he accepted the opinion of his critics: he took little interest in politics and was always anxious to fit in with whatever company he was keeping. But by nature he was conservative. In a letter addressed to "Comrade Laurenski," Ralph Richardson's wife told Olivier: "Nothing that you can say can convince Ralphie that you are other than A TRUE BLUE CAPITALIST who will fight with him to the last Bentley." Ralphie was right. Olivier voted Tory in 1945, the one election when many committed Conservatives strayed to the Left. In 1926 it never occurred to him not to identify himself with the traditional ruling classes and do what he could to keep the country running.[12]

He won his permanent place in the Birmingham Rep. by securing a part in a tour of Eden Phillpotts's successful rustic comedy *The Farmer's Wife*. It was "a sheer revel of wholesome laughter," judged a local paper: Olivier was not mentioned in the review, but the accompanying photograph showed him in a clinch with the leading lady. He anyway did well enough to earn Barry Jackson's approval. In the course of the next twelve months he appeared in fifteen plays: a grueling but enormously valuable experience. His parts became steadily more important. "I was terribly promising," said Olivier. "I was considered the most promising actor they'd had for years and so they risked things on me." One of the most remarkable risks was to entrust him with the title role in *Uncle Vanya*, giving a nineteen-year-old boy a part specified in the text as being for a man of forty-seven. A "brave and compelling" performance, judged the *Birmingham Post*. It marked the start of a lifelong devotion to Chekhov, curious in a man who in his character seemed the polar opposite to the typical male of Chekhovian drama. "Once one has experienced the gift of his marvelously poetic realism," he wrote to a Russian correspondent, "it must of course exist to a certain extent in almost all one's dramatic deliberation." His status as a director was to be a matter of controversy, but when Chekhov was in question no one doubted Olivier's masterly touch.[13]

In 1928 Barry Jackson moved for a season to the Royal Court in London. The next few months established Olivier as an important player on the London stage. "Most people from the Rep. took advantage of being in London to have a good time," wrote Jackson. "Not Larry! While other performers were out carousing in London pubs he would be back in the empty dressing rooms reading aloud from this, that or the next play. He became monkish about it." His reward was to be offered by far his most substantial part to date, that of the Saxon King in Tennyson's monumental, and monumentally dull epic *Harold*. John Gielgud had hoped to be given the part and, being far better established than Olivier, seemed the clear favorite, but Olivier had the effrontery to insert a three-minute speech from *Harold* into the previous play in the repertoire, Shaw's *Back to Methuselah*. Jackson, it seems, must have been both amused by Olivier's cheek and impressed by his delivery. The part was his.[14]

Not everyone envied him. Richardson remarked that there was "a distinct absence of normal jockeying among the Rep.'s actors to get the part . . . Everyone was afraid of the role because of its ponderousness and the ponderousness of the play itself. But not Larry. He was aching for a lead role." Apart from anything else, the part was dauntingly long. "It would have taken over a month to get a part like Harold down to the point where I could do a rehearsal without help," said Richardson. "Larry did it in a week and was letter perfect. He was a 'genius' when it came to learning lines, better than any of the rest of us."[15]

He must have wondered whether the effort had been worthwhile. It was by far the best rewarded role of his career to date—he was paid a princely £20 a week—but the play appealed neither to the critics nor the public. To make matters worse, the first night coincided with the opening of *Gentlemen Prefer Blondes*, an option preferred by most of the leading critics. When they did get round to *Harold* they for the most part damned the play, but were cautiously approving of Olivier. One of the most important critics of the period, St. John Ervine in the *Observer*, said that he was "excellent on the whole. His faults are those of inexperience rather than those of ineffectiveness." But Harold Hobson in the *Christian Science Monitor* struck a cautionary note that Olivier was to remember in a few years' time. "He might improve his delivery of blank verse . . ." wrote Hobson. "We do not want the beautiful and pleasing art of verse-speaking to pass everywhere from our stage."[16]

The monkishness remarked by Jackson was more apparent than real; like many monks Olivier was not immune to the temptations of the flesh. From childhood, wrote his sister, he had been prone to fall in love—he was always returning home saying: "Clare is so pretty, Mommy," or "I love Sarah. She has such sweet little teeth." With adolescence, admiration became desire; he hungered for sex but, for religious reasons, felt that his lust should not be indulged except in marriage. The result was frustration and a determination to get married before common sense might have told him he was financially or emotionally ready to do so. But though sex was important it was always clear to him that it must not be all-important. His career came first. "Don't let your romantic fantasies disturb your life," he was to advise his son Tarquin. "You see, these wild horses, that natural instincts are, are things that you must be sure to have control over. See that the *reins* are firmly in your *hands*. Don't let them take you where they will, because they don't know what's good for you, or care . . . Just remember that all the romantic ecstasies, all the rosy reveries, the stoppings of the heart when the phone rings, all the existing and bewitching variations of love's sweet dreams that mankind is subject to, are basically, simply and solely, wicked old Dame Nature's cold-blooded, calculated bribe to bring children into the world." Except perhaps for the first few years of his relationship with Vivien Leigh, Olivier *did* keep the reins firmly in his hands. Those who believe that love must conquer all will view his attitude as timorous and cold-blooded. No doubt there was a lack of true romance about his approach to sex. But the theatrical life of Britain might have been impoverished if his priorities had been different.[17]

Be that as it may, Olivier was in quest of a wife before he was twenty-one. Peggy Ashcroft claimed that he was on the point of proposing to her when a lavatory flushing in the next room made the gesture seem inappropriate. The opportunity did not occur again. He claimed that he was "madly in love" with Dorothy Turner, a fellow member of the Birmingham Rep., but she had neither money nor connections and the madness did not stretch to making so unpropitious a match. Then he found himself playing opposite Jill Esmond, an actress a few months younger than him but better established in the theater. Her father had written a number of successful comedies, her mother had acted in many of them. Her father was now dead; his widow, Eva Moore, lived in considerable comfort, if not affluence, in a large house in Berkshire. She still enjoyed many useful connections in the theatrical world and decided that Olivier had a future and would make an excellent husband for her daughter. Jill was of the same opinion and, without too much reflection, Olivier agreed. Jill was pretty, she was amusing and intelligent, she was a strong personality, inclined to be bossy, but not letting this show in the first throes of a new relationship. Olivier was not "madly in love," but he was quite ready to tell himself he was: "With those antecedents," he explained in his autobiography, "though not *dazzlingly* attractive, she would most certainly do excellent well for a wife." This sounds, indeed was, somewhat cold-blooded. "I suppose, unconsciously, I used all my wives to further my journey up the ladder," he admitted to Sarah Miles. "Something in me is lacking. No ability to love just for the sake of it . . ."[18]

Jill Esmond, whether or not she detected something less than passionate in Olivier's wooing, was not going to be rushed into any rash commitment. Instead, she took advantage of the fact that the play in which she was then appearing was transferred to New York, to put the Atlantic between herself and her putative lover. Olivier was left to his own devices. There were several possibilities to choose between. In December 1928 he was asked to take the leading part in an unknown play by an unknown playwright being put on for a couple of performances at one of the Sunday Play Societies that then proliferated in London. The hope was that it would catch the eye of a producer and be transferred to a West End theater.

Olivier recognized the merits of his part, but he did not have high hopes for the play as a whole. The author went to a rehearsal and found Olivier looking "bored and restless. I got the feeling that he was wishing he hadn't come." He was right, when a more promising possibility turned up Olivier jumped ship with alacrity. The author was R. C. Sherriff; the play, *Journey's End*, ran for two years and is still frequently revived today. To make Olivier's chagrin still sharper, the actor who replaced him, Colin Clive, was deemed to have made a great success. The *Daily Mail* quoted the play's director as saying: "In point of fact it is my opinion that Clive is far the better of the two actors in the part. We were never entirely happy with Mr. Olivier."[19]

As to the more promising possibility, it turned sour. P. C. Wren's adventure story of the French Foreign Legion, *Beau Geste*, had been an immense success as a film, with Ronald Colman playing the hero. Olivier had seen it in Birmingham and had appeared that evening with his hair cut in Colman style and a little mustache painted in. "I'm going to play *Beau Geste* when we get to London," he announced. When the book was reworked for the stage the leading role in it was eagerly sought after: "I was the envy of all the juveniles there were; it was *the* part." But they could not recapture the spectacle and excitement of the film. Olivier began to feel doubts before the rehearsals were far advanced. Possibly they affected his performance. Basil Dean, the director, was unimpressed. "For Christ's sake, boy, show us some charm!" he shouted. It was "a horrible bit of cruelty," thought Olivier, but he took the order to heart: "I was always very good at accepting criticism." He showed some charm, but it was not enough; the play failed to grip the audience and soon closed. "It wasn't much of a piece of work," Olivier reflected. But he accepted that part of the blame was his. "I hadn't sufficient star quality," he admitted. He still had some way to go before he could match Ronald Colman as a romantic swashbuckler.[20]

He was now offered the chance of pursuing Jill Esmond to New York. The play in which he was to appear, a trivial thriller called *Murder on the Second Floor*, proved a failure; he himself got some pleasant reviews, but not enough to give him any sort of established position on the American scene. He enjoyed himself extravagantly, however; loved the buzz and hectic excitement of New York life; better still, persuaded Jill Esmond to agree to an engagement. The marriage did not last, but the affection for New York, indeed for the United States, never faltered. He was always British in his loyalties, never contemplated settling in Hollywood or anywhere else abroad, but every time he set foot in the United States it was with the expectation that something interesting and unexpected was bound to happen and that it would almost certainly be good. One of his few complaints was about the American press. When he arrived in New York a journalist asked him whether he did not agree that Katharine Cornell was the greatest living actress. He answered that he much admired her, but he but would hesitate to put her above such fine British actresses as Edith Evans or Peggy Ashcroft. "Unknown British actor thinks Cornell stinks," was the banner headline the following day. Olivier resolved that in the future any journalist, British or American, but particularly American, should be treated with circumspection as a potential enemy.[21]

Back in London he at last found a part in a worthwhile play. In *The Last Enemy* he played a shell-shocked survivor of the Royal Flying Corps. "I'm awfully glad Larry has another job," Jill Esmond told her mother. "He's the luckiest fellow I know." When his luck ran out after ten weeks—not because audiences were lacking but because the theater was booked for another production—he could congratulate himself on some outstanding reviews. *The Last Enemy*, he wrote, with that curiously warped syntax that marked so much of his writing, "brought me friendly and timely establishment as a leading character juvenile." It did not, however, bring a guarantee that interesting roles would always be available on the London stage. Instead, he made his first film. By now the cinema was well established in Britain. There were more than sixty serious film-producing companies, most of them clustered around London. Olivier's first film, however, was not made by one of these but by a German company in Berlin, shot simultaneously in English and

German. Olivier did not take it very seriously, indeed he did not at this time consider that any film could deserve to be taken seriously, but it earned him some money and gave him an opportunity for an orgy of opera-going—thirteen in just over three weeks. The money was most acceptable, even essential. His marriage to Jill Esmond was fixed for July 25, 1930. He realized and was unworried by the fact that she would, at least at first, be richer than him, but he had no wish to venture into matrimony empty-handed.

By then, however, his career had taken a momentous turn. He was, of course, well acquainted with the work of Noël Coward, had admired the shockingly controversial *The Vortex* and reveled in the wit of *Hay Fever* and *Bitter Sweet*. He had admired Coward from afar, however, and, though he longed to get to know him, had no reason to believe that this would soon come about. Then, on June 18, he was summoned to the presence. A new life began.

CHAPTER THREE

BREAKTHROUGH

Coward had a proposition to make. His new play, *Private Lives*, was essentially a vehicle for himself and Gertrude Lawrence but it had two other parts that, although uninteresting, were by no means insignificant. One of these he offered to Olivier. Olivier needed to be associated with a success, he said; *Private Lives*, he was confident, would be enormously successful; Olivier would be ill advised to reject the opening. Olivier needed little persuading, especially since his pay would be far more generous than anything he had so far earned. He accept without demur. Years later he asked what Coward had thought of his visitor. "I liked you very much," Coward said. "I found you very attractive, wildly attractive, but you were a bit pro-y." "I suppose I was," admitted Olivier. "A young actor showing off his professionalism." It was not enough to deter Coward. The fact that he found Olivier "wildly attractive" may have been a factor in his thinking. He made it very clear that he would like their relationship to be physical as well as friendly. Olivier always felt guilty that he did not respond; it would have cost him little and given great pleasure to his benefactor. The idea, however, both repelled and alarmed him; he rejected the overtures and Coward bore him no grudge.[1]

Olivier always revered Coward as well as enjoying his company. More than twenty years later, after the first night of *Titus Andronicus*, by which time he had unequivocally entered the ranks of the great, Dulcie Gray noticed that, while telling an anecdote, he kept his eyes on Coward to see the effect that he was having. "Does it

really matter to you if Noël laughs or not?" she asked. "Certainly,"
Olivier replied. "Noël was my first leading man and the gap never
lessens." He was an "incredibly brilliant man," Olivier insisted, "better educated than me by a long chalk." He told Olivier that he was
"the most illiterate boy I have ever met" and prescribed a reading list, consisting, rather bizarrely, of *Wuthering Heights*, *The Old
Wives' Tale* by Arnold Bennett and Somerset Maugham's *Of Human
Bondage*. Whether Olivier read them or not is uncertain but he
claimed to have done so. Many years later, when asked to name five
books that had influenced him, Olivier cited these and added *The
History of British Civilization* and *The Reason Why*. He might have
been embarrassed if challenged to expound their contents.[2]

The knowledge that, in *Private Lives*, he had a profitable and, with
luck, long-lasting job awaiting him on his return meant that Olivier
went to his wedding and honeymoon with a light heart. It would be
surprising though if, in those last few weeks, he did not ask himself
whether he was making a mistake. "I love you. Oh, my dear, I do
love you," Jill Esmond assured him, and in her way she did, but was
it Olivier's way, and did *he* really love *her*? The honeymoon got off to
an inauspicious start when they found that the house in Dorset that
had been lent to them was occupied by the owner's two daughters,
who seemed determined to accompany their guests everywhere
except into the marriage chamber. Perhaps it would have been
better if they had followed them even there. The first night was a
disaster: Olivier was inexperienced and notably inexpert; his wife
had physical problems that were not sorted out for several months.
Even when the teething pains had been overcome, it became agonizingly evident that while Olivier possessed the most vigorous sexual appetites, Jill found the physical side of marriage distasteful if
not repellent. She came out as a lesbian after their marriage ended.
Olivier later claimed that he had known about this from the start:
"I thought I could cure her. I was wrong. I didn't realize how strong
nature was . . ." It seems unlikely that this is true: both parties to the
marriage were strikingly innocent and Jill would probably not even

have understood what lesbianism was. As it was, Olivier felt cheated and frustrated.[3]

Private Lives, when it did open in August 1930, proved to be very much as Coward had predicted—an immense success for the author and the principal players with scant attention paid to the supporting roles. "Gertrude Lawrence is amazing," T. E. Shaw—Lawrence of Arabia—told Coward. "She acts nearly as well as yourself. I was sorry for the other two. They were out of it." His was a "stooge role," Olivier thought. But he made something of it. "In this comedy, in which every other line was a belly laugh, I had two half-laughs. By the time we finished, I got myself another two." People who knew saw that the part was a difficult one and admired his handling of it. Most importantly, Coward himself approved. When John Mills saw the play Coward asked him what he had thought of Olivier's performance. "Well," said Mills, "I couldn't believe that anyone as good-looking as that could be such a rivetingly good actor." "I'll tell you something," replied Coward. "In my much-sought-after opinion that young man, unless something goes radically wrong, will, before long, be acknowledged as our greatest actor."[4]

Successful or not, Olivier did not enjoy the play. Coward told Robert Stephens that, some years later, Olivier had admitted to him that he had been "eaten with jealousy" every time he witnessed the triumph of the leading players. "The thing about Larry was that he was jealous of everyone, whatever they did, if he felt they did whatever they did better than he could." Or that they enjoyed an opportunity he had been denied. Or played a part he felt to be his own. Usually he kept such feelings under control, sometimes they burst out. His jealousy made his life a lot less tranquil and caused him much unhappiness.[5]

After his London triumph Coward took *Private Lives* to New York. Adrianne Allen, the actress who had played opposite Olivier in the London production, was not free to make the trip so Jill Esmond was recruited to fill the gap. In spite of the fact that he was doomed to play second fiddle to the stars, there was a great deal about the season for Olivier to enjoy. Noël Coward and Gertrude

Lawrence were invited everywhere and their junior partners usually traveled in their wake. They made many friends, among them
Douglas Fairbanks Jr., who remained a close friend of Olivier all
his life. Together Olivier and Fairbanks went to the Russian Club,
where they watched a man whose act consisted of swallowing
almonds, sewing needles and goldfish and regurgitating them in the
order demanded by the audience. To add to this esoteric entertainment he offered them cocaine. Nervously, they accepted. Fairbanks
survived more or less unscathed. Olivier, Fairbanks remembered,
"never very robust, got sick to his stomach and asked us to leave
early so as to throw up." Such mishaps apart, he enjoyed his forays
into New York high society. But the tour was not a total success. For
one thing Jill Esmond not only disliked her role but thought she
was miscast: "I was very bad in the part." For another, irrespective
of the merits of her performance, more attention was paid to her in
New York than to her husband. She was already to some extent an
established figure and the gossip columns covered her doings more
often than those of Olivier. "Many of the local bigwigs dismissed
him as a nice but stiff young Englishman," remarked Fairbanks.
"They said Jill was the one to watch and that Larry's future was limited." Olivier professed not to mind this in the least, but in fact was
put out: it did not make the already slightly shaky marriage progress
more smoothly. Halfway through the run Gertrude Lawrence fell
ill and the Oliviers took advantage of the gap to spend a few days
beachcombing in Nassau. Perhaps some time alone together would
have helped them sort things out; Coward, however, decided to join
them. "We didn't really want to be joined," said Jill Esmond wistfully. "We were quite happy by ourselves."[6]

The run over, Jill Esmond was anxious to move on to Hollywood,
where she knew profitable work awaited her. Olivier was doubtful:
apart from his professed conviction that the cinema was an inferior
art form he was conscious of the fact that he had not fully mastered
the art of acting to camera and was reluctant to expose himself
to the risk of failure. In the end, he decided that he should give it a
go. Coward was disdainful when he was told of their plan: "You've

got no artistic integrity, that's your trouble . . . Hahlleewood!" The reality was even worse than Olivier had envisaged. "He has no chance," said a studio executive. "He tries to look like Ronnie Colman but his face is too strong and his looks are too rugged. When it comes to rugged actors we don't need Englishmen." Worse still, the director Victor Schertzinger said that Olivier had no idea how to perform before the camera: "He acted the way he did on the stage—all broad gestures and a face forever busy with expressions." David Selznick, one of Hollywood's most powerful producers, was more favorable, deeming Olivier an "excellent possibility," but even he admitted that most people thought Jill Esmond "more desirable for stock." In any case, he considered their salaries "way out of line for beginners, especially as we have no parts in line for either."[7]

Though underemployed, and fobbed off with indifferent parts when he *was* employed, Olivier never lost his confidence in his powers. Fabia Drake, one of his oldest friends, was acting with a company putting on a repertoire of classical plays in Los Angeles. Night after night Olivier came to the theater. How could he bear to spend his time watching other people act? she asked. "Well, you see, I'm going to do them all one day," he replied. But he was not going to do them on the West Coast of America. After three years, with only three second-rate films to his credit but a reasonable cache of dollars in the bank, he decided it was time to return to London.[8]

To Jill, things looked rather different. It seems that she was likely to land the most important role in Clemence Dane's *A Bill of Divorcement*. "Whoever played that, unless they were an appalling actress, could not help being a success," remembered Jill sadly. "It was a wonderful part." To secure it, though, she would have to sign a seven-year contract. What happened then is obscure. Olivier claimed to have seen papers on Selznick's desk that made it clear that the young Katharine Hepburn had already been signed up at a high salary and that Jill was merely being strung along. David Selznick claimed that this could not be the truth. The contract with Hepburn was not signed until after the Oliviers had left Hollywood, so Olivier could not have seen it. He was determined that his wife should not be a bigger star than he was: "Larry is the most selfish man I have ever met." If Olivier did invent the story of Hepburn's contract it would have been not so much to sabotage his wife's career as to ensure that she returned to London with him. It does not seem, anyway, that it played an important part in her final decision. "Larry," she said, "wanted very much to go back to England . . . Naturally a part of me wanted to stay on but I wasn't unhappy having made the decision."[9]

Back in London, they decided that they must live in a style more appropriate to international stars. For the first year of their marriage they had rented a tiny apartment in Roland Gardens with a bed, a dining room table and chairs and almost nothing else. A Mrs. Johns cooked for them when they had company. Her style was as unpolished as the surroundings. Once they plucked up their courage and asked Noël Coward to dinner. Some culinary disaster occurred and the three of them laughed heartily. "It's all very well to laugh," said Mrs. Johns, "but suppose someone important had been here!" Things were going to be very different in the future. They moved into a house on Chelsea Embankment, boasting a huge room that had been Whistler's studio. In it they installed an imposing stone fireplace, a tapestry and a grand piano and prepared to entertain the cream of Bohemian London. Bohemian London duly rallied to the call. Their first large party was a flop. "We were too grand," admitted Jill Esmond. "We invited too many grand people and, if you have too many grand people everyone wants to talk." They learned by their mistake; in future parties the more voluble celebrities were interspersed with people prepared to listen. But the dollars were running out and though Olivier was offered one or two interesting parts and got excellent reviews, the plays were not sufficiently successful nor the financial rewards high enough to support the life style to which he had become accustomed in America. Like it or not, he had to return to films.[10]

It is curious how long it took Olivier, a most perceptive actor and one who would repeatedly show himself as an innovator, to realize that the cinema made demands on the performer quite different from those posed by the stage. In part this was because he continued to despise the medium. "There's something rather terrible and cold-blooded about acting in a film studio," he told his sister Sybille. "Films can help you to buy your mother a smart car or your wife a house in the country, but I still don't believe they can help you to act." When Alexander Korda, the man who got nearer than anyone else to creating an English Hollywood, gave Olivier opportunities to play important parts, he only accepted them disdainfully: "I felt unhappy in the medium, and was using most of my energy trying to build strong performances on the stage in the evenings.[11]

Korda played an important part in Olivier's life. He needed Olivier, because in the early 1930s there was still only a small pool of actors who operated exclusively in the cinema and producers looked to the stage to find their casts. Olivier needed Korda, because the cinema was where the money was. Olivier respected and, up to a point, trusted Korda; Korda admired Olivier. Yet they were in opposite camps, the relationship between them was always cautious. "There were times when I was frightened of him," Olivier admitted, "when he seemed to have a sort of power thing." Korda was determined that Olivier should play opposite Marlene Dietrich. Olivier refused "because Jill was rather ill, and I thought that if I was in a picture with Dietrich it would worry her." When he tried to explain this to Korda, he met with ridicule. "I hated him at that moment," Olivier remembered. J. B. Priestley tried to convert him to the potentialities of cinema. "I'd like to do a film with you sometime," he wrote. "I think a bit better of them than you do—as long as one hasn't some half-witted producer sitting on one." Olivier was not convinced.[12]

Half-witted producers were only part of Olivier's quarrel with the cinema; the whole film world seemed alien to him. He was convinced that the dislike was mutual. "God help any man, woman or child who tries to get into the films through me," he protested to George Devine, "as I am very unpopular with them." Even when he had made his breakthrough and come to terms with the medium, even when he had become a major film star, he never seemed altogether at home on the screen. Orson Welles remarked that Olivier was the master of technique and that, if screen acting depended only on technique, he would have been supreme master of the medium. "And yet, fine as he's been in films, he's never been more than a shadow of that electric presence that commands the stage. Why does the cinema seem to diminish him? And enlarge Gary Cooper—who knew nothing of technique at all?" He might equally have cited Marilyn Monroe; a woman who barely knew what acting was yet who, twenty years later, was to outshine Olivier in every scene.[13] *

His view of the world of cinema was by no means enhanced by his expedition to Hollywood to star opposite Greta Garbo. In July 1933 he went back to Los Angeles to play the Spanish lover of Garbo's Queen Christina. Garbo at this time was the best-known film star in the world. To costar with her would have been an important step forward in Olivier's film career; it would also have been a risky one, since Garbo's screen presence was so overwhelmingly powerful that any man opposite her was likely to be eclipsed. This was a risk Olivier was more than ready to take; he haggled over terms, but he was never in any real doubt that he must accept the invitation. He had reckoned without his costar's idiosyncratic tastes. She seemed not so much to dislike him as to be unaware that he was there. With increasing desperation he tried to get through to her; launching a blitzkrieg of charm, wit and wistfulness in an effort to break down her Nordic indifference. She allowed him to rattle on with detached unconcern; then shrugged and sidled away with an enigmatic: "Oh vell, live'sh a pain, anyway." The following day the producer told him that, while M.G.M. still had total faith in Olivier and was eager to keep him under contract, in this particular part, perhaps . . . In fact, it may not have been so exclusively Garbo's decision as Olivier imagined; the casting director concluded that "he didn't have enough maturity, skill and acting weight . . . he was too

---

* See below pp. 206–209.

young and inexperienced for Don Antonio." At the time it seemed, indeed was, a humiliating rebuff; in the interests of his long-term career it was perhaps a good thing. If Olivier had acted opposite Garbo and achieved even moderate success the pressure to remain in Hollywood and make a fortune would have been hard to resist. We might never have seen his Henry V, his Richard III, his James Tyrone; the history of the National Theater might have been very different.[14]

So it was back to the stage and parts that became steadily more important and more testing. If one had to pick out three or four plays that defined the development of Olivier's career, the first would certainly be *The Green Bay Tree*. William Wyler, the great American filmmaker, saw it on its opening in New York and found it "a dark and puzzling drama about a homosexual relationship." It "shocked and astonished" its audiences. It shocked and astonished Olivier, too, who disliked the part though recognizing the great opportunity that it gave him. It was memorable for him because it was directed by Jed Harris. He had known Harris before, and found him charming, but as a director he was transformed into "a dreadful man," a "cruel little bastard"; "I've never been so grateful to leave anything in my life." He claimed to have in part modeled his Richard III on memories of Harris. But for all his defects, Olivier had to admit that he had "a theatrical brain of rare excellence" and that his ideas about the play were "sound and illuminating." Harris had no doubts about the importance of his contribution. "The reason Olivier was halfway good in *The Green Bay Tree* was because I made him good," he wrote dismissively. "I took none of his childish shit about 'forming' his character and his 'choices' in reading lines. I just told him to read his lines my way, and if he didn't like it to get the hell out of the play." Harris left an enduring mark: "he gave Larry a sense of discipline and seriousness about the theater that he's not had before," said the director and critic, Harold Clurman. The very fact that Olivier felt ill at ease in the part, playing a weak and devious homosexual, forced him to introduce new depths into his acting to a degree that he had not so far achieved. "He was sensational," remembered Noël Coward, "it was a marvelous, an extraordinary performance." Olivier agreed. It was his first personal success in New York: "They thought I was wonderful and I *was* very good."[15]

He came back to a far more congenial role in London, though he had not expected to get it. Gielgud was directing Ralph Richardson as Bothwell in Josephine Tey's *Queen of Scots*. Eight days before the opening night Richardson threw up the part. He disliked the play, was not enjoying acting opposite Gwen Ffrangcon-Davies and, above all, hated being directed by Gielgud. "Johnnie was an awfully inconsiderate director," said Olivier. "He didn't give a damn what he said to anybody. I think probably he'd done that with Ralph and Ralph bloody well walked off the stage." At twenty-four hours' notice, Olivier walked on. "I shall always remember the gallant way you took over the part, the way you worked at it those last crowded days and the peace and reassurance your coming brought," wrote the grateful author. Within a week he had memorized the role while rehearsing fourteen hours a day. All did not go smoothly. In rehearsals Gielgud was very rude to him, "but I took it because it was my habit. I decided I would always take, and think, and listen, and not act proud and stalk off." He overstated his readiness to accept hostile criticism. Increasingly, he grew to resent instructions from those he felt less experienced than himself and on at least one occasion he stormed off in protest against an overassertive director.

But on the whole he took direction calmly and, even if he considered that his judgment as an actor was more sound, would contrive to compromise or to get his own way without direct confrontation. Richardson regretted his own impetuous departure, especially when the play ran for several months and was then only closed because a heat wave emptied the theaters. He felt vaguely aggrieved, however, at the alacrity with which Olivier had taken over his part: there was no outright quarrel between the two, but for a time the relationship was cool.[16]

It was Olivier's next play, though, which won him his first popular following. Once again he got it by chance. He was engaged by

Coward to play the swashbuckling hero of *Theater Royal* during its provincial tour, after which the part was to be taken over by Brian Aherne. He was so good, however, that Aherne volunteered, or was persuaded, to opt out. It was the sort of dashing young hero role that Olivier could have played with little effort; he elected, though, to fling himself into it with reckless zest. His first entry involved a spectacular leap onto the stage from the top of a steep staircase. There was no need to make so energetic an appearance, but Olivier was determined to impose himself on his audience from the outset. It was not the only physical excess in which he indulged. Michael Meyer, the biographer and translator, was only a boy when he saw the play. Fifty years later he told Olivier what an impression the leap had made on him. "Ah, yes, but do you remember how I slid down the banisters?" Olivier replied. He seemed hurt when Meyer admitted that he did not. *Theater Royal* ended in predictable disaster. Olivier broke an ankle in his leap and, though he only missed a handful of performances, his athleticism was sadly curbed toward the end of the run. His career was to be punctuated by such mishaps. "I am a moral and physical coward," he maintained. Moral cowardice is hard to pin down; Olivier seems to have suffered from it less that most. Physically he was one of the bravest of men. Time and again he subjected himself to extravagant and sometimes quite unnecessary risks. Usually he got away with it; the fact that sometimes he met with disaster never in the least deterred him. Nor did he hesitate to involve others in his adventures. Once, without stopping for oncoming traffic, he drove Ralph Richardson at fifty miles an hour over the junction of the Croydon bypass and the Purley road. "I shall never forgive you for that," said a shaken Richardson. "Old man, what are you fussing about?" inquired Olivier. "It is a well-known thing that when you get to a point of danger, you must get over it as quickly as you can."[17]

John Gielgud was one of the many who admired *Theater Royal*. "It made me envious of Larry's marvelous use of physical technique," he remembered, "and his mastery of timing was breathtaking . . . I had a sense that Larry was suddenly my rival. He was younger

than I and I had the disagreeable notion that he was now in a position to surpass me." Olivier was similarly ready to acknowledge the
greatness of Gielgud. He went with Roland Culver to see *Richard II*:
"He was transfixed by Johnny's performance—by the grace of it, by
the insight that flowed from its understated eloquence." He found
Gielgud's first, and greatest Hamlet equally memorable: "fabulous,"
he called it. "He made it intensely real, very well felt and very well
modulated." But the consciousness of rivalry was always there; only
a few days after Olivier had seen Gielgud's Hamlet he surprised Jack
Hawkins, who was playing Horatio, by saying that "he'd like to give
old Hamlet a try, to see if he couldn't do it better than Gielgud."
The relationship between Gielgud and Olivier was correct but edgy.
Told that Olivier had failed to contribute to a collection of tributes
that Ronald Harwood was assembling, Gielgud remarked drily:
"Larry was always jealous of me." For his part Olivier saw things
differently: "He always says awful things about me," he complained.
Even in the 1980s, he maintained, Gielgud would harp back to flaws
in Olivier's performances as a young man. "That's forty-five years
ago, you know. You don't have to harbor nasty things about people
for forty-five years."[18]

The contrast between the two men was indeed striking. Olivier
was power, passion, animal magnetism; Gielgud precise, exquisite,
melodious. It was the difference between Nature and Art, Kenneth
Tynan suggested; between burgundy and claret, Alan Dent more
prosaically suggested. Gielgud, three years older, was better established on the London stage and was shortly to try his hand as an
actor-manager; Olivier had stolen a march by venturing into film.
Apart from Richardson there were not many other giants in their
age group. Frederick Valk and Ronald Colman belonged to an earlier generation, Emlyn Williams possessed a considerable talent,
but he was somehow never in the mainstream, Alec Guinness was
still barely visible. Donald Wolfit and perhaps Charles Laughton
were the only figures considerable enough to challenge the big
three. Wolfit could produce performances of real majesty—most
notably as Lear—but surrounded himself with a team who were

too often not even second rate. Olivier's Othello was a *tour de force*, went Hermione Gingold's unkindly quip, Wolfit's a forced-to-tour. Olivier disliked him: "He had extraordinary guts," he admitted, "and at the height of his career he had a tremendously gutsy voice," but he was selfish, arrogant and bad mannered: "We all thought he was awful." When Wolfit was put up for the Garrick Club during the war, Olivier stopped short of blackballing him, but he did his best to thwart his entry; "standards had slipped," however, and Wolfit was elected.[19]

Olivier himself became a member of the Garrick early in 1936. He was, he thought, the youngest member at the time and he was very conscious of the distinction: "I was thrilled to bits." He deplored the prejudice of those members who blackballed Noël Coward—"stupid clots, hidebound, absolutely immovable anti-homosexuals"—but did not contemplate resignation in protest. To be a member of the Garrick was a necessary part of belonging to the theatrical establishment. Being a member of the establishment— theatrical or not—mattered to Olivier. He was not clubbable by nature, but at times he belonged also to The Players in New York, Boodle's, Buck's, the Beefsteak and the R.A.C. Membership was a visible sign of his eminence in his profession. He would have been inordinately grateful if he had known that James Agate, perhaps the leading critic of the day, when asked who were the contemporary equivalents of the Irvings and Ellen Terry, had answered that they were John Gielgud and Edith Evans, "with a reservation in favor of Laurence Olivier as the most promising young actor."[20]

CHAPTER FOUR

BIRTH OF A
CLASSICAL ACTOR

It was Gielgud who now propelled his rival into the next stage of his career. He conceived the idea of producing *Romeo and Juliet*, alternating the roles of Romeo and Mercutio between himself and some other actor. His first choice for a partner had been Robert Donat, who was unwilling or unavailable. He then tried Olivier, who at first said he planned to put on the play himself with Jill Esmond as Juliet but changed his mind when he heard that Gielgud had signed up Peggy Ashcroft for the part with Edith Evans as the Nurse. It was generous of Gielgud to offer this opportunity to someone he considered a dangerous rival; part at least of his calculations may have been that he would be taking on Olivier on what he felt to be his own ground, on which he was confident he could outshine the young pretender.

Up to a point he was proved right. Olivier was the first to play Romeo and he was savaged by many of the critics for what they saw as his inability to speak the poetry: "His blank verse is the blankest I ever heard," wrote the reviewer for the *Evening Standard*, while James Agate in the *Sunday Times* accused him of an "inexpertness that approached virtuosity." Olivier was appalled. His intention was, and always would be, to speak the verse "as if that is the way you speak naturally." If that was unacceptable then he had better give up the part altogether. His offer to resign was refused. Not all the critics condemned his approach: St. John Ervine in the *Observer* said he had "seen few sights so moving as the spectacle of Mr. Olivier's Romeo, stunned with Juliet's beauty, fumbling for words with which to say his love." "Larry was the definitive Romeo," thought Peggy Ashcroft, "a real, vigorous, impulsive youth."[1]

When Gielgud took over as Romeo the contrasting approaches became more obvious. Gielgud was concerned most of all with the beauty of the words, Olivier with the reality of the action. "Larry had the advantage over me in his vitality, looks, humor and directness," wrote Gielgud, "I had an advantage over him in my familiarity with the verse and in the fact that the production was of my own devising." Alec Guinness, a relatively junior member of the cast, was less generous. "We all admired John greatly," he said, "but we were not so keen on Larry. He seemed a bit cheap and vulgar, striving after effects and making nonsense of the verse." But Olivier's was the way of the future. Over the years he much improved his delivery of Shakespearean verse, but he never yielded in his belief that it was the sense that came first. Gielgud, he said, sang Shakespeare. "I've always despised Shakespeare sung. I don't think it's opera; I think it's speech." After his Romeo everything changed; ten years later the Gielgud school of declamation would have seemed almost absurdly old-fashioned. Gielgud himself was to modify his style. As to which was the better in 1935, Gielgud himself summed it up with concision. "I spoke the poetry much better," he told Patrick Garland, "but Larry got the girl."[2]

When it came to Mercutio, the critics treated Olivier more kindly. He had appealed to Ralph Richardson for advice on how to play the part. Richardson denied that he could help: "You should be much better than me—don't forget you could color Bothwell which drove me right out of the stage door." He did offer two useful tips: Olivier was not to take Mercutio's great "Queen Mab" speech too fast, and on no account was he to get drunk during the one hour and twenty minutes in which he was offstage: "This takes years of skill and cannot be overestimated." Oddly enough, Gielgud was more put out by Olivier's rendering of Mercutio than he had been by his Romeo. He complained about the "loudness and extravagant tricks" of Olivier's performance and speculated that the critics would treat it with even greater harshness. Possibly he feared a too conspicuous Mercutio might distract the audience from his Romeo. The public did not seem to have seen any problem: *Romeo and Juliet* ran for six months and was still playing to full houses when the show had to close.[3]

Any ill feeling between Olivier and Richardson had faded. They decided to produce and star in a play together, joining forces with the prolific and, usually, most successful dramatist, J. B. Priestley. Unfortunately, Priestley was having an off day; there was nothing much wrong with *Bees on the Boat Deck* but its sour tone lacked popular appeal and though ten years later the names of Olivier and Richardson would have been enough to carry an unappealing play, in 1936 more was needed. It soon closed. The failure did no damage to Olivier's reputation, but it did to his bank balance. He lost some £700, say £30,000 at current values. By the standards of the day Olivier was paid well for his labors, and he had money left from his American filmmaking, but he never knew how to save. Money was there to spend: he lived well, was extravagantly generous and gave no thought for the morrow. Jill Esmond was little better. When Soṫka Zinovieff came round seeking to get a job as secretary she suggested that she should be paid £16 a week. "Give her £25," Jill called from the next room. Olivier was happy to oblige.[4]

Something that in the end was to cost him far more, in money, time and emotional strain, was in the offing. In the middle of July 1936 filming started on Alexander Korda's new patriotic epic, *Fire Over England*. In this Olivier played a heroic sailor who almost single-handedly defeated a dastardly Spanish plot to assassinate Queen Elizabeth. "It was an excellent part," he recalled. "I just wasn't very good in it." He exaggerated both the excellence of the part and the inadequacy of his acting. Michael Ingolby was the sort of energetic young hero whom Olivier could have played in his sleep. Possibly, indeed, he would have been more successful if he *had* played it in his sleep: if anything, he tried too hard. He could do "the hysterical type of young romantic with ease," remarked Graham Greene

with mild contempt. The reviews were not ecstatic, but his performance brought him no discredit. It had, however, other, more lasting consequences. The hysteria that Greene noted was not induced
just by the excesses of the plot. Opposite him, playing the object of
his passionate devotion, was a young actress called Vivien Leigh.[5]

They had not met for the first time on the set. Vivien Leigh had first
seen him in *Theater Royal*. "That's the man I'm going to marry," she
is said to have announced. Her companion pointed out that she was
already married. "That doesn't matter. I'll still marry him one day."
Jean-Pierre Aumont, the French actor, claims to have seen them at
separate tables in a restaurant, exchanging glances across the room.
"That couple are madly in love," he announced. His companion,
who knew them both, laughed dismissively and said they'd never
even met. "Whether they had met or not didn't really matter," concluded Aumont. "Their love shone across the restaurant."[6]

Vivien Leigh was a young actress. She had made her name the
previous year in *The Mask of Virtue* and was now at least as celebrated as Olivier in the world of cinema. The word "beauty" is
one that should be used with exceeding caution, but Vivien Leigh
was unequivocally, triumphantly beautiful. She was clever, funny
and, when she wanted to be, exceptionally charming. She was no
more an intellectual than Olivier and not much better read but she
had quick wits and a retentive mind and could give the impression of deep culture; her taste was excellent and she furnished a
series of houses with pictures and furniture of real quality. She was
also manipulative, cunning and determined. What she wanted she
almost always got. She wanted Laurence Olivier. Her nice, intelligent
barrister husband, Leigh Holman, was irrelevant to this pursuit: she
had married him for the sake of security, she would abandon him
without a qualm.

The couple had grown to know each other well before they met in
Fire Over England. The progress of their relationship can be charted
through Olivier's diaries. On June 27, 1936, he took her out to lunch
(a fortnight later he was giving lunch to the beautiful actress Ann

Todd, so his interest at that time was by no means exclusive). They met again five days later. From then on they met at intervals, both separately and as families. Olivier was an obsessive keeper of statistics. In his pocket diary he noted his watch number, season ticket number, pass book number, his size in boots (8–9), in collars (15½), in hats (6 ⅞), his height (5ft 10¼ inches), his weight (10 stone 7 pounds). At the beginning of each year he put in certain significant anniversaries: "Anniversary 1st night on stage," "Anniversary 100th Perf. Henry VIII." The list included the birthdays of his intimates: his father, his brother, his sister, Jill. On November 5, 1936, Vivien's birthday was added.[7]

It has been suggested that Korda knew of the relationship and set them to play against each other in *Fire Over England* for that reason, either to make mischief or because he felt that their growing love would make for some lively filming. Olivier dismissed the idea: Korda made the casting "for no purpose beyond the fact that we were two of his contract players and we looked right for those parts." Korda would indeed have been prescient if he had known what was going to happen; Olivier himself was not aware how deeply he was becoming entangled. When they first met on the set Vivien Leigh remarked politely how glad she was that they were going to act together. "We shall probably end up by fighting," prophesied Olivier. "People always get sick of each other when making a film." His words were soon proved spectacularly untrue. Alexander Knox, who had a minor part in the film, said that it was almost immediately obvious to everyone that the pair were in love and that "the intensity of their affair is noticeable in all their scenes together." By the time the film was finished Olivier's marriage was, to all intents and purposes, at an end.[8]

But it was to be a long time before that became evident to all the world. In the meantime Olivier had a career to advance. Swashbuckling roles in silly films might serve well to earn some money, but his performance in *Romeo and Juliet* had convinced him that he wanted most of all to make his future in classical plays on the London stage. The classical theater meant, above all, Shakespeare and Shakespeare meant the Old Vic. Under the leadership of the formidable Lilian Baylis this scruffy, shabby theater unfashionably south of the Thames had become the Shakespearean center for the country, indeed the world. "I was always determined to be a sort of top actor," Olivier much later said. "I knew that if you continued to not quite bring off the classics, you were never going to make it . . . I had to go on . . . and after about a year the press referred to me as 'that Shakespearean actor.' Then I knew it had been done." To reassure himself that he was doing the right thing he rang up Richardson, who was acting in New York. "Shall I go to the Old Vic?" he asked. "Think it's a very good idea," was the terse reply. It was done.[9]

Olivier was confident that he would be welcomed with enthusiasm. "I was a snip," he explained. "They had to have a so-called star . . . I'd done these films, you see, and I had a fantastic name for them." In a few years the name would indeed be fantastic, in 1937 the adjective was still a touch vainglorious. He was right, however, in thinking that Lilian Baylis would be delighted by his advent, particularly since she knew he could easily have earned ten times as much by pursuing his career in Hollywood. Tyrone Guthrie, director at the Old Vic and one of the few figures of such stature whom Olivier both liked and respected, made it clear that, within reason, he could pick whatever parts he chose from the repertoire, the more of them the better. The more the better for Olivier, too. Always gluttonous for hard work, he wanted not only to play a full house of major roles but to play roles that were as different from each other as could be managed. His ambition always was to *be* the character that he was portraying and the more those characters differed, the happier he would be. "I wanted to be completely different in every performance," he wrote, "I like to appear as the chameleon." He deplored the kind of actor who regularly won a round of applause on his first entrance: his ambition was to take people by surprise; to be perpetually unexpected.[10]

Superficially, Olivier's wish to *be* the character he was playing seemed reminiscent of the fashionable doctrine of Konstantin Stanislavsky. In fact it was very different, almost its antithesis.

Stanislavsky, to reduce a complex and sophisticated argument to a sentence, believed that to act characters properly it was necessary first to conduct an exhaustive study of their background and psychology. Olivier claimed that he could tell when young actors had first read Stanislavsky by observing their arriving at the theater an hour earlier than would have been the case before and "wandering thoughtfully about the set, touching the furnishings affectionately and familiarly." Stanislavsky believed that the actor must penetrate to the very heart of the character and then work outward; Olivier preferred to build up the outward appearance of the character and then work in. He thought that "The Method," as the philosophy of Stanislavsky developed in New York in the 1930s and 1940s came to be called, was a futility: "I'd rather work through a scene eight times than waste time chattering about abstractions. An actor gets a thing right by doing it over and over." Acting for him required a peripheral approach, it was naturalism or truthfulness that came first. The difference between the two approaches was often more philosophical than real; what happened on the stage was little affected by the theoretical debate that preceded it. The conflict was a real one, though, and sometimes impinged sharply on the actors. There were moments in Olivier's career when he had cause to curse Stanislavsky and his Method.[11]

In his first eighteen months at the Old Vic Olivier played six major Shakespearean roles. He began with Hamlet. For a man who claimed to deplore theorizing, his approach was unexpected. Professor Ernest Jones, the influential psychoanalyst and biographer of Freud, had propounded the theory that Hamlet had been a victim of the Oedipus complex, passionately in love with his mother. Probably at the initiative of Guthrie, Olivier, Guthrie and Peggy Ashcroft went to see Jones and were converted. Olivier's performance was marked by his lustful fondling of the Queen—or that at least was the idea; most of the critics failed to notice this interpretation. What they did remark was the energy, the fury, the athletic vigor of his performance. Not all of them were sure that they liked it.

James Agate remarked that Olivier, while playing Hamlet, had offered the best performance of Hotspur that his generation had ever seen; he "does not speak poetry badly. He does not speak it at all." His fellow actors too were critical. Michael Redgrave, who played Laertes, thought he was "a bad Hamlet. Too assertive and too resolute," while Alec Guinness, Olivier's understudy, was outraged by "the gymnastic leaps and falls" in which he was expected to indulge if called upon to replace his principal. No one questioned, though, the power and excitement of his performance. After a few weeks, too, his playing evolved. "He has been visited by another spirit," wrote George Buchanan in the *News Chronicle*. "Feeling has been released in him that was unsuspected . . . His Hamlet is not anymore the good chap in a tight corner."[12]

Olivier, who always expected the best from the reviewer, was disappointed and discouraged. But though his delivery of the verse still gave rise to complaint it was far more muted than after *Romeo and Juliet*. John Gielgud did not like Olivier's performance but, talking to Peter Brook, he claimed that he had never been jealous in his life, then added thoughtfully: "But I admit I burst into tears when Larry Olivier got such good notices for his Hamlet." Whatever Olivier may have believed, the general view was that the performance was something not to miss. It was during the run of *Hamlet* that Olivier first indulged his propensity to make speeches at the end of the performance. "Ladies and Gentlemen," he announced on January 30, 1937, "tonight a great actress has been born. Laertes has had a daughter." Considering the age of Vanessa Redgrave at the time, Olivier was being remarkably prescient.[13]

After Hamlet came Toby Belch in *Twelfth Night*: a part, as Olivier remarked, "designed to demonstrate my staggering versatility." Henry V came next. By instinct Olivier was patriotic, but he was not immune to the prevailing mood of the times. In 1937 heroism was out of fashion, appeasement had not yet become a dirty word. "I think you will be *very* good as Henry V and I don't think he's a shit at all," Peggy Ashcroft encouraged him, but he was unconvinced. He appealed to Ralph Richardson for advice. "Henry V?"

said Richardson. "He's a scoutmaster. But he raised scoutmastership to godlike proportions . . . Of course you must play him." Olivier concurred, but with a marked lack of enthusiasm. So wan was
his performance that Guthrie turned on him and accused him of
betraying the sense of the play and letting down his public. "I was
fortunate to have him directing me," wrote Olivier. "I followed his
eye. He knew."[14]

He did not have the benefit of Guthrie's eye for the *Macbeth* that
followed. The French director Michel Saint-Denis was imported for
that production. He was "a fine director with a wonderful imagination," considered Olivier, "but he let his imagination run amok." It
was a gimmicky affair, in which the principal characters had their
faces swallowed up under grotesquely heavy makeup. Usually Olivier reveled in elaborate disguises, but even he was taken aback by this
excess. "Larry's makeup comes on," remarked Vivien Leigh, "then
Banquo comes on, then Larry comes on." It was "not an unparal-
leled success," Olivier wrote in his memoirs, and he felt he had done
nothing to redeem it. As was so often the case, he exaggerated his
own inadequacy. It was mock modesty perhaps, designed in part
to distinguish himself from the common ruck of actors who over-
praised their own performances, but his self-deprecation was on the
whole endearing and enhanced the value of his judgment on those
occasions when he claimed to have achieved something altogether
special. The critics rated his Macbeth higher than he did himself.
"He brings off some magnificent vocal effects," wrote James Agate.
"Mr. Olivier will probably play this part twice as well when he has
twice his present years." It was shrewd comment: it was in fact eighteen years before Olivier provided what all agreed was a great and
some felt must be the definitive Macbeth. In this production he
sought to cover up his unease with a display of hectic energy. His
shriek on seeing Banquo's ghost was so loud and protracted that it
gave him laryngitis while the dueling became so vigorous that the
man who played Macduff once needed to be taken to the hospital.
Olivier had to be reminded that he was supposed to lose the fight: "I
always fought with too much vigor. That came from a sort of pride."[15]

He had intended to follow Macbeth with Richard II, but Gielgud protested that he planned to do them both in his own season at the Queen's Theater. Olivier acquiesced: *Richard II* was dropped from the Old Vic repertoire. It was one of the few great Shakespearean roles that Olivier never played; it would not have come naturally to him, but he had shown in *The Green Bay Tree* that he could play weakness and self-pity and it would have been a memorable experience to see him seated on the ground, telling sad stories of the death of kings. Instead, he played Iago to Richardson's Othello. According to the designer, Roger Furse, both men tried to persuade Guthrie to cast the women of their choice, in Olivier's case Vivien Leigh, as Desdemona. They failed, Guthrie instead chose Curigwen Lewis. "This is where I saw the generosity of Larry," wrote Furse. Though he deplored Guthrie's failure to employ Leigh, "once it was decided he worked in real harmony and generosity with Curigwen. The others didn't." No amount of harmony could redeem what proved to be a disaster. "It wasn't good," Olivier considered. "I feel a bit churlish saying it, but it wasn't good simply because Ralph wasn't good." The initial reading had gone well but Richardson never improved on it, he "tried to keep within the nice cozy feeling of his reading, and you can't." Guthrie was in despair and at one time threatened to call off the production. Olivier, partly because he felt Richardson's Othello imposed on him the duty to bring some life into the play, partly because it was always his instinct to seek out the comedy in any figure, however malign, played his Iago for laughs. "He was a comedian by instinct, a tragedian by art," considered James Agate. Olivier would have seen nothing offensive in that judgment. "I maintain," he wrote, "that a pure tragedian isn't going to move an audience except by the sheer sound-value of a glorious voice, which, to my mind, is not the true nature of acting . . . Your studies of humanity are going to be far sharper if you're a comedian." Almost any part would be the better for a little humor, though he confessed, "It's jolly hard to get a laugh in 'Lear.'" But though he felt that he had been right to play Iago as he did, he did not think that it had been a success. "What I missed entirely," he concluded, "was the essential value of the part"—an opaque comment that presumably implied that he had oversimplified Iago and not done justice to the complex emotions that shaped his conduct.[16]

Five major roles at the Old Vic and none of them totally successful: he had done more to establish himself as a Shakespearean actor than his own self-criticism would suggest but it had still not been a triumphant progress. There remained Coriolanus. Lewis Casson was the director and his wife, Sybil Thorndike, refused to play Coriolanus's mother, Volumnia, unless Olivier promised to do what her husband told him. "His orders were that Larry was to get rid of all his experimental ideas and tricks, and act Coriolanus in a natural, straightforward way." Olivier accepted the ruling meekly. He allowed himself one extravagance. *Coriolanus* was a "jolly ripping entertainment," he told Basil Rathbone. "Whatever happens, you must do a magnificent fall at the end. I did a peach, I remember, a perfect peach." It was to be still more of a peach when he repeated the part in 1959, but it was already spectacular enough. Otherwise he followed Casson's bidding. "It was a great delight to watch you," wrote Esmé Percy, who one suspects might have been briefed by Casson on what to say, "in a production that left you free to give your whole strength to the Play, without 'stunts' or eccentricities. How fine I thought you were, I cannot tell you, and how passionate and sincere your reading was. One may say you have been trying out all this year parts not yet quite within your compass. But that is what I feel has been so splendid for you . . . Now these memories are in your bones. They have given you range and depth and force." Olivier had been growing in experience and stature ever since he had joined the Old Vic. With *Coriolanus* he came of age.[17]

His success was the more remarkable because of the strains put on him by his tempestuous private life. Early in 1936 it became evident that Jill Esmond was pregnant. So far as Olivier was concerned this seems to have been unintended, for Esmond it was a despairing effort to save a sinking ship. As the filming of *Fire Over England* went on it became ever more evident that Olivier's infatuation for

Vivien Leigh was not a passing fancy. Jill Esmond knew well what was going on but, preoccupied by pregnancy, she preferred to think of it as little as possible. "All that, from my point of view, was pretty nasty," she remembered. Perhaps she hoped that, when their child was born, her husband's love would be miraculously rekindled. When he came, they called him Tarquin: "It came to me in a mad moment," Olivier admitted. "It has such dramatic overtones." But Tarquin brought no great improvement to his parents' marriage. Olivier took a proper interest in his son but withdrew still further from any real engagement with his wife.[18]

Formally the marriage survived. Vivien Leigh went to inspect the baby a few days after it was born. "It is really *very* attractive," she told her husband. "Larry says it is like Edward G. Robinson; which is a little cruel. He has already started reciting Shakespeare to it." To the outside world she was still no more than a friend of the family and it was to remain that way for the best part of another year. But the veneer on the marriage was wearing thin. When filming *Fire Over England* finished, the Oliviers took off for Capri. Vivien Leigh was soon in pursuit, presumably with Olivier's consent. She was escorted by an elderly friend, Oswald Frewen, who viewed with dismay the development of a relationship that sooner or later, he felt sure, was bound to end in disaster. He pleaded with Leigh not to break up her marriage: she agreed that the advice was excellent, but she did not take it. Olivier, for his part, seems to have made occasional efforts to escape the thrall. Raymond Massey claimed that, when the filming of *Fire Over England* was almost completed, Olivier told him that: "He was consumed by guilt. He was putting an end to it, he said. He loved Jill and he'd been a fool. With Vivien, well, it was just a wild infatuation, but it was to Jill he owed his loyalty. He had talked to Vivien about it. She had agreed to a cooling-off period." Massey can hardly have invented the exchange, but Olivier's words do not ring true, especially so far as Leigh's role is concerned. Even if he said something along those lines he cannot have done so with much conviction. Jill Esmond, anyway, seems to have had few illusions. "After all, she was one of the most beautiful women there have ever been," she accepted with resignation, "and he fell desperately in love with her in a way he'd never been in love with me."[19]

Things came to a head when the Old Vic company set sail for Denmark, to put on *Hamlet* at Elsinore. It was in many ways a memorable visit. The plan was to perform in the open air at the castle of Kronborg but the first night was made impossible because of heavy and continuous rain. It was a gala performance with royalty present, so Guthrie was determined not to cancel it altogether. Instead it was switched to the ballroom of a nearby hotel. For a frantic few hours the cast, with Olivier very much in the lead, labored to reorganize the production so that it could be acted with chairs banked all around the stage. The cast rose to the challenge, the audience appreciated the effort and were determined to enjoy it. The evening was deemed a complete success. More significantly, it convinced Guthrie that Shakespeare not merely could but should be played on a proscenium stage with the audience on both sides of as well as in front of the players, not merely viewing them in a box cut out of a wall as in the more traditional theaters. Olivier reached the same conclusion. The shape of the National Theater, first at the Old Vic, then in its present building, owes much to the success of this one performance on a rainy night in Denmark.[20]

The visit was also important for the effect it had on Olivier's marriage. According to his own account, he was taken aback when Guthrie suggested that, for the Danish tour, the part of Ophelia should be taken by Vivien Leigh: "Of course, I tried to mask my feelings, and said 'Oh, yes.'" A more convincing account maintains that it was Olivier who pressed for the change. Guthrie at first refused. Vivien then made an hysterical scene and Olivier threatened to withdraw from the excursion if he did not get his way. Probably the truth was somewhere between the two. In any case, to the annoyance of the woman who had played Ophelia in London, Olivier won the day. For reasons that are obscure, Jill Esmond decided, or was persuaded, that she should come too. "I shouldn't have done. It was a mistake," she admitted later. The result was open humiliation.

Olivier and Vivien Leigh were unable to conceal their love for each other; indeed made very little effort to do so. Alec Guinness was delegated to look after Esmond when Olivier was acting or rehearsing: to stop her being bored, he was told; to leave the field open for the lovers to display their emotion freely, Guinness assumed. By the time they returned to London all attempts at secrecy had been abandoned. "I decided that it was time to pack up and go away," is Esmond's account of what came next; "Jill told," was the terse entry in Olivier's diary for June 11, 1937. Whichever side took the initiative, the result was the same: the marriage was over.[21]

Olivier wanted to postpone a public breach for as long as possible. He had already received offensive letters denouncing his behavior; he was convinced that a storm of abuse would follow as soon as it was known that he had left his wife for another woman, especially a woman who was married and as celebrated a star as Vivien Leigh. For another year he remained formally committed to Esmond while cohabiting more or less openly with Leigh and taking her for long, self-indulgent trips across France. It satisfied nobody; it was a "furtive life, lying life. Sneaky," Olivier wrote in his memoirs. In July 1937 he wrote a will. It left the house in Cheyne Walk and the fruits of all his insurance policies to Esmond. The rest, including Durham Cottage, the charming semirural retreat a powerful stone's throw from the Royal Hospital, Chelsea, in which he had made a home for Leigh, he left to her. He concluded: "It is my most earnest wish that my wife and Mrs. Holman [Vivien Leigh] shall live in friendliness and harmony of spirit, both forgiving and forgetting any possible bitterness that may perhaps lie between them. My dearest love, in the proportions that they know they own it, be with them and my family, my son and my good friends forever." The concept of Esmond and Leigh meeting in radiant harmony, presumably to discuss the merits of the deceased Olivier, is both bizarre and distasteful. Olivier does not emerge with credit from the break-up of his marriage: in his defense it can be said that he was besottedly in love. At least he made no attempt to justify his behavior. He was from time to time to complain about Esmond's deficiencies as a wife, but he never denied that he had been at fault and she misused. He accepted his responsibilities as a former husband and as a father and was as generous in the financial provisions that he made for her as he had been sparing in his love.[22]

Things were moving toward a resolution. William Wyler, probably the most distinguished and certainly among the most prominent of American film directors at the time, was pressing him to go to Hollywood to star in what would be his most important film to date. Early in November 1938 he sailed from Southampton on the French liner, the *Normandie*. A new chapter began.

CHAPTER FIVE

FILM STAR

The film in which Wyler wanted to involve Olivier was *Wuthering Heights*; Olivier, of course, being destined to play the tempestuous and vengeful Heathcliff. He was not the first choice for the part. He had been told that Colman had been preferred to him but was not available: "That makes me the poor man's Ronald Colman," he observed. He would have been still more disconcerted if he had known that Wyler had then transferred his favors to Robert Newton. "Newton magnificent Heathcliff. He has strength and power that Olivier lacks," he told the producer, Sam Goldwyn. Ben Hecht, who wrote the script, argued for Olivier. He was "one of the most magnificent actors I have ever seen," he told Goldwyn. "He could recite Heathcliff sitting on a barrel of herring and break your heart." Goldwyn thought Newton too ugly; Douglas Fairbanks, who was also in the running, would be too weak for the part. Olivier was the safest bet.[1]

But Olivier himself had doubts. He thought of making it a condition that Vivien Leigh should take the leading female role of Cathy. Goldwyn would only promise vaguely that she would be offered an important part. Then Ben Hecht's script arrived and Olivier realized what a splendid role it would be for him. When it became clear that Vivien was to be fobbed off with the secondary part of Isabella he protested, but not to the point of turning down the offer. He did not believe that the woman whom Goldwyn had chosen to play Cathy, Merle Oberon, could be of Vivien's caliber, but he had heard good things of her and concluded that it was worth accepting the second best. When Vivien decided that Isabella offered too little to make the part worth accepting, she and Olivier realized that they must temporarily separate. To confirm that he had made the right decision Olivier once again turned to Ralph Richardson for advice. "Yes. Bit of fame. Good," said Richardson, and Olivier was on his way.[2]

He had worked in Hollywood before, but never for a director with the skills of Wyler, nor in a production that had the potential to be important, perhaps even great. His first reactions were favorable. Things were better run than in England, he wrote to Sybille. "I am horrified to have to tell you that the American workman beats the English workman hollow in efficiency, acceptance and above all in enthusiasm . . . which make working conditions very much more pleasant." As for Wyler: he was "an Alsatian of great artistic integrity and photogenic brilliance . . . one has the comforting knowledge that his artistic conscience will not permit anything to 'go by' that is not good or better than good." But the two were destined to clash. Olivier still felt that film was an inferior medium, that real acting had to be done on a stage. "I was frightfully pompous, frightfully pleased with myself, overwhelmingly opinionated," he recollected. When Wyler made it clear that he found his star's performance extravagant Olivier retorted: "I suppose this anemic little medium can't stand anything great in size like that." For Olivier the problem was that Wyler was quick to complain about what his Heathcliff was doing wrong but reticent when it came to suggesting how it might be done better. Even Wyler admitted that there was "a lack of communication and articulation on my part." Olivier would produce what seemed to him a splendid rendering of some lines, Wyler would tell him to do it again. One scene was shot seventy-two times without a single constructive comment from the director. "How do you want it?" demanded an exasperated Olivier. "I've done it calm, I've shouted, I've done it angry, I've done it sad, standing up, sitting down, fast, slow—how do you want me to do it?" "Better," was the only answer. In retrospect, Olivier concluded that Wyler was waging a war of attrition, trying to reduce him to a point where he would see for himself that cinema demanded a radically different approach to acting on a stage. In the end it worked: Olivier was never wholly to repress an urge to overact but by the time "Wuthering Heights" had been completed he had come to terms with the medium and, perhaps even more important, accepted that it was a medium with which it was worth coming to terms.[3]

The lesson was reinforced, though in a very different way, by David Niven, who was playing the relatively minor role of Edgar. Niven already knew Olivier and was to become one of his closest friends. He had no pretensions to be a great tragic actor and did his modest bit with studied casualness. Olivier watched him play and thought: "He isn't even trying to act and here I am working my bloody guts out. He is going to look bad on screen." But he didn't; nobody could have transformed Edgar into a memorable role, but Niven made him convincing, as if there was no other way he could have been. Olivier acknowledged as much, and admitted too that Niven's performance had taught him a great deal. "I thought when we first started working on the picture that I knew much more about acting than he did. And I did, when it came to acting on a stage, but he had a natural gift for screen acting, which I had to work at."[4]

Another problem for Olivier was his leading lady. He was prepared to forgive Merle Oberon for not being Vivien Leigh but not for what he saw as her pretensions and incompetence. She was indeed neither as vital nor as attractive as the ideal Cathy would have been. "Of course, we were at daggers drawn," Olivier recalled. "We spat at each other. We hated each other." The spitting was literally the case. Once Oberon protested when Olivier's spittle landed on her face. Olivier called her "a silly little amateur bitch" and told her that it was bound to happen in scenes of this kind. Oberon stormed off the set and Wyler insisted that Olivier should apologize when she returned. "Over with your tantrum, dear?" was the best Olivier could do; an apology that neither Wyler nor Oberon felt met the needs of the situation.[5]

Sam Goldwyn proved to be another problem. Though he was responsible for Olivier getting the part, he had his doubts once filming got under way. "A sordid story, but artistic," he deemed

Wuthering Heights, and on at least one occasion it seemed to him that Olivier was exaggeratedly sordid and not nearly artistic enough. He chanced to come onto the set at a moment when Olivier was playing Heathcliff at his most disreputable and uncouth. Puce with fury, Goldwyn shouted: "Thees actor es the ogliest actor in pictures, thees actor will ruin me!" Wyler defended his star and Goldwyn grumbled off. Olivier subsequently surmised that the incident had been contrived so as to create a rapprochement between actor and director. This could be true but credits Goldwyn with greater subtlety than he was accustomed to display. Anyway, it did no harm, and provided Olivier with one of his favorite anecdotes with which he would entertain dinner parties for many years.[6]

In spite of these vicissitudes Wyler prevailed; Olivier produced a performance finer than anything he had done on screen before. His Heathcliff was passionately natural: extravagant, of course—nothing was going to turn Heathcliff into a normal member of society—but terrifyingly convincing, a magnificent study of humiliation breeding hatred and the hunger for revenge. Not everyone was satisfied: Graham Greene for one complained that this Heathcliff "would never have married for revenge. Mr. Olivier's nervous, breaking voice belongs to balconies and Verona and romantic love." The vast majority of the critics, however, and still more the public, hailed a great achievement. Wyler for one had no doubts. Merle Oberon publicly made some disparaging remarks about Olivier's performance. "The truth is, Merle," Wyler wrote, "that his dynamic performance is *the* most important contribution to the artistic success of *Wuthering Heights*, far more than yours or mine."[7]

Before the filming of *Wuthering Heights* had even begun Vivien Leigh had joined Olivier in Hollywood. She came because she missed him and could not bear to be parted from him any longer, but she had another reason too. For the last few months the papers had been full of speculation about who would play the role of Scarlett O'Hara in the film that David Selznick was making of Margaret Mitchell's successful novel *Gone With the Wind*. It was conceived on a vast scale; enormously expensive; star-studded; the film, it was predicted, of the decade. All the great names of Hollywood had been canvassed: Tallulah Bankhead, Bette Davis, Katharine Hepburn. Paulette Goddard was the current favorite. Vivien Leigh had decided that the part must be hers. She knew that she was a complete outsider—an Englishwoman little known in Hollywood—but that did not weaken her determination. Olivier was skeptical about her chances but eager to help in any way he could. As his relationship with Jill Esmond had shown, he was not a man who liked to be outshone; he knew that if Vivien won the part of Scarlett she would be propelled into the ranks of superstardom; the fact that he nevertheless supported her in her efforts was a measure of how intense his love had become.

His agent in Hollywood was Myron Selznick, brother of David. Olivier planted in Myron's mind the idea that Vivien Leigh would make a perfect Scarlett. Myron took to the idea; to place one of his clients in such a role would enormously enhance his reputation. Together the three visited the set where *Gone With the Wind* was being filmed. The need to settle on a Scarlett was growing urgent; a decision had to be made within a few days, a fortnight at the most. They arrived on the evening that the spectacular burning of Atlanta was taking place. The flames were just beginning to die down as they approached the spot where David Selznick was standing. Vivien Leigh was silhouetted against the flames, spectacularly beautiful, her face glowing with the excitement of the moment. "Hello, David," said Myron. "Meet Scarlett O'Hara."[8]

Of course, it was not as easy as that. There were screen tests, anguished debate about her English accent, her relative obscurity, but in a remarkably short time the matter was settled. Vivien Leigh felt that the part of Rhett Butler, her putative lover, ought to be played by Olivier. Olivier agreed. With Leslie Howard playing Ashley Wilkes, however, that would have meant that English actors were playing the three most important parts in this great American epic—a palpable absurdity. Anyway, the part was already pledged to Clark Gable. Gable had the reputation of always sleeping with his leading ladies, but in an interview with the press he insisted that he and Vivien Leigh had "neither fought nor fucked." Leigh affected to find this a little hurtful; she asked him whether he had thought she looked a bad lay. Not at all, replied Gable. It was all Olivier's fault. "Never have I seen a girl more completely hooked on a guy than you. You couldn't think or talk or dream of anything or anyone else on earth. I really began to think I was slipping." There were, indeed, many witnesses to the fact that the couple were conspicuously in love. "They were more like teenage lovers than two adults who had been married before," said Myron Selznick's secretary, who had been deputed to look after Leigh while the filming was in progress; while Douglas Fairbanks noted that they "seemed to be constantly impatient to get the trivialities of everyday life over with so they could just rush madly back to bed. Or anywhere else handy and preferably private . . . Vivien was extremely libidinous." Formally, they lived separate lives, but Olivier's hotel room became celebrated as "the least slept-in bedroom in Hollywood." David Selznick feared that there might be a scandal that would damage the prospects of his film, and so put a night porter outside Vivien Leigh's house, with instructions that he was to keep Olivier out. Vivien protested, whereupon Selznick relented and changed the orders: the porter was to let Olivier in and keep out everybody else.[9]

Once the filming of *Wuthering Heights* was over, however, no amount of fornication would have kept Olivier in Hollywood. The constant efforts of the English set to draw him into their midst bored and irritated him. "We didn't play cricket and always go about together," he remembered, distancing himself from the Anglocentric group that clustered around Sir Cedric Hardwicke. "Nobody liked the English because they were English, though the English seemed to think they did. It embarrassed us terribly." More important than that, however, was the fact that no work of any real interest was offered him. "I was never the sort to let a romance interfere with my career, never," he admitted or perhaps boasted, "so when I saw the way the land lay I said, 'I'm sorry, darling. I'm going to get a job in New York.'" Vivien Leigh accepted his defection with apparent equanimity; subsequent events suggest that it caused her a great deal more grief than Olivier realized, or chose to realize.[10]

The "job in New York" had, in fact, already been secured. Olivier was to play opposite Katharine Cornell in S. N. Behrman's new play, *No Time for Comedy*. Cornell was one of the most, perhaps *the* most distinguished actress on the American stage. Unfortunately, however, she had relatively little experience of playing comedy and this, in spite of its title, was what Behrman's play was. She was a great deal below her best. "Poor old Kit," said some critic condescendingly. "Poor old Kit!" echoed Olivier derisively. "The most successful woman in the American theater. The richest, the most beautiful, the most sought after, the most distinguished, the most loved. Poor old Kit indeed!" Privately he was rather less enthusiastic: "I'm afraid I came out a little bit ahead of her," he claimed, "because I did know how to do it and she didn't really. I don't think she was terribly happy, poor darling. I'm afraid it was *my* success." A success it was, a resounding one, but it was marred for Olivier by a sudden appeal from Selznick to rush to Hollywood to succor Vivien Leigh. Gruelingly hard work coupled with her separation from Olivier had proved too much for her; she was hysterical, close to a breakdown. It seemed that the vast investment that had been made in *Gone With the Wind* might be in jeopardy. Olivier could only be away for three days but in the short term it was enough. He successfully applied emotional first aid and Leigh was back at work by the time he left. For Olivier it was an alarming shock. He had always known that she was highly strung and suspected that she might prove unstable— "Vivien was barking fucking mad from the word go," he once told Derek Granger—but this was the first time he had encountered any serious disorder. All seemed to be well, but he must have had apprehensions about the future.[11]

To add to his preoccupations, his father died just before the first night of *No Time for Comedy*. He had been ill for some months and was getting little pleasure out of life, but his death was sudden and unexpected. Even if he had wanted to, Olivier could not have got back in time for the funeral. "I can feel no sorrow whatever at Fahv's dying," his sister told him. "I'm thankful for his sake and everybody else's." Olivier did not feel differently, but, almost in spite of himself, he had warmed to his father in recent years. "I got fond of him because he got fond of me," he confessed. But he was conscious of the fact that his father's affection was related closely to his own success as an actor. "More and more, old Son, I congratulate you on your wonderful success," he had written when Olivier's Hamlet was first beginning to attract attention. "Everybody about here is raving about you." Olivier could not help contrasting this adulation with the scorn, if not hostility, which his father now showed toward his elder son. Dickie's job in India had come to an end, through no fault of his own, and he had returned to England more or less penniless and with dismal prospects of finding rewarding employment. His father seemed to delight in pointing out that he had been a failure. Once Olivier came to the house and Fahv offered him a whisky. Dickie asked if he could have one too. "Good God, no, what do *you* want a whisky for?" Fahv demanded. "It was brutal, shocking," remembered Olivier. "I was afraid of him and never was able to give it to him straight. My weakness, my cowardice, was to blame more than anything else." It was Olivier who gave Dickie the money he needed to stay afloat while searching for a job. He did it with good grace and without a trace of patronage, but it must still have been humiliating for Dickie to depend upon the charity of his younger brother. The Rev. Gerard not merely did nothing to alleviate that humiliation, he seemed to rejoice in it. Any warmth that Olivier felt toward his father was weakened by the indignation he felt on behalf of Dickie.[12]

Jill Esmond came to her father-in-law's funeral. Sybille told Olivier that she had never seen her look prettier or more contented. "I don't think it was an act, either," she wrote: "I think she really has gained a measure of stability and happiness that she'd never have achieved while staying with you." Part of it *was* an act. Jill was lonely and distressed, but her feelings toward her husband had stopped well short of passion and she was doing a good job of making a new life for herself. She, too, wrote to Olivier after Fahv's funeral, agreeing with Sybille that his death was the best thing that could have happened. She gave news of their son, Tarquin. "It's impossible to describe him to you as it's so long since you've seen him and you don't know him at all . . . all I can say is, he really is heaven and makes me laugh a lot." She had been to see "Wuthering Heights": "I have never thought you a really first-class film actor before, but I do now . . . We wept buckets." Only on page sixteen of a twenty-three page letter did she turn to "our jolly little divorce." Did Olivier want to go through with it immediately, which would involve Vivien Leigh being cited as co-respondent and the risk of a lot of disagreeable publicity, or would he be content to wait another year and then be divorced for desertion—a process that, with luck, would attract less attention? She was in no particular hurry herself. "Without our being together or you loving me, I can't feel I'm your wife," but, "as yet I haven't met anyone I want to marry . . . Of course, if I meet someone I want to marry I shall want a divorce at once."[13]

It was a brave letter, and one that must have cloaked much unhappiness. Olivier *had* met someone he wanted to marry and he *was* in a hurry, but he saw the force of his wife's argument. He dreaded the publicity, which would be all the worse now that Heathcliff and Scarlett O'Hara had given him and Vivien Leigh a prominence that normally they would have courted but which at that moment seemed undesirable. Besides, it was not just he who needed a divorce. Leigh was still married to Leigh Holman. Esmond was quite ready to get together with Holman so as to sort out the details of the divorce, but this had to be done with caution since any hint of collusion would have been enough to see the petition dismissed. Regretfully Olivier penciled in the summer of 1940 as being the earliest moment he could hope to remarry. Till then their furtive relationship had to carry on. It was disagreeable for both of them. Selznick continued to do all he could to keep their entanglement out of the public eye. When Vivien Leigh said that she wanted her lover to come to the grand opening of *Gone With the Wind* Selznick vetoed the idea out of hand. In that case they would have to manage without her either, said Vivien Leigh. Selznick gave way and invited a few other

celebrities in the hope that Olivier's presence would thus be camou-
flaged. Olivier found himself in a carriage with Claudette Colbert
and Carole Lombard. They were agreeable company but were not
enough to make the occasion pleasurable for him. He hated playing second fiddle and real though his love was for Vivien Leigh he
found it displeasing to figure only as one of her admiring retinue.[14]

Hollywood held better things. David Selznick was scheduled
to make a film based on Daphne du Maurier's *Rebecca*, a romantic
novel that had come close to *Gone With the Wind* in its popular
success. It was to be directed by Alfred Hitchcock, who had made
his name triumphantly with *The Thirty-Nine Steps* and *The Lady
Vanishes* and with whom Olivier was particularly anxious to work.
It seemed that he was bound to have his wish: the role of the moody,
slightly saturnine Maxim de Winter, though not a particularly testing part, was so obviously within his range as to make it likely that
it would be his if he wanted it. "I was an absolutely natural choice
for it," he argued. "I was the obvious chap. I was the top English
actor." Selznick was not so sure. "Colman is the only perfect man,"
he wrote, but once again Colman was unobtainable. William Powell
was next choice, but he would have cost $100,000 too much. Oliv-
ier was, if not *faute de mieux*, at least considered a second or third
best. Once he had the part Vivien Leigh decided that the role of
the anonymous but omnipresent heroine should be hers. Selznick
thought that to cast an actress so recently distinguished as the dashing, headstrong Scarlett as the hesitant, self-effacing second Mrs.
de Winter, would be to destroy the balance of the film. Olivier professed to disagree with him. He maintained that Vivien had done an
outstanding test and that it was only Selznick's wish to show that he
could create a new star that had led to her rejection. In fact Selznick,
while thinking she would not be right for the part, had great respect
for her ability and had by no means ruled her out. If Olivier had
pressed strongly he might have got his way. But, as he later admitted, "I didn't really want her to get the part. There was already so
much strain in our personal lives, our divorces, leaving a wife and
child and a husband and child in England . . . It was perhaps better

for us to have a little vacation from constant togetherness. Vivien thought I didn't try hard enough for her . . . Well, I didn't. I hadn't felt she was right for the part, if the truth be told."[15]

Instead, he found himself playing opposite the little known Joan Fontaine. He disliked her from the start, finding her skinny and unattractive—"I didn't really understand what Max de Winter could see in her." The generosity that Roger Furse had remarked when Olivier had played opposite Curigwen Lewis was conspicuously lacking.* He told Hitchcock that he thought she was no good in the part and Hitchcock passed it on. "You can imagine how that made me feel," Fontaine said. "I was as friendly and cooperative as I could be. But after what I'd been told, if I convinced Olivier of my good feelings toward him then I *really* deserved an Oscar." She won no Oscar—for that piece of acting at any rate. "I felt she didn't like me . . ." was Olivier's conclusion, "she never said anything hostile to me, but she scarcely spoke to me at all." In spite of this unpromising preamble, the partnership worked pretty well. Fontaine, Olivier admitted, "gave an amazing performance"; as for himself: "I literally walked through the part—it had nothing to do with the real work of acting." His was, indeed, an understated performance in an undemanding role, but it was what the film needed and what the public wanted. "Most people thought I was excellent . . . That, of course, was the bloody exasperating thing about film acting. The less acting one did the better one came across." Another way of putting it would have been that Olivier had fully come to terms with the medium. *Rebecca* confirmed what *Wuthering Heights* had already suggested; that Olivier was now in the first rank of international film stars.[16]

This to some extent consoled Korda for what seemed to him Olivier's rank treachery. "Am amazed at information you have contracted to play 'Rebecca' for Selznick," he cabled. "You are, of course, aware your exclusive contract with us is still subsisting and

* See page 58 above

was only suspended to permit you to play New York. Please cable immediately that information received is unfounded." Olivier replied blandly: "Am amazed at your resentment . . . Am under definite impression no contract with you exists. However, am willing to discuss new one with you upon my return end of the year, also most happy to see you." Perhaps Korda was not sure of his ground, perhaps the conciliatory note of the last few words convinced him that, in the long run, it would be better not to quarrel with his inconstant star. He was to get his reward some years later when it was Selznick who cabled indignantly to complain about Olivier doing work for Korda while still under contract to the American producer.[17]

In August 1939 Selznick had another preoccupation. What would happen if war broke out and Olivier, George Sanders and the other British members of the cast were ordered to report for duty in England? "We would be in a fine pickle—not so much of a pickle as Poland, I grant you, but still a pickle." The question does not seem to have caused Olivier serious worry. International affairs meant little to him; he rarely studied a newspaper except to read reviews of the new plays and films. The Munich crisis had not passed unnoticed, but he had many other things on his mind that seemed more pressing. On September 3, 1939 he was on Douglas Fairbanks's yacht off the Californian coast. Everyone had been drinking heavily and when Neville Chamberlain broadcast his baleful pronouncement that Britain was now at war it seemed only sensible to drink some more. Olivier, said Fairbanks, "was the only one who got really and truly drunk." With some difficulty he lowered himself into a dinghy and began to row round the fleet of expensive yachts that infested those waters. "You're all finished!" he shouted as he passed the boats. "You're done! Drink up. You've had it! This is the end!" The occupants of the yachts, who did not share Olivier's view that they were done or that this was the end, complained to the authorities that a mad Englishman was rowing around, abusing them. Unfortunately, they identified the miscreant as Ronald Colman, whose yacht was also in the area. Colman was accused of insulting behavior and had some difficulty proving his innocence. Meanwhile, Olivier rowed back to the Fairbanks's yacht and went to sleep. He woke next morning with a hangover and considerable uncertainty as to what he should do next.[18]

CHAPTER SIX

WAR

Drunken extravagance was all very well, but was no solution to the problem of what Olivier should do now that his country was at war. He told Oswald Frewen that he didn't know whether to stay where he was, to enlist or to be a conscientious objector. "Truly the 'to be or not to be' spirit has entered into him," Frewen commented. The conscientious objector possibility cannot have been advanced very seriously. Olivier was by nature belligerent and any fashionable antiwar sentiments he might have held a few years before had long vanished. This, he believed, was a just and necessary war and he wished to play his part in it. But what part should that be? His first instinct was to hurry back to England to be of whatever use he could. Yet what use *could* he be? At his age he knew that there was no possibility of his being able to join up for several months at least, perhaps longer. It was likely that most of the London theaters would be closed: there was no filming in the offing: there seemed little point in rushing back to London only to hang around doing nothing.[1]

And yet he felt this was what he ought to do. He disapproved of, indeed disliked, most of those English in Hollywood who decided to stay there. They held endless meetings to discuss how they could do this without giving an impression of cowardice or irresponsibility. "They had plans for getting publicity, having cricket matches for charity. I don't know what bloody nonsense they didn't get up to." Angrily he told them that he would have nothing do with it all; he was going home. At least he preferred the honesty of George Sanders, who had acted with him in *Rebecca*. When Olivier told him he was determined to return to London, Sanders replied: "Of course, I admire your courage and all that, but *I'm* not going back because I'm a shit and I don't give a fuck who knows it!" Olivier was not a shit and he was very anxious that nobody should think he was. If only to preserve his good name he felt that he must leave.[2]

It was David Niven who first shook his resolve. The British Embassy had told Niven that he could serve his country best by staying in the United States and making propaganda for the Allied cause. He had been a regular army officer however; he had a regiment to join; he felt he must go back. "Why don't you ask Larry Olivier, though? He's dying to do something for the war effort and it'll be a while before he gets home." Olivier was a friend of Duff Cooper, who he knew was close to Churchill. He approached him for advice. "Stay in New York," came the reply. Alexander Korda was going there and had projects in mind in which Olivier could play a useful part.[3]

It has been suggested that there was more to it than that. A recent biography puts forward the theory that Olivier had been recruited by S.O.E., the Special Operations Executive, to work for a propaganda organization. This made him a target for German undercover agents and put him at risk of assassination. He never said anything himself to support this theory, but he was quite happy to let a touch of mystery color his activities in the United States. When asked why he was not more communicative he replied coyly: "My ego is too great to reveal my secrets. It serves my ego to keep things to myself." In fact it seems unlikely that he had any secrets of consequence to reveal. He would have been useless to any intelligence organization and one can imagine no reason why any such body should have sought to enlist him. Where he could serve his country was by making patriotic films that might speed America's entry into the war or at least promote the British cause. If he had asked the Embassy for advice he would have received no more than generalized encouragement to strike a patriotic line.[4]

Though he was rarely picked out by name, Olivier found himself, or at least felt himself included in the condemnation of those actors who had opted to stay in America. In the *Sunday Dispatch* Michael Balcon denounced "deserters" and insisted that "for the isolationists the curtain should be run down." "We've got a good word in Lancashire to describe the people who have run away," declared the ukulele-playing George Formby, "and it's a bit stronger than desertion!" Such charges hurt, the more so for being unfair, but it was to be several months before Olivier was engaged in any activity that was intended to serve the war effort. In the meantime he prepared himself by taking flying lessons. He had begun these as long ago as 1935 but had let them lapse; now he engaged in an intensive course. "Larry is learning to fly every day, so that means he will be good," Lynn Fontanne told Noël Coward. "He says he is going to be an ace." He was never going to be an ace, but nor was he conspicuously unsuccessful. The legend grew—fostered largely by his delight in making a good story out of very little—that he had merely to step into a plane for some disaster to ensue. Olivia de Havilland wrote how he had repeatedly written off both his own and other people's planes: "There were at least ten incidents and it was really hilarious. Larry was undaunted, fearless, oblivious." Undaunted and fearless he was, but there was no long chapter of accidents of which he needed to remain oblivious. The notes of his hypercritical instructor suggest that he was no worse than most of his fellow students and better than some of them. He completed his two hundred hours of solo flying—"which is a great deal," commented Jill Esmond—and was issued his certificate of competence.[5]

His first contribution to the war effort was to be the making of a patriotic film with Alexander Korda but there was another commitment to be undertaken first. Though M.G.M.'s version of *Pride and Prejudice* took what any self-respecting Janeite must consider outrageous liberties with the plot, it was in fact a quite creditable effort to put Miss Austen's best-known if not best novel on the screen. Olivier, of course, was Darcy: a part that he was quite as capable of walking through as he had been when playing Max de Winter.

He considered that his Elizabeth should be Vivien Leigh and this time he seems not to have had any of the private reservations he had admitted to in the case of *Rebecca*. Instead, Greer Garson was imposed on him. Where he had disliked Joan Fontaine, he thought well of Garson, but this did not reconcile him to the casting: "I hated it, and I thought it was disgraceful, and I was awful, and I thought darling Greer was as wrong as could be." Instead of being sharp and level-headed as the plot demanded, she was, he claimed, "the most silly and affected of the sisters." It seems almost as if he saw some other version of the film to that enjoyed by the rest of the world. He was not "awful." Darcy was hardly a testing role but he acted it with all the necessary arrogance and panache—while Greer Garson was neither silly nor affected but something very close to the high-spirited and opinionated heroine Jane Austen had created.[6]

Now the war effort could begin. This time, though, Vivien Leigh was included. "Larry and I are to do a picture about Nelson and Lady Hamilton," she told the man who was still her husband. "I am extremely dubious about it. But now one does not plan a career much, as it seems futile, and we are certainly only doing this for financial purposes." She did not do herself or Olivier justice. Money mattered, since their children were coming over from embattled Britain and would need support, but they could have earned far more if they had not chosen to put themselves at Korda's disposal. Olivier was initially as doubtful as Leigh about the project. Had he heard of Lady Hamilton? Korda asked him. "She was the tart who fucked Nelson, wasn't she?" replied Olivier. Korda agreed that this more or less summed it up, but he stressed that what was planned was a patriotic extravaganza, tailored to the needs of the day, with Nelson/Churchill mouthing slogans about the "unconquerable valor of the British nation." Olivier was allowed a large input into the production—"We did a lot to make it sound more natural and that sort of the thing"—and the result was a slightly absurd but exciting adventure story. Olivier read energetically around his subject—"In those days I did quite a deal of research"—and tried to make his part realistic as well as romantic. His research omitted one detail. Shooting was about to begin when he asked which arm it had been that Nelson lost at Santa Cruz. None of the available portraits elucidated the point, naval historians were scarce in Hollywood. Then someone remembered that an elderly Hungarian opera singer living nearby had once played Nelson in an operetta in Vienna. He was sent for and Korda interrogated him. For a few minutes he pleaded forgetfulness, then admitted that he had got so bored playing the role that he had alternated, sacrificing his left arm on one night, his right on the other.[7]

Olivier, always the perfectionist, was outraged by what he saw as Korda's slapdash practices. The most important scene was the one in which he said goodbye to Lady Hamilton before leaving on what was to be his final voyage. For some reason he made a fearful hash of it. Twice he dried up, once he caught his scabbard in his cloak. To his dismay, Korda then called for the next shot. "Alex," said Olivier. "You must be mad. It's the worst acting I've ever done in my life. I must have another go at it." "Larry, my dear boy," Korda replied, "you know nothing about making pictures. Sometimes there must be bad acting. Next shot."[8]

"It was a damned good film," Olivier concluded. "It stands up." He did not find it an easy part to play, though. It was "quite fraught with traps and dangers." It is probably true to say that, if the traps and dangers had not been there, he would have invented them. "I can't remember if I ever found a part simple," he once said. "Each one has always been a delicious problem, there's been something always to fight a way through." Each play or film for Olivier was an enemy, to be confronted, outwitted, battered into submission. The stiffer the resistance, the more Olivier loved it. That is why he believed *Hamlet* to be the greatest play ever written; because however many times he thought he had defeated it, it would reveal some unexpected and inexplicable subtlety, would escape from him again. *Lady Hamilton* possessed no comparable delights but it was good enough to be getting along with. It won him a powerful admirer. Churchill thought it the best film about war ever made and watched it seven times, though it was probably the battle scene that appealed as much as Olivier's performance. He even sent a copy to Stalin who had notched up three viewings by the time he discussed the film with Churchill at a dinner during the Tehran Conference in 1943. The critics were not quite so enthusiastic, though they were generous enough: James Agate had little good to say about Vivien Leigh's performance but thought Olivier made "a brave, unaffected and successful Nelson."[9]

This was not the only patriotic rodomontade in which Olivier became involved. The Ministry of Information asked Michael Powell to make a film that might help persuade the Americans to join in the war. He came up with the story of a group of survivors from a U-boat that had been sunk in Hudson's Bay, who decided to make their way across Canada to the United States. "Goebbels considered himself an expert on propaganda but I thought I'd show him a thing or two," remarked the screen writer, Emeric Pressburger, and the Germans were portrayed as a bunch of murderous thugs. Olivier, who charged only half his ordinary fee as a contribution to the war effort, played a French-Canadian trapper who was one of the Germans' victims as they savaged their way southwards. His part was a small one but made memorable by his singularly bloody death. His sister Sybille asked him how this had been contrived. "I'm a marvelous actor, my dear," he answered. "I can cough up a hemorrhage whenever I want to." Pressed for further details he confessed that two tablespoonfuls of liquid chocolate—the film, *The 49th Parallel*, being shot in black and white—had provided the basis for his spectacular demise.[10]

Their films, though not vast moneymakers, had helped Leigh and Olivier to build up a comfortable reserve that would suffice to support their respective children when they arrived as evacuees. They managed to lose most of it in an ill-fated venture in the theater. It was George Cukor who suggested that if they wanted to make a lot of money quickly and at the same time burnish their theatrical reputations they could not do better than act together in a production of *Romeo and Juliet*. How could it go wrong? "Never has there been a happier and more colorful combination of principals and production," wrote one interviewer. "Two internationally famed lovers of fact projecting themselves into the two most famed lovers of fiction." Olivier flung himself into the enterprise: selecting the cast, fussing over the costumes, planning the provincial tour that would precede the New York opening, even providing the music. "Larry has suddenly started *composing* music and nothing will stir him from the piano," Vivien Leigh told her mother. He had completed his own entrance music and was now doing the same for Juliet—"unless I can do it myself," Leigh concluded.[11]

One result of this was that Olivier wore himself out. He was never fully able to accept that there was a limit to what he could achieve and in 1940 he had not even begun to learn the lesson. By the time the play opened in San Francisco he was mentally and physically at his limit. The result was a debacle. For the end of the balcony scene Olivier had devised a dramatic exit from the Capulet garden that involved him bounding lithely over the wall and disappearing into the night. Unfortunately he was so much weakened by his efforts that he missed his footing and was left floundering, clinging to the top of the wall but quite unable to surmount it.

After this unpropitious start, things improved. "By dint of strenuous rehearsals it is getting better and better," Vivien reported, "and by the time we open in N.Y. it should be alright." What they did not take into account was that, while the reviews were reasonably friendly, the newspaper coverage that they received, particularly while in Chicago, was having the worst possible effect in New York. "See real lovers make love in public," had been the tenor of the reporting. A squalid romance was being vulgarly exploited, was the response of the more austere New Yorkers. Besides, Olivier and Leigh were known in New York as film stars; *Gone With the Wind* and *Wuthering Heights* were playing to packed cinemas. It was deemed significant that the venue where *Romeo and Juliet* was to appear, the 51st Street Theater, had been known till recently as the Hollywood Theater. The case was proven. Something very remarkable would have had to have happened between Chicago and New York for the critics to treat the production with even a degree of charity.[12]

Up to a point their complaints were justified. Olivier, by his own admission, was not at his best. Edmund O'Brien, who played Mercutio, agreed that it was a lifeless performance. Not for the first time, Olivier was accused of muting his performance so as to enhance the showing of Vivien Leigh. "He thought the whole thing should be Viv's show," O'Brien said. "Olivier believed the pure power of his stage presence would carry him through, and that American audiences wouldn't know the difference between a great portrayal of Romeo and a lackluster one." If Olivier really thought this he was swiftly disillusioned. The critics denounced his performance: "Sheer, savage, merciless cruelty," he described their judgment. Brooks Atkinson of the New York Times, most influential of all American theater critics, was one of the more temperate. "Mr. Olivier in particular keeps throwing his part away," he complained. "The superficiality of his acting is difficult to understand. He is mannered and affected, avoiding directness in even simple episodes. As his own director," Atkinson concluded, "Mr. Olivier has never heard himself in the performance. This is just as well; he would be astonished if he did." In the course of his career Olivier was often to direct plays in which he played a leading role. It was always a risky business, but his astonishing energy and ability to keep an almost impossible number of balls simultaneously in the air usually carried him through. In 1940, inexperienced and perhaps distracted by the need to sustain a faltering Vivien Leigh, he met with disaster.[13]

If they had had any doubts about the scale of their failure these would have been dispelled the night after their opening when they went to a "War Relief" ball that Noël Coward had organized. Coward greeted them with a sympathetic but embarrassed smile. "My darlings," he murmured, "how brave of you to come." Goldwyn put it more brutally. After the first night Vivien Leigh told him that she would not be able to make another film for him as they would be leaving for London once the run was over. "So soon?" replied

Goldwyn. The public read the reviews and flocked to the theater to cancel their bookings and get their money back. "Let them all have it," Olivier instructed. In her draft biography his sister suggested that he did this because gangsterism was rife in New York and, if he had offended too many people, he risked having the theater burned over his head. "No, no, no," Olivier protested in mock American. "It was only for the first two weeks of the run we handed the money back . . . but after two weeks I stopped it, as pride was becoming too expensive. It wasn't that we were sceered, it was that we was proud."[14]

Romeo and Juliet struggled on for several weeks. Vivien Leigh was horrified by the reviews and in no way comforted by the fact that, on the whole, she had got better notices than Olivier. Whenever she was not on stage she hid in her dressing room, leaving it to Olivier to do what he could to sustain morale. "He continued to behave as if everything was fine," said Joan Shepard, a member of the cast, "inspecting everyone's makeup and costumes each night and treating everyone with the utmost courtesy." It was a gallant effort on his part, to cover what had been a most painful shock. It was one of the few times in his life that he had been guilty of over-confidence. "We still feel that at any moment the laughter will stop and the tomatoes will begin," he wrote many years later when describing life on the stage. "I don't think that there has ever been any true actor who has not felt this. To this day I still feel it." On the whole he escaped with a small proportion of tomatoes against a mountain of adulation; the failure of *Romeo and Juliet* was the most unpleasant and the most unexpected exception.[15]

It was also among the most costly. "Larry has just lost $40,000 on *Romeo and Juliet*," Jill Esmond told her mother, with what one suspects might have been mild *Schadenfreude*. "Vivien did not put one penny of *her* money into it. She has more sense." Olivier found himself short of money. Any satisfaction Jill felt at this must have been diminished by the fact that she and Tarquin had by now crossed the Atlantic and so would be dependent on Olivier for financial support. She met him in Toronto in July 1940. "He is quite the film star now and suffering from a persecution complex," she reported. "He is terrified of being recognized and distrusts everybody . . . He got on very well with Bumpin [Tarquin] but didn't seem really very interested, in fact he seemed lacking in interest in almost all things except himself and his point of view." Things were little better when she called on him in New York. Vivien Leigh came in while she was there: "Her eyes were hard and cruel. We were *so* charming to each other and so insincere. She left me quite cold—I might have been talking to a fish." Jill had no idea why Olivier had wanted to organize the meeting; it had been a waste of time and "I gained nothing from it except the fact that he meant nothing to me and I don't want to see him again." She had to admit, though, that he was being as generous as he could be on the financial front and that he appeared genuinely concerned about the well-being of herself and their son.[16]

By the time they met again, on Christmas Day, the divorces had come through and he and Vivien Leigh had been married. The fact that the situation had thus been regularized seems to have removed some of the restraint that had soured his relationship with his former wife. He was "charming, quite his old self," Esmond told her mother. "I still think he's a nice person. I don't think I would have loved him if he hadn't been really nice—he was just *very* weak, and still is." Even though her sexual tastes developed in different directions and she grew further and further apart from her former husband, she never ceased to love and miss him. She wrote to her mother comparing the love that she had had for Olivier with her mother's feeling toward *her* former husband. "Both our lovers had their faults and gave us great pain in various ways but at least we had a hell of a good time while it lasted and we both had a completeness of both body and soul that comes to very few . . . We have been very lucky that we have known the best that life has to offer."[17]

Olivier and Leigh had been married at the end of August 1940. "I hope he finds happiness, but I very much doubt it," wrote Esmond grimly. The relationship had for the first time come under strain some months before when Leigh won an Oscar for her Scarlett O'Hara while Olivier was passed over for Heathcliff. Olivier stoically survived the banquet and preserved an expression of feigned delight when Vivien was receiving her award, but his suffering was dreadful. On their way home together, he told Tarquin many years later, he took her Oscar from her: "It was all I could do to restrain myself from hitting her with it. I was insane with jealousy." He no doubt exaggerated his resentment, but the pain was very real. By the time of their marriage the offense had been forgiven if not forgotten, but his new wife can have had no doubt that, earnestly though he might seek to advance her career, there were limits to the level of competition he could endure.[18]

For their marriage they slipped away to Santa Barbara where they could escape the attention of the press. They were so far successful that by the time they had joined Ronald Colman on his yacht at San Pedro an hour or two away not a word had been heard in public about the wedding. Olivier congratulated himself on his cunning and professed to hope that the silence would continue. A news bulletin made no mention of the marriage: "Excellent," said Olivier, in mild dismay. An hour later there was still silence. The Oliviers were patently disconcerted. "We certainly pulled it off, didn't we?" Colman said. "We certainly did," agreed Olivier gloomily. At last, at ten o'clock, the story broke. "Too bad!" said Olivier, with evident relief. "Too good to last," sighed Vivien with an incandescent smile. "After that we had a very happy evening."[19]

The delay had proved worthwhile. People in Great Britain in September 1940 had things on their mind rather more urgent than the matrimonial vicissitudes of even their most celebrated actors and actresses. Olivier received a handful of letters, written more in sorrow than in anger, reproaching him with breaking sacred ties, but there was nothing like the torrent of abuse he had anticipated. They had no reason to expect any violent reaction when they returned to Britain. Six weeks earlier, Lynn Fontanne had told Noël Coward that the British Government had ordered Olivier home: "He doesn't know when, as there are a hundred thousand young men of military age in America and they must wait until the facilities for getting them over are completed." In fact there was no question of an order: the British Government would have been content if he had chosen to remain in the United States; might, indeed, have preferred it. The facilities were a problem, though. It was the very end of 1940 before the Oliviers got berths on the American ship *Excambion* destined for Lisbon. It was an uncomfortable voyage, not least because the captain was a German and most of the other passengers seemed to be German or German sympathizers. Olivier feared lest the ship be intercepted by a U-boat and the British passengers taken off into captivity. All passed off peacefully, though, and after a few days in Lisbon they managed to board a plane for England. This stage of the journey was no less hazardous: Vivien Leigh's costar in *Gone With the Wind*, Leslie Howard, was to be shot down and killed on the same flight the following year. But without mishaps, they arrived in Bristol on January 10, 1941. An air raid was in progress and the anti-aircraft guns were firing. They spent the night in a bomb-damaged hotel without heating and with the outside wall of the building replaced by a flimsy tarpaulin. They had come home.[20]

CHAPTER SEVEN

NAVAL OFFICER

Olivier's intention was to follow the example of Ralph Richardson and join the Fleet Air Arm—it had always seemed to him that the Royal Navy was the most estimable of the armed services and the Fleet Air Arm would give him a chance to exhibit his prowess as a pilot. Not everybody thought that this would be the most sensible use of his abilities. Sidney Bernstein, then working in the Ministry of Information, asked for his ideas on the best way to influence American opinion and added his thanks for "promising to make films for the Crown Film Unit." Olivier had made no such promise or, at least, had made it clear that his military service must come first. He at once applied to the Admiralty, attended a medical examination and, to his dismay, was failed for some defect in his hearing. He could now, with honor, have taken up Bernstein's offer and reverted to what he did best—acting. Instead he reapplied, a few discreet strings were no doubt pulled, and on February 18, 1941, he passed his medical and was accepted for the Fleet Air Arm. If he could get through his flying test he would immediately be commissioned. A day or two later he chanced to meet his old school friend, Douglas Bader. Bader was by now a hero, having already shot down more than twenty enemy aircraft and been awarded the D.S.O. and bar and the D.F.C. and bar. "I want to congratulate you," he said to Olivier. "I think it's a thoroughly good show your coming back to join up like this. I want to say 'Bravo!'" Olivier cast a respectful eye on the glories attached to Bader's breast. "I want to say more than 'Bravo,'" he replied.[1]

After a brief stay at the Royal Naval Air Station at Lee-on-Solent Olivier moved on to his first serious posting at Worthy Down, four miles north of Winchester. His unexciting though useful role was to fly trainee air gunners around the skies while they honed their skills in preparation for more serious operations. It was typical of Olivier that he not merely carried out his duties with competence but looked absolutely right in the part. "I always thought my performance as a naval officer was the best bit of character acting I ever did," he once remarked. Ralph Richardson paid a half-mocking tribute to his transmogrification. "He looked fine," he remarked. "The uniform was perfect: it looked as if it had been worn long on arduous service, but had kept its cut. The gold wings on his sleeve had no distasteful glitter; only the shoes shone . . . His manner was naval, it was quiet, alert, businesslike, with the air of there being a joke somewhere around." Richardson found his friend's performance mildly comical, but he was impressed by the contented atmosphere of the unit and the relationship between Olivier and the people who served under him. He knew all the Wrens and seamen, remembered their names and details and was liked and trusted. "Larry did that very well indeed," thought Richardson as he left the base. "Then a thought crossed my mind: 'I wonder if he rehearsed it?'" Olivier probably had rehearsed it—he left as little as possible to chance— but the leadership qualities that were so evident at Worthy Down were in time to figure to still greater effect in the National Theater.[2]

Though nobody would have detected it from his demeanor, Olivier did not feel at home in the Fleet Air Arm. "I'm always filled with the most affectionate admiration for the 'lads,'" he told Jill Esmond, "tho' many officers I don't think much of." Olivier found nobody in the Officers' Mess to whom he could relate. He could impersonate an Air Force officer and even relish his performance, but he could not enjoy the company of his fellows. They knew nothing of the theater and had no wish to learn about it; he for his part could only pretend to share their preoccupations. A somewhat narrow approach to life was one of his more noticeable characteristics. He was always reluctant to venture far outside his designated

territory. A friend once asked him to dinner. He accepted with pleasure. "I've got some banker friends coming," his friend continued.
"I can't do it," Olivier protested. "Writers, directors, actors O.K.
Otherwise, I can't do it." He *could* have done it and would, no doubt,
have provided a most convincing performance as a banker, but he
would not have enjoyed it. He coasted through his life in the Fleet
Air Arm without engaging thoroughly with it. "I occasionally hear
from somebody who says 'Do you remember me at Worthy Down?'
and I probably don't, but I say 'Of course I do,'" Olivier recalled forty
years later. "There were very few people with whom I had anything
in common."[3]

Any chance that he would fit more easily into life in the Officers'
Mess was lost when he got permission to move into a bungalow
he rented two or three miles from the aerodrome. "Larry not very
happy," Noël Coward noted. "Think it a great mistake for him not
to live in Mess." Possibly he would have been less happy if he *had*
been living in Mess. At least, Vivien Leigh, who was enjoying a
long run in *The Doctor's Dilemma*, was able to join him in the bungalow on Sundays. It was embellished with Indian rugs, an Aubus-
son carpet, paintings by Sickert and Boudin. Other friends visited
him from time to time. For him it was an oasis of civilization in a
barren world.[4]

One reason for his discontent may have been that, by the high
standards that he set himself, he was not a particularly good pilot.
The legend of his unique incompetence, that Olivia de Havilland
had rejoiced in while he was training in the United States, still clung
to him. There was as little reason now as there had been then. He
had one accident before he even took to the air and damaged two
aircraft as a result, but this seems to have been only in part his fault.
"I think I may describe myself as a decent pilot," he wrote; and the
description was not overflattering. But he was no more than that,
though he would have liked to have been acknowledged as a master.
Instead he was mocked for his inadequacy. Cyril Cusack was trav-
eling back to London by train in the same compartment as Vivien
Leigh. She dropped off to sleep. Two Air Force cadets came into the

compartment. "Isn't that Vivien Leigh?" one of them asked Cusack. He said it wasn't. "Just as well. That husband of hers is our training officer and he couldn't fly his way out of a paper bag."[5]

Another cause for gloom arose when Ralph Richardson was given a half-stripe and thus gained seniority over his friend. Richardson had joined up several months before, so his promotion was justified, but Olivier admitted that this extra stripe "almost killed our relationship. I didn't want one particularly; I wouldn't have cared at all if it hadn't been for Ralphie having one." It made him very pompous, Olivier complained: "There was no talking to him, he became a different person." It was not the first or the last time that Olivier resented his friends being awarded distinctions that he would never otherwise have coveted for himself.[6]

Whatever their judgment of his merits as a pilot it became ever more obvious that the authorities felt he could be more usefully employed making propaganda and encouraging the public to contribute to various aspects of the war effort. His activities ranged from a tour of the countryside around Winchester, appealing to the local inhabitants to contribute unwanted books to a Salvage Drive, to performances in a packed Albert Hall ending with a spirited rendition of "Once more unto the breach." The change in emphasis in his activities can be traced from the entries in his pocket diary. At the beginning of every month he would enter the various training courses and flights to which he was committed. More and more often these were crossed out and some propaganda duty substituted: a lecture on Ship Recognition, for instance, became an appearance at the Lyceum in Sheffield. Tyrone Guthrie, who had moved the Old Vic to Burnley and believed that it was vital that the theater should be kept alive, argued that even this was not enough. The country did not need Richardson as a staff officer or Olivier as a second-line pilot, trolling air gunners about the skies. Nor was the occasional flag-waving foray a proper use of their talents. They had better and more important things to do. Regretfully, Olivier accepted that this was true. He was no more than an airborne taxi driver. He should move on.[7]

He made a final effort to play a more active role. The Walrus was an amphibious aircraft designed to be catapulted from the decks of battleships or heavy cruisers. If he could qualify to fly them he would at last be able to undertake some real operational flying. He was frustrated once more. By the time he had completed the course the Walrus, already recognized in some quarters as a cumbersome antique, was withdrawn from active service. It would be back to the taxi work again. The blandishments of those who felt he would be better employed making films became more and more difficult to resist. Even before he had finished the course he had agreed to undertake a full-length film. It would be some time yet before he was discharged but effectively his life in the Fleet Air Arm was behind him.

His first film after his liberation was *Demi-Paradise*, a propaganda exercise intended to make average Britons feel more warmly toward their Russian allies. As Olivier pointed out, Russia was at that time high in public favor; the exercise seemed superfluous. So great was his relief, though, at finding himself once more doing the work he loved, that he rated the film more highly than it deserved. It was, in fact, slight and rather silly, but it gave Olivier a chance to try out his Russian accent and was enjoyed by most of those who saw it. Anthony "Puffin" Asquith, who directed the film, had no illusions about its importance but felt that Olivier had produced "a truly creative performance." Ivan, the Russian hero of the film, played by Olivier, was "so thoroughly imagined and so consummately realized that he contrives to exist quite apart from the film." Asquith was not the only person to believe that the film represented a step forward in Olivier's career: Dilys Powell, already one of the most respected of cinema critics, claimed that this performance put him for the first time in the top flight of British film actors.[8]

Another tempting possibility was dangled before Olivier while *Demi-Paradise* was being filmed. Michael Powell had decided to make a film based upon David Low's farcical cartoon character, Colonel Blimp. It was to be a satirical attack on all that was most hidebound and atrophied in the British establishment. Who better to play it than Olivier, who had himself had the chance to study blimps at first hand during his service with the Fleet Air Arm? He put forward the idea. "Larry stooped like a hawk . . . Larry is, above all, an inventive actor who has to find the secret pass-key that makes a character work for him . . . What bitter, burning satire he could bring to bear from his own experience of a diehard Blimp." Unfortunately, the Secretary of State for War, Sir James Grigg, who himself was not altogether free of blimpish traits, saw little merit in a film intended to mock the stuffier elements of the British military establishment. He rejected any suggestion that Olivier should be released from the services to make such a film.[9]

Meanwhile, Olivier was making desultory efforts to keep in touch with his son and former wife. He could fairly plead that he had a great deal else to do, but even so he could have tried harder. Jill Esmond wrote wistful letters reporting on their son's progress. Tarquin loved gardening, like his father, but had inherited the impatience that led Olivier to dig up each plant a few days after it had been put in the ground so as to see how it was getting on. "I think it is awfully difficult to bring up a boy entirely without a man and I'm determined that he will never be a mother's boy," wrote Esmond. Could not Olivier make more effort? "I wish you would write him a letter; he can't quite understand why you don't, as other boys here have their Father."[10]

The truth was that what energy Olivier had left over was devoted almost exclusively to Vivien Leigh. The successful production of *The Doctor's Dilemma* had brought her to London—"Amazing, the appeal of the film star," wrote Gielgud superciliously. "She is still madly in love with her husband—who adores her—and is convinced he is a much greater person than herself," Cecil Beaton wrote in his diary. William Wyler, who saw them several times at this period, agreed that they were "still very much the newlyweds—and it's very refreshing to see." About her feelings for him there can be no doubt; Selznick's London office assured him that the only reason she did not honor her contractual obligations and return to Hollywood was that Olivier forbade it: "She is still terribly in love with him" and "refuses to listen to any criticism of Larry." Olivier's feelings are not quite so clear cut. "No one has ever been made so happy as Vivien makes me," he wrote in September 1942. "She's my whole life." But there are some suggestions that he was beginning to find her devotion a little oppressive and to be alarmed at the force of her emotions. The situation was complicated by her failing health. In 1944 she was diagnosed with tuberculosis. She seemed to have recovered and was at work on a film of *Caesar and Cleopatra* when she found that she was pregnant. She should have given up the part but filming was by then far advanced and she struggled on. One scene, in which she had to beat an offending slave, proved too taxing for her. She collapsed, miscarried and suffered a fresh bout of tuberculosis. Grief for her lost baby and the protracted nature of her recovery did permanent damage to her psychological balance. She had always been subject to violent mood swings; after this trauma they became dramatically worse. The marriage between Laurence Olivier and Vivien Leigh would endure for many years yet, but it was under threat. It was not, to employ a trite but telling phrase, the beginning of the end, but it was the end of the beginning.[11]

Olivier himself had other and, if he was honest with himself, more important things on his mind. He was about to embark on the enterprise by which he is best remembered and which established him most firmly as a figure celebrated not only in his own country but across the world.

According to his memoirs, the suggestion that he should undertake a film of *Henry V* came first from the Ministry of Information, who presented it to him in a package that also contained *Demi-Paradise*. With the Normandy landings not too far ahead, the swashbuckling heroics of Shakespeare's most patriotic play seemed very much to chime with the popular mood. Only a few weeks before, Bernard Miles had conceived the idea of putting on the play in the West End with the characters clothed in modern battledress. "Larry didn't go for it. Larry only likes ideas of his own," he commented sourly. But when it was a question of a film with full governmental backing, things were different. The idea was a daring one. Since the coming of sound to the cinema, producers had shied away from Shakespeare, believing that a mass audience would not be able to cope with the arcane language. In the previous fifteen years there had only been four serious efforts to put Shakespeare on the screen: Olivier's own contribution, *As You Like It*, having been one of the most notable, though by no means a total success. Far from being deterred by this, Olivier saw it as a reason to take it on. "You have always been loath to have a bash," he told Tarquin. "I used to be a bit like that, but not for a long time now." It must indeed have been a long time; Olivier seems to have been eager to have a bash almost from childhood. That he would have a bash at *Henry V* was never in doubt.[12]

But how much of the work should he undertake himself? It was clear from the start that he would play the King. Who should direct? Olivier's first idea was Terence Young, at that time relatively inexperienced though much later to achieve fame through his direction of several of the James Bond films. Young, however, was still in the armed forces. Olivier invited James Grigg, the War Minister, to dinner to try to persuade him that Young should be released. He "got him drunk as a skunk," Young recalled, and secured a promise that Young could be freed for ten weeks. The dates didn't work, though; Young's name was scratched off the list. Garson Kanin was then approached, then William Wyler—both turned the invitation down. Michael Powell, Korda's favorite director, was next on the list. Olivier expounded all the ideas he had for the film. Powell listened attentively and then told Olivier that it was obvious he should direct *Henry V* himself. "Do you really think I could?" ventured Olivier. It has been suggested that this had been his intention from the start and that he had gone through the rigmarole of inviting others so as to make it clear that the task had been forced on him. Possibly by the time he approached Powell the idea that he should take on the direction himself had begun to seem more feasible, but there is no doubt that at the start he had been hesitant. One of the people whom he most trusted was Roger Furse. "I remember poor Larry's heart-searching," wrote Furse, "and how he questioned me and others as to whether he should take it on. He seemed to be as nervous and uncertain as a virgin."[13]

Once he had taken the plunge, however, all doubts were put behind him. Furse recalled "the tremendous vigor and confidence he exuded to all around him." He told Terence Young that, Young having been ruled out, he was relieved to be doing it himself. "The torturous business of balancing one second-rate director against another and trying to decide which would be worse, was too much. It really feels better to be riding a terrible great horse myself than pretending to trust somebody else whose riding I suspect." Neither Wyler nor Kanin fit into the category of "second-rate" directors and Powell too might have been affronted by the description. The phrase can hardly have been carefully considered but it reflects Olivier's exhilaration at having made up his mind and mounted his "terrible great horse."[14]

Having done so, he had no intention of sharing the ride with anyone. Dallas Bower of the B.B.C. had written the original script for a film of *Henry V* and took it for granted that he would be the director or producer of the current version. His pretensions to the director's role were brushed aside and to his dismay he found that he was soon bypassed as producer too. Olivier, he told Derek Granger, "in fact invited me to be the producer, and I *was* the producer, although he liked to take the production credit to himself. I think it is now generally accepted by everybody that it was a pretty selfish thing to do." He had reason to be aggrieved—Olivier had been at the least guilty of inconsiderate behavior—but one can only rejoice that Olivier kept the reins of his horse firmly in his own hands. Since he was so totally in charge, he told his son, "it'll be all my fault if it's no good. I'm afraid I've made rather a mess of a good many things in my time; let's hope this will be an exception." It was an indication of his total absorption in his work, as well as his relationship with his son, that he absentmindedly signed the letter "Larry Olivier," then crossed out the "Olivier" and added "(well well well)."[15]

Olivier never forgot that, while he intended to produce a great film, he had been commissioned to conduct a propaganda exercise. The Ministry of Information had suggested that he should follow Bernard Miles's plan and clothe the troops in modern battledress. Olivier would have none of it, he had envisaged a setting of spectacular beauty along the lines of the Limbourg brothers' book of hours, *Les Très Riches Heures du Duc de Berry*. The film, however, was dedicated to "The Commandos and Airborne troops of Great Britain the spirit of whose ancestors it has been humbly attempted to recapture," and immense pains were taken to emphasize the supposed parallels between the patriotic fervor of the fifteenth century and the present day. There was no mention of treason within the state of England and inconvenient details like the King's order to kill all the French prisoners were omitted.

Olivier had hoped to cast Vivien Leigh as Princess Katherine, but Selznick ruled that it was a miserable little part that could only damage her reputation. She had already enraged Selznick by refusing to honor her contract and return to the United States; to defy him still further would have been foolhardy. Reluctantly she bowed out. Gielgud admitted that he had hoped to be invited to play the Chorus but was too proud to ask: either the idea never occurred to Olivier or, as Gielgud suggested, "he feared I should be likely to show off my verse-speaking again at his expense, and he chose Leslie Banks instead." The boldest piece of casting was Robert Newton as Ancient Pistol. Newton was a fine actor but a notorious drunk. Olivier warned him that if he ever appeared "pissed, as we all know you've been on many occasions—no matter how far we've got in the script, I'll sack you and start with someone else." Newton complied and as a result put in an anemic performance instead of the rumbustious rendering expected of him: "I don't know how to do it, Larry boy," he pleaded, "show me how." Olivier obliged, coaxing the sober Newton into the sort of performance that a drunk-but-not-too-badly-drunken Newton would have provided. "It is doubtful," wrote Esmond Knight, who played Fluellen, "if Newton would have undergone that kind of torture for anyone other than Laurence, and he certainly would not have trusted anyone else to show him how to act." One of Olivier's bolder improvisations was bringing in the veteran comedian George Robey to play Falstaff in a scene pillaged from *Henry IV, Part Two*. "I felt I needed it," Olivier said, "because he was the definitive part of the comic . . . I had to have those comics, otherwise it would have been Henry, Henry, Henry, through an entire two hours." The obvious person to have asked to play Falstaff was Ralph Richardson, who was in time to achieve glory in the role. There is no evidence, however, that Olivier ever invited him to do so. Perhaps he did, but Richardson was reluctant or unavailable. More probably Olivier feared that he would intrude rather too conspicuously into what in his own mind he did intend to be "Henry, Henry, Henry, through an entire two hours."[16]

Olivier always paid great attention to music. "For goodness sake, I implore you, don't give up on your music," he wrote to a girl who had asked for his advice. "It is a higher art; a more rewarding art; a greater weapon for your soul's purpose than the questionable craft of acting." His experiments with *Romeo and Juliet* had convinced him that composition had best be left to professionals, but he was determined that *Henry V* should be entrusted to a composer of vision and passion as well as technical ability. Dallas Bower put forward the name of William Walton: "He's a bit modern," he said, but he still writes a good tune. "Modern? Oh, very good. That will be splendid," replied Olivier, who did not know much about contemporary music but liked the idea of modernity. He claimed that, once the decision was taken, he left it entirely to Walton to produce what he thought right. Walton on the contrary maintains that Olivier had strong views on the subject and did not hesitate to voice them. His ideas were not always helpful. "Now this is a beautiful tune I've thought of," said Olivier, humming a few bars. "Yes," replied Walton. "It's a lovely tune. It's out of *Meistersinger*." But, however much he may have been tempted to interfere, Olivier soon concluded that he could have total faith in Walton. Their partnership, based on real affection as well as mutual respect, was to last for many years.[17]

Making *Henry V* "changed my entire career," Olivier believed. "I discovered that I was capable of being an extremely capable film director. I took to it like a duck to water." Not everyone agreed. "His method of direction was simply extraordinary," said Dallas Bower. He would play each part himself as he conceived it and expect the actors to copy it. Though Robert Newton welcomed the treatment, some of the other senior actors felt that they were more than capable of conceiving their performance by themselves. Olivier was insistent, though; not indifferent to their opinions but determined to impose his overall vision on the production. In the end, Bower noted with mingled dismay and admiration, the players concluded: "Well, if this is what he wants, we'll simply have to do it." With *Henry V* Olivier established a reputation for being one of the most demanding and perfectionist of directors. "Ruthless would be too strong a word," Harry Andrews felt. "Single-minded, I'd say. Single-minded in doing what he thinks is right for him." Right for him, and right for the production. *Henry V* was not the creation of one man, but every aspect of it bore the mark of one man's authority.[18]

His resolve to serve as both producer and director, not to mention playing the lead role, imposed a burden that even with his great energies he found hard to bear. Making a film in wartime Britain created problems far beyond those that ordinarily plagued a producer. "The various Ministries and Secretaries of Supply, War, Manpower, Labor, Information, etc. that all have to be wooed with such abandon, in order to get anything done at all, leave one gasping at the end of the day," he complained to Terence Young. Sometimes his patience cracked under the strain. He could be unreasonable. Laurence Evans, the production manager, once asked him how many horses he would need for a certain shot. "I don't know how many fucking horses I want," Olivier truthfully but unhelpfully replied. More often he was exemplary in his command of detail and of his precise requirements. "Because I was an artist and a dreamer and an actor, I didn't want them to say 'Ah well . . . ,'" he recollected. "I wanted to be the most professional director they'd ever had." Of course he depended on the expert help of others. Nowhere was this

more the case than where the financing of the operation was concerned. In this field, his task would have been far harder, perhaps
even impossible, if it had not been for the support of the Italian
Filippo del Giudice, a cheerful extrovert with a nose for money,
who made sure that the necessary funds were always there when it
seemed that otherwise filming might have to be halted.[19]

His most innovative and daring departure from the cinematic
norm came at the very beginning of the film. He was worried what
effect Shakespearean verse would have on an unschooled audience
when superimposed on the naturalist background against which
most of the film would be shot. The solution came to him after a
long evening's discussion with Alan Dent in the Garrick Club. The
two men made their way to their respective homes, then, in the
small hours of the morning, Olivier telephoned Dent to expound
his ideas. The action would begin in a mocked-up version of the
Globe; the actors, performing with stagey theatricality, would create
an atmosphere of conspicuous artificiality. Then would come liberation; the camera would desert the theater and soar over medieval
London into the realistic setting of the embarkation for Harfleur.
Relieved of the trappings of the Elizabethan theater the dialogue
would seem natural, even modern. A few critics complained that the
mixture of approaches marred the integrity of Shakespeare's play;
most of them and, to judge by the film's rapturous reception, the
general public, felt that it was a brilliantly conceived and executed
enterprise that provided one of the most memorable moments of
cinema history.[20]

Though Shakespeare's play, for obvious reasons, did not dwell
on the battle of Agincourt itself, Olivier was determined to avoid
the traditional rendering of a handful of soldiers dashing on and off
leaving occasional corpses in their wake. Why make a film at all if
one was not going to exploit all its potentialities? He wanted a cav-
alry charge that would surpass all previous charges, he wanted an
array of archers who would blacken the sky with their deadly arrows.
But where, in wartime Britain, could one find enough horses and
able-bodied extras; where were there enough open spaces free of

pillboxes and other such wartime encumbrances; where were there skies not afflicted by passing airplanes? It was Bower who suggested the battle scenes should be shot in Ireland. Olivier felt guilty about it, though a more authentic French setting would patently have been impossible and England was no more appropriate than Ireland as a venue. "Dear old boy, I feel we're perpetuating the swindle of the century," he observed as he and Bower got off the boat at Dun Laoghaire. It was a swindle that was both expensive to mount and difficult to bring off. It was triumphantly worthwhile. The filming in Ireland took eight weeks to produce only ten minutes of screen time, but those ten minutes provided images that linger in the mind more than half a century after they were first created.[21]

From the start, Olivier was determined to lead by example. They would be asked to do things that were difficult and sometimes even dangerous, he told the seven hundred assembled extras, but never would they have to do anything that he would not be prepared to do himself. They took him at his word. At one point an extra was required to drop some twenty feet from the bough of a tree onto a horse cantering below and drag the rider from its back. "I'd like to see you do it first, Mr. Olivier," said the destined victim. Olivier climbed the tree, performed the leap, landed heavily on his ankle and tottered to his feet in agonizing pain. "There, you see," he gasped through clenched teeth. "Quite easy, really." This was not the only injury he suffered. He was behind a camera that was filming a galloping horse. The results seemed disappointingly dull. He urged the rider to aim for the camera, only swerving to avoid it at the last moment. The horse misunderstood the instructions and plowed straight into the camera, driving the viewfinder into Olivier's upper lip. The scar remained with him for the rest of his life. It did not mar his looks, indeed Jill Esmond said it actually improved his appearance. His mouth had used to be soft and sensitive, after the accident it was stronger and narrower. At least his various contretemps won him sympathy where he most wanted it. "Oh my darling are you alright," cabled Vivien Leigh from Gibraltar. "Desperately worried your back arm shoulder knee lip and what o what else cable immediately baba do stop I worship you dying to see you."[22]

The Irish extras loved him. At the end of the filming they clubbed together and presented him with a handsome bog-oak walking stick inscribed to "Mr. L. O'livier." This showed, thought Roger Furse, that they had accepted him as a real Irishman, "and it showed something more . . . It was, as the Navy say, a happy ship, and that is always due to the Captain." For a man who was by nature short-tempered, Olivier showed miraculous patience when people blundered or things went wrong. By an unaccountable and exceptional lapse Furse provided armor for all the other actors but failed to produce anything for the King himself. When he admitted that this was the case, Olivier looked quizzically at him and then roared with laughter. "What was so lovely about it was the way he took it," said Furse. "I know of no, repeat NO, actor, let alone starring director, who would have taken it in quite that way." Furse was, of course, an old and valued friend, but when a cameraman made a disastrous mistake and failed to record one of the most dramatic battle scenes, all Olivier said was: "We can't afford to let this happen again!"[23]

It was very different if he thought there had been laziness or deliberate ill-will. On one occasion he was leading a group of technicians around the battlefield, planting flags and quantities of red tape to show where the shots were going to be. After a while the camera crew announced that they did not think that this was the sort of work they should be undertaking: "So I sent word back that if they would rather do nothing and watch me working, that was alright with me, as they weren't much help anyway." Later the same day a member of the crew showed himself "temperamental, sulky and awkward." "I hope things will be alright," Olivier told Vivien Leigh, "but if not I shall get rid of him, and anybody who doesn't pull his weight. The Irish are being so marvelous that it's just not good enough to take any nonsense from our own people." Stephen Greif, who was later to work with Olivier at the National Theater, compared him to the boxer, Muhammad Ali. "There was no fucking around. He did it. He never hid. And that's what makes him great."

Greif wished that the actor and the boxer could have met: "They were fearless and courageous and they had a master plan. They were birds of a feather."[24]

Olivier took immense and justified pride in his achievement. "It doesn't date at all," he said more than thirty years later. "It has a sense of permanence about it. People refer back to it as one of the great films. The Americans have always put it somewhere in the top ten, if not five. They're mad about it in America . . . I just bloody well thank God I knew what I was doing." The film ran for eleven months in London and the same in New York, even though it did not make a profit for nearly twenty years. The profession, said Olivier, were worried that, when the Oscars were awarded in 1945, he would make a clean sweep by winning the categories of best actor, best director and best producer. The judges dodged the issue by giving him a special award. "It was a complete fob-off," he said indignantly. The announcement was greeted with "the greatest applause that has ever been heard at any Academy Awards." It was not, Olivier surmised, inspired by admiration for his work so much as relief that the three categories were still open for somebody else to win.[25]

It was a spectacular conclusion to what turned out to be a distinct stage in his career. Olivier was not to make another film until 1948. By then he would not merely have reestablished himself on the stage but have played a leading part in what many still believe to have been the golden age of British theater.

CHAPTER EIGHT

THE OLD VIC

When does a good actor become great? Good actors are, if not two-a-penny, at least relatively common; two or three hundred of them, perhaps, in the British Isles at any given moment. Greatness is something different. "If theater is to affect life, it must be stronger, more intense than ordinary life," wrote Kafka. Similarly, if acting is to achieve greatness, it must be stronger, more intense than ordinary acting. No actor can show his greatness in every part: Richardson was a sublime Falstaff yet barely competent as Othello. Nor, when the greatness is there, need it necessarily manifest itself on every occasion; even the greatest actor will have the occasional off night. Yet where it exists it can always be recognized and its presence can suffuse a theater so that an audience will be almost literally intoxicated by what it is watching and hearing.[1]

It is something quite distinct from mere celebrity. "You can't make yourself a star," Olivier once said. "You can make yourself very, very good; other people make you a star." The concept of "a star," with its connotations of worldwide recognition and mass acclaim, may sometimes coincide with true greatness but is by no means the same. Olivier was a great actor as well as being a star, but he would still have been a great actor even had he not been a star. "Make up your mind, dear heart," he said to Richard Burton, "do you want to be a household word or a great actor?" Burton wanted to be both and the world was thereby robbed of his potential to be truly great. Olivier was acclaimed as a star and enjoyed it but in his scale of priorities he would never have put specious celebrity before the quality of his performances.[2]

"Between good and great acting," wrote Kenneth Tynan, the most brilliant if also, at times, the most erratic dramatic critic to have illuminated the London stage in the twentieth century, "is fixed an inexorable gulf, which may be crossed only by the elect . . . Gielgud seizes a parasol, crosses by tight-rope; Redgrave, with lunatic obstinacy, plunges into the torrent, usually sinking within yards of the opposite shore; Laurence Olivier pole-vaults over, hair-raisingly in a single animal leap. Great acting comes more naturally to him than to any of his colleagues." Tynan listed the qualifications that he believed necessary if an actor was truly to be great. First came the capacity for complete relaxation, then powerful physical magnetism. He must have commanding eyes that are visible at the back of the gallery and a commanding voice that is audible, without effort, at the back of the gallery. His timing must be superb and he must possess chutzpah, "the untranslatable Jewish word that means cool nerve and outrageous effrontery combined." Last and rarest was the ability to communicate a sense of danger: "Watching Olivier, you feel that at any moment he may do something utterly unpredictable; something explosive; possibly apocalyptic." Asked in what way his acting differed from Olivier's, Richardson replied: "I haven't got Laurence's splendid fury." It was this sense that, when he was on the stage, an eruption was imminent, the improbable likely, the impossible conceivable, that set Olivier aside from the other great actors of his generation. "It was the danger that produced the excitement of his performances," wrote John Mortimer. "You had to watch him closely, every second, because you simply had no idea what on earth he was going to do next."[3]

The commanding voice that Tynan stressed was essential for the great actor was something that Olivier cultivated sedulously and in which he took great pride. Doing a turn at the birthday party of a mutual friend, Chico Marx took up a microphone. Olivier berated him: "One thing we've got in the theater is the human voice." His own had more the quality of brass than strings, Tyrone Guthrie considered. "I have never been able to understand those critics who are not aware of the intense musicality that infuses all his performances—a rare sensitivity to rhythm, color, phrasing, pace and pitch." The brass and strings analogy is revealing. Gielgud was strings; more exquisite, more melodious than Olivier but unable to match the power and forcefulness of the latter. So magnificent an instrument was Olivier's voice that it could sometimes transcend the bounds of his dramatic vision. Comparing him to Charles Laughton, Simon Callow remarked that his "physical command of both the text and his own instrument resulted in performances that far exceeded the limitations of his interpretations. The part instilled itself in his chords and limbs, and took on a life of its own."[4]

It was not only his voice that he trained with such disciplined intensity. His body was as much an instrument of his genius. He exercised ferociously; subjected his limbs to the most arduous tests and strains; took physical risks that most actors would have sought to avoid. Some people thought that he carried his physicality too far. He "got caught up in this mystique of his physical power and neglected other vital aspects of his craft," said Jack Hawkins. True, he had ended up a great actor, but "he might have been greater yet." He could so dominate a stage that he would distort the balance of the drama. There were occasions on which his pyrotechnics seemed, to the rest of the cast, to be extravagant and unwelcome. These were rare, however. Olivier did not often forget that he was a member of a team and that, if a team is to operate successfully, no single member must so stand out as to disturb its rhythm. He could command his body as he could command his voice and turn both into instruments in a greater harmony. When he thought it necessary, indeed, he could efface himself to the point of near invisibility.[5]

Samuel Butler's observation that genius is an infinite capacity for taking pains is only half true; taking pains has been responsible for creating mountains of dross that have added little to the cultural or intellectual treasures of the world. When added to a creative imagination, however, it is indeed a formidable instrument. Olivier must have been among the hardest-working and most thorough of all great actors. He was always the first person to know his lines, he would wrestle with a part, battering it into submission, never relenting until in his own mind he had created a complete and detailed vision of its every nuance. When with his family or friends, he would without warning withdraw into an inner world, working out in his own mind the exact speed or intonation with which certain lines should be delivered; oblivious to those around him he would spend hours moving a chair, picking up a glass, until he had satisfied himself that he had got the movement right. Nothing was left to chance, the extemporaneous was anathema to him. "Week after week, day after day, hour after hour, practice makes perfect, practice makes perfect," wrote Peter Brook. "It is a drudge, a grind, a discipline . . . Laurence Olivier repeats lines of dialogue to himself again and again until he conditions his tongue to a point of absolute obedience—and so gains absolute freedom." For Ronald Pickup, one of the best of the talented young actors whom Olivier gathered around him at the National Theater, it was the precision of Olivier's acting that was the most impressive. "What I've learned from him is always to deal in specific very concrete intentions, never in generalizations. You have to know exactly why you're doing and saying anything at any moment." In one of the plays that Pickup acted in at the National, he marveled at the pains Olivier was at to find a watch strap that it seemed to him would have suited the character he was playing. Nobody in the audience would know it was there, but Olivier knew. Having chosen the suit that he thought appropriate for the role, he wore it for several days before the dress rehearsal. It would take time before he had got used to the suit and the suit to him.[6]

Olivier needed to know what he looked like before he knew who he was. It was sometimes said of him that he started with the shoes, more often it was the nose. William Gaskill, one of the most talented of National Theater directors, was a great believer in masks, which he used in several productions and as a teaching tool. Olivier scorned such fanciful devices, but, as Gaskill pointed out, he was "the great mask actor of our time, working inwards from the externals of makeup and costume." Once, before rehearsals for a new production had even started, Gaskill found Olivier sitting in front of a mirror with his false nose already molded, trying on wigs. "I understood that he couldn't start work until he knew what he was to look like." When he was playing a historical figure he would go to great pains to ensure he looked as much like his subject as was possible. For Shaw's *Caesar and Cleopatra* he procured a copy of what was believed to be the only contemporary likeness of Caesar and wrote a letter to the man responsible for his appearance with five paragraphs on the appropriate style of wig along with anxious inquiries about the nose: "Could you not take a cast of Caesar's nose from the bust and a cast of my nose from mine, and get the material between the two of them?" John Dover Wilson, the great Shakespeare scholar, unkindly pointed out that new research made it seem almost certain that the bust was in fact not of Caesar. But at least, he went on more comfortingly, it was what Shaw had in mind when he wrote the play.[7]

Olivier, Christopher Plummer suggested, had every attribute of the great actor except pathos. "Oh, he manufactured pathos to the hilt—he acted it expertly, wonderfully. He knew all its ingredients, and yet none of them came naturally to him." The judgment is a curious one: to be able to act wonderfully something that does not come naturally to one is surely the attribute of a great actor? Did the malign wickedness of Richard III come any more naturally to Olivier than the pathos of a Tyrone or an Astrov? Not everyone agreed with Plummer: Ernest Milton, an Old Vic veteran, after see-ing Olivier as Caesar, wrote to congratulate him on his "extraor-dinary gift of pathos." Of all the actors he had seen or had played with, only Bernhardt and Owen Nares could stand comparison. But Olivier himself was inclined to agree with Plummer. He had, he admitted, "something Philistine in me that produces a pretty invin-cible resistance to pathos—Pagliacci, He Who Gets Slapped, Laugh Clown Laugh." That he could nevertheless affect it so masterfully was a great tribute to his professional skills but he felt more at ease when his part required him to rage, clown or make love.[8]

In 1965 a young beginner asked Olivier whether he would ever make a great actor or even a good actor. Olivier could—and frequently did—humbug and flatter extravagantly, but where his professional judgment was concerned he could not lie. "I think your personality is very nice," he wrote, "your presence and your appearance. To be absolutely frank, I do find the lack of an essential quality in our job, and that I can only describe as an absolute grip that makes any part that we are playing, a true part of ourselves, belonging to ourselves." "Absolute grip" is an imprecise phrase that could mean different things to different people but it does suggest the intensity of purpose, the relentless determination, which Olivier brought to every role. Ian McKellen and Antony Sher were once dining together, discussing the state of the theater in general and the achievements of Olivier in particular. "We can't match him—none of us can—ever," said McKellen gloomily. Sher shrugged in silent acquiescence. "The combination of beauty and self-hatred, and, of course, talent, colossal talent and imagination," he wrote. "His characters remind me of Michelangelo's monumental portraits; they have an almost marble feel, awesome yet quite cool." It was the glorious paradox of Olivier's acting that he both sublimated himself totally in his acting and yet remained ever present. He is a great actor, Michael Billington has written, in a perceptive analysis of Olivier's strengths, "partly because he shows us so much of himself in all his performances, partly because he is unafraid to reveal those elements in his personality that most are trained to keep hidden." He held nothing back yet, in the last analysis, gave nothing away. He could be everything; he could, if he so wished, be nothing. Whatever the mood, whatever the needs of the moment, his integrity was total, his authority absolute, his grip never failed.[9]

Sometime toward the end of 1944, the first year in which Olivier played in repertory at the resurrected Old Vic, a man came to the box office and asked for a ticket for "a Laurence Olivier play." "*Which* play?" asked the ticket seller. "It doesn't matter. Whatever Olivier is in." The response does not suggest any great sophistication on the part of the would-be theatergoer, but it shows that, in the eyes of the public at least, Olivier had earned the status of the "great actor" par excellence.

There were a handful of other actors who could aspire to the same grandeur. One of these was Ralph Richardson. It was he who did more than anybody else to get the revived Old Vic under way. There was precious little except its name and its reputation to help in the resuscitation; the building itself had been badly damaged during the war, the management long disbanded. The Old Vic Board invited Richardson and Tyrone Guthrie to take over the New Theater and, with some financial help from the government, put the show back on the road. Guthrie's role was ill-defined, he was heavily involved with the ballet at Sadler's Wells and was not going to be able to provide much more than encouragement and, from time to time, advice. Richardson was eager to take it on but knew that he could not manage single-handed; he insisted that he must be able to recruit partners who would share the burden of the acting as well as the management. The first two men to whom he applied were Laurence Olivier and John Gielgud. "It sounds a hare-brained scheme," Olivier wrote to his American accountant, "but we feel very strongly that the Theater should have some national representation in London, particularly at this time." The Lords of the Admiralty were approached and, with almost offensive insouciance, agreed that he should be released from what were anyway increasingly nominal duties in the Royal Navy. His salary was to be a derisory £15 a week as a director; if he was also acting this would rise to £40. In recognition of the fact that he could earn many times as much if he returned to the cinema, it was agreed that from time to time he would take leave to make a film. In the summer of 1944 he resumed his career as an actor in the theater.[10]

Gielgud proved more difficult to tie down. Richardson sent him a cable when he was performing for the troops in Cairo suggesting he should join himself and Olivier in this new enterprise. "I should like nothing better," Gielgud told his mother, "if it is a partnership and plays and parts that I like." Then he seems to have decided that in fact it would *not* be a true partnership. Probably he would have been more enthusiastic if Richardson had been the only other person involved. The thought of entering a triumvirate with Olivier was unappealing. "It would be a disaster," Gielgud is said to have told Richardson. "You would have to spend all your time as a referee between Larry and me." He already had his own independent company and decided it would be best to keep it going in competition with the Old Vic. In time he came to wonder whether he had made the right decision. When the Old Vic produced a series of unequivocal triumphs Gielgud admitted ruefully: "I was a bit down . . . I was very aware they had beaten me to the post and that he [Olivier] was now a much bigger star than I was, but I swallowed that, I was only sorry that I couldn't live up to it. I enormously admired what they did." Probably he was right in thinking that he and Olivier would never have made a happy partnership. Writing to a friend about his return from the United States in 1946, in which he happened to find himself on the same liner as the Oliviers, Gielgud remarked: "I hope to make the grade on arrival by hanging firmly on Mrs. Olivier's other arm as soon as the photographers get on board and refusing to be shaken off." Deference and contempt could hardly have been more neatly blended.[11]

The fact was that neither man was entirely easy in the other's company. Each had reservations about the other's style of acting: Gielgud thought Olivier was too often vulgar, exhibitionist, over-physical; Olivier accused Gielgud of being anemic, insubstantial, over-musical. Each admired the other's strengths. Writing to Gielgud about his performance as Andrew Crocker-Harris in Rattigan's *The Browning Version*, Olivier wrote: "Your old friend was bursting with pride and admiration. Your performance was quite flawless and dreadfully moving. It haunts me still." Gielgud wrote appreciatively of Olivier's "acting genius and his gift for leadership." Both admitted that they were sometimes jealous of the other: Olivier's jealousy being the more frequent and the more consuming. Yet there was also a sense of solidarity and common purpose. When Gielgud was arrested for soliciting in a public lavatory Olivier's response was to propose him for membership of the Garrick Club (he was blackballed, though elected later). A homophobic actor set to work putting together a group with the aim of getting Gielgud expelled from Equity. He was ill-advised enough to appeal to Olivier for support. Olivier summoned him to his dressing room in the intermission of the play in which he was then acting. Delighted at the prospect of securing so prominent a backer, the actor rushed to the theater. "Mr.———," said Olivier. "If you persist in this resolution I shall make sure that you never appear on any British stage again."[12]

Richardson and Olivier, then, would provide the main driving force behind the revived Old Vic, but someone else was needed to furnish the nuts and bolts of the operation. John Burrell was chosen, a theater director in his early thirties working with the B.B.C. Burrell has sometimes been represented as a mere administrator who meekly carried out the bidding of his overpowering partners. This is unfair: he was himself a strong personality with ideas of his own. But he was inexperienced, little known outside a narrow theatrical circle and inevitably outshone. He became an indispensable part of the organization, but if Richardson and Olivier were both resolved on a course of action there was little hope that Burrell would be able to deflect them from their course.

In the simplest analysis, there are two ways of putting on plays: deciding on the play and then looking for the actors, or engaging the actors and then looking for a suitable play. For the sort of ensemble acting that the Governors had in mind for the Old Vic, the emphasis would in principle be on the latter. In practice the process was almost always a patched-up compromise: reflecting a multitude of requirements. The needs of the permanent members of the company were certainly one, perhaps the most important, but there was also the need to present a balanced theatrical diet with a fair amount of Shakespeare as well as Ibsen, Shaw, Chekhov or Brecht and an occasional obeisance in the direction of contemporary British drama. It had been decided that the play to open the

London season should be Ibsen's *Peer Gynt*, so the first batch of actors had to be selected with that in mind. The cast required for *Peer Gynt* was, however, substantial and since by the time it began the Old Vic would already have opened in Manchester with Shaw's *Arms and the Man*, it was obvious that the management could not afford the luxury of employing actors who were too narrow in their specialties. One of the first to be approached was Renée Asherson, a talented young actress who had played opposite Olivier in *Henry V*. Olivier urged her to keep the fact that she had been invited to herself. "It is a vague plan still," he told her, "and we do not want to invite catty conjectures or exaggerated musings in the press . . . The offer, roughly, is that you should be our juvenile girl." To the layman that sounds a rather unappealing proposition, but since Olivier went on to say that she would be asked to play such parts as Anne in *Richard III*, Hero in *Much Ado About Nothing* and Sonya in *Uncle Vanya*, it must have been clear to her that she would not be starved of challenging roles. "Three of these plays will be performed every week," Olivier concluded, "so I think and hope it will be more fun to act in the Theater than we have known it to be before."[13]

In the event, Renée Asherson could not escape from her existing contract. There were other refusals, too. Ursula Jeans at first agreed to appear but then recanted because she wanted to act in a new play by Peter Ustinov. "I hope that when you come to see us next, you will bring your coffin with you, because you will need it," Olivier wrote indignantly, concluding with: "My appalled, incredulous but always devoted love." But such cases were the exception and occurred usually only when the actor concerned was committed elsewhere. Most people leapt at the opportunity of acting with Olivier and Richardson in such surroundings and agreed that it was likely to be "more fun" than an appearance in the conventional theater. They did not do it for the money, though. Sybil Thorndike, Margaret Leighton, Alec Guinness, Miles Malleson, all of whom had appeared earlier at the Old Vic, were well-established figures much in demand on the West End stage. They could not have earned anything approaching the money that Olivier would have been offered if he had returned to Hollywood, but they could still have done a great deal better for themselves elsewhere. Olivier and Richardson had constantly to bear in mind that many of their most valued performers were making a sacrifice in working in the Old Vic and that their continued loyalty could not be taken for granted.[14]

The most powerful force in the London theater at the end of the war was Hugh "Binkie" Beaumont's company, H. M. Tennent. Beaumont dominated the West End stage; at one point eleven out of London's thirty-six theaters were playing his productions. Many of these were of high quality, but his main concern was that they should make money: he eschewed the experimental and had little use for any except the most popular of classics. He was, as Michael Billington put it, the Fortnum & Mason of London theater. Beaumont did not fear the Old Vic—he had no reason to—nor did he seek to do it down, but he presented a powerful counter-attraction. Even the most high-minded actor would hesitate to reject out of hand an overture from this magnetic figure. Olivier himself could afford to ignore his blandishments, but even he—apart from the fact that he rather liked him—hesitated to thwart him too overtly and realized how powerful his attraction was for many members of the company.[15]

When dealing with potential adversaries like Beaumont Olivier was adept at using kid gloves; in other circumstances he was ready to resort to knuckledusters. He was on the whole sensitive to other people's feelings, anxious not to offend, taking care to wrap up criticism or bad news in a rich cocoon of treacle, but if he felt his patience was being abused or that he was being in some way put upon, his anger could be terrifying. A Mr. Wanbon protested that he was being fobbed off with trivial roles and not treated with the consideration he deserved. "You talk about being thrust into a walk-on part as if you were deserving of something better," retorted Olivier. "I have not been able to discover what should give you this idea . . . Your allegation that this very busy organization should spare time to frame intrigues against you personally is, of course, absurd. The 'ability' that you speak of did not emerge sufficiently clearly to justify your engagement. Your letter is wild to say the least of it, and the manner of it endorses the reports of your behavior. I should most strongly advise you to behave yourself and to fulfill your dearest ambition in a way that will not be a nuisance to other people. I wish you luck, but I doubt if you will have it unless you change." Not many people fared as badly as the unfortunate Mr. Wanbon, but Olivier was always liable to explode and if he was in a bad mood his anger could lie heavy on the whole building.[16]

That building, until the Old Vic had been patched up, was the New Theater in London's West End. Space for rehearsal was limited, so the company borrowed the National Gallery, which was standing empty pending the return of its pictures at the end of the war. Unfortunately this coincided with the arrival of the V-Is, the buzz bombs. To stand under the vast expanse of glass that roofed the Gallery while a V-I chuntered overhead cannot have been a soothing experience. Diana Boddington, the stage manager, claimed that neither Olivier nor Richardson ducked or flinched. If they did manage to keep up such an appearance it reflects great credit on them: Olivier remembers that they both went green and "wished we were back in uniform in a nice, comfortable mess." They were spared, but most public meeting places in London were closed and at one point the Old Vic was one of only five theaters in London still open.[17]

Olivier could not indulge his temper with Richardson and Guthrie as he could with Mr. Wanbon, yet at the time they were discussing the apportionment of roles in the first season, he found himself consumed by barely concealed indignation. The plan was that, so far as was practical, he and Richardson would each play small parts in the production in which the other was starring: this would both help the spirit of ensemble and please the audience. But Olivier convinced himself that Richardson's small parts were not nearly as small as his own. "My small part was so fucking small you couldn't see it—it was the Button Molder in *Peer Gynt*. I was on the stage for all of three minutes. And I resented it." In *Arms and the Man* their parts were more or less the same size, but Olivier disliked playing Sergius and was convinced that Richardson had once more outmaneuvered him. But the most profound grievance arose when Richardson and Burrell both insisted that Olivier, as his main role, should play Richard III to balance Richardson's Peer Gynt. Olivier hated the idea, mainly "because that cunt Wolfit had made an enormous success only a year or eighteen months before. And I didn't want to be compared with him because I knew bloody well the press would compare me ill with him because they adored Wolfit." He protested that the part would be all wrong for him—he would play Richard II if they liked. They would have none of it: "'Now, come on, old chap. We both think you ought to do it. We're sure you'll get through being compared with Wolfit alright!' They could afford to be sure, couldn't they? . . . I thought the other two were really piling on top of me in order to take down my position of popularity owing to being a film star, which Ralph certainly wasn't . . . They thought it would be good for me not to do as well as Wolfit. They thought they'd got me where they wanted me." Even Mr. Wanbon could hardly have shown more paranoia. He voiced these thoughts—"thoughts," perhaps, is hardly the right word— nearly a quarter of a century later. If he had felt so bitterly about it at the time would he not have continued to refuse to play the role? As it was, he gave in pretty quickly. The Old Vic's first season was taking shape.[18]

Tyrone Guthrie does not seem to have taken much part in these deliberations, though he played an important role as director. Indeed, his rather nebulous supervisory role counted for little. At the end of the year Richardson and Olivier seem to have decided that they would be better off without him. "Do you mind leaving us alone?" they said. According to Olivier, Guthrie was exhausted and happy to shed the responsibility: "I understand. You want to be independent. Go ahead, I'm not necessary. No hard feelings!" Olivier deluded himself. Guthrie did indeed understand, but there *were* hard feelings. In due course he was to get his revenge.

One of the plays Burrell had directed was the Old Vic's first production with Olivier and Richardson—*Arms and the Man*.

Convinced from the start that Richardson had got the better part, Olivier as Sergius put up a lackluster performance and won few laughs. When Guthrie nevertheless congratulated him on his performance, Olivier made it clear that he thought the part was a weak one and his own rendering of it still worse. "Why, don't you like the part?" asked Guthrie. "Don't you love Sergius?" "Love that stooge? That inconsiderable . . . !" "Well, of course, if you can't love him you'll never be any good in him, will you?" Olivier claimed that this was the richest pearl of advice that he ever received and that it transformed his acting. It took him a week to adjust to the idea, but "by the end of it I loved Sergius as I'd never loved anybody." He learned to love Sergius's faults, his showing-off, his absurdity, his blind doltishness: his rendering of the part was transformed. It is hard to understand why Guthrie's remark came as such a revelation to Olivier. Had he not loved Coriolanus? Had he not loved Heathcliff? Perhaps it was not so much a new concept as a reminder. Olivier had dismissed the part with contempt and so had not allowed himself to establish any real rapport with the man he was portraying. It was not so much a matter of love as of intimate identification. Encouraged by Guthrie, Olivier got to know Sergius, absorbed Sergius, was absorbed by Sergius, became Sergius. In the provincial tour Richardson had secured far better notices, Olivier's part had been almost ignored. When it opened in London, though Richardson still got more space, it was clear that two great actors were playing the principal roles and that both deserved attention.[19]

By then the Old Vic season in London had already begun with *Peer Gynt*. "A tatty, artsy-craftsy production," Noël Coward thought it. "Larry wonderful, but only on for five minutes at the end." Meeting Olivier in the Garrick a few months later, by which time *Richard III* had already achieved immense success, Donald Wolfit merely observed: "Liked your Button Molder." Olivier took this to be a calculated insult, and so no doubt it was meant to be, but in fact, by a display of extraordinary virtuosity, Olivier did make his tiny part into something memorable and much commented on.

It was still very much Richardson's evening, however; and, until the third play, *Richard III*, very much Richardson's season.[20]

This was the play that Olivier had wished not to do and which still filled him with dread. The shadow of Wolfit hung over him. He himself thought Wolfit's treatment of the part "unspeakably vulgar, really bad and cheap and pantomime comic." "*Richard III*, Wolfit. Phew!" was the somewhat cryptic entry in his diary after he had been to see it. His own portrayal of the role was in part at least inspired by his determination to be as unlike Wolfit as he could contrive. But he could not escape the fear that he might fail. His friend and fellow actor John Mills was coming to the first night. He and his wife were surprised to get a message asking them to go round to Olivier's dressing room half an hour before curtain up. They found him fully made-up and dressed. "I just want you to know that you are going to see a bloody awful performance," Olivier blurted out. "The dress rehearsal was chaotic. I dried up at least a dozen times. It's a dreadful production, and I was an idiot to let them persuade me to play the bloody part . . . Anyway, I just wanted you to know that *I* know. Also, I don't give a damn. I'm past it." Mr. and Mrs. Mills tottered across the road to fortify themselves with double brandies before the forthcoming debacle.[21]

There followed what Mills describes as "the most majestic and inspired performance I have ever seen." Few performances can have had so many superlatives lavished on it. "The most theatrically overwhelming performance of the period"—J. C. Trewin; "absolutely terrific . . . even Binkie raved"—John Gielgud; "I think the greatest male performance I have ever seen in the theater . . . He is far and away the greatest actor we have"—Noël Coward; "*il m'a donné la plus grande émotion théâtrale de ma vie*"—Albert Camus: one could fill pages with such commendations. Robert Stephens believes that, until the very last minute, Olivier had not decided how to play the part: it was only when his first entrance provoked a roar of laughter because of his exaggeratedly grotesque appearance that he realized the part must be played as comedy. This cannot be the whole story: Olivier had concluded from the start that the relish with which Richard III gloats over his villainy was always going to contain a whiff of the ridiculous and that to enhance it by adopting what Alec McCowen called "a slightly spinsterish deportment and manner of speech" was bound to make the performance more coherent as well as more entertaining. But though his Richard III raised many laughs, they were uneasy laughs; it was Olivier's achievement to be at the same time ridiculous and infinitely menacing. Never for an instant did the audience doubt that it was in the presence of unadulterated evil. Guthrie's advice, Olivier claimed, "had inched its way under my skin. When I came to it, I loved Richard and he loved me, until we became one." Melvyn Bragg has suggested that part of Olivier's reluctance to take on the role might have been the fear that it would permanently sear him: "Henry V left him in some way forever heroic, might not Richard leave him malevolent?" Whether or not the thought entered Olivier's mind, total immersion, night after night, in a hot bath of such steaming evil must at the best have been uncomfortable, at the worst positively dangerous.[22]

The effect on the rest of the cast was dramatic. Infected by the gloom of their leading actor, they had embarked on their first night in a mood of resigned depression; within a few minutes they found themselves caught up in a gale that bore them away to triumph. For Roger Braban, then only a boy and playing a very minor part, it was like being "a speck of dust on a carpet with a bloody great Hoover coming at it." Olivier exuded evil. The cast shrank from him. It was his voice as much as anything that gave force to his performance: "It is slick, taunting and enviously casual," wrote Tynan, "nearly impersonal . . . pulling and pushing each line into place." "The thin reed of a sanctimonious scholar," is how Olivier himself described it. It was hard to believe that only a few months before that same voice had been urging on the English troops: "Once more unto the breach, dear friends, once more!" It is perhaps his death, though, which lingers most tenaciously in the mind. Writhing like a demented spider, arms and legs shooting out in fearful convulsions, seeking to bring down his enemies even though himself doomed, he performed what Harold Hobson called "a horizontal dance." James Agate, harking back to Hazlitt's celebrated description, says that this is how Kean must have done it. Olivier himself admits—or perhaps claims—that he took Kean's performance as a model. In the case of Shakespeare he always found the legacy of the past particularly rich, sometimes oppressive: "Almost every bit of business that does occur to one makes one feel that it had been thought of before."[23]

Within a few moments of the curtain rising Olivier knew that the audience was with him; by the end of the evening the theater was permeated by "that sweet smell (it's like seaweed) of success." It was "a fabulous hit: the first time in my life I ever felt equally a junction of successful acceptance by public, critics and my colleagues." He managed not to let it go too obviously to his head. At the end of the first run he was persuaded by Sybil Thorndike to make a curtain call. ("He needed much pressure as he modestly wanted to give the others *all* the credit," David Boyle told Duff Cooper—an observation that suggests that Olivier's histrionic skills were employed as much in dealing with his admirers as in playing the King.) His speech, Boyle went on, was "so simple and from the heart that it will be treasured by all who heard it." Some exultation could have been forgiven him, but he had little time to gloat over his success. This was London in wartime. His cousin, Edith Olivier, went round to see him in his dressing room when the play had been running for three weeks or so. He was exhausted and could hardly speak, yet he was just about to go on duty "as a Firewatcher in the Theater, in which he has to take his turn each week."[24]

The most generous tribute came from John Gielgud. In 1939 his mother had given him the sword that Edmund Kean had worn when he played Richard III in the early nineteenth century. "It will be a nice thing to be handed on again to another young hopeful when I am too old to play Hamlet anymore," Gielgud wrote in his letter of thanks. Olivier could hardly be described as a "young hopeful," but Gielgud judged the time had come to pass it on. He had the sword inscribed by a master of the trade—the man who had inscribed London's tribute to Russian heroism, the Sword of Stalingrad—and charged Alan Dent with carrying it to Olivier in the New Theater. He suggested Dent should "carry it on a tray, like John the Baptist's head." Such a gesture, toward a man who was not only a rival but in direct competition, was almost sublimely magnanimous. Olivier treasured the sword. He did not emulate its previous owner by passing it on to a young challenger but it was among the trophies that were processed up the aisle in Olivier's memorial service in Westminster Abbey.[25]

As if it were not enough to have completed the film of *Henry V* and triumphed in *Richard III* within a few months of each other, Olivier now took on his first serious work as a stage director. He was reading every new play that came his way with a view not only to acting in it himself but also finding a part for Vivien Leigh. He was sent a new play by Thornton Wilder—an American dramatist whom Olivier knew, liked and thought well of. *The Skin of Our Teeth* was rambling, incoherent, brilliantly intelligent, provocative and enormous fun. Olivier would have liked to play the leading role himself, but he was fully committed at the Old Vic; the part of the maid Sabina, however, which had been played by Tallulah Bankhead on Broadway, would, he saw, be a marvelous vehicle for his wife. Whoever directed it would have an unusually free hand, for Wilder had given no instructions of any kind. Olivier leapt at the opportunity. "I always encourage actors to invent like mad," he claimed. This was a piece of self-deception. More often, he invented like mad on their behalf and expected them to follow his bidding. Roger Braban, age twelve, found himself forced for financial reasons to leave school and go onto the stage. Olivier, who knew his recently deceased father, offered him the chance of playing a baby elephant in *The Skin of Our Teeth*. The boy looked dubious. Olivier then got on to all fours and cavorted around the floor in baby elephantine mode. "Can you do that?" Olivier asked. "Yes, but I don't want to." "Then why are you wasting my time, ungrateful brat?" He got the job all the same and was enormously impressed by the

trouble Olivier took to help him along the way. He had the pleasure of burying his head in Vivien Leigh's skirts and was patted on
the head by George VI when the King visited the theater and went
behind stage after the performance.[26]

Olivier as a director could be fiercely protective of his actors
and, most of all, his wife. On the first night James Agate was late
coming back into the theater after the intermission and groped his
way toward his seat. "Sit down, damn you!" snarled Olivier, striking Agate on the shoulder. "Who's that?" asked the bemused critic.
"You know who I am!" said Olivier menacingly. In spite of, or perhaps because of this, Agate gave the play an excellent review. "That's
the way we should treat critics," Olivier told Binkie Beaumont with
satisfaction. "We should do it more often." Agate was not the only
critic to praise the production; it got a rapturous reception and
Vivien Leigh in particular was acclaimed for her performance. Best
of all, Thornton Wilder came to one of the earlier performances. "I
never knew I'd written such a play," he said in awe.[27]

The Skin of Our Teeth opened in May 1945. It had already been a
year of miracles for Olivier. There was more to come.

CHAPTER NINE

HAMLET

"**A**mazement upon amazement," Olivier wrote to Jill Esmond in the autumn of 1944, "all wonderful successes . . . quite unbelievable. Nothing like it has ever happened to me before." By the time he wrote the Old Vic had already embarked on the second phase of its triumphant progress. The two parts of *Henry IV* will be remembered above all for Richardson's Falstaff. No performance of any part can be definitive, but few indeed of those who saw him doubted that they were witnessing something that they could never hope to see rivaled in their lifetime. But though Richardson was the hero—and admitted by Olivier to be so   Olivier was much praised for his extraordinary virtuosity. In *Part One* he played Henry Percy, that paradigm of hot-headed and turbulent fighting men; in *Part Two* the twittering and absurd Justice Shallow. The contrast between the two characters could hardly have been more striking; but these were merely sighting shots for what was to be one of the most ambitious and audacious performances of his life.[1]

It seems to have been Olivier's idea that there should be a double bill, in which *Oedipus* would be followed by *The Critic*: the supremely tragic Oedipus by W. B. Yeats out of Sophocles followed by that prattling ninny, Sheridan's Mr. Puff. Olivier cheerfully admitted: "I wanted to show off. Ralph had had everything up to then." The purists were outraged: "Would Irving have followed Hamlet with Jingle?" demanded the *Sunday Times*: "No!" But Garrick might, as Bryan Forbes has pointed out. "I feel that there are more than passing similarities between Garrick and Olivier," Forbes went on to say, "even a certain physical resemblance and certainly numerous parallels in their approach to the art of acting." Garrick or no Garrick, Tyrone Guthrie was opposed to what he saw as unspeakable vulgarity. "Over my dead body!" he declared. "That could be arranged," was more or less Olivier's response. Guthrie recognized that he could do nothing to stop the performance and returned, fulminating, to New York. *Oedipus* and *The Critic* had their first showing in October 1945, two months after the Japanese surrender and the end of the Second World War.[2] Since the end of the war in Europe in May, the London theater had been regaining its former vigor. There could not have been a better time for Olivier and the Old Vic to strike gold.

What sticks most vividly in the mind of those fortunate enough to have seen Olivier as Oedipus was the great cry he uttered when he discovered that the prophecy had been fulfilled; he *had* killed his father; he *had* committed incest with his mother, he *had* driven his mother to suicide and, despairing, he gouges out his eyes with the gold pins from his mother's dress. He based the cry, he claimed, on the anguished protest of an ermine that has licked salt scattered on hard snow and found itself held fast and unable to escape. Both this explanation and the cry itself teeter on the edge of absurdity. Henry Root, the inspired creation of the satirist William Donaldson, showed how it could be parodied when he explained that the cry was based on the mating call of the North American bull moose: "Ever a perfectionist, Olivier spent nine months practicing in a forest thirty miles from Quebec. With such success, in fact, that he got shot four times." Only an actor of extraordinary powers could have made this ghastly denouement convincing to a sophisticated London audience. "I never hoped for so vast an anguish," wrote Tynan. "Olivier's final 'Oh! Oh!' when the full catalog of his sins is unfolded must still be resounding in some high recess of the New Theater's dome: some stick of wood must still, I feel, be throbbing from it."[3]

An intermission devoted to a change of costume and of mood, and Olivier was on stage again as Mr. Puff. Some critics felt that he overdid the comedy; that Sheridan's wit was weakened by indulgence in slapstick. Tynan thought that it was a bad example of an actor not trusting his author; Noël Coward, on the other hand, thought it "quite perfect. Technically faultless and fine beyond words." For Olivier it was a glorious relief after the rigors of Oedipus. If he took it lightly this did not mean that, for a moment, he relaxed his rigidly professional approach: Alan Dent remembered him withdrawing "from the company of his wife and myself [to] practice Mr. Puff's fantastic ways of taking snuff for quite ten minutes on end, totally unaware that we were gazing at the solo rehearsal from the other end of the room." He also took physical risks. He evolved an elaborate device by which he would be swept up into the flies, borne to earth again on a painted cloud, propelled violently into the heavens and finally delivered back to earth where he performed a somersault. It was a prime example of the extravagance that Tynan condemned; it also nearly cost him his life. The equipment somehow went awry and Olivier found himself dangling thirty feet above the stage with no apparent means of extricating himself. Eventually the flyman managed to lower him to the ground. "And that," he wrote, "was how my very favorite invention became a living dread for the next six months." It never occurred to him, however, to cut out or even to reduce the scale of this piece of business. He had convinced himself that it was an important element in his success; there could be no question of accepting anything below the best; the show must go on.[4]

There was to be one more major role that season. Olivier had never thought that he would play King Lear; he knew Richardson coveted the part and was happy to let him take it. But when the time came to apportion the parts between them, Richardson had first pick and chose Cyrano de Bergerac. Olivier wanted the part for himself and, as a means of wresting it back, made Lear his first selection. Richardson looked disconcerted and Olivier felt sure that, after the meeting, it would be possible to swap the one part for the other. When it came to the point, however, it became clear that Richardson had no intention of surrendering Cyrano. Olivier was stuck with Lear. It is often said that Lear is the impossible part: by the time one is old enough to play it one is too old to play it. Olivier, only thirty-nine, was too young. Next time he played it he would be too old. He underestimated the problems ahead of him. "Frankly, Lear is an easy part," he claimed boldly. "We can all play it. It is simply being straightforward . . . He's like all of us really, he's just a stupid old fart . . ." This somewhat insouciant approach led to a Lear that was bad-tempered, blustery, eccentric from the start and not particularly royal. "His Lear was a failure," judged Max Adrian. "I hated it, and I told him so." Not many people were so bluntly condemnatory. Gielgud thought him "brilliantly clever and absolutely complete in his characterization, but it is a little doddering King without majesty or awesomeness. However," he added wryly, "the critics were lyrical, and I hope I am not jealous." "Lyrical" was perhaps too generous, but on the whole Olivier was highly praised. It is remarkable, however, that given his capacity to dominate a stage, the image that even today often predominates in the memory of those who saw the performance is not of Olivier's Lear but the chill, stark white face of Alec Guinness's infinitely pathetic Fool. "Not Larry's part, I fear," said Wolfit with satisfaction. "You see, Lear's a bass part, Larry's a tenor." He was right in thinking that Olivier never felt that he belonged in "Lear." He made a sound try, but by his own standards he fell short of triumph.[5]

Not content with playing the King, Olivier elected to direct the production as well. Margaret Leighton, who played Regan, thought he was brilliant as a director. "He astonished me by having everything worked out in great detail. He had planned every single move for Regan and each move was in accordance with the text and helped to explain it . . . It was a marvelously meticulous piece of direction, and at the same time he made me understand not just my own part but the whole play." There were some who thought he worked everything out in *too* great detail; his vision of each part was so clear-cut and imposed with such authority that spontaneity was lacking. The duty of the director was to direct, Olivier believed—at least when it was he who was doing the directing—and the duty of

the actor was to take direction. Where the two were in potential conflict, it was the director who prevailed. Olivier the director did no
favors for Olivier the actor; if the needs of the play demanded that
Olivier the actor should be reined in, then Olivier the director would
make sure that it was done. Lawrence Langner of the Theater Guild
in New York had been told by Burrell that the actor who played Lear
would traditionally hog the limelight and cut down all the other parts
to enhance his own. "I looked at the program to see who had directed
the play with such a sense of integrity as to make King Lear himself but one of the series of fine portrayals. It was Laurence Olivier."[6]
He was harsh on himself, but he could be quite as harsh on others.
He would be interested in other people's points of view, and might
even from time to time take account of them, but he would not tolerate sustained dissent. Marian Spencer, who had been the original
choice for Regan, was summarily sacked. "I found very soon that the
part did not suit you," wrote Olivier. Nor was she "sympathetic to my
view of the part." If she had been younger and more inexperienced he
might have tried to force his view on her, "but I really did not think it
right to attempt this with an actress of your standing and knowledge."
So out she went; a dire warning to other members of the cast that if
they crossed the will of their director they would be likely to regret it.[7]

Even by the end of its first season, in April 1945, the Old Vic had
achieved the sort of cult status normally associated with the more
celebrated crooners or pop stars. On its last night St. Martin's Lane
was closed for an hour while 2,500 delirious fans massed outside,
cheering any actors who showed their faces and setting up a wild
chant of "We want Larry! We want Larry!" Eighteen months later,
though the hysteria might slightly have died down, the reputation
of the company had not ceased to grow. Between August 1944 and
December 1946 the Old Vic Company had rarely fallen below the
level of excellence and had produced some of the finest performances that can ever have graced the London stage or, indeed, any
other stage. For this the credit, above all, must be given to Richardson and Olivier. It would be futile to speculate which made the
greater contribution. Two superlatively fine actors at the peak of

their powers, they complemented each other to perfection. For the most part their relationship was harmonious but inevitably there was tension and a sense of rivalry. When Richardson was given a knighthood in the New Year's Honors in 1947, wrote Olivier in his memoirs, "You should have heard the screams of fury." He professed to be disapproving—"artists should not accept honors of this kind"—but recanted six months later. "When the offer came along," he cheerfully admitted, "I found that I liked the idea tremendously, and so did Puss [Vivien Leigh]." The fact that he could write about it with such self-mockery suggests that the fury did not run very deep, but it was fearsome while it lasted.[8]

Richardson, more phlegmatic, not so prone to jealousy, felt the rivalry less keenly, but there was sometimes rancor on his side as well. In his second book, *On Acting*, Olivier describes a bizarre incident when the company was on tour on the continent and had arrived in Paris. Richardson was annoyed that they had opened with *Richard III* and that Olivier's predictable triumph had stolen the limelight from his own Peer Gynt. A drunken Richardson seized Olivier and held him over the edge of a balcony, sixty feet above the cobbles below. Olivier remained calm and suggested it would be sensible if Richardson pulled him back. "I saw in his eyes that if I'd done anything other than I had, he'd have let me go. For a brief moment he wanted to kill me." In his official biography Terry Coleman has suggested that this anecdote was fantasy or at least grossly exaggerated. It does indeed sound most improbable. However, when Derek Granger asked Lady Richardson about the incident and suggested that it had never happened, she replied. "Oh, no; it was even worse." She, of course, was not a witness to the incident but Michael Munn, another of Olivier's biographers, records that once when he was present, Gielgud asked Richardson: "Why did you try to kill Larry?" "Oh, I was just annoyed with him for being smug." "You tried to kill Olivier?" put in Munn, incredulously. "Oh, just for a moment or two when I felt like throwing him from a great height." At least it seems there may have been some kind of confrontation, proving, perhaps, no more than that when great artists are pitted against each other, passions are likely to run high.[9]

What should come next? Olivier and Richardson assumed that they would remain with the Old Vic for several years, but though this gave them great professional satisfaction it did not provide enough in the way of income. "Television is taking America by storm and throwing the film industry into panic," wrote Anthony Bartley, Deborah Kerr's husband. Would Olivier encourage the actors at the Old Vic to espouse this new medium and, by implication, might he consider gracing it himself? It had taken Olivier long enough to admit that the cinema should be treated as a significant art form; it would be many years before he would do as much for television. He was even cautious when it came to committing himself to making a new film. Terence Rattigan pressed him to do so in the spring of 1946. He saw little chance of undertaking one before 1948, he replied. He would go back to the Old Vic for one more play and then had "other plans, rather vague" in other parts of the world: "As you know I am really in a very tired condition, and when the present is so formidable one has to take the future little bit by little bit." He was being disingenuous. By the time he told Rattigan that he had no plans to make a film he must already have discussed with del Giudice the possibility of making a film of *Hamlet*. By the end of 1946 the decision had been made. It was to rank with *Henry V* as the most important, if not the most successful film he ever made.[10]

As with *Henry V*, he was determined to be in sole charge. He would produce, direct and star. The financial rewards for this were substantial, if not approaching what he could have earned in Hollywood. He was to be paid £1,000 a month as producer, the same as director, and £2,000 a month as actor, with a cut of the profits if there turned out to be any. But the load he accepted in return for this was overwhelming. "No one unacquainted with film work can appreciate the burden that a man shoulders in taking on the direction of such a picture as *Hamlet* and acting the Prince himself," wrote Harcourt Williams, who played the First Player. "What is matter indeed for the Recording Angel is the fact that Olivier, working day after day, month after month, maintained a perfect equilibrium and sanity of outlook." As producer he would be among the first to arrive; as director and actor he would be active throughout the day; as producer, again, he would be among the last to leave. Sometimes he worked a sixteen-, even an eighteen-hour day. No normal human could have endured the strain; Olivier was exhausted, but relished every minute of it.[11]

The first task was to cut a play lasting four and a half hours to a film script that would run for something near half as long. Alan Dent was called in to help with this, but, according to Olivier at least, he contributed almost nothing except approving nods. Rosencrantz and Guildenstern vanished; to the subsequent confusion of people like Ronald Harwood who had come to *Hamlet* by way of the film and could not understand what Tom Stoppard's brilliantly witty comedy *Rosencrantz and Guildenstern are Dead* was all about. But Olivier was as ruthless with his own part. One of his noblest soliloquies—"How all occasions do inform against me"—was likewise removed. It tore his heart out, Olivier said, "but you have to cut it, because it was just dangerous to get discursive there, from a film put-together point of view." Whenever in doubt whether a passage would be obscure or over-complex, the "Gertie" test was applied— Gertie being a hypothetical girl in the cheap seats who had barely heard of *Hamlet* and whose powers of concentration were limited. If Gertie would not understand a passage, out it went.[12]

The film was to be in black and white. "I see it as an engraving rather than an oil painting," Olivier would answer loftily when asked why he had made this decision. "The fact is," he admitted later, "I was having a blazing row with Technicolor and wouldn't do another film with them." Another reason was that he wished to differentiate between *Henry V* and *Hamlet*. In *Henry V* he had gloried in the opportunities to escape the theater and luxuriate in wide landscapes and grandiose battle scenes. *Hamlet* was confined, almost claustrophobic; occasional glimpses of the sea beating against the castle walls was the only relief from the gray rooms and staircases in which the play evolved.[13]

For his mother Olivier cast Eileen Herlie, eleven years his junior. She managed to age herself convincingly but was still a most attractive woman, reinforcing the Oedipal message that had been conveyed in Olivier's stage *Hamlet* some ten years before. The situation would have been still more bizarre if, as Vivien Leigh had hoped would happen, she had played Ophelia, thus being five years older than her putative mother-in-law. The possibility cannot have been taken seriously. Probably Olivier realized it would not work, instead the actress he described as "a ravishing sixteen-year-old," Jean Simmons, was given the part and did it uncommonly well.[14]

His style of direction had become still more autocratic. His courtesy was unfailing, said Harcourt Williams, "but his conviction that his way is the right one is unshakeable. Indeed, argument with anyone who knows so surely what he wants would be a waste of time." Peter Cushing, who played Osric, noted that early in the filming Olivier was considerate and patient, ready to take into account other people's points of view. "At first it was 'Let's try it this way' or 'What do you think about . . . ?' But toward the end it was 'Do it this way and don't argue, God dammit!'" There was little resentment among the cast: partly because, though Olivier's way might not be the only, or even the best one, it was never obviously wrong; partly because they realized the strain that he was under and accepted that he did not have the time to debate each point. "Olivier was an autocrat, no doubt about that," said John Laurie, a humble sentry in this production, but later to win fame as Private Frazer in *Dad's Army*. "But in his position he had to be."[15]

His physical energy was as amazing as his mental. Esmond Knight as Bernardo, with Marcellus and Francisco, had the job of trying to hold Hamlet back when he wanted to accost the Ghost. "It was like holding a Bengal tiger," he remembered. "He was immensely strong." When dueling with Terence Morgan, who played Laertes, Olivier encouraged his adversary to attack more vigorously. "Just try and punch it into me," he said. "Don't worry. I'll parry it." He didn't, Morgan pierced his shirt and blood spouted. Undisturbed,

Olivier paused only to apply a dressing and then was at it hammer and tongs again. But it was the great leap in the final act, when Olivier launched himself from fourteen feet above onto the King below, that proved the most testing feat of all. The stand-in who was to make the jump seemed to Olivier insufficiently dramatic. He brushed him aside and took on the task. He might kill himself, he reckoned; he might damage himself for life; he might hurt himself seriously; he might hurt himself slightly; or he might escape unscathed. He thought that there was an equal chance of any one of these outcomes. In the event he got away with it; it was the unfortunate King who was knocked unconscious. As he left the scene Olivier heard one of the cameramen mutter to another: "Good old Larry! He gets on with it."[16]

Desmond Dickinson, the director of photography, had his doubts about some of Olivier's ideas but said that nevertheless he had learned "that Laurence Olivier is quite plainly a genius, and *Hamlet* is his film, every foot of it." His overriding concept was made clear before a word had been spoken, when the preamble reads: "This is the tragedy of a man who could not make up his mind." He had stolen it from a Hollywood film starring Clark Gable, he admitted. Someone asked Gable what he was reading. "*Hamlet.*" "What's that?" "It's about a man who couldn't make up his mind." This approach was one to which Olivier adhered. When a student teacher appealed to him for advice on how to play Hamlet, Olivier advised him not to worry about psychological niceties: "It is simply a play about a man who could not make up his mind . . . he just can't and you must just feel that he can't, that's all." It was a reasonable and tenable approach. The trouble was that Olivier patently *could* make up his mind.[17]

Olivier himself admitted that he was better suited to more positive and straightforward character roles, like Hotspur or Henry V, and that he was somewhat at sea in the "lyrical, poetical role of Hamlet." Guthrie put it more brutally. "The film makes absolute nonsense of its premise," he wrote, "for it showed a person . . . who shouldered aside all opposition with splendid vigor, but paused now and then to say

a few reflective words that were completely at odds with the appearance and behavior of their speaker." Olivier was far too good an actor
to put in a bad performance, but he failed to achieve greatness or
even to be convincing. With one or two conspicuous exceptions—
"Technically pedantic, aurally elephantine," Tynan deemed it—the
film got deferential, even glowing reviews. Particularly was this
the case in the United States, where its reception bordered on the
ecstatic. *Hamlet* won four Oscars, including Best Picture and, for Olivier, Best Actor. Not conceivably could it be called a failure. But Olivier
was not right in the part and his satisfaction at the popular success was
tempered by his private conviction that it did not show him at his best.[18]

J. Arthur Rank, who gained the most financially from the film's
success, had every reason to be delighted. Olivier had treated
him pretty roughly while filming was in progress. Rank had been
forbidden access to the studios and denied a view of any of the
rushes. (It is said that one of his executives managed to see half an
hour of it. "What's it like?" demanded Rank. "Mr. Rank, it's wonderful. You'd never know it was Shakespeare.") But when it came
to the promotion and distribution of the film, he could no longer
be kept at arm's length. Olivier had doubts about Rank's adequacy.
"The picture is being made with the most marvelous enthusiasm
and co-operation by all concerned and unusually intensive hard
work," he wrote severely. "It is neither fair nor just if the ultimate
exploiters of the film cannot be expected to take the same amount
of trouble over their part of it." The great mogul of British cinema
can rarely have been so sharply rebuked. Olivier had no cause to
repeat the reprimand. Rank did him proud. It was not merely in
Britain and the United States that the film performed sensationally at the box office. It was a hit in Singapore, with Chinese subti-
tles. In Romania it ran for eighteen weeks from ten in the morning
till eleven at night with every seat sold in advance. "Altogether it
would seem that the deserved fruits of fourteen months' blood,
toil and sweat are beginning to tumble from autumn's branches,"
wrote the musical director, Muir Mathieson, with unwonted
lyricism.[19]

After this triumph Rank would have let Olivier make any film he wanted. But did he want to? The Old Vic was awaiting his return, but would not another season there merely be repeating what he had done before? He had acted recently on Broadway and felt no immediate wish to return to Hollywood. But southeastward, look, the land was bright.

CHAPTER TEN

AUSTRALASIA

Olivier's decision—and it was almost entirely his own personal decision—to take a company to Australasia in 1948 seemed to everyone surprising and to some inexplicable. The idea had been suggested by the British Council, but without any real expectation that it would be taken up. Australia and New Zealand, if not a theatrical desert, were short of fertile areas. They were also a very long way away—more than four weeks by boat. Olivier says that the main reason for his decision was his belief that it was not enough for the Old Vic just to consolidate its London base: what was needed was a second company, so that one would be permanently on tour. "I think I ought to piss off now," he told Ralph Richardson. "I'll go to Australia for the best part of a year and I promise you there'll be a decent company by the time that I come back." The distance was a recommendation: the journey out would provide an opportunity for rehearsals while, on the way back, they could prepare for the next Old Vic season.[1]

Another consideration must have been the relief at escaping for the best part of a year from the whirlpool in a goldfish bowl that his life in London had become. Olivier had already had to fight desperately to preserve what little was left of his private life. In spite of the pleading of his publicity team he refused to receive in his home anyone who was not a personal friend: "Were this slender gate broken down it would be quite impossible to conduct our lives in any degree of privacy." But outside his home the pressure was almost unendurable. He compounded his problems by his inability—due

partly to good manners, partly an inbuilt conscientiousness—to
ignore approaches that most people in his position would have
consigned immediately to the wastepaper basket. He was bombarded by letters from actual or would-be theaters—youth, repertory, amateur, professional, urban, rural, Polish, Kenyan—asking
him to be their President or Patron, to attend their performances,
speak at their annual conferences, provide financial support. Usually he declined, but always with apologies. To the Hall Green Little
Theater in Birmingham he agreed to serve as President, but "on the
solemn understanding that it is only my name you want, and only
my name you will ever get." Always such promises were made; rarely
were they adhered to. Even the cranks and lunatics got replies. One
correspondent, a Jane Smith, had "a strange feeling, perhaps you
can call it sixth sense," that Olivier was her stepbrother. She repeatedly told Olivier that this was the case, suggesting a test by which
the matter could be proved. Eventually Olivier lost patience. He
had written many times, he said: "I say now, quite definitely and
for the last time, I am not your stepbrother, nor have I a scar on the
back of my right hand." Mr. James Jackson of California addressed
his letter to "Mr., Sir, Knight Laurence Olivier, Greatest Actor, London, England." The Post Office had no trouble delivering the letter;
Olivier found more difficulty in allaying Mr. Jackson's concern that
the Communist Party, disguised as the First Baptist Church, was
poisoning his (presumably Jackson's rather than Olivier's) grand-
mother and had previously disposed of the Duke of Windsor, President Nixon and nine American astronauts. At least Olivier was
spared letters of this kind when aboard the S.S. *Corinthic* bound to
Perth, Western Australia, from Liverpool.[2]

Olivier suspected that he was knighted in the Birthday Honors of 1947 so that the Australians would not feel shortchanged
by having a mere "Mr. and Mrs. Olivier" in their midst. Whatever
the explanation, it meant that he had caught up with Richardson.
Less to his taste was the fact that he had got ahead of Coward and
Gielgud who had not been given knighthoods, it was assumed, for
sexual rather than professional reasons. He wrote to them both to

apologize and duly received their assurances that they bore him no grudge. Gielgud told his mother that he had had an "enchanting letter" from Olivier. Richardson had also written. "They are both touchingly sincere and generous in saying that they feel embarrassment in being recognized over me." How Gielgud was able to measure Olivier's sincerity is difficult to say, but, having got in first, there is no doubt that Olivier was genuinely pleased when Gielgud was finally recognized.[3]

The journey out set the pattern for the whole expedition. Olivier and Vivien Leigh were exhausted by the time the *Corinthic* sailed. The cast had expected them to spend most of the journey in their suite, emerging only for rehearsals and occasional communal meals. For a day or two that was the case, but long before the liner reached Cape Town Elsie Beyer, who was largely responsible for looking after the welfare and program of the Oliviers, was reporting that they were "very, very happy and wonderfully fit . . . You just can't keep them out of the public rooms, the dining saloon, the games deck, sundry cabins, etc., etc.! They are adored by everybody . . . and voted the best mixers ever."[4]

It was Vivien Leigh who took the lead. When she was there and on form, Olivier was happy to leave public relations in her hands. "She was enormously popular in the company," Alec McCowen said of her on one of the American tours. "She was really much more of a company lady than he was." But Olivier was always ready to intervene when necessary. Peter Cushing had been reluctant to join the party because he did not want to be parted for so long from his new wife. "I'll have none of that," said Olivier. "There was too much of it forced upon most of us during the war. You bring Helen with you." The Oliviers worked energetically as a team. Every member of the party received a poem urging them to report if they had a birthday coming up:

> A lonely birthday is no joke.
> And we "parentis" are "in loco,"

> We also love you very dearly
> And are always yours sincerely . . .

When the occasion arose the birthday celebrant was given a party, loaded with presents, made to feel a cherished part of the family. "I have to thank you for your ever-gentle guidance," wrote Cushing, "your untiring efforts with my Speech and many imperfections and all the dear, friendly, sympathetic interest you have so generously given me to benefit my present and future life." Effusions of this kind can mean very little, but there are enough such tributes paid by members of the party to convince any doubter that this ship was indeed a happy one. The Oliviers were equally happy with their companions. "The Co. are absolute angels," Vivien Leigh told Ralph Richardson's wife Meriel—"Mu"—"and we're all very happy together in that direction."[5]

But it was also "incredibly strenuous," she went on. Once they were in Australia they constantly found themselves on their feet "saying a few words." It terrified her but "Larry is getting wonderful at it." They were not merely running a theater company and acting most of the principal roles, they were also making a royal progress with all that that involved in the way of gracious speeches, grandiose dinners and receptions and endless visits to institutions in which their interest was something less than passionate. "I was substitute royalty," Olivier observed of one A.N.Z.A.C. day celebration. "I didn't actually say 'The Queen and I' but it was not far off." Once was quite amusing; endlessly repeated it became a stressful chore. Required while at Melbourne to make two speeches within three hours, Olivier thought he would relieve the monotony by dropping into Australian slang, referring to his audience as "beauts" and saying that the company was having "a bonzer time." At once he was accused of being patronizing and of disparaging Australia's cultural achievements. More often he played safe and struck a patriotic note. The British, he told a Melbourne audience, were truly grateful for the food parcels dispatched from down under, but if they thought they were provoked "by that feeling of pity that is akin to contempt" they would far rather do without. "Britain is not finished." So far as the Australians were concerned, even better than hearing the Oliviers in the theater was meeting them in the flesh. Everyone who was anyone thought he had the right to at least five minutes of their time. Mrs. Donnell, acting as their secretary, had to call in additional help at each stopping place to deal with the fan mail and sort out the would-be callers.[6]

On the whole the reviews in the Australian press wavered between the enthusiastic and the ecstatic and most of the coverage given to the party was extremely friendly. Olivier for some reason however—perhaps because he was so exhausted—decided that he was being victimized. "The most unpleasant press I've found in the entire world," he remembered many years later. "I've never known myself feel so under attack." It is true that the press were ready to take offense if they felt their visitors were being high-handed or supercilious, but such occasions arose only rarely. "Never, and I mean NEVER," wrote the correspondent of the Melbourne *Argus*, "have I seen the men and women of the press fall so heavily . . . for the charm of a couple they were all keyed up to resent." Melbourne felt itself to be the most sophisticated of Australian cities and so was likely to be the quickest to object to any real or imagined slight. In fact the reviews of *The School for Scandal*, *Richard III* and *The Skin of Our Teeth* (with Olivier taking over the part of Mr. Antrobus) were excellent. What Olivier remembered, however, was the casual comment in one newspaper: "We have better Richard IIIs here in Melbourne." Eager to engage such significant new talent for the Old Vic, wrote Olivier, he sent out his talent scouts to track down the putative King Richard; they returned with the news that there was no professional theater in Melbourne.[7]

The opening in Perth showed them some of the perils ahead. *The School for Scandal* was put on in a monster hall that had not been used for live theater for more than ten years. "It was quite a task," Olivier commented, "to bash over Sheridan's gossamer trifles in a way that would be appreciated by 2,280 people." When he first saw the auditorium he observed gloomily: "We'd better dress up as

Christians and throw ourselves to the lions." In the event, the audience were respectful, but loath to laugh. It turned out that few of them could hear. Reluctantly Olivier agreed that people from the University could install amplifiers; it offended his sense of theatrical propriety, but at least it meant that the subsequent audiences could take in what was going on. For the last night at Perth Vivien Leigh decreed that at the end the cast should sing "Waltzing Matilda." "Nobody knows the words," she was told. "It doesn't matter," she insisted. "The audience will join in and you can pretend to sing." The audience did not oblige. The first verse was more or less alright but by the end "all you could hear was Vivien's little voice singing solo." The experiment was not repeated.[8]

In the mind of Olivier the various stops along the way were marked as much by the pressure of social events as by the quality of the performances. In Hobart, where the company spent three full days, only *The School for Scandal* was mounted. This might suggest an opportunity to rest. Instead Olivier found himself calling on the Governor, attending a party given by the Tasmanian Arts Council (speech required), visiting the repertory company (speech), attending the Lord Mayor's party (speech), inspecting the local hospital and the University, spending an hour at the Governor's tea party and giving an Old Vic party for local residents who had been helpful. After all that, asking as many members of the cast as possible to lunch, tea, dinner or beach picnics must have seemed a rest cure.[9]

The pressure was almost beyond endurance. By April, when the party had reached Canberra, Elsie Beyer was reporting that the Oliviers were "terribly exhausted . . . I had been feeling uneasy about them for the past couple of weeks because they just did not seem to be able to get on top of their feelings of exhaustion." Then, early in July, in Sydney, on a day on which he was playing Richard III both in the afternoon and in the evening, Olivier tore a cartilage in his right knee. The pain was acute, but he carried on with the aid of crutches: "which he used to splendid effect in *Richard*, culminating in breaking one over the unfortunate Brackenbury's head, in one performance," wrote Vivien Leigh. By the time he reached New

Zealand lumbago added to his problems. He had to have injections before he could play. "Poor chap, he is going through it," Michael Redington, a junior member of the party, wrote to his family. "I don't know if he is going to have an operation when we get back to London." In fact he decided to have it in New Zealand and to convalesce on the journey home, but he put the operation off to the last minute and continued to act until a few days before the time of sailing. The tour of New Zealand was overwhelmingly successful. "You may not know it," Olivier told a reporter in Dunedin, "but you are talking to two walking corpses." The dead can rarely have appeared more quick. The tour took them to Auckland, Christchurch, Dunedin and Wellington: every house was packed, every audience appreciative. The Governor, Bernard Freyberg, sent Olivier a case of whiskey. "My congratulations on your conquest of New Zealand," he wrote, "and my thanks for all you have done. I know it has been hard work but it has been so very well worthwhile."[10]

Olivier, fresh from the hospital where he had had his operation, boarded the ship on a stretcher. He was carried aloft by a crane and which lowered him triumphantly on the deck: it was an exit as theatrical as any he could have contrived for himself.

The tour of Australia had been greatly eased by the labors of a young Englishman working for the British Council, Peter Hiley. Hiley won the hearts of both Oliviers and in return adored both of them and the life they represented. By the time the party sailed for England he had become part of the family. He was to remain a vital part of Olivier's life for the next forty years.

All his ministrations had been needed. The tour of Australia and New Zealand was marked for Olivier by two crises that seemed at the time at least as pressing as anything that was happening on the stage. The first was resolved relatively easily. Before he left England he had encouraged, or at any rate authorized, his sister Sybille to write his biography—more because it would give her a chance of earning a little badly needed money than because he thought she would do it well or that there was much point in writing about a life

that was far from complete. She went to work and by July had finished a first draft. The publisher was keen to have it in the bookshops
by October. Olivier took fright. He was worried, he told his agent
and confidant, Cecil Tennant, about the biography appearing without his knowing what it said. "Really think it should be inspected
by one of us," he cabled. Tennant had no intention of accepting sole
responsibility. The text was sent to Olivier in Australia. "You MUST
react very quickly," Tennant urged him, as otherwise the publisher
would have begun to set the text and it would be too late to alter it.[11]

Editing a manuscript of some 70,000 words on top of all his
other responsibilities can hardly have been a welcome challenge,
but he undertook it with characteristic thoroughness. He made a
lot of changes, some factual, many more of emphasis or phrasing,
then suddenly repented of the whole exercise. "I must implore you
not to publish biography as it is now," he cabled his sister. Too much
of it, "involving people's feelings," was inaccurate, and the balance
of the book required a lot of thought. If it went ahead as it was he
would feel bound to dissociate himself from it "in ways that would
only hurt and discredit you." The disgruntled publisher had to be
bought off and Sybille compensated for her wasted work, but in the
end Olivier had his way: the draft was abandoned and now rests,
with Olivier's amendments, with the rest of his archive in the British Library.[12]

Reread today, it is hard to see why he took so strongly against
it. It was not a great work of literature but it was quite as well written as Olivier's own later efforts. It was affectionate throughout and
the occasional blemishes that it revealed in its hero's behavior and
character were far less acerbic in tone than the criticism to which
Olivier from time to time subjected himself. Sybille would have
been happy to accept any changes that her brother wished to make.
The most probable explanation is that, when it came to the point,
Olivier could not bear that his sister should write his life. Many
years later, when Mark Amory seemed set to ghost the autobiography, Olivier decided that he would instead do it himself. As with the
plays or films that he produced, directed and starred in, he had to

be in charge. If some outsider had been undertaking his biography he could have affected indifference; when his sister was involved it came close to home, he could not avoid a measure of responsibility. But for Olivier a measure of responsibility was an intolerable concept. Too late Sybille discovered what she should have known from the beginning; her brother was generous, loyal and affectionate but where his own territory was involved he would tolerate no trespassing. The responsibility must be his and his alone.

The second crisis had consequences far more profound. On July 15, 1948, Olivier received a letter from the Chairman of the Old Vic, Lord Esher, thanking him for all he had done to build up the company but saying that the Board felt that in the future it should not be run by actors but by some full-time administrator who would devote himself exclusively to the work. The contracts of Olivier, Richardson and John Burrell would not be renewed after the end of the 1948–9 season. Rumors that something untoward was in the offing had reached Olivier a few weeks before. "Private and confidential communication from Old Vic makes many changes in the future outlook," he had cabled Cecil Tennant in mid-June. "Would you contact Burrell immediately and seek confidential information?" Burrell does not seem to have had much idea as to what was going on; at all events nothing had prepared Olivier for the terse dismissal that he had now received.[13]

Ralph Richardson had been more prescient. It had been some time since Lord Esher had reached an implicit agreement with Oliver Lyttelton, later Lord Chandos, chairman of the committee that controlled the hoped-for but still nebulous National Theater, that when the National secured governmental backing and financial support, the Old Vic would supply the hard core of its operations. Though formal governmental acceptance still seemed a long way off, those on the inside reckoned there was a more real possibility of a functioning National Theater now than had been true for many years. The decision to involve the Old Vic in the operation was obviously a sensible one. Both Olivier and Richardson rejoiced at the prospect. But Richardson foresaw the implications for the current management. "It won't be our dear, friendly semi-amateurish Old Vic anymore . . ." he told Olivier. "They're not going to stand for a couple of actors bossing the place around. We shall be out, old cockie"[14]

Olivier had not been convinced. He noticed, though, that a new formality, a bureaucratic element, was seeping into his relationship with the Board. A trivial incident brought it home to him. Shortly before they left for Australia, the egregious Mr. Wanbon, whom Olivier had so fiercely dismissed sometime before,* lurked outside the Oliviers' London home, Durham Cottage, until they came home late at night, accosted them and, presumably drunk, tried to kiss Vivien Leigh. In the ensuing brawl Olivier broke a finger. Legal proceedings followed, and Olivier hired a counsel to represent him. Since Wanbon's attack had been inspired by his resentment at the Old Vic treatment of him, Olivier took it for granted that the theater would cover his costs. A couple of years earlier they would have done so without demur; now they grumbled that it was not their responsibility and that there had been no need to retain a counsel. In the end they paid only half the costs, and that with bad grace. Things were not as they used to be, Olivier considered. He became suspicious about what was going on. Perhaps Ralph Richardson had a point. While in Australia he was concerned that so many of what seemed to him the most promising productions at the Old Vic had been crowded into the first half of the season while he would be away. "I can't help thinking there is the tiniest bit of hanky-panky going on," he told Cecil Tennant.[15]

Hanky-panky or no hanky-panky, what was in effect outright dismissal took him by surprise. To have been eased out gently might have been acceptable, to be notified in a brief and not in the least apologetic letter when he was at the other end of the earth and engaged in what he saw as Old Vic business seemed to him intolerable. For more than three years, at considerable financial sacrifice,

---

* See page 118 above.

he and Richardson had devoted themselves to the affairs of the Old
Vic, they had raised it to the position of the finest repertory company in Great Britain, possibly the world. To dismiss them, to his
mind at least, was not simply gross ingratitude but folly, since it
could only doom the Old Vic to the obscurity from which they had
rescued it. Harold Hobson compared the deed to the dismissal of
Winston Churchill by the electorate in 1945, the triumph of medi-
ocrity over elitism, the ungrateful spurning of the great leader who
had brought his country to glorious victory. The analogy begged
many questions, but it had a certain poignant force.[16]

There was, of course, another way of looking at the matter. It was
put by Tyrone Guthrie, who was himself probably the individual
most responsible for the dismissal of Olivier and Richardson. The
two great stars, he admitted, had done wonderful things, but: "The
period of glory was brilliant but brief. In spite of enormous houses
no money was saved." They were more concerned, Guthrie suggested
even if he did not directly state, with their own careers than with the
future of the theater. When Olivier took his company to Australia he left Richardson and Burrell to run the show in his absence;
Richardson, however, acting within the terms of his contract but at
variance with the spirit of the agreement between the two stars and
the Board, took off for Hollywood. Burrell was left to do the best he
could. He had a powerful team to support him—Sybil Thorndike,
Alec Guinness, Trevor Howard, Edith Evans, would have been most
producers' acting team from heaven—but the Old Vic audiences
had grown used to seeing either Richardson or Olivier, preferably
both, in every play. A series of lackluster productions made matters
still worse. The Comédie-Française visited London in 1948 and the
critics took some satisfaction in pointing out how much better it
was than its British rival. Attendances fell away; the Old Vic 1948
season lost £26,000. The only critically acclaimed new production
was *The Cherry Orchard* and that, said Olivier, was an economic
disaster and led to "the Governors getting the bloody wind up."[17]

Lord Esher, supported if not egged on by Guthrie, felt that the
Old Vic had become too dependent on its two stars. A situation

in which the success of the theater depended on their presence could not be allowed to continue. The spirit of repertory was being eroded. He was not alone in his doubts. Barbara Ward, one of the most vociferous and influential members of the Board, firmly believed that the director of a putative National Theater should never be an actor. She had some strong arguments on her side. From the point of view of the long-term future of the National Theater a change in the style of management was desirable. But the way in which the Board handled the matter—by long-distance correspondence and without a glimmer of consultation—was disastrously inept. The proper course would have been to let Olivier and Richardson return from their travels and then to explain the Board's feelings in a face-to-face meeting. Even if a compromise had not proved possible, the sense of grievance on the part of the two stars would have been less strong, or at any rate, less justified.[18]

As it was, the change of regime caused indignation if not outrage. There was to be no official announcement until after Olivier's return, but within the profession the news spread quickly. One member of the Board, the publisher Hamish Hamilton, resigned in protest: "I cannot remain a member of a body that has treated you so badly," he told Olivier. George Chamberlain, the general manager of the Old Vic, claimed that the conduct of the Board seemed "to have been borrowed from international politics" and was inexcusable. Olivier realized that when he got back he would have to decide whether to go quietly or to stoke up resentment and make his remaining months as a director unpleasant for everybody. For the moment there was little to do except stay quiet and complete the tour. Richardson seemed disposed to take the less aggressive and easier course. "Aha, dear fellow," he wrote when Olivier had reached New Zealand. "You seem as sad as I am about the Old Vic. You must be sadder, you are doing so much more than I am for the cause. It was a happy dream that we might take a share in piloting that ship for years to come . . . I suppose we will have to look around for another job . . . I feel the need for something on a long-term basis, not just hopping from job to job. I long to lay my head with yours in this matter."[19]

Ill-health, crippling fatigue, a lost job—what would anyway have been a sad end to the Australian tour was made worse by suspicions that his marriage was going awry. "Somehow, somewhere on this tour I knew that Vivien was lost to me," he wrote in his memoirs. This pronouncement was over-dramatic. He had not lost Vivien and was not finally to lose her for another decade. But there were signs that the relationship was under strain; it would never be glad confident morning again. Olivier put his gloomy comment in the context of their meeting with Peter Finch. Finch would in time play an important part in the disintegration of the Oliviers' marriage, but in 1948 he was no more than a talented but almost unknown young actor whom Olivier had seen playing Argan in *Le Malade Imaginaire* in Sydney. Olivier was enormously struck by his potential. He wrote to Cecil Tennant to report that "an exceptionally clever, I repeat exceptionally clever young Australian actor is on the way . . . I cannot express too much what a very, very bright boy I think he is." Vivien Leigh seems to have shared her husband's enthusiasm. But at that stage there was no more to it than that. Finch was married; happily so, so far as the Oliviers could judge, and Leigh hardly did more than exchange a few words with him.[20]

Other factors, though, were threatening the Oliviers' marriage. There had been tension even during the preparations for the tour. One day an acrimonious argument over lunch had been followed by an ugly scene during the rehearsal of *Richard III*. Olivier ruled that Lady Anne, played by Vivien Leigh, should fall off her chair at a certain point. Leigh refused to do so, saying that it would be out of character. Through clenched teeth, Olivier retorted: "The Lady Anne will fall off her chair if I have to bloody well push her off myself!" This may have been no more than a tiff between two highly strung artists under pressure, but it would not have happened two years before. Another such confrontation was reported on the tour. At Christchurch Leigh refused to go on stage without her red slippers, which had been mislaid. "Put on any shoes and just get on up there," Olivier ordered. She refused. He slapped her face, saying: "Get up on that stage, you little bitch!" She slapped him back: "Don't you dare hit me you—you bastard!" The trainee student who recalled this incident may have been exaggerating—no other member of the party recorded anything similar—but though the couple generally kept up a brave front in public an uneasy feeling that all was not well hung over the later stages of the tour.[21]

Though she usually managed to put on a good show when others were present, it was obvious to all who knew her well that Leigh was under great strain and was growing increasingly unpredictable in her reactions. "My birth sign is Scorpio and they eat themselves up and burn themselves out," she told a reporter. She spoke lightly, but she must have believed that there was truth in what she said. Olivier was realizing that the tuberculosis that had so alarmed him in 1945 was only part, and not the worst part, of her problems. To a friend who asked how she was, Olivier replied that it was difficult to be sure: "Her sort of trouble is rather veiled in mystery and it is hard to get conclusive and satisfactory news." That was in 1946; two years later the veil of mystery was as thick as ever but Olivier was becoming more convinced by the day that something was badly wrong. It was to be several years before the full horror of the situation dawned on him, but during the Australasian tour it became ever more clear that there was trouble ahead and that things were likely to become a great deal worse.[22]

During the last weeks in New Zealand and on the ship going home this manifested itself in an irresponsibly conspicuous flirtation between Vivien Leigh and Dan Cunningham, a young man who, according to Emma Brash, the wardrobe mistress, was not much of an actor but "terribly funny and very attractive and elegant and a really charming person." Olivier was first having the operation to his knee, then more or less confined to his cabin: it was understandable that Leigh should hanker after some entertainment and welcome the attentions of an eligible young man happy to squire her around. There is no reason to believe that there was more to it than that, but the relationship was indiscreet enough to create much gossip and cause her husband some unease. In the end, as he described in his memoirs: "I pleaded with her not, please, to make her flirtation with one young man in the company so obvious . . . I really couldn't see that it was justified that I should be so humiliated." Rather to his surprise, she took the rebuke meekly and promised that the gossips would have no further material on which to exercise their talents.[23]

The Oliviers docked at Tilbury on November 16, 1948. There would be another six months to serve with the Old Vic. After that the future appeared a great deal more uncertain than had been the case a year before.

CHAPTER ELEVEN

LIFE WITHOUT THE OLD VIC

One of the first things Olivier did after his return to London was to confront Lord Esher. He and Richardson had by then agreed that there was no point in contesting the Board's decision: if they were not wanted, they were not wanted, there were plenty of opportunities for them elsewhere. Esher oozed appreciation of all that the existing directors had done to get the Old Vic up and running; the time had come, however, to entrust the enterprise to a single man who would devote himself wholeheartedly to carrying it to still greater heights. According to Olivier, he went on to suggest that that single man should be Olivier himself: now that Richardson and Burrell had resigned, the way was clear for the third, and most effective, member of the triumvirate to assume supreme power. Olivier answered that he could not betray his friends in such a way. Barbara Ward, who made a similar approach, was similarly rebuffed: "I couldn't let them be fired . . . It would have been rather ugly. But they couldn't see that, these bigwigs." The scenario is not convincing. It seems more likely that Esher was referring to a time—he hoped only two or three years away—when the Old Vic would be reborn as the National Theater and a fresh start would be needed. Olivier, however, must have found it pleasing to portray himself as standing by his friends and spurning a chalice which, if not poisoned, would still have left a nasty taste in the mouth.[1]

To replace the dismissed directors, Hugh Hunt was brought in from the Bristol Old Vic. "Quite a respectable director, nothing thrilling," Olivier dismissed him. Guthrie, too, returned to the fold to supervise the move back to the now-restored Old Vic building south of the river; he compounded Olivier's indignation by bringing in Donald Wolfit to play Tamburlaine. Hunt was anxious to keep Olivier on board in one capacity or another. He had only accepted the position after much self-questioning, he wrote: "On the one hand every sense of loyalty to John [Burrell], you and Ralph pulled against it; on the other, I felt the alternatives were not in the Vic's interests." He besought Olivier not to turn his back on the theater: would he play Malvolio? Would he play Othello? "I realize that this is a very great deal to swallow from your point of view, but I can only make a very personal plea."[2]

Olivier was unmoved: he was resolved to work out the last six months of his contract and then to shake the dust of the Old Vic from his feet. In the meantime his main responsibility was the staging of a refurbished version of *The School for Scandal* which had been a great success on the Australasian tour. Cecil Beaton had done the costumes and Olivier's lengthy letters to him illustrate the perfectionism and keen eye for detail that marked his approach to any theatrical enterprise with which he was associated. He did not spare Beaton's feelings: Lady Sneerwell's day costume was "a bit common"; Maria's outdoor costume "honestly, dear boy, does not come off"; Charles Surface needed to be dressed in "a more crudely, hail-fellow-well-met fashion." Almost as an afterthought, Olivier ended: "This letter does not convey to you one thousandth part of the brilliant success that your work has been." Beaton swallowed the criticism, worked on the costumes and thought the results were sensationally successful. When he went round to see them after the London opening, however, he found, or thought he found, that Vivien Leigh snubbed him and Olivier was frigid: "No smiles, no back-thumping, and no 'old mans' or 'old cocks' . . . I knew that, such is my unforgiving, unforgetting nature, no matter how hard the Oliviers might try, one day, to make up for this evening, I would have no further interest in them." He did, of course. The Oliviers were far more important to Beaton than Beaton to the Oliviers and he was frequently to work with them in the future. Olivier, neither unforgiving nor unforgetting and not the most sensitive of men, probably failed to notice that Beaton had taken offense. But their relationship, at its best not close, would never be the same again.[3]

It remained only for Olivier to leave the Old Vic as gracefully as possible. His farewell speech contrived to say nothing critical of the Board while leaving a strong impression that he had been misused. Esher, for his part, wrote a letter of effusive insincerity to record the Governors' "sense of loss at the termination of so stimulating a connection," and to express his "confident hope that time will bring us together again." It depended on what he meant by "us." If he meant himself as an individual Olivier would have as little as possible to do with him; if he meant the Old Vic transformed into the National Theater then time would indeed bring them together again in the not too distant future.[4]

The years between his severance from the Old Vic in 1949 and the opening of the Chichester Festival in 1962 were far from barren for Olivier—he played important roles, both in the theater and on the screen, and established himself as an actor-manager—but in terms of his overall career they were a period of marking time. The one thing of which he professed himself certain was that he did not wish to undertake another tour on the scale of the Australasian adventure; occasional forays to New York and Hollywood or European tours were the limit of his ambitions. Nevertheless, at one point he seems to have been contemplating some sort of theatrical expedition to Africa. "Why on earth we do such things, I can't think," he told Sybil Thorndike. "We loathe these capers once we start on them."[5]

That project was abandoned, but one caper nearer home proved almost equally testing. Olivier had conceived the idea of directing Vivien Leigh in Tennessee Williams's *A Streetcar Named Desire* while he was still with the Old Vic. By the time he got back from Australasia, however, Binkie Beaumont had intervened. He told the producer Irene Selznick that Vivien Leigh was a very great friend and that she was eager to play the role of Blanche DuBois. When

Selznick asked whether Olivier would be ready to act himself, or at least direct the play, Beaumont was more evasive. "Well, that might be managed," was the gist of his reply. "I detected less enthusiasm and no intimacy." It soon became clear, though, that Leigh would only act if her husband were to be the director. A deal was done with Selznick and Beaumont. Rehearsals were scheduled to begin in the autumn of 1949.[6]

At this point Olivier had only glanced at the play. When he read it properly he realized that it was powerful, tragic and certain to cause trouble with the censor. His wife's part was magnificent but harrowing, requiring her to play a vulnerable victim who gradually crumbles into insanity. He defended the play against those who dismissed it as obscene sensationalism. "It is a tragedy in the purest sense of the word," he told one critic. "The object of the theater is not only one of entertainment, or even only one of uplift, the basic object of tragedy is to shock the soul." But he also thought it repetitious and verbose. He resolved to cut it, but found that the author felt it had been cut to the bone already. Twice the men met to thrash out the matter, twice they failed even to address the issue. Olivier then took the law into his own hands. "Surely it's a director's prerogative to take out anything he wants and to rearrange things as he sees fit?" he claims to have asked Irene Selznick. "Who's going to stop me?" Whether or not he in fact expressed himself with quite such arrogance, he proceeded to take considerable liberties with the text. The author took fright: "See that everything possible is done to protect *us* and the play," he cabled, "as distinct from Sir Laurence and his lady." In the end a compromise was reached. Irene Selznick seems to have come off better; almost all the major cuts were restored. Olivier was dissatisfied. "If only real geniuses would listen to practical old craftsmen sometimes," he cabled to Garson Kanin. All seems to have ended happily, though. When Williams came to London to see *Streetcar*, according to Olivier, he "saw for the first time how intensely amusing the play was for all its tragedy and stark grimness. He absolutely died laughing. He loved it."[7]

The principal victim of the play was Vivien Leigh herself. Olivier believed that he had done a masterly job of direction. "If it hadn't been for me Vivien would have been no good in *Streetcar*," he claimed. "This sounds like a terrible lack of humility; I'm sorry . . . You sometimes need a guy who knows what the fuck he's talking about and can tell you how to get it, and whatever else I am, I know the hell of a lot about the business. I'm very, very good at giving people the right advice." But in claiming responsibility for her remarkable performance he also accepted responsibility for the damage it did her. Instead of shedding the burdens of the role at the same time as she took off her makeup, Leigh seemed somehow to have become locked into Blanche DuBois and was permanently scarred by the experience. "I think it was the beginning of the illness, the seeds of the illness," wrote Olivier. It was neither the beginning nor the seeds of the illness, and on other occasions Olivier accepted that his wife's condition could be traced back for many years, but the strain of playing the part marked a notable step in her disintegration.[8]

Streetcar was an immense success with the critics and, still more, with the public. More than ten thousand people applied for tickets on the first night; people were queuing for seats in the gallery three days before. Olivier came in for some criticism for sponsoring so shocking a play. In a speech J. B. Priestley remarked that the world of show business encompassed everything from the bearded lady or elephants playing hockey to Vivien Leigh in *A Streetcar Named Desire*. Olivier complained bitterly about this juxtaposition. It encouraged the sort of audience, he said, who normally went only to the Windmill (a Soho theater celebrated for the display of naked women) and who "sat squirming, giggling, coughing, hoping for the worst to happen. This had made Vivien's task, already cruelly arduous, almost impossible to bear." It seems, in fact, unlikely that many habitués of the Windmill found their way to Vivien Leigh's performance but criticism of this kind from so august a figure as Priestley increased her unease and made her still more vulnerable to the self-doubts that consumed her.[9]

The final curtain fell on *Streetcar* in June 1950. "I think I'm almost more grateful about it than she is," wrote Olivier. "It's been a most ghastly strain for her, poor darling." The strain was not yet over for there was still the film to be made, but it was in the nature of acting for the cinema that the emotional pressure of the stage performance was relieved if not removed. It was also made more acceptable for Vivien Leigh by the fact that she was playing opposite Marlon Brando. It proved a memorable experience. Though far less experienced and versatile, Brando was one of the few actors who could match, even surpass Olivier for sheer explosive power. He also had a reputation for always sleeping with any actress who played opposite him. But not Vivien Leigh, it seems: he is quoted as having said, "I was so anxious to bed my costar that my teeth ached," but Olivier was also in Hollywood at the time and "I liked him too much to invade his chicken coop." Brando, with Danny Kaye, Henry Ainley and others, is among the men with whom it is alleged that Olivier had a homosexual fling. Olivier to some extent brought this on his own head by his cryptic reference in his autobiography to his "nearly passionate involvement" with another man. He went on to say, however, that he had never had any sort of homosexual relationship. In his memoirs and elsewhere he frequently accused himself of far more serious offenses; there is no reason to believe that he lied in this respect. He would hardly have bothered to deny the charge if it had been true: he saw nothing reprehensible about going to bed with another man, it was merely that the idea did not appeal to him. A high proportion of his theatrical friends and acquaintances were homosexual: not admitting publicly to it and thereby risking prosecution, but taking little trouble to conceal their leanings. Olivier was intrigued—he took a somewhat salacious interest in other people's love lives and offended Alec Guinness by cross-examining him on whether Gielgud had or had not tried to seduce him—but he felt none the worse of them if their tastes lay in that direction.[10]

Gielgud himself was no less curious. He was fascinated to read in Donald Spoto's biography that Olivier was supposed to have had an affair with Danny Kaye. "Quite unexpected news," he wrote, but then he remembered that Kaye had plied him with drink at his home in Hollywood. "Perhaps he conceived making a pass at me and thought better of it when he actually saw me . . . You never know, and I never shall." Others among Olivier's friends who were quite as well qualified to speak on such matters, thought they *did* know. Noël Coward, having established that his godson, Tarquin Olivier, was not on offer, confessed that Tarquin's father had proved equally obdurate. Terence Rattigan tried to persuade Olivier to play Diaghilev: "Yes, I know . . . you're frightfully normal and couldn't bring yourself to love a mere boy . . . but there's no one else who *could* play it or *should* play it." Cecil Beaton, in his diary, said that he had seldom come across "someone who has so successfully mastered the conundrums of his life . . . He's 100 percent male and sure of the basic things in his life." The evidence most often cited by those who claim Olivier was bisexual is a remark by Vivien Leigh to the effect that Robert Helpmann had shared a bed with her and her husband, but this, even if true, is no proof of homosexuality. Helpmann himself claims Olivier once said: "I'm sorry to say this in front of you, Cocky, but I don't think there is any place in the theater for queers"—a curious observation given the sexual predilections of many of those at the Old Vic but one that Helpmann claimed to understand.[11]

Olivier's appetite for women, on the other hand, was rapacious and enduring. He could hardly wait to get every new acquaintance into bed. It has been said that, when he got them there, his performance was not particularly distinguished, but that does not seem to have stopped them coming back for more. "I don't know anybody who had more sex appeal," said Rosemary Harris—Elena to Olivier's Astrov in *Uncle Vanya* in the celebrated Chichester program: "Everybody, whatever sex you were, whether you were a cat, a dog or a mouse, you were in love with him." "You were and are the DISHIEST man who ever lived," announced Claire Bloom, who had a brief affair with him. To those unacquainted with theatrical mannerisms he gave some grounds for doubting his virility. He could be

extremely camp; he was by instinct tactile, quick to lay an affectionate arm on the shoulder of another man or woman; his epistolary
style, even by actors' standards, was extravagant—"Darling boy," he
began a letter to David Niven, ending "All my love dearest friend in
the world, your devoted Larry." Nobody who knew him well, however, can have doubted that he loved women, lusted after women
and would have considered a sexual relationship with another man
a pitiful substitute for the real thing.[12]

As a father Olivier knew he had been inadequate. Since his divorce
from Jill Esmond he had barely seen his son. He dutifully sent foreign postage stamps to him when he was aboard, he was conscientious about birthday presents, but meetings between the two were
rare. "Some years ago," he told Tarquin in 1951, "I arranged my life
so that I could never be a father to you in the accepted sense of the
word." Now he felt he should be making up for lost time. Vivien
Leigh helped in the process; indeed, she was much better than
he was at establishing a relationship with Tarquin. Olivier found
it difficult to have any sensible conversation with a schoolboy. Jill
Esmond urged him to make greater efforts: "He very much wants to
get closer to you . . . He said that if in the next two years or so you
and he still remain strangers, after that it would be too late . . . He
has reached an age when Mom ought, for the time being at least, to
take a back seat—his problems are male and should be discussed
with a male." Olivier was left with a feeling of guilt, but still had
neither the time nor the will to do much about it. Nor did the business of day-to-day communication get easier. "I do hope you don't
mind my being untalkative," he wrote apologetically. "I am rather
prone to long silences, I know, which makes me jolly dull company
at times." Tarquin, of course, was left suspecting that it was he who
was the dull company; an additional cause for unease in their faltering relationship.[13]

But Olivier was still concerned about his son's future. Shortly
after he was ejected from the Old Vic, he told Jill Esmond that he
was determined to own a theater before he died, "with the vague idea

that Tarkie might like to inherit it." He never achieved this ambition but he at least made a start in that direction when, in 1949, he took a four-year lease on the St. James's Theater. It was a decisive step forward for the limited company that he had set up in 1946, Laurence Olivier Productions, usually referred to as L.O.P. In origin L.O.P. was little more than a tax avoidance scheme whereby the Oliviers could channel all their earnings into a company and make that company responsible for most of their expenses. At its first meeting Anthony Bushell, one of his closest friends, was appointed business manager. Cecil Tennant, the managing director, announced at the second meeting that £2,000 had been borrowed from Laurence Olivier, interest being paid at the commercial rate, and that the first substantial undertaking had been the purchase of a Rolls-Royce. It was all very cozy, certainly legal, and, from a tax point of view, beneficial. At first the only directors were the Oliviers; as the activities of the company became more ambitious, Roger Furse and Alexander Korda were added to the Board. Now, in occupation of the St. James's Theater, L.O.P. was taking a new initiative. Leslie Banks wrote to say how thrilled he was that "an Actor has managed to PRY his way back into real Actor Management again. It is the reward for all the imagination, the vitality, the team-work, the loyalty to a craft, the family feeling in a curious way, of us English actors."[14]

The pity is that imagination, vitality and teamwork were not enough. The St. James's Theater, though superficially attractive, had bad acoustics and sight lines so deplorable that only once, when the Oliviers were playing *Caesar and Cleopatra* eight feet up center stage on the paws of the Sphinx, were both leading players visible to the whole of the audience. Financially speaking, Olivier was not a good manager. He would never accept second-best, whether in terms of cast, scenery or costumes, and the cost of his productions was so great that, even with a full house, the margin of profit was only £60 a week. Perhaps most of all the age of the actor-manager was over, not because there was no one fit to wear the mantle of Booth or Irving but because, as Tyrone Guthrie put it, "the garment has become unwearable. A general devolution of tasks has taken

place. The production of a play is now undertaken by a corps of spe-
cialists." Even with a powerful machine behind him Olivier was to
find it overwhelmingly difficult to act, direct and at the same time
run the National Theater. At the St. James's Theater he was working
more or less single-handed.[15]

To make matters worse, his choice of plays, though not always
unsuccessful, failed to generate any great popular success. The first,
James Bridie's new play *Daphne Laureola*, was in fact put on before
he had acquired the St. James's Theater and was still at the Old Vic.
Wyndham's, where it first played, was back-to-back with the New
Theater where the Old Vic was still based. It starred Edith Evans
and there was a part for Olivier's Australian protégé, Peter Finch.
Harold Hobson was awestruck by the audacity of this enterprise. "It
is doubtful," he wrote, "if in the 350-year history of the London theater, there exists any really comparable case: when a world-famous
actor, appearing himself in one theater, presented a world-famous
actress in a rival attraction at a theater only a few yards away . . .
Sir Laurence unites in himself an influence in the cinema and the
theater never before concentrated in the hands of one man." The
play itself was less remarkable than the circumstances of its production but it did well enough to encourage Olivier to move into his
own theater.[16]

For his first play at the St. James's he turned to the most fashionable dramatist of the day, Christopher Fry. Viewed in hindsight, it
is hard to understand how this sophisticated, frothy and basically
frivolous versifier was once ranked with T. S. Eliot as the inaugu-
rator of a new age of poetic drama. His words sounded very nice,
though—even if he did not have much to say—and *Venus Observed*
gave the public what it wanted and had come to expect. Olivier's
extravagance was liberally displayed. He himself headed a powerful cast, a six-piece orchestra was employed, the women's dresses
were all changed after the first night, Roger Furse let himself go
with the sets. The author was expelled from rehearsals after the
first read-through: "Since I'm both acting and directing," Olivier
told him, "I should only show off if you were here." Accepting this

somewhat dubious premise, Fry withdrew and the next thing he heard was that the dress rehearsal was scheduled for the following day. He phoned to find the time. "Well, you're a nice author, I must say," said Olivier. "Never coming near us!" "Larry, I've been waiting for you to ask me to come," Fry protested. "Well, it's too late now." It was too late: the production was not at all what Fry had been expecting, but though the two men talked until four in the morning, not much could be done about it. Olivier had other, to him more pressing matters on his mind. On the one occasion outside the theater when Fry thought a serious discussion was beginning, Olivier's only question was: "What sort of nose do you think . . . ?" "It's a wonderful success," Olivier told Garson Kanin, "and I am so very happy in what I like to kid myself is my own theater." The play ran for seven months, which was success enough, but by the end of its run it had not generated enough profit to justify the enterprise on commercial grounds. For the cast, though, it had been a rewarding experience. "The last six months have been for me the most exciting, inspiring, and indeed the happiest that I can remember," wrote Denholm Elliott. "Thank you for teaching me so much, so patiently, and for pretending not to notice my nervousness at the beginning of the run."[17]

Rex Harrison took over Olivier's role when the play opened in the United States. "Larry and I got on splendidly," Harrison wrote. "I'd never worked with him before, and now I found him a marvelous director." In fact, according to Patrick Garland, the two men, "so similar in many ways, egocentric, supremely gifted, insecure, envious, deeply attractive to women," disliked each other. When Harrison asked whether some role could be found for him at the National Theater, Olivier rebuffed him: "For the sake of the *amour propre* of the company I do not want to practice more than I can help a constant settling on top of them of visiting stars." The philosophy was sound enough but it would have been more convincing if Olivier had not already engaged Peter O'Toole, every inch a visiting star, for his first production. Harrison, anyway, was not pleased. When some years later he was invited to play opposite Olivier in

The Dance of Death his reply is said to have been: "Dance of Death? Only on your grave, dear boy."[18]

In the first years of L.O.P. at the St. James's that was as good as it got. One aborted disaster was *The Damascus Blade*—a play by a new writer called Bridget Boland. Noël Coward dismissed it as "badly constructed, fairly tedious" and the public concurred. John Mills had been persuaded to play the principal role and, like others before him, said that he had never before encountered a director "who had so meticulously worked out every single move and every single piece of business." On the whole he thought the system was successful but, personally he would have preferred "more freedom at the early rehearsals." Whether because of or in spite of Olivier's directing—probably the latter—the play limped painfully around the provinces. By the time it reached Edinburgh it was clear a London opening would be calamitous. What followed illustrates Olivier's striking propensity to rewrite history to suit his view of what should have happened. In his memoirs he says that John Mills got cold feet and begged him not to bring it to London; Olivier was reluctant to let down the author but "valued Johnnie's friendship too much to refuse." In the interviews on which his memoirs were to be based his recollections were still more stark. It had the makings of an excellent play, but Mills "hadn't the courage to go on with it . . . I hated giving way . . . He was unfortunately a great friend; if he'd not been I'd have said: 'You fucking get in there and earn your money!!'" In fact he wrote to Mills: "Listen, Johnnie, you are my dearest friend. The last thing I want to do is to bring you into town and have you find yourself with a flop on your hands. Would you be very upset if we accepted defeat and called it off?" To Leslie Banks he explained that the play "didn't add up, if you know what I mean," and was not "a worthy enough thing for dear Johnnie's return to London."[19]

Increasingly Olivier seemed to be casting around in search of something that would fill his theater. He asked Evelyn Waugh if he could have an option on *The Loved One*, his novel about American funeral practices. Olivier "thinks it will make a film," Waugh told his agent incredulously. "He must be insane." (In fact it was made into a film—not very successfully in 1965 with John Gielgud in the cast.) Waugh thought Olivier's idea so eccentric that he asked Anthony Bushell whether there had been a muddle and the offer should have referred to *Brideshead Revisited*: "If so I should be most excited, as I believe there is a really good film in it and an excellent part for Lady Olivier, tho' I am less sure about Sir Laurence." Olivier had probably not even read *The Loved One*. Certainly he did not mean *Brideshead*; it was to be more than thirty years before he played the tiny but imposing role of the aged Lord Marchmain in the television series.[20]

Don't come back to Britain, Olivier urged a female acquaintance who had written to him, presumably hoping that he would offer her a job. "Life is not at all easy. There are restrictions, there is austerity amounting to what would certainly seem like hardship to people not used to it. We have taken rather a toss with our last two plays, and so are having to be careful in any case." L.O.P. was not on the rocks, but it was close to them. Something special would be needed for 1951, the year of the Festival of Britain.[21]

CHAPTER TWELVE

DISINTEGRATION
OF A MARRIAGE

Meanwhile, the Oliviers' marriage wore inexorably more thin. The trouble was that they were both too self-centered, too preoccupied by their own lives, to address themselves fully to the problems of the other. Olivier genuinely cared about Vivien Leigh's career and worked actively to forward it, but in the last resort his own concerns took first place. Leigh admitted and admired her husband's greatness, but was quick to resent it if she felt that her own preoccupations were taking second place in his mind. In the first fury of their passion they had been prepared to make serious sacrifices for each other; when the relationship subsided into something nearer the humdrum they grew to resent the demands that their marriage imposed on them. To the outsider their life together seemed idyllic, but this was more a reflection of the fact that they were both professional actors than that all was well between them. She became slightly bored with him, he grew irritated by what he saw as her affectations and pretensions. They were falling out of love.

In London their home was still Durham Cottage. Vivien Leigh, who had admirable taste and an indefatigable appetite for forays into the more expensive zones of shopping, furnished it lavishly: "It was tiny and sweet and bijou," remembered a friend of the Olivier's, Anne Norwich. "I had an awful feeling of Larry being like an unfortunate bull in a china shop . . . I could hardly move for objects; it was an almost claustrophobic prettiness that Vivien surrounded herself with." It was unequivocally *her* house and except in his crowded and defiantly untidy study, Olivier always seemed slightly out of place. Leigh was not good at being alone and loved to surround herself with a band of decorative and chattering friends, not necessarily theatrical but almost always smart. Olivier, on the other hand, disliked parties and was happiest when *à deux* with an attractive woman or gossiping over a glass of whiskey with one or two old cronies. Athene Seyler remembered a wonderful party at Durham Cottage but also recalled that "Larry, who had been filming all day and was very tired and rather dirty, suddenly came in and saw his cottage filled with people all drinking and shouting and talking, and she really paid no attention to him at all . . . He went off to bed. She wasn't always very considerate."[1]

Durham Cottage was not their only house. Toward the end of the war Olivier had bought for a bargain price Notley Abbey, a semi-stately home near Thame in Oxfordshire. Ralph Richardson had left his mark at Durham Cottage when he arrived there for a party armed with fireworks that he set off in the garden. A rocket went astray, zoomed through the window of the recently decorated drawing room and did much damage. When in due course he was invited to Notley, the memory of this mishap disturbed him. "I won't put my foot in it this time," he promised. Olivier took him up into the attic to see the frescoes on the ceiling of what had been the great hall. He had made a narrow walkway from which visitors could admire the artwork. Richardson expressed rapturous enthusiasm, stepped back to get a better view, put his foot in it and brought down the ceiling in the bedroom below.[2]

Much of Notley, including the ruins of the Abbey itself and the Abbot's Lodging in which the Oliviers lived, dated from the Middle Ages. Cardinal Wolsey is supposed to have lived there while Christ Church, Oxford, was being built. According to the somewhat starry-eyed estate agent, it had a ghost, a dining room that would comfortably seat twelve, ten bed- and dressing rooms, a wine cellar, a potato room, fifty-six acres of land, eleven rooms for grooms, menservants etc.—in fact all the appurtenances desirable in the residence of a distinguished actor who wished to establish himself as a country gentleman. "I never had anything in my life I loved like that house," Olivier remembers. "It was absolutely idolatry . . . I've always been over-romantic about antiquity." Vivien Leigh, after some initial doubts, took to the concept and decorated whole-heartedly: too much so, in the minds of some. Kenneth Clark, the art historian, admitted that he had preferred it before it had been embellished: "The drawing room, when it was finished, was too big for me and made me feel I was staying in Petworth."[3]

Whatever one thought of it, Notley was grand and intended to be so. "It is very romantic in a medieval way," Cecil Beaton told Greta Garbo. "The life they lead is most suitable for Shakespearean actors. The whole atmosphere of the place is suitable for perfor-mances of *Twelfth Night, Midsummer Night's Dream* and *Hamlet*." It was designed for entertaining: without company it was dimin-ished. Vivien Leigh made sure this rarely happened and her fero-cious energy ensured that her many guests had a taxing as well as enjoyable experience. The author Godfrey Winn described a typi-cal weekend. The party drove down after the theaters closed on the Saturday night and a substantial dinner was served at 1:30 a.m. Lilli Palmer, another guest, then "caused some surprise and dismay by going to bed." Winn stuck it out for another hour or so; he hoped to sleep on in the morning but was woken early to be told that Leigh, "looking as fresh as a girl of eight," was recruiting him for a game of bowls. There had been talk of an early night for Olivier on Sunday, but it was not to be: it was 2:00 a.m. before supper finished and he had to leave early on Monday morning for the film studios. He returned at lunchtime and the remains of the party left for Lon-don in time for the evening performances. "Thank goodness we can have an early night this evening and go to bed directly after the show," said Olivier with relief. "Oh, Pussy, not tonight," cried Leigh in dismay. "It's Bea Lillie's opening at the Café de Paris, and we promised to go to her party afterward." The clash between Leigh's supernatural energy and hunger for diversion, and Olivier's all too natural need for privacy and a decent amount of sleep was one of the factors that undermined their marriage.[4]

Olivier at Notley took particular delight in the grounds and the farm. He planted avenues of trees, acquired an impressive knowledge of the Latin names for trees and shrubs, put up greenhouses. More land was bought and a herd of Jersey cattle established, all given the names of Shakespearean heroines. Olivier used to train his voice by bellowing at his cows: "It was a glorious, warm sound," remembered Tarquin. "Not a snarl, more like the roar of a lion." It was a place where, if only he could escape his wife and her guests, he could learn his parts and rehearse in peace. With John Mills he took a boat onto the River Thame so as to be able to rehearse *Othello* without interruption. They became absorbed in their task and had drifted five miles downstream before they noticed what was happening.[5]

Delightful though such pursuits might be, they did not cure the malaise that was poisoning the Oliviers' relationship. No two people of their skills, ambitions and restless temperaments would have found it easy to share a life. "Have you read Henry James's *The Turn of the Screw*?" Eileen Beldon, an Old Vic actress who had been on the tour of Australasia, wrote to Sir Barry Jackson. "Larry and Vivien remind me of the two children—charming, talented, exquisitely mannered, diabolical and bewitched and completely immature." Immature or not, Olivier was protective toward his wife and constantly worried about her state of health, psychological as well as physical. Sally Anne Howes remembered that, when Leigh was playing Anna Karenina, Olivier used to telephone every morning at eleven and every afternoon at four to ask how she was. Equally, he was often exasperated by her selfishness and indifference to his needs. Even before her breakdown became apparent he was more sinned against than sinning. Then, in the spring of 1949, when they were sitting in the porch at Durham Cottage, out of the blue if Olivier's version of events is to be accepted, Leigh almost casually remarked: "I don't love you anymore." "I felt as if I had been told that I had been condemned to death," Olivier wrote. "The central force of my life, my heart in fact ... had been removed." Olivier was never one to underplay his emotions. It is easy to suppose that both Leigh's statement and Olivier's reaction have been overdramatized. Richard Olivier, however, his son by his third wife, Joan Plowright, took his father to a homeopathic doctor some months before he died. After various tests the doctor announced that Olivier's series of crippling illnesses had their origins in "a massive trauma to the heart" which he had suffered in March 1949 or thereabouts. Olivier, when told this, claimed not to have had any special problems around that date, but Richard worked out that it might have stemmed from the moment at which Vivien Leigh told her husband that she no longer loved him. This, of course, proves nothing. Whether it is even evidence of anything depends on the importance one attaches to the opinions of homeopathic doctors in general and this one in particular. But from about this time, the marriage took a sharp turn for the worse.[6]

She was not in love with anyone else, Leigh explained, but she now looked on Olivier as a brother. "Somewhat to my surprise," he commented drily, "occasional acts of incest were not discouraged." Peter Finch was now on the London scene, but though Leigh thought him attractive and good company it does not seem that at this point the relationship was more than friendly. Then came *Streetcar*, with all the pressure that that involved. The marriage limped on until, at the end of 1951, the couple found themselves acting together in New York in the two *Cleopatras*, which had already been a substantial success in London.* It was at this point that Leigh's illness ceased to be a threat grumbling in the background and took over her life. The terrifying swings between elation and black despair, which marked what we used to call manic depression but now know more prosaically as bipolar disorder, overtook her life. In New York above all it was a time of despair. They were staying in Gertrude Lawrence's elegant but rather depressing apartment. Olivier would come back to find his wife "sitting on the corner of the bed, wringing her hands

* See page 182 below.

and sobbing, in a state of great distress." Olivier would refuse invitations to parties knowing that they would be too much for her; she would acquiesce but would then search frantically through the papers to see if their absence had been noted. In the theater, Olivier claimed, she never gave more than 85 percent—"which was worth their bloody money" but not good enough. Then her condition became still worse: "it started to become manic. I tried to be patient. I tried to make everything alright." For him the problem was exacerbated by her ability, except when she was at her worst, to put on a convincing display of normality. Olivier told Noël Coward that he thought his wife was having a bad nervous breakdown: "Darling boy," he asked, "what do you think I ought to do about Puss?" Nonsense, Coward retorted. "If anybody's having a nervous breakdown, it's you."[7]

At the end of 1952 Leigh was asked to play in a film called *Elephant Walk* which would involve much filming in what was then Ceylon. Olivier was invited to costar. He refused but was indignant when someone suggested that he had turned down the invitation because he was exhausted: "I've never been exhausted by anything in my life. I just thought it was a fucking awful film." He was also engaged on other projects; something that Leigh presumably knew when it was suggested that he should join her in Ceylon. When Korda asked her who she would therefore like as her leading man, she replied, "in altogether too airy a voice," that she thought Peter Finch would fit the bill. Asked later whether he thought that there was already some romantic attachment between his wife and Finch, Olivier replied: "If there wasn't, it was very clear to me that it was imminent. As soon as they got to a nice location in the heart of Ceylon, there was no question what would be going on in the bushes." Finch seems to have had some pangs of conscience; he told one of the senior technicians that he was "well aware that he owed more to Larry than anyone in the world," but that he found Leigh "totally fascinating." The compunction does not seem to have run deep. Finch is said to have asked Olivier's biographer, Thomas Kiernan: "Is it my fault that Viv picked on me to cling to? I was just trying to act in Larry's best interests. Would he rather have her fall into the clutches of some assistant cameraman?"[8]

A few weeks into filming, when Olivier was staying with William and Susana Walton in Ischia, there came a frantic message from the producer in Ceylon: Vivien Leigh was impossible, the work on the film was being disrupted, could Olivier please come out and try to help? Olivier was pretty certain that nothing he might be able to do would make any lasting difference, but dutifully he flew to Ceylon and did what he could to talk his wife into reason. He seems to have had a little success: the caravan moved on to Hollywood to continue filming and Olivier went back to Ischia. Within a few days he was told that his wife had suffered a still more catastrophic breakdown. There was little possibility of resuming filming; there was talk of summoning Elizabeth Taylor to take her place; in the meantime Leigh was in need of rescue. It was back to the airplane. Olivier found his wife wholly out of touch with reality: "When she spoke to me it was in the tone of halting, dream-like amazement that people in the theater use for mad scenes." With the help of Stewart Granger and David Niven—"I had always thought of David as a darling person but definitely a fair-weather friend, but he turned out to be the most fantastic friend I've ever had"—he managed to get his wife sedated and on an airplane back to England. From there it was a nursing home and the promise that she would be unconscious for three weeks or more. Emotionally and physically more exhausted than he had ever been before, Olivier returned to Ischia.[9]

It was to be the best part of ten years before the Oliviers finally divorced. During this period they put up a convincing display of marital unity, they appeared in public together, they acted together, for most of the time they cohabited in reasonable if imperfect harmony. But the marriage, in its full sense, was over. After the nervous breakdown, Olivier remembers, "She was an entirely different person. I never really knew her again."[10]

One of the most successful of the Oliviers' joint enterprises had come in 1951. Olivier's original project had been a gala revival of

The School for Scandal" that would put him and his wife on a stage
with Richardson and Gielgud. Gielgud in principle welcomed the
idea of doing some play with his two great rivals—"there is again
some murmur of *Caesar* with Ralph and Larry that would greatly
appeal to me if it could be arranged," he told his mother—but he
decided against this particular project on the somewhat contradic-
tory grounds that it would be a mistake to combine such talent in a
single theater, thus dooming the rest of the London stage to medi-
ocrity. "Of course, dear fellow," Olivier replied, "your whole attitude
is entirely and absolutely understood by me." He cast around for an
alternative. The Caesar motif still appealed to him: Shaw's *Caesar
and Cleopatra* would provide a wonderful part for Vivien Leigh and
suit him well. But was it challenging enough to catch the imagination of the public?[11]

It was Roger Furse who suggested that Shaw's play could be
doubled with Shakespeare's *Antony and Cleopatra*. He advanced it
partly as a joke—the company would save on advertising costs by
having two Cleopatras—but the idea appealed to Olivier. Vivien
Leigh was initially horrified at the thought of playing the Shakespearean role, but her husband persuaded her. "You've got to do it,"
he told her. "We've got to make one hell of a mark in the West End."
John Mason Brown, most eminent of American critics, claimed that
the two plays complemented each other admirably, "fitting together
as neatly as if they were installments in a novel." Olivier was not
concerned about the logic of the enterprise: he saw two splendid
parts for both the stars and an eye-catching project that would be
sure to draw large audiences. He had reservations about *Antony and
Cleopatra* as a play, however, thinking it dragged on after Antony's
death. Nor was he entirely happy about the traditional rendering of
Cleopatra's character. She was much less complicated, he believed,
than she was usually portrayed. Shakespeare's Cleopatra, after all,
would have been played by a boy of fourteen. Given that, he told the
Shakespeare scholar John Dover Wilson, "I can't quite believe that
all the various vicissitudes of character attributed to Cleopatra by
many purists can really have been intended." He sent Wilson a list

of his proposed cuts and changes, admitting that he knew he would be charged by some with vandalism. Wilson was not among them; he took exception to a few of Olivier's alterations but agreed that, on the whole, the changes were for the better. Encouraged, Olivier went ahead.[12]

His readiness to take direction, always meager, was soon tested beyond its limits. He fell out with the director, Michael Benthall, with whom he had worked amicably in the past but who seemed to him to be adopting a wrong-headed approach to the two Cleopatras, particularly Shakespeare's version. Either you must accept his way of doing things or take over yourself, advised Glen Byam Shaw: "If you try to muddle through I think it will be very dangerous and the Company will be confused, nervous and unhappy . . . I suspect that if you take away his confidence he may collapse. You must remember the enormous power of your personality and authority, particularly in your own theater." The warning was a wise one. Olivier's was an overwhelming presence and if he chose to exert it there were few indeed who could stand up to him. It is to his credit that, provided whatever opposition there might be seemed to him based on sensible premises and was well argued, he was almost always ready to give it a hearing—not necessarily to accept it wholly or even in part but at least to take it into account. That seems to have been the case with the Cleopatras: Benthall remained in charge and the rehearsals, if not always uncontroversial, went off without too much acrimony or the demoralization of the company.[13]

The success of the enterprise would depend above all on the two stars. Even under pressure Vivien Leigh was professional enough to ensure that they seemed to act together in well-drilled harmony. No member of the public would have had reason to suspect that the relationship was fraying. Even within the company there was little speculation about the marriage. Yet there were signs that all was not well. Vivien Leigh was "sensational," thought Maxine Audley, but "there were definite undercurrents that she and Larry weren't getting on too well together. Now and again there were little flare-ups."[14]

Olivier was as critical of Shaw as he was of Shakespeare. Shaw, he complained, gave Cleopatra a marvelous first act and then lost interest in her and lavished all his attention on Caesar. "I call it very bad play-writing," he told someone who suggested he had disliked playing Caesar: "Though to be truthful," he added, "it is not often that I can actually enjoy acting in the usual meaning of the word." What he meant by this last remark is obscure; perhaps that acting made such demands on those who did it that they were unable to derive conscious pleasure from their performance. If that was what he meant, he deluded himself. If he knew that he was acting well in a worthwhile part Olivier drew not merely enjoyment but delight from his activities: if it was a great performance in a major role, then delight became ecstasy. Shaw's Caesar was not one of the roles likely to stand out in a great actor's career, but it was quite good enough to give pleasure to a man who was almost as preoccupied by his wife's performance as by his own.[15]

His Antony was more questionable. Tynan was not alone in thinking that Olivier's rendering of the part was diminished by his wish to see Vivien Leigh succeed. He "subdues his blow-lamp ebullience to match her," Tynan wrote. "Blunting his iron precision, leveling away his towering authority, he meets her halfway. Antony climbs down: and Cleopatra pats him on the head." Tynan seldom missed an opportunity to denigrate Leigh and to exalt Olivier, but there were others who felt that she was not fit to play Shakespeare's Cleopatra. "She [is] beautiful to look at, but not grand enough for so superb a part," judged Harold Nicolson. The play was commercially successful and on the whole got very friendly reviews, but few claimed that it was among Olivier's greatest successes.[16]

It was a different matter when they took the plays to New York. "The Oliviers are a sensational hit here," reported Tennessee Williams. It was as if the critics felt guilty about the bad reception they had given *Romeo and Juliet* ten years before and were resolved to make up for it. "There's no doubt at all that these two are very serious artists," Olivier quoted them as saying. "They have changed completely in a few years; they've learned all sorts of lessons." Olivier probably thought that the critics were the ones who had learned the lessons, but he was not disposed to quarrel with them. His only cause for regret was his wife's deterioration. Publicly, Olivier emphasized the physical symptoms of her malaise. She had missed two performances of *Caesar*, he told Alan Dent. "At the moment she is sitting up in bed and not allowed even to whisper, so I am blessed with that dream of all husbands, a dumb wife. She has been awfully poorly and very brave and gallant and utterly darling." He was deceiving Dent; perhaps he was deceiving himself as well. To Jill Esmond he reported that they had been playing to huge houses and making an enormous amount of money: "Our season here has been very decently successful, but somehow it doesn't seem to feel awfully happy."[17]

One of the audience for *Antony and Cleopatra* while it was in London was Winston Churchill. As he had done when he had come to *Richard III* some years before, Churchill recited the lines from memory, providing a muted accompaniment to Olivier. Instead of chiding the great statesman for a practice that must have been irritating to those sitting near him, Olivier congratulated him on his phenomenal memory. "Oh, well, I learned that at school," said Churchill, going on to say that any actor had to remember much more. Olivier admitted that, if he had not played a part for more than three weeks, he would have to learn it all over again. "You mean you don't carry it all in your head?" said Churchill in surprise. "That must be a great saving of burden for you." Churchill took a fancy to Vivien Leigh: "She's a real clinker," he remarked to Christopher Soames, his son-in-law. He invited them to Chartwell, his home in Kent, and made much of them. Olivier knew next to nothing about politics, but he could recognize a hero when he saw one. If Churchill had advised him to do so he would have voted Fascist, Communist or for a Flat-earth candidate. At first he felt shy in Churchill's company. He was by nature shy, he maintained—something that those used to seeing him dominating any gathering would have found hard to credit, but which was essentially true. When it was Churchill who was the host, anyone might have been excused for feeling abashed. But Churchill, Olivier remembered, "made such a palpable effort to put one at one's ease that it would be terrible not to do so." It worked, and by the time the Oliviers left they felt very much at home.[18]

As well as being by instinct if not party allegiance a Conservative, Olivier was a monarchist and a patriot. Though he once refused to call on the Duchess of Kent on the grounds that "We don't want to mix with that sort of person; we may have to offend them some day," his attitude toward royalty was deferential if not obsequious. He was equally traditional in his reverence for home and country. When del Giudice tried to involve him in some of his European adventures, Olivier replied: "I can't do this, Del dear. I belong in England." This may have been inspired by doubts about del Giudice's financial acumen as well as by his own love for Britain, but his dedication to his homeland was never in question. Only when the demands of patriotism clashed with the obligations of his profession did he show that there were limits to his ardor. He agreed to join the Executive Committee of the George VI National Memorial Fund, attended the first meeting in May 1952, but then missed every subsequent meeting. The Lord Mayor asked him to consider how the theatrical profession could best contribute to the Fund. He passed the baby to Bronson Albery and eventually opted out altogether, protesting that the existing demands on his time made it impossible for him to organize any sort of matinée.[19]

When theatrical politics were in question he felt a greater obligation to intervene. Early in 1951 he caused a stir by denouncing the unreasonably large proportion of the income from films that was taken by the exhibitors. From every £1 million taken at the box office the Government took 40 percent in tax, the exhibitors took a further 40 percent, the producers were left with only 20 percent to cover all expenses. His stance caused a storm of protest. Olivier ignored the heavy costs of running a cinema, argued the Cinema Exhibitors' Association, and in *Today's Cinema* F. J. Partner pointed out that film actors and producers could live in "palatial residences in London or country estates and take yachting cruises between pictures. How many exhibitors can do this?" Olivier was on safer ground when he complained that the 30 percent quota of films shown in Britain reserved for homemade products was too small, but even here he stirred up resentment. Tom O'Brian of the cine-technicians' union was at one with Olivier on this issue, but he cherished a grudge against him for his opposition to restrictive practices on the employment of foreign actors. "I have no time for a milk-and-floury hypocrite who stands on a platform and condemns United States films," O'Brian was quoted as saying, "having himself come back from Hollywood with his wife after making a small fortune in dollars." Olivier took counsel's opinion on whether these comments were libelous and was told that he would have to prove special damage—which would be difficult if not impossible. He was not naturally litigious and he dropped the idea of taking legal action with some relief.[20]

His plea that Equity—the trade union representing arts and entertainments—should accept that the best actors or directors should be employed in every case, irrespective of their race or domicile, did not go down well with the more protection-minded members of the Union. O'Brian turned to Churchill for support. If Olivier "enters the field on one side in matters of acute controversy, he must incur the scratchings on the other side . . . My own personal admiration for Sir Laurence is second to none, and you as a friend can do more probably to bring this issue to a satisfactory conclusion than anyone else." There is no evidence that Churchill responded to this appeal—it was hardly a matter on which he would have felt it appropriate to intervene—but Olivier paid the price in popularity within the profession. In 1951 he had come second in the election for the General Council of Equity with 741 votes, in 1952 he got only 561 votes, coming ninth, and in 1953, 506 votes, coming eleventh (it may have been some consolation that Donald Wolfit secured a mere 300 votes and was not elected). Though he hated not to be popular, it would in fact have suited Olivier quite well if he had lost his seat. "My life is so jolly full, and I am such a frequent absentee," he told the President of Equity, Felix Aylmer, "that I do feel . . . I am keeping some more active and useful Counselor out of it."[21]

It was not only the affairs of Equity that made him feel that his life was "jolly full." Early in 1949 a publisher urged him to write his autobiography. "Even if *you* don't agree, it is generally assumed that you are now at the peak of your career," Herbert Thompson of Michael Joseph told him. Only if he undertook the job himself would it be possible to check the flow of inaccurate and sometimes malicious accounts of his life that were appearing. "Even if I could find the energy for it," Olivier replied, "I would be harder put to it than I am able to cope with to find the time for such a venture." But he was alarmed by the threat of a flood of unauthorized biographies and he would have checked it if he could. A possible solution seemed to be to organize a biography which, without being formally authorized, would still be known to have the blessing and the cooperation of the Oliviers. Felix Barker, of the *Evening News*, was encouraged, first to write a series of articles on both Olivier and Vivien Leigh, then to inflate them into a book. In exchange for their cooperation and after an initial payment to the author the royalties were to be split two-thirds to L.O.P., one-third to the author. The Oliviers, Cecil Tennant told the editor of the *Evening News*, "never ceased telling me how nice it was to work with Mr. Felix Barker." This is discouraging for the reader: the biographer of a living person is under no compulsion actively to quarrel with his subject, but too cozy a relationship is to be deplored. Barker's book is pleasantly written and entirely harmless but of interest mainly as showing what the Oliviers wanted to be the truth rather than revealing what it really was.[22]

When Olivier did finally take to his pen it soon became obvious that the written word was not his forte. At this stage in his life he wrote for publication only with reluctance. *This Month*, a New York magazine, offered him $100 for a piece of 1,500 words on the Old Vic. Olivier demanded $200 but added: "I am not a practiced writer and it may take a longer time than would seem to be justifiable." It did; *This Month* is still awaiting it. He was asked by Fruity Metcalfe, the Duke of Windsor's great friend, to contribute to a series of "Great Thoughts from Great Men" for the Sunday edition of the *New York Herald Tribune*. This time it was $200 for only two hundred words. Wavell, Halifax, Shaw and Lady Astor had already obliged. "This will take time, dear boy, and thought, and I am up to my eyes in it," Olivier replied. "But I'll do my best." His best was not good enough. His Great Thoughts never reached the New York reader. He did succeed in finishing a foreword for *School for Scandal*. It was, judged Alan Dent, "at a moderate estimate, the worst article ever written by an adult Englishman in the English language." Dent was perhaps piqued at not having been asked to write it himself; it is not as bad as all that. But it leaves the reader in no doubt that Olivier was more profitably employed in acting or directing.[23]

One of the subjects on which Felix Barker was keen to interview Olivier was television. "Honestly, I don't feel I have any definite enough ideas about this little, newly born medium," Olivier replied, "and I couldn't be a bit interesting about it." It was only recently that he had fully reconciled himself to cinema; it was to be some time yet before he considered television a suitable vehicle for his skills. Films, however, were very much to the fore in the early 1950s. First he played Hurstwood in the film of Theodore Dreiser's novel, *Sister Carrie*. For Olivier the project had two main attractions: it would take him to Hollywood while Vivien Leigh was also there making *Streetcar* and it was to be directed by William Wyler. "It was always wonderful to work with Wyler," Olivier remembered. "Though we couldn't bear each other in *Wuthering Heights*, we got on like a house on fire in *Carrie*. By that time he respected me . . ." He would have been disconcerted if he had known that Wyler was at first opposed to him playing the part. "I honestly don't know what to say," David Selznick replied. "I still am crazy about the idea of Olivier, and wish you would see it. I think he has every single thing the part requires . . . He would give the picture the great distinction it should have. He would bring it extraordinary freshness. If it were my picture I would be breaking my neck to get him."[24]

Eventually Wyler was persuaded and Olivier contributed a moving depiction of a man who has everything in his favor but is in the end destroyed by love. But making the film was not a happy experience. His leg was hurting badly and his ill temper often showed. He refused to do more than the bare minimum to help publicize the picture and made a furious scene when visitors to the set made a slight disturbance. Eddie Albert was an American actor playing his first major dramatic role. He found himself opposite Olivier at a point when the hero, Hurstwood, had lost his temper. "Olivier whipped himself up into a frenzy and started playing the role. I looked at him, and the guy is looking back at me like he's going to kill me. I was in awe." A few days later, at a party in Albert's house, the wine ran out, so the host and Olivier, "both badly sloshed," went down to the cellar to get some more. The door was locked, the key was mislaid, a hinge had to be removed. Albert got a screwdriver and began to fumble ineffectively at the hinge. "Old boy!" said Olivier. "Let me have a dash at it." He took the screwdriver. "It was scary. His eyes changed. Everything changed. He became a bloody giant in total control. In no time he had the hinge off. It told you that anybody who got in his way, watch out. If he puts the heat on you, you're in trouble. Try to make it to the border."[25]

Few things gave Olivier greater pleasure than demonstrating his virtuosity by playing starkly contrasting roles. Oedipus and Mr. Puff he had managed in a single evening, it was a year or more before he was able to follow the tragic Hurstwood with the lightweight swashbuckling of the highwayman Macheath, in a film of Gay's *The Beggar's Opera*. This involved Olivier in a substantial singing role. His voice was pleasant enough and he took lessons for several months, but he had never sung a significant role on a set or stage before. He and Stanley Holloway were the only singers who were not dubbed by professionals. The result was that, in terms of sound, his performance was manifestly inferior. He suggested that the rest of the cast should also be amateurs, but the director, the young but talented Peter Brook, near the start of his meteoric career, would have none of it. Brook, who had anyway originally wanted Richard Burton to play Macheath, suggested that Olivier too should be dubbed. Olivier in his turn would have none of it. To complicate matters still further, while Brook conceived Macheath as a ragged proletarian, Olivier saw him as a debonair playboy, exercising his nefarious skills with nonchalant elegance. Brook's Macheath would have been painted by Hogarth, Olivier's by Lawrence at his most flamboyant. Brook was the antithesis of Olivier in that he believed a play should evolve during rehearsals, as much because of the input of the actors as of the director. A director still had to direct, however; he could not surrender control to an actor, however eminent. But in *The Beggar's Opera* the chain of command was confused. As well as acting Macheath Olivier was coproducer, and this put him in a position where he could usurp much of the power that should have been Brook's alone. "The position of a director who has less authority than his leading man is a rotten one," Olivier admitted, "and poor Peter had an utterly miserable experience."[26]

Brook would have echoed those words. He had deluded himself that, when it came to the point, Olivier would be as flexible as he himself was prepared to be. "But I did not know Olivier. He was a strangely hidden man. On stage and on screen he could give an impression of openness, brilliance, lightness and speed. In fact, he was the opposite. His great strength was that of the ox. He always reminded me of a countryman, of a shrewd, suspicious peasant taking his time . . . What I never realized was that, once a conception had taken root in him, no power could change the direction in which the ox would pull the cart." According to Brook, Olivier at one point tried to get him removed and to take over as director himself. "Somehow I resisted, but between us we spoiled much of the picture." With this judgment at least Olivier would have concurred. "I just hope and pray," he wrote, "that my personal flop in *The Beggar's Opera* will be the worst that I shall ever disenjoy."[27]

CHAPTER THIRTEEN

STRATFORD

Scratch an actor and you find an actor, Olivier was accustomed to remark. "I don't know who I am," he confessed to his son, Richard. "I've played two hundred characters in my life and know them all better than I know myself." If even he did not know himself, what hope could there be for anyone else? Michael Meyer was talking about Olivier to Richardson and Gielgud. "I've known him as well as I've known you, Johnnie," Richardson said to Gielgud. "Marvelous actor. Love the fellow. But I've no idea what the real man's like." "It's extraordinary," Gielgud agreed. "I've known him all these years and I admire him as you do. He's always been most generous to me . . . And he's such wonderful company, such a marvelous mimic and raconteur. I always adore seeing him, but I've no idea what he's really like." He's not really like anything, was Kenneth Tynan's view. "He's like a blank page and he'll be whatever you want him to be. He'll wait for you to give him a cue, and then he'll try to be that sort of person."[1]

Olivier did have an almost magical capacity to blend in with whatever company he was keeping. Put him at the bar of a golf club, a synod of the Church of England, an agricultural fair in Durham and he would be within minutes a golfer, a clergyman, a farmer. It might take him a little time to master the jargon, but so good was his ear and so quick his wits that within a few minutes he would be able to convince anyone that he was in his natural element. He might even convince himself. He would have made a wonderful bishop or ambassador, or rather, though he would not necessarily have been very good at the job, he would have seemed far more episcopal or ambassadorial than any real incumbent of those offices would presume to be. Partly this was unconscious: it was his instinct to play the appropriate role. He was like a stick of Brighton rock, said Oscar Lewenstein, moving spirit of the Royal Court, "but with the word 'Actor' going right through." Partly it was conscious. At one level he convinced himself that he was a bishop or ambassador, at another he was secretly aware that it was a sustained and enjoyable hoax. He spared no pains to prepare for and sustain the current role. When he was preparing himself for a filmed interview with Melvyn Bragg he procured a fawn, leather-buttoned cardigan, of a style affected by Simenon and other writers, and a pipe—an accoutrement to which he was obviously unaccustomed. "A good prop, you see," he explained. "All authors smoke pipes, don't they?"[2]

With the urge to conform went the ability to render himself inconspicuous. The actress Billie Whitelaw—Samuel Beckett's "perfect actress"—said that the first thing she noticed about Olivier was that "in the street I wouldn't have noticed him at all. Offstage, Olivier looked as if he might have worked in a bank." He was capable of leaving a theater, outside which a dense crowd was waiting to cheer him, and disappear round the corner without anyone realizing he had been and gone. He gloried in his ordinariness. Interviewers, he complained, "always want to give me eccentricities, they want me to be quaint and Dickensian and full of character, very romantic." He was none of those things. He was an ordinary man of extraordinary talents. Where he was extraordinary as a human being was in his lack of humanity, his failure to connect with others on anything except a superficial level. Up to a point he could love but he could not feel deep and lasting affection; he could represent characters to perfection on stage, but he could not truly understand them outside the theater. Wyndham Lewis in 1936 painted a canvas called "Players upon a Stage," in which a group of actors, composed of an assembly of props and bits of costume, perform to an audience of their own reflections. It was a scene in which Olivier might have felt himself at home.[3]

Early in 1952 Olivier was invited to take a company to Canada in the following year. He refused. "It is not easy to visualize what sort of a company we shall be having around us so far in the future, or what nature of repertoire we shall have to offer (should we in fact have any such)."[4] He felt unusually uncertain about the future. L.O.P. needed something substantial, to do in Coronation year what the two Cleopatras had done during the Festival of Britain, but what that something should be he had no idea. Orson Welles offered readings from *Moby-Dick*, but even had this been aesthetically desirable the Board of L.O.P.—in effect Olivier himself—decided that it would not be "a good economic undertaking." Terence Rattigan came to the rescue. At his best Rattigan was a playwright capable of work that was both well constructed and socially challenging. *The Sleeping Prince* was not in this category. It was a frothy romance about the Crown Prince of Carpathia, who fell in love with a chorus girl. Olivier claims that Rattigan thought this would suit the Oliviers very well; Rattigan says he thought it all wrong for them: "my little 'occasional fairy tale' couldn't contain *one* of those two gigantic talents, let alone both."[5]

Olivier had taken on the play largely because he thought it contained an excellent part for his wife. In this he was wrong. As Rattigan himself observed, she was "one of nature's Grand-Duchesses," unsuited for her chorus-girl role. When Rattigan went backstage in the intermission on the first night Olivier asked him: "Tell me, Terry, how are they liking Puss?" "Very much indeed," said Rattigan. "I don't think so. I don't think so at all. I don't think she's going over as well as she should be." Rattigan thought Olivier's performance was "magic . . . I would watch, in rehearsal, utterly spellbound as, over the weeks, he built his performance slowly and with immense application from a mass of tiny details, some discarded, some retained." But, confronted by his wife's difficulties in the part—compounded by the fact that she had by no means recovered from her breakdown—Olivier reined in his performance. It was not a disaster, commercially indeed it was a tolerable success, but the critics for the most part thought little of it. "Once upon a time," wrote Kenneth Tynan, "there was an actor called gruff Laurence Olivier, whose wife was an actress called pert Vivien Leigh, and a playwright called clever Terence Rattigan wrote a play for them with a gruff part for him and a pert part for her, and to nobody's surprise it ran happily ever after, with twice weekly matinees." It was, he said, "a quilted cushion of a play."[6]

With some gallantry Olivier, on behalf of his wife and of himself, as both actor and director, apologized formally for mucking up the play. "Darlings," Rattigan replied, "please accept my apologies for having written such a mucky, trivial, little play." Noël Coward, who witnessed this orgy of humility, then contributed: "Children, may I say that as an author, producer and actor I have frequently managed to muck up my own acting, plays and productions and still survive." After that, everyone felt better.[7]

"It is so wonderful to see him relaxed and relieved and happy about *Sleeping Prince*," Vivien Leigh told Mu Richardson in an undated letter, presumably written when rehearsals were still in progress. "We have only seen *The Country Wife* since we got back. It is a huge success but I can't honestly say we cared for it much except for Miss Plowright who is very engaging." Too engaging by half, she would no doubt have thought a few years later.[8]

It was a bad season otherwise—"the worst anyone can remember," in the opinion of the *Daily Sketch*. The Royal Court, where the engaging Miss Plowright was enjoying such success, was one of the few beacons of hope in the London theater. Olivier looked to Stratford. Before then, however, he made his third great Shakespearean film: *Richard III*. Vivien Leigh, according to Angela Baddeley, opposed the project—in part, at least because she had been denied the chance to play Princess Anne. Olivier was too old, she said; he would make himself ridiculous. Anyway, she needed him to be with her that summer: "Larry was betraying her by putting his career first." In fact he was still prepared to make great sacrifices to sustain his wife, but when it came to the point, as always throughout his life, he would put his acting first. He had hoped to produce the film with

Mike Todd, believing that that would ensure he would get Richard Burton as Richmond and Orson Welles as Buckingham, but in the event he settled for Korda instead. His relationship with that charismatic yet evasive figure remained equivocal. Olivier found Korda "very amusing, very witty, fantastically well self-educated," but "there was something about him I didn't like and didn't trust." On this occasion he did Olivier proud: neither Burton nor Welles but Gielgud, Richardson and Cedric Hardwicke—making an unprecedented quartet of theatrical knights—and Claire Bloom as Lady Anne. Claire Bloom was not merely seduced by Richard III on the screen but by Olivier off it. Neither party seems to have attached great importance to the affair.[9]

This plethora of stars caused some jostling for position. Gielgud and Richardson insisted on equal billing with Olivier in all the advertising. Olivier agreed. But they were still suspicious. What about the line: "Laurence Olivier presents"? Would that be of the same size too? Again Olivier promised it would. "But I had it in copperplate writing, so it looked a bit different," he remembered with satisfaction. The rivalry continued in the filming. Gielgud's "false, fleeting, perjur'd Clarence" was much praised but it was noticed that his scenes were poorly lit. "Was this the director's jealous hand at work?" speculated Gielgud's biographer. Probably it wasn't; but it could have been. As for Richardson, he matched Olivier in his reluctance to take direction. Olivier wanted Buckingham to be an out-and-out villain, almost as nefarious as Richard III himself; Richardson, either through perverseness or a genuine inability to summon up the necessary nastiness, played the part for sympathy; thus, in Olivier's eyes, upsetting the balance of the production.[10]

"Olivier was superb, really superb . . . Oh my word, what a film!" was Harold Nicolson's breathless verdict. It was, indeed, a memorable performance in what, on the whole, was a successful film. And yet the rabid fury of Olivier's stage performance failed to translate to the screen. He seemed, curiously, to be in a different production to the rest of the cast. "I felt a lack of reality about Larry," wrote Kenneth Williams in his diary. "It was indeed a theatrical Richard, with funny walk, crook back, unformed hands and a plasticine nose. This, surrounded by so many realistic performance, looked somewhat bogus." Olivier himself was dissatisfied but undiscomfited: "I call it a waggish performance," he said. "I mean, it was pretty clever." It was quite successful enough to whet his appetite to produce, direct and play the lead in at least one more of the great Shakespearean dramas. If it was humanly possible, that play would be *Macbeth*. In the end it turned out not to be humanly possible, but at least in 1955 he was able to play the part at Stratford in a season that was also to include some of the finest Shakespearean performances of his life.[11]

Olivier was then at the summit of his powers. There was much still to come and a whole new world yet to open in the running of the National Theater, but his total mastery of the Stratford stage produced one of the great glories, perhaps the greatest glory, of the twentieth-century theater. This was the more astonishing given that his private life was in tatters and that he insisted on playing all the major roles with, as his partner, a wife who was not merely unfaithful when off the stage but teetering on the edge of breakdown when on it.

It should have been an easy start, for Vivien Leigh at least. Viola in *Twelfth Night* is an important but not particularly taxing role, and well within her powers. "She was enchanting," wrote John Gielgud, who was supposed to be directing the play, "but she was torn between what I was trying to make her do and what Olivier thought she should do." She survived relatively unscathed, which is more than can be said for Gielgud himself. He went against Olivier's concept of Malvolio—"like a Jewish hairdresser, with lisp and an extraordinary accent." When Olivier insisted on falling backward off a bench in the garden scene—"though I begged him not to do it"—Gielgud roundly, and in front of the whole cast, accused him of vulgarity.[12] Olivier was offended. "You've no idea how damaging that is," he protested (another version has him saying: "Johnny, you just winged me"). From that moment it was open war. Angela Baddeley, who was playing Maria, said: "The basic antagonism

between Larry and Johnny came out during rehearsals. I think
Larry was a bad boy about it. He was very waspish and overbear-
ing and Johnny became intimidated by him. Almost everyone in
the cast sided with Larry, laughing at his wisecracks about John's
direction. I felt very sorry for Johnny." Gielgud himself admitted
that he was "very restless as a director and very apt to change my
mind"; under Olivier's bombardment he became even more inde-
cisive and the production seemed to be drifting toward disaster.
"Darling John," Olivier finally flung at him, "please go for a walk
along the river and let us just get on with it." Gielgud's summary of
the affair in a letter to his friend, Stark Young, is a perceptive and
on the whole generous comment on his rival.

> Olivier is brilliant as Malvolio, though he is ultra-realistic
> in his approach and his gift of mimicry (as opposed to crea-
> tive acting) sticks in my gizzard at times. His execution is so
> certain and skilled that it is difficult to convince him that he
> *can* be wrong in his own exuberance and should occasionally
> curb and check it in the interests of the general line and pat-
> tern of the play. The truth is he is a born autocrat and must
> always be right. He has little respect for the critical sensitivity
> of others; on the other hand he is quite brilliant in his criti-
> cism of my directing methods and impatient with my hesita-
> tion and (I believe) necessary flexibility. He wants everything
> cut and dried at once, so that he may perfect with utter cer-
> tainty of endless rehearsal and repetition—but he is good for
> me all the same.[13]

He was good for himself as well. "Larry was absolutely superb,"
wrote Coward in his diary. "He's a great actor, and that's all there is
to it." Most of the critics and, to judge by the volume of applause,
the vast majority of the paying public, agreed: his performance was
extravagant, even self-indulgent, but it delighted almost all who saw
it. Gielgud continued to feel that Malvolio unbalanced the rest of
the production, but, as he handsomely told Olivier: "The character

is brilliantly conceived and consummately executed—and I know you will delight with it." Vivien Leigh fared less well. In the early rehearsals she was anxious and uncertain. It could still work, Gielgud thought, if Olivier "would let me pull her little ladyship (who is brainier than he is but *not* a born actress) out of her timidity and safeness. He dares too confidently while she hardly dares at all and is terrified of overreaching her technique." This is a little unfair—it is the combination of Olivier and Gielgud that seems to have disturbed her, rather than either one of them—but the result was that her performance, though competent, seemed lackluster compared with the explosive vitality of her husband. Tynan described it as being one of "dazzling monotony." "It was absolutely untrue," said Olivier. "She rang every vocal change that anybody could do." But it did little for her morale in the buildup to what was to be her stiffest test.[14]

Olivier had had doubts about *Macbeth*"; not for his wife but for himself. "Glennie, I've played Macbeth. I'm no good as Macbeth," he told Byam Shaw. He allowed himself to be persuaded without too much difficulty. Byam Shaw knew that Olivier was going through "a difficult and worrying time," but, he wrote, "I believe that the greatest achievements are often accomplished through the most difficult circumstances, and so I feel that your Macbeth may well be your greatest of all triumphs." As for Vivien Leigh as Lady Macbeth, Byam Shaw hoped that their partnership would help "bring about a perfection of subtle reality between those two great characters": an observation which, if taken literally, seems to suggest a somewhat unenthusiastic judgment on the Oliviers' marriage. What the partnership *did* bring depends on whose judgment prevails. Olivier himself maintains that his wife was up to the part—"she was good, she was marvelous in the sleep walk." "Wonderful," thought Godfrey Winn, "wonderful," echoed Christopher Fry: both men adding that they preferred her performance to her husband's. But this was not the opinion of most of the critics who, with Tynan as ever at their head—"more niminy-piminy than thundery-blundery" was his verdict—dismissed her as a lightweight who wilted when exposed to the blazing fury of her husband. Probably Gielgud got it right. Olivier, he considered, was "the finest Macbeth I have ever seen"; Leigh's performance was, "I think, almost the best thing I ever saw her do—but on a small scale. She would have been enormously effective if a film had been made."[15]

Olivier continued to protest at any suggestion that he was lowering the level of his performance so as to accommodate his wife. "I was keeping my end up for all I knew how," he protested. "I was acting opposite her as if I was acting opposite Sarah Bernhardt. I was doing my nut to act her off the stage. I couldn't." In fact this charge was leveled at him more often over *Twelfth Night* than *Macbeth*; the critical response to his Macbeth was adulatory, even awestruck. Harold Hobson, by now the doyen of British theater critics, rarely missed a chance to praise Olivier and on this occasion outdid himself. "As distress and agony enter into him, Laurence Olivier multiplies in stature before our eyes until he dominates the play, Stratford-upon-Avon and, I would say, the whole English theater. The performance is full of unforgettable things . . . I don't believe there is an actor in the world who can come near him." His physical presence on a stage, always daunting, became overwhelming. Keith Michell, who played Macduff, was one of the few actors in Britain who would not have been eclipsed by him. They flung themselves into the fight in the last act with an abandon that left the rest of the cast aghast. "We both enjoyed it more than any other two people who fought on the stage, I swear it," Olivier remembered. "We were wonderful together . . . two peacocks who weren't afraid of hurting each other." Or of being hurt. Other actors were less hardy and protested that their lives, or at the least limbs, were being put at risk. "Oh, I'm so sorry," Olivier exclaimed. "Have I hurt the dear boys? I'll do better in the future, but I do like to show there's life in the old dog yet."[16]

Rattigan told him that his was the definitive Macbeth. Olivier made no bones about agreeing. "I just thought of it the right way," he explained. "It was just the right mixture of style and down-to-earth bone reality. I found the right cocktail, the right ingredients and the right proportion. I'm very proud of it."[17]

Third and last in this majestic season was *Titus Andronicus*, a horror comic with some magnificent poetry but so macabre a plot that it is not often staged. Any play that accommodates thirteen deaths, two mutilations, a rape and a cannibal banquet at which a mother inadvertently eats a pie made out of her two sons, must teeter on the brink of absurdity. T. S. Eliot considered it "one of the stupidest and most uninspiring plays ever written"; more importantly for the purposes of this production, Olivier himself had doubts about it. "I don't think I really admire *Titus Andronicus*," he told Basil Rathbone, while to Colin Blakely he complained that he would rather play characters like Richard III or Macbeth than Titus, who was "one of the moaners. Those are the difficult ones, the ones that do nothing but suffer." But he moaned majestically. Peter Brook was the director. It was the first time the two men had worked together since the ill-fated *Beggar's Opera*. Brook arrived determined to impose his will from the outset to find that he was beating at an open door; Olivier was resolved "to show himself a model of acceptance and flexibility . . . Not only could I understand and admire his amazing talent, but the way he played the central role gave the whole production an intensity and reality that no other actor at the time could have brought." Brook admitted that he never felt close to Olivier—"He was most polite and attentive, but behind the gesture there was always a sense of strain; even his laughter was acted, as though he never ceased remaking and polishing his mask"—but on this occasion at least their professional relationship could not be faulted. Olivier praised Brook as a "master interpreter," who had "not only the genius for the job but also the generosity to make me a partner in his thinking"; Brook wrote Olivier gushing thanks for "being such an extraordinary, great, true, breathtaking actor on one hand and for being so endlessly sweet, understanding, helpful and encouraging on the other."[18]

As so often, Tynan found the most compelling phrases to praise Olivier's performance. "It was," he wrote, "an unforgettable concerto of grief . . . One hears great cries that, like all of this actor's best efforts, seem to have been dredged up from an ocean-bed of fatigue. One recognizes, though one has never heard it before, the noise made in its last extremity by the cornered human soul." But again—as so often—Tynan could not resist a dig at Vivien Leigh. She received, he wrote, "the news that she is about to be ravished on her husband's corpse with little more than the mild annoyance of one who would have preferred foam rubber." Such criticism from Tynan might have been expected, but Gielgud, usually ready to defend her, was equally condemnatory. She seems in a very bad way, he told a friend. "She is utterly ineffective on the stage—like paper, only not so thick, no substance or power." Worst of all, Olivier himself agreed. "I was terribly disappointed," he recorded. "She didn't act the part at all, she was beyond it then, she couldn't bloody well act. For the first time I felt ashamed of her."[19]

It was during the run of *Titus Andronicus* that Vivien Leigh moved irrevocably closer to total breakdown. It was not just her lackluster acting that signaled what was happening. Offstage, wrote Gielgud, she is "haunted, avid, malicious and insatiable, a bad look-out for the future and for poor Larry, who is saint-like with her." Noël Coward visited Stratford and thought *Titus* "a very, very silly play with some good moments." Afterward: "Vivien was in a vile temper and perfectly idiotic. Larry was bowed down with grief and despair . . . Personally, I think that if Larry had turned sharply on her years ago and given her a clip in the chops, he would have been spared a mint of trouble." The comment does not suggest that Coward had the remotest perception of what lay behind Vivien Leigh's behavior, but, coming from a man who up till then had tended to think of her as more sinned against than sinning, it illustrates vividly the pressures under which Olivier was now living.[20]

In spite of his own resounding success, Olivier did not enjoy the Stratford season. He was longing for an end to it: "I feel I cannot take any more of that lowering Stratford atmosphere," he told Mu Richardson. It was not so much Stratford as the state of his marriage that caused the atmosphere to lower. Peter Finch, whether there or not, seemed omnipresent. Olivier accepted the relationship yet resented it. He told Hamish Hamilton how much it pained him "to go into her dressing room and see the photograph of that god-damned Finch on her dressing table." She made no effort to keep her feelings hidden and seemed almost to exult in the pain she caused her husband. She told Trader Faulkner, a close friend since the tour of Australasia, how "warm, sweet and thoughtful Peter was, like a wild, sensual Pan," while "Larry could think of nothing but his career." Peter was "an old soul, full of timeless wisdom," Larry "a new soul with a plastic Karma." At least Finch was only present at Stratford in photographic form; at Notley, where they went almost every weekend, he was a regular visitor. Leigh would bombard him with telephone calls and send her car to collect him; when he was there her devotion to him was obvious and, to Olivier's friends at least, embarrassing. "The best you could say about them," wrote Finch's biographer, Elaine Dundy, "was probably the worst you could say about them; they did nothing behind Olivier's back." To the casual observer it seemed as if Olivier condoned or at least was indifferent to his wife's behavior; in fact he felt rejected and resentful. Once there were fireworks after dinner. "I had the distinct feeling," wrote Susana Walton, "that Larry was pointing a rocket directly at Peter, but reluctantly changed his aim at the last minute."[21]

Olivier's pride told him that he should not make a scene or show how deeply he was being hurt; on the other hand, the situation could not drag on indefinitely. The trouble was that he still liked Finch and could not blame him for what was happening. Eventually, he decided that there must be a confrontation. The two men met in the library after dinner but, although Olivier was resolved to settle matters, somehow the encounter evolved into an enjoyable conversation. It was broken by Vivien Leigh putting her head round the door to ask which of the two men was going to bed with her. In the end it was the guilty couple who brought things to a head, by escaping together to the South of France. Olivier pursued them and pleaded with Leigh not to make a public scandal that would damage his career and destroy hers. Possibly the flames of passion between her and Finch were burning lower, possibly discretion overcame her romantic urges; at any rate, she returned to the fold. For a time, in the public eye at least, the marriage was reestablished. "Larry and Vivien have decided to present a united front," Noël Coward noted early in 1956. He wished them well; especially since she was on the point of appearing in his new play. He was less pleased when the rapprochement was followed by the news that Leigh was going to have a baby and so he would have to find another star. Yet more annoying, Binkie Beaumont heard about the pregnancy before he did, so injured pride was added to his irritation. In a letter to a friend Coward indulged in some disobliging reflections on the likely destiny of the unborn child. "To be born into such a turbulent *ménage* might possibly be far from easy, what with Daddy shrieking 'Fuck!' and bellowing 'Macbeth,' and Mommy going briskly round and round different bends, and never less than twenty people to lunch, dinner and supper." When Coward met Olivier in Dublin he made a violent scene, then realized he had gone too far and apologized for being so clumsy and self-indulgent. "The only possible excuse was that I had been miserably hurt by being shut away from your confidence," he wrote. "This, considering that I have been so intimately concerned with your and Puss's troubles for so long, made me very angry and hurt like hell. After all, you *are* both very dear to me."[22]

Olivier professed himself, and probably was, delighted by the prospect of becoming a father again at the age of fifty. He told the *Daily Sketch* that he thought he would prefer a girl; if it were one she would be called Katherine. He hoped that a child would cement his marriage and give Vivien Leigh a measure of stability. "Thought it might help her," he told Tarquin. "I was worried I was sterile. Tests showed I'm as fertile as Hercules." Perhaps the baby would have helped; Leigh had shown immense pleasure at the thought of being a mother and a nursery was already planned for Notley. In the fourth month of her pregnancy, however, she miscarried. Though neither of them knew it at the time, the last hope for their marriage was extinguished.[23]

One person who had not looked forward to the birth was the putative Katherine's half-brother, Tarquin. He had been very reasonably affronted when he read of his stepmother's pregnancy in the newspapers rather than hearing of it from his father, and he made his resentment clear. Olivier groveled. He had suspected that Tarquin would be upset by the news, he wrote: "Believe me, I do understand your feelings. When my father threatened me with the same possibility, I felt sick." As a result he had put off passing on the news until it had leaked to the press and then it was too late. He urged his son to look on the bright side: "I beg of you to try and feel happy about it, it is a thing that pleads for joyful feelings." Now the joyful feelings were in abeyance: Vivien Leigh seemed to be more settled but Finch was still in the background and the possibility of another breakdown had obviously not disappeared.[24]

Even when she was calm the pace of her social life remained hectic. Notley was not a place where Olivier could hope to relax; every weekend the house was filled with guests and loud with parties. In London they had abandoned Durham Cottage as being too small and spent a few months squatting in the Waltons' house in Lowndes Square. They tried to buy a house in Lord North Street, but were beat to it by Harold Macmillan and finally settled for "a beautiful new apartment" in Eaton Square. He and Vivien both loved it, Olivier told William Walton. "She is exceedingly bonny and better than she has been for ages, and all is merry song in the birdcage." That was late in 1957. Walton was one of Olivier's closest friends and he would not have sought to mislead him. He must have suspected, though, that the merry song was not going to last for long. The pace of her social life grew ever more frantic; even in a period of remission her mood swings were unpredictable; it could be no more than a lull.[25]

CHAPTER FOURTEEN

L.O.P.

At the end of the Stratford season Olivier made a speech on the stage, without notes, in the course of which he thanked ninety-seven people by name; including the box-office staff. At the end he apologized in case he had forgotten anybody—"I never was any good at names." "It was a show-off," he cheerfully admitted. It was also one more illustration of a memory that was at the worst excellent, at the best prodigious. Roger Furse paid tribute to his "stubborn memory," his alarming capacity to conjure up pieces of information that had been given him many years before and which the original informant had long forgotten. He had told Churchill that once he had stopped playing a part it vanished quickly from his mind. He belittled his capacities. The part had in fact not been forgotten, merely filed in a waiting tray from which it could quickly be recovered. At the age of forty-eight the sharpness of mind that had enabled him to learn a part in half the time needed by Ralph Richardson had perhaps been blunted, but he had perfected techniques that helped him retain otherwise evasive material. One of them he called "the Green Umbrella." He was playing a part that was proving particularly intractable. Then, in a shop window, he saw a green umbrella and knew at once that it was the sort of thing the character would have owned and cherished. He bought it, carried it at every performance and never forgot another line. Not all talismans proved so miraculously effective, but in one form or another green umbrellas became a valuable weapon against the terrors of a failing memory.[1]

It was partly because it was not necessary to keep a long part in one's head that he had felt the cinema to be a lesser calling than the stage. By 1956, however, that feeling had evaporated: he was immensely proud of his Shakespearean films, particularly *Henry V*. He was above all anxious to add *Macbeth* to the list and devoted almost as much time and effort to trying to set up a production as he had done to making any of its predecessors. He had been playing with the idea for several years; a screenplay and detailed production notes show how much thought he had given to the project. The problem, of course, was the cost. *Macbeth* was not a film that could be made on the cheap. The appearance of Scone, he considered, should be "a little more effective than its present-day aspect would seem to suggest that it was." Any other thousand-year-old castle would look a thousand years old, which would clearly be unsatisfactory. It would therefore be necessary to build a castle. The early battlefield scenes could be on a small scale, but Birnam Wood could not come to Dunsinane without some significant display: at least eight hundred extras would be needed. *Henry V* had made a profit of £100,000, Olivier pleaded, *Hamlet* more than £300,000, *Richard III* £400,000, "which I think shows that the public were being educated to these Shakespearean epics." He did not mention how long it had taken for each of them to reach these happy conclusions, nor were the figures immune to challenge; most accountants, for instance, would have said that *Richard III* was still in the red. Economically, the timing was unfortunate. "The production of *Macbeth* under present conditions is, of course a highly speculative proposition," warned John Davis of Rank.[2]

Mike Todd had seemed the most likely backer, but his death had ended that hope. Korda at one moment seemed interested, but he deferred a final decision until he too was dead. Filippo del Giudice claimed he could raise the money, but he inspired little confidence. William Walton thought he had found an American millionaire, but he too proved a will-o'-the-wisp. Sam Spiegel appeared to be more promising and the National Film Finance Corporation promised a loan of £65,000. Lord Wemyss agreed to let the film be shot on his estate at Gosford in East Lothian.³ Olivier got as far as commissioning Walton to compose the music. At one point confidence was so high that a bottle of champagne was opened and a toast drunk to the new enterprise. And then came closure. *Macbeth* had been "indefinitely postponed," Olivier told Walton. "We went on and on until things got to a point at which . . . the building would have had to have started in Scotland on the following Monday, and we could no longer continue without the money." It was one of the most bitter disappointments of his life. "Don't worry, I'm not too discouraged," he told Tarquin. There was still a faint hope, but "even if it does come off, the recent peddling has tired my spirits and dulled my enthusiasm." More than most people, Roger Furse knew how much Olivier had invested in the enterprise; financially but, more, emotionally. It must have been a terrible strain on his nerves and a grievous disappointment at the end: "But you're a great boy at taking it and the reward for your courage and patience will be great." If he meant that the film might still one day be made, he deluded himself. Olivier's film of *Macbeth* was lost forever. Not merely was posterity robbed of a permanent record of one of his finest performances, but another question had never been resolved. Was Gielgud right when he speculated that Vivien Leigh's Lady Macbeth would have been stronger and a better complement to her husband if she had played it on the screen? If so, the film would have been memorable indeed.⁴

L.O.P. was not short of other projects. "There have been some changes in the setup of my Company, for financial reasons, and I am not quite the little autocrat that I was," Olivier told Michel Saint-Denis, when regretting he could not offer to bring the French company to London. It was a convenient excuse, but in fact the members of the Board—Bushell, Furse and Korda—were either not closely enough involved or too much in awe of Olivier to prevent him from doing anything on which he had set his heart. This did not mean, though, that his liberty was unrestricted. He wrote to T. S. Eliot, asking if he had a new play coming up that might be suitable for him. He was "gratified and flattered," Eliot replied. Unfortunately, he was committed to Henry Sherek as producer, but if Olivier wanted to play "a leading part (*the* leading part) I should like nothing better." He was finding it hard to finish the play he was working on (presumably *The Elder Statesman*) and it would be a year or more before it was likely to be ready. By then Olivier was engaged elsewhere. He did not miss much: Lord Claverton was a bleak part and when the play reached London it quickly closed. Another aborted project was a film of Graham Greene's *The Quiet American*. Olivier admired the book, but he was nervous of it "because I would never wish to be thought anti-American." Joe Mankiewicz, the director, assured him that he had no intention of putting "a Coca-Cola swilling, crew-cut, Mom-loving, dollar-waving Yankee on the screen." In fact, his script did the opposite and ended up with a bland hero-cum-villain who, Greene thought, betrayed the message of the book. Olivier was still doubtful, however; if he did make the film, he insisted, there must be no changes made to the agreed script: "I'm not a difficult person, you understand, but a teensy bit too old to have my pants removed with becomingly boyish submission." In the end he read Mankiewicz's outline, disliked it and turned it down.[5]

Another project that at once attracted and repelled Olivier was a film of Nabokov's brilliantly written story of the girl-child Lolita and her seduction by, or perhaps of, the middle-aged Humbert Humbert. In the end Olivier recoiled. "Having scrutinized the book curiously and intensely during the last week," he told Stanley Kubrick, "I do not find my mind grasping a film conception of the subject . . . The chief merit of the book lies in the author's brilliant, original and witty descriptive powers, and I can't see how this particular virtue is photographable. I fear that, told in terms of dialogue, the subject would be reduced to the level of pornography." It was a shrewd judgment and was proved right by the final film which, though not a disaster, was far from a success. A part of Olivier, though, still hankered after the challenge. Some years later, he was filming in Paris with Sarah Miles, his mistress at the time, when he heard that James Mason was to play Humbert Humbert. Miles noticed that he seemed disappointed and asked whether he wished he were doing it himself. "I suppose so," Olivier confessed. "But I'd sooner live it," he added as an afterthought. "He gave me a sleepy look. 'I never ever dreamt that I'd be tempted by anyone so young.'"[6]

One venture that did come off was the filming for television of Ibsen's *John Gabriel Borkman*. Until then Olivier had dismissed television with lofty scorn. He didn't want to appear "in a medium where squiggly lines appeared across the screen every time a car went past." Television, he pronounced, was "intellectually unrespectable as well as technically primitive." But recently, both intellectually and technically, things had got better. Olivier was still not ready to accept the new medium as being the equal of theater or cinema, but provided the money and the producer were right he would give it a go. His agreement to play in *John Gabriel Borkman*, wrote Michael Meyer, "was a great turning point for television in Britain. At a stroke it made it respectable." He was far from satisfied with his own performance, though; believing, in particular, that he had made a mess of the great final scene on the mountain. So strongly did he feel about it that he refused to allow the recording to be shown in America: "which was bad luck for the rest of us," Meyer wistfully observed.[7]

Olivier guarded his reputation the more jealously because he felt—and was justified in feeling—that his status was unique and that anything he did or endorsed was thereby invested with an importance out of proportion to its true significance. Harold Nicolson attended a grand dinner given by Kenneth Clark for the departing French Ambassador, René Massigli. The heads of all the professions were there, he noted: "Tom Eliot for literature, the Oliviers for the theater, Margot Fonteyn for the ballet, William Walton for music, Graham Sutherland for art." Olivier, rightly or wrongly, was deemed by the world to be at the head of his profession: he knew it, he loved it, and yet he felt the role carried with it duties and responsibilities as well as prestige.[8]

His grandeur was not confined to the United Kingdom. He went to the first night of the film of *Richard III* in Washington. He had been invited to lunch at the White House that day and had been told that it was possible but unlikely that President

Eisenhower would attend. He prepared two speeches: one in case
Ike was there, one in case he was not. At the last moment he was
told that Eisenhower was coming. "A great lump of pride came into
my throat," he told Tarquin. "It was the first time he had ever done
such a thing and it was for a British picture and all that, and I was
moved beyond anything to think that our little picture had got the
Queen in London and the President in Washington." "Our little
picture" was a fine example of the unconvincing self-deprecation
in which he habitually indulged. He reveled in such marks of distinction. The fact that he would be an honored guest at even the
grandest houses in Britain and the United States gave him especial
pleasure. During the provincial tour of *The Sleeping Prince* he and
Vivien Leigh drove from one venue to another. He boasted to Tarquin that on the way they stayed with "some very sweet and rather
swell friends that your pals at Eton wouldn't be ashamed of—the
Buccleuchs at Drumlanrig and the Northumberlands at Hotspur's
old haunt at Alnwick." He would never have allowed hobnobbing
with Presidents and dukes to interfere with the serious business of
acting, but it was a very enjoyable bonus all the same.[9]

He knew, though, that however brightly he might shine in the
theatrical firmament there were people in show business who,
regardless of their skills and abilities, were always going to be more
widely known than he was. One such was Marilyn Monroe. Monroe conceived—or had the idea sold to her—of buying the film
rights to *The Sleeping Prince*, playing Vivien Leigh's part herself
and persuading Olivier to direct and act opposite her. Rattigan,
Olivier and Cecil Tennant hastened over to New York to discuss
the matter: she kept them waiting for an hour, but thereafter all
went swimmingly. "I am going to fall most shatteringly in love
with Marilyn," Olivier decided. "She was so adorable, so witty, such
incredible fun and more physically attractive than anyone I could
have imagined."[10]

There were soon hints that all would not run to plan. Even
before filming started the script caused problems. Rattigan had
assumed that, once Olivier had fed in a few ideas, the serious

work would be left to him. Olivier, however, insisted on "complete collaboration" and at one point the two men fell out so thoroughly that it seemed the enterprise might founder. Reason prevailed, a *modus vivendi* was established and they retreated to Gleneagles to complete the job in comparative amity. But Rattigan cabled his New York agent: "Have feeling Larry really prefers his authors dead."[11]

Once filming got under way what was left of the euphoria was rapidly dissipated. Monroe arrived with her recently acquired playwright husband, Arthur Miller, so all thoughts of dalliance had to be put aside. To make matters worse, Olivier did not take to Miller. "A self-satisfied, argumentative pseudo-intellectual," he described him. "He talks a great deal better than he listens," Olivier told Noël Coward, "but I never found his talk very entertaining."[12]

Miller was at least a professional who could be relied upon not to interfere. Far more dangerous was Monroe's adviser and confidante, Paula Strasberg. Strasberg was the wife of the most enthusiastic proponent of "The Method" and herself the repository of innumerable half-baked, half-understood and passionately held notions that she preached with idiotic fervor. She came with excellent credentials from Garson Kanin—"a sensitive creature; sound and discreet. Her considerable talents, used to the full, can benefit you and the film enormously"—but what those talents might be Olivier was at a loss to guess. She saw her main function as being to boost Monroe's morale, which she did by assuring her that she was the greatest actress since Sarah Bernhardt and that she must never allow herself to be pushed into any course of action that did not seem right for her. If she did not feel in the mood to act then she must not do so—too bad if other people were inconvenienced. She was putting up the money for the production so she had every right to indulge her whims. Mrs. Strasberg was tiresome enough; Olivier tolerated her existence so as to avoid a bust-up with Monroe. His never very notable patience snapped, however, when he heard that her husband Lee had arrived in London and was proposing to take over his wife's responsibilities. "I'm the fucking director of this fucking film," he shouted. "I'm the fucking producer too. I won't allow Lee Strasberg on set. Call the studio police and have him stopped. Fuck him!"[13]

Lee Strasberg, by one means or another, was stopped; but it made no difference to Monroe's behavior. Olivier, professional through and through, punctual and well-ordered, was outraged by her unpunctuality, horrified by what seemed to him her willful inability to follow his direction, offended by her discourtesy—she failed even to acknowledge gifts of flowers and lavish presents that the Oliviers had given her. She had "the brains of a possum," he exclaimed; teaching her how to act was "like teaching Urdu to a marmoset," she was incapable of learning five lines by heart.[14]

It was still more irritating when Sybil Thorndike—an immensely distinguished old lady who was kept waiting hour after hour by this Hollywood addle-pate—praised Monroe's warmth and charm. "She has a ravishing smile—no airs and graces at all—simple and quite fun. I like her awfully." When Monroe forgot her lines for the umpteenth time and Olivier berated her, Thorndike sprang to her defense. "Don't you realize what a strain this poor girl is under? She hasn't had your years of experience. She is far from home in a strange country . . . Are you helping or bullying?" Olivier, indeed, was unsuited to the task of directing Monroe. He shot one scene twenty-nine times, achieving nothing but the misery of his leading lady. "I really think," wrote Colin Clark, a young assistant director and an amused yet horrified witness of all that was going on, that Olivier "wanted to break all records as proof . . . of how difficult it was to work with her." Arthur Miller, who had a pretty clear perception of his wife's strengths and weaknesses, was critical of Olivier's methods as director yet supported him—to little purpose—against the appalling Mrs. Strasberg. "As for Olivier," he wrote in his memoirs, "with all his limitations in directing Marilyn—an arch tongue too quick with the cutting joke, an irritating mechanical exactitude in positioning her and imposing his preconceived notions upon her—he could still have helped her far more than Paula with her puddings of acting philosophy."[15]

In some ways the most irritating thing for Olivier—though it was also a consolation—was that Sybil Thorndike proved to have been right when she had predicted that it would only be Marilyn Monroe whom the public looked at: "She's really giving everyone else lessons in acting for the cinema." *The Prince and the Showgirl*, as it was eventually titled, was not a great film but it was enjoyable and the enjoyment lay principally not in Olivier's adequate performance but in Monroe's warm and wayward charm. She exercised a miraculous rapport with the camera that transcended her inexperience and limitations of technique. Olivier was generous in accepting that this was so. Many years later he admitted that by the time the film had been made "my hatred for her was one of the strongest emotions I had ever felt." But only a few days earlier a friend had insisted on his watching it: "I was *amazed* what a good film it was," commented Olivier, "and flabbergasted how wonderful Marilyn was."[16]

As if this experience had not been grueling enough, within a few months the Oliviers embarked on a European tour of *Titus Andronicus*. Olivier told Noël Coward that, after the claustrophobic horror of internment in a studio with Marilyn Monroe, he found the prospect of "darting like hysterical bumblebees" from Paris to Warsaw by way of Venice, Belgrade, Zagreb and Vienna decidedly pleasing. The rehearsals were characteristically thorough. Michael Blakemore, who had just joined the company and so was a new boy to *Titus*, was amazed by the attention paid to even the most minor parts. He felt that Olivier was always watching him—"His eyes kept swinging over the newcomers, assessing us perhaps or just practicing which name went with which face." Blakemore only had a single speech and one day felt that he had delivered it badly. Olivier turned to him and said: "You've got a very good voice, a fine voice, but if I might just suggest, try pitching it further forward. Up here"—he tapped his frontal sinuses—"Just for a day or two to see how it goes." It was excellent advice, Blakemore thought, but even more "what bucked me up was the fact that I had been noticed and, however briefly, thought about. Those few considered words warmed my entire afternoon." Blakemore believed that Olivier was not merely concerned to have a better production but was anxious to help a young actor at the start of his career. When the actor became established it was a different matter. "Now he had a competitor, and he assessed him according to his weaknesses, not his strengths, and often with a marked lack of generosity."[17]

In the theater the tour was a triumph: in Paris the applause was so loud and so prolonged that it seemed Olivier would never be allowed to leave the stage. Offstage it was another matter. "I had all sorts of intensely and agonizingly personal complications in my life," he recalled. "It was a very tough one for me indeed." The main, indeed the only complication was his wife. In public, the Oliviers still kept up a united front. As in Australia nearly ten years before they struggled to keep up the spirits of the company and to foster a sense of unity. In Belgrade the Oliviers and one or two of the other, more senior members were invited to dinner at the Embassy. Olivier replied that he had made everyone bring clothes suitable for grand receptions and, if the Ambassador wanted him, he would have to invite the company as well. A buffet supper was substituted for the *intime* dinner that had been planned. It was bad luck on the Ambassador, who had looked forward to lionizing the Oliviers, but from the point of view of the morale of the company it was an excellent affair.[18]

Vivien Leigh would have supported him in this enterprise and been on her best behavior at the Embassy but her hold on the proprieties of everyday civility grew ever more tenuous. "It was impossible not to admire her pluck," wrote Blakemore, "though by this time we had grasped that it had an edge of craziness. She was like some Italian *principessa*, absolute in her whim, reigning over a small state in Renaissance Italy. The company was her principality, and she could be as charming or as deadly as the mood took her." Olivier, of course, bore the brunt of it: he fussed over her "very like a lady's maid" and tried to ensure that she was in the right place at the right time. But as the tour wore on her behavior became ever more unruly, her drinking was unbridled, she roamed the streets at night, got into a fight with an Italian policeman, refused to board the train with the rest of the party. "Unprovoked. Bad scrap," is a scribbled note in Olivier's diary written in Belgrade, which gives some hint as to what was going on in the seclusion of their hotel suite. "When I woke her up in the morning, very, very gently, she was absolutely sweet for about five minutes and then when I went to have my shower, she got up in a rage and smashed the mirror against the wall."[19]

In 1954, in a late night show for charity, Olivier had found himself paired with Jack Buchanan. I "would find nothing in the world more exciting than to dance with you," he told Buchanan. "I've always had a great leaning that way." After twenty hours of intensive busing they ended up with a two-minute dance routine that was judged by the—no doubt indulgent—audience to have been a riotous success. "I was really happily swollen-headed about my dancing," Olivier recalled. The word spread of his new accomplishment. "*J'ai lu même que vous apprenez la danse*," wrote Jean-Louis Barrault. "*Quand allez-vous vous livrer à la pantomime?*" This fleeting experience was not responsible for Olivier taking on *The Entertainer*, but it disposed him to look kindly on a project that he might otherwise have felt to be outside his range.[20]

He was anyway in a mood to seek adventure. He felt that his life had settled into a predictable rhythm: a classical or semi-classical film, a play or two at Stratford, a nine-month run in the West End. "I was going mad, desperately searching for something fresh and thrillingly exacting. I really felt that death might be quite exciting compared with the amorphous, purgatorial *Nothing* that was my existence." As was not unusual, he grossly overstated his case.

By the standards of most people his life was crowded with incident and variety; even by his own standards most days brought a new and interesting challenge. Nor was he as discontented as he suggests; he was restless and ambitious but unless things were going badly he was on the whole a happy man. But he did have an uneasy feeling that he had got into a rut and ought to be looking for some new experience. He sought it in the Royal Court Theater off Sloane Square in London.[21]

The establishment of the English Stage Company at the Royal Court in April 1956, followed by the visit of the Berliner Ensemble to London only a few weeks after the death of its founder, Bertolt Brecht, profoundly affected the development of British theater over the next decades. The Court, under the direction of its great founder, George Devine, became not merely renowned for the spare, vigorous, exquisitely integrated ensemble acting that was the Brechtian trademark, but also as a center of rebellion and challenge to the established order. Outrage at the Anglo-French adventure at Suez, a crusading campaign for the abolition of nuclear weapons: these were not necessarily causes overtly espoused by the Royal Court, but they were part of the atmosphere in which it existed. Nothing was sacred; everything was open to challenge. Olivier, if he had considered the issues at all, would probably have favored intervention at Suez and the retention of a nuclear deterrent. But he wanted a change; he recognized the quality of the Royal Court's productions; he might deplore some of the methods and the causes it espoused, but the basic thrust, the energy, the passion, stimulated his jaded palate. He was ready, almost determined, to be converted.[22]

John Osborne's *Look Back in Anger*, with its ferocious yet brilliantly entertaining assault on patriotism, paternalism and all the values of the middle classes, was the most celebrated or notorious example of this new rebellion. Olivier at first disliked the play. "It's just a travesty of England," he told Arthur Miller, "a lot of bitter rattling on about conditions." Although, he added, "some people think it's fairly good satire." Miller was intrigued and decided to go. Olivier went with him and was convinced by Miller's enthusiasm that, even if the sentiments were not to his taste, Osborne's was a powerful talent and his work heralded a tsunami of new drama on the crest of which it would be possible to ride into a challenging and exhilarating world. A few weeks later Olivier came again to the Royal Court to see Osborne act in Nigel Dennis's *Cards of Identity*. He went behind afterward to congratulate the cast. "You're my kind of actor," Olivier told Osborne. "You like hiding behind makeup." He was evidently Olivier's kind of dramatist as well; to Osborne's amazement Olivier went on to ask him whether he would consider writing a play with a part suitable for him.[23]

Osborne denies that he wrote *The Entertainer* specifically for Olivier: this tragicomedy about a seedy music-hall performer whose career was already declining from its never very considerable heights had been conceived and half written before the possibility of Olivier playing the leading role had even been considered. It was George Devine who persuaded Osborne to send over the first two acts for Olivier's inspection. There were doubts on both sides. Osborne was afraid that Olivier's fame would disturb the balance of the play, leading the audience to view it merely as a vehicle for his talents. Besides, would Olivier's style of acting fit happily into the Royal Court? They were accustomed to something more homespun—as they saw it, more real, more feeling—than the scintillating but somehow heartless Olivier. Olivier for his part had doubts about what he saw as being the unpatriotic thrust of the play. Spiteful jokes about Eton—which Tarquin had so recently adorned—seemed to him in poor taste. His friends advised him that it would be a most misguided enterprise. "I must say that I formed the opinion that most of his friends were very stupid people," Osborne observed waspishly. But in the end the Royal Court's realization of how valuable it would be for them to have Olivier on their stage and Olivier's conviction that, like it or not, this was the new wave and he wanted to be riding on it rather than drowned under it, overcame all hesitation. *The Entertainer* opened at the Royal Court in April 1957, went into abeyance for four months or so to allow Olivier to tour Europe with *Titus Andronicus*, and then reopened at the Palace Theater.[24]

Olivier's original idea, based on his reading of the first two acts, had been that he should play Archie Rice's father, Billy—a gruff, courageous old-school patriot who would have come much more naturally to him than Billy's doomed and pathetic son. He swiftly recognized, however, that Archie Rice was what the play was all about: in his fatuity, his fecklessness, his clutching at the coattails of a largely imaginary glory, he embodied all that Osborne thought was wrong with British society. "It comes nearer to the true concept of tragedy than any other modern play I have been in," Olivier told a friend, "the original purpose of which, as laid down by the ancient Greeks, was to give the audience a good kick in the stomach and make it think again." He based the music-hall activities of Archie Rice on what he remembered of the performances of Max Miller, though having to scale down Miller's "incredible, masterly technique" to suit the abilities of his second-rate or even third-rate hero. To be a great actor playing the part of a bad actor must be uncommonly testing: Olivier played Rice in a way that was both inept and almost unbearably poignant. More than any other part he played it took him over, invaded his offstage life. One of the part-time jobs that he took on during the run of *The Entertainer* involved Bible readings; he was dismayed to hear, when he listened to the recordings, that he had developed "ever so slightly doubtful vowel sounds." None of his friends said he sounded common, but he suspected that they must have thought it. "This is the real me," he told the designer Jocelyn Herbert when she saw him in his makeup. He was joking but, she thought, "in a funny way he meant it."[25]

William Gaskill, who had been one of the most uncertain about Olivier's suitability for the Royal Court, was the first to admit how misjudged his doubts had been. "It would have been very easy for the work of the Court to have been a fringe activity performed by a group of left-wing cranks," he told Olivier. "The moment you decided to play Archie Rice it became a movement of importance to the theater." Olivier knew that whatever he had given to the production was more than balanced by what he had gained from it.

Before the first night he sent an effusive letter to Osborne. "Thank you for the thrilling and lovely play . . ." he wrote. "Thank you for the most deeply engaging part, perhaps barring only Macbeth and Lear, that I can remember—certainly the most enjoyable . . . Hope I don't fuck it up for you tonight." He did not fuck it up; on the contrary he produced a performance of such startling versatility that the critics were left struggling for new superlatives: "You will not see more magnificent acting than this anywhere in the world," wrote Harold Hobson. In a sense Osborne's fears were borne out; the play was distorted by Olivier's presence. "Olivier is fabulous in the part of Archie Rice and wonderful to act with," Joan Plowright, who took over from Dorothy Tutin as Rice's daughter, told her parents, "but the rest of the play's characters don't really mean very much." Yet Osborne had no complaints. His compliments to Olivier were quite as fulsome as Olivier's to him: "Whatever might become of me in the future, nothing could deprive me of the memory of your tremendous, overwhelming performance, nor the experience of working with such greatness."[26]

But though each man knew how much they owed the other, they never got on well. When the play went to New York Osborne put a paragraph in the program denouncing the American theater critics. Olivier felt that this could only harm its prospects. "It was the action of a cunt," Olivier observed, "but then he was a cunt." While Olivier's performance was lavishly praised, the play itself got a poor press. "Darling heart, they're not good, not good at all," Olivier told Osborne after reading the reviews. "Well, not good for *you*, anyway. I shouldn't read them." He said it without a trace of irony, Osborne remembered, "only concern." It would be surprising if the concern was not tinged with a touch of *Schadenfreude*. Olivier himself was disappointed because the Tony award that he felt he ought to have been given was instead awarded to Ralph Bellamy, who was playing Franklin Roosevelt elsewhere on Broadway: "As a performance, well, to put it mildly, I didn't think it outshone mine." The excuse was that he had just been given a special prize for his performances of Shakespeare. "I do congratulate you on the invention of this wonderful prize," he said sourly in his acceptance speech, "and the effective removal of my candidature for the Tony . . ."[27]

Some people were shocked by what they saw as Olivier's indecorous descent from the pedestal of classical theater. "I appeal to you," wrote the Rev. David Parton, "to put the wretched, vulgar thing behind you." But for every one who deplored the vulgarity, a hundred wondered at the exceptional versatility and, indeed, courage of an actor who, at the age of fifty, was prepared to thrust forward into unknown territory and risk his reputation in the quest for a new horizon.[28]

One hazard during rehearsals was the frequent attendance of Vivien Leigh. She would slip in unobtrusively, sit in the dress circle and make no attempt to advertise her presence; but the fact that she was there was disturbing; as distracting, as Osborne rather bizarrely put it, "as an underwear advertisement at a Lesbians for Peace meeting." No doubt she paid particular attention to Dorothy Tutin: Olivier's daughter on the stage and, as she no doubt knew, his mistress off it. But such minor escapades cost her no real anxiety. She would have much more cause for worry a few months later. Tutin withdrew, to be replaced by the rising star of the Royal Court, Joan Plowright. Olivier had first seen her in *The Country Wife*, had been immensely impressed by her acting and enchanted by her appearance and personality. He would have taken steps to ensure that she took over from Tutin, but fortunately found that the management had reached the same conclusion with no help from him. She for her part had worshipped Olivier in the film of *Henry V* and then, under the influence of the Royal Court, come to see him as a fustian figure, more a celebrity than a serious actor, even perhaps a bit of a ham. When Olivier came backstage after *The Country Wife* she was partly awestruck, partly derisory. Once she was enlisted to play in *The Entertainer* and began the rehearsals that all changed. "He got down on the floor with us," she said. "Larry won us over with sheer talent, and when you have that it pulls everyone up on their toes. There was no side about him—no nonsense at all. His sleeves were rolled up and his braces were showing. He was one of us."[29]

By the time *The Entertainer* opened in New York they were most evidently in love. Joan Plowright viewed the relationship with some caution. She knew Olivier's reputation for casual liaisons that ended after a few months; she was resolved that she would not be just one more name on that dissatisfying list. Vivien Leigh too was still on the scene: Plowright knew that Olivier felt that his marriage must be near its end but she knew too of Leigh's terrifying instability and Olivier's feeling that he should not do anything that would precipitate a crisis. Things were to move slowly and uncertainly. Nearly two years after the run of *The Entertainer* in New York came to an end Olivier stayed with Noël Coward at his house in France. "He was absolutely sweet and at his most beguiling best," Coward wrote in his diary. "I really am becoming more and more convinced that he won't go back to Vivien. He's happier than I've seen him for years. I *hope* he won't get a divorce and marry Joan Plowright, but I have grave fears that he will."[30]

CHAPTER FIFTEEN

MARKING TIME

Between the last performance of *The Entertainer* in May 1958 and the start of rehearsals for the Chichester Festival in March 1962, Olivier's working life was relatively uneventful. To describe as "uneventful" a period that included four plays, four films for the cinema and two for television may sound a misnomer, but even though one of the plays and two of the films were of some importance they were, in Olivier's mind, secondary to a longer-term development with which he was resolved to be associated: the opening of the National Theater.

There had been talk of a National Theater since the mid-nineteenth century; foundation stones had been laid, dug up and relaid; the foundation and development of the Shakespeare Memorial Theater at Stratford-on-Avon had clouded the issue—was this perhaps what had been intended all along? In 1948 the scheme had taken on a new life when the London County Council made available a site on the South Bank and, in the following year, while Olivier was in Australia, the Government pledged financial support. Still there was quibbling, haggling, one step taken backward for every two forward. Without the resolute pressure of a group of devotees, notably Oliver Lyttelton, who in 1954 became Lord Chandos, the process would have stalled indefinitely. As it was it remained falteringly alive. By 1956 Chandos and Lord Esher were joint Trustees. They felt they needed someone from the theatrical profession to lend some practical expertise to their deliberations. The obvious choice was Tyrone Guthrie, but he proved reluctant.

"There are plenty of old duffers around who would jump at the chance . . . It needs new blood," he ruled. There was no guarantee that whoever was appointed a trustee would be the first Director of the National Theater, but he would plainly be well placed to challenge for the job. The Director would have, in Guthrie's view, to be "someone of an almost heroic stature: infinitely patient (to deal with committees), of an unassailable theatrical reputation (to attract the support of the political establishment) but also sufficiently flexible to absorb the ideas and style of the new generation." Esher and Chandos did not have this job description to hand when they turned to Olivier, but they must have had in mind the possibility, even probability that whoever they asked to join them would end up in charge of whatever National Theater finally opened on the South Bank. Olivier put it more modestly. "We don't believe you'll be much use," he alleged Esher had told him, "but what we need is a glamour-puss, and you're it."[1]

Olivier later claimed to have had some doubts about the desirability of an institutionalized National Theater. If he did, he kept them to himself. When Kenneth Rae, the Secretary of the Board, wrote in June 1958 to announce that Olivier had been elected as a Trustee to serve on "what is really the only important Committee, the Joint Council of the National Theater and the Old Vic," he accepted with alacrity. It might be many months before there was a meeting, Rae warned him. In fact the pace quickened, there were more meetings than Olivier could conveniently attend and by early 1960 the fact that he would be the first Director had been agreed if not yet crystallized in a legal contract. Long before then it had been the pole star of his ambitions. Anything that he undertook in these uneasy years was of secondary importance: the main challenge lay ahead.[2]

One man who, in his own mind at least, was a plausible rival for the role of directing a National Theater was Donald Wolfit. Wolfit had far more experience than Olivier at running a theater company and was one of the few other actors of his generation who was capable of greatness. Olivier disliked him heartily and would have been appalled if Wolfit had been preferred to him for the National, yet there was still some solidarity between them, evidence that, however much actors might vie with each other, they do make common cause when assailed by those outside the profession. Early in 1957 Kenneth Tynan reviewed Wolfit's performance in Henry de Montherlant's *Malatesta*. Wolfit, he concluded, was not up to the part; Olivier would have been the better choice. For some reason not immediately obvious to the layman Wolfit considered this line of criticism impermissible. "Can nothing be done about this man Tynan?" he asked Olivier. "What a generation of critics for bitter venom!" Olivier claimed to be out-raged. "I don't read Mister T. myself," he told Wolfit (a statement that was not entirely accurate), "but what he had said was shown me by friends." He had intended anyway to write to Tynan "to point out the error of his ways. It was the first letter I have ever written to a dramatic critic [another questionable assertion], so you may judge that I felt strongly moved. I did not make it a public letter as it is against my principles to cross swords with the bastards." He was as good as his word. Comparisons between actors, he complained to Tynan, though sometimes inevitable were invariably odious. This one was gratuitous, as well. Anyway "I must beg you to remind yourself that Donald Wolfit is an actor of considerable qualities who has given some very greatly admired performances and, as a courageous Actor-Manager, has rendered in his own way substantial services to the cause of the theater." The words "in his own way" gave a certain ambi-guity to this testimonial, but it satisfied Wolfit, who wrote a grateful letter. "We don't really know each other," he concluded, "and I wish we did. Lunch at the Beefsteak?" It would be pleasant to record that this overture was well received and many happy lunches followed. The row with Tynan was still rumbling on, however, when Olivier in Zagreb got the news that Wolfit had been knighted. He had already been awarded the C.B.E., Olivier told Maxine Audley, "'And that gives him precedence over me!' He was furious."[3]

One of the more interesting films Olivier made in this period was an adaptation of Bernard Shaw's *The Devil's Disciple*. He costarred with the American duo, Burt Lancaster and Kirk Douglas. He said in his memoirs that he was tired, depressed and far from at his best; also, that he found it impossible to remember which of his co-actors was which—he habitually addressed Burt Lancaster as "Kirk." Privately he admitted that Lancaster, who was coproducer but not director, infuriated him by forever making suggestions as to how he should play his part, the British soldier General Burgoyne. In the end he took Lancaster aside and said apologetically: "I wonder if you could help me. I'm sure I'm being stupid but I'm finding it a little difficult to apprehend what it is you're trying to say to me. Do me a favor, let's go somewhere quiet and you read to me the scene as it ought to be done." Flattered, Lancaster obliged and launched into his rendering, then became self-conscious under Olivier's quizzical gaze, and came to a stammering halt.[4]

The following year Olivier was reunited with Kirk Douglas in the film *Spartacus*, a no-expenses-spared epic in which Olivier played a Roman general and Douglas a heroic Thracian slave. This time it was Douglas who took on the role of mentor; again Olivier became irritated, again he invited his costar to give his rendering of the part, again the American broke down in the face of Olivier's rapt attention. "It was all very shocking and very childish," Olivier admitted, "but I didn't care to be taught acting by those two." He had read Howard Fast's novel on which the film was based and thought that it had tremendous potential, but when the script arrived he decided it was "pretty awful. The more money they pour into a film, the more ordinary and conventional they make it." Fortunately a fair amount of the money came his way—$250,000, to be precise—and since the part made small demands on his skills and he had old friends like Peter Ustinov and Jean Simmons in the cast, it was a relatively painless way of earning his living. Kirk Douglas, he told Tarquin, was a good actor, but "he does not feel heroic enough unless he is being fearfully physical all the time, consequently the thing is gummed up with calisthenics and flagellation."[5]

Charlton Heston was another American superstar with whom Olivier found himself dealing. Heston had already played four major roles on Broadway when, early in 1960, he appeared in Benn Levy's *The Tumbler*, with Olivier as director. He might therefore have resented Olivier's somewhat dictatorial style. Unlike Lancaster and Douglas, however, he viewed Olivier with some awe. "Today I lunched with Larry, which I've not yet been able to call him, of course," he wrote at the end of 1959, when rehearsals were just getting under way. He was convinced that Olivier somehow had access to the elixir that would transform him into a major actor: "If I'm ever to reach any special creativity, it surely must happen with *this* part, *this* director." It never happened though: "Everything Olivier says adds a touch, and he's unfailingly good humored and light about it, but the sad fact is I'm not measuring up to my standards, thus can hardly be reaching his." He appealed for help to his director: "Star acting is really a question of hypnosis," Olivier told him, "of yourself and your audience." Heston's hypnotic powers proved faltering: "This plane's like an overloaded bomber straining down the runway," he moaned, "I can't lift it." The bomber crashed, the reviews were disastrous, at the first-night party at Sardi's "the knowledge of failure seeped like ink through the happy drinkers." "I don't know if *The Tumbler* could have been made to work," Heston mused. "Certainly Olivier made an enormous effort with it. He was heavily burdened at the time with the disintegrating fragments of his marriage with Vivien Leigh." The only profit Heston derived from the production, he wrote, was "what I learned from Larry." He was to win an Oscar for *Ben-Hur* and global renown for his performance in *Planet of the Apes*, but his failure in *The Tumbler* haunted him all his life.[6]

The oddest play in which Olivier acted at this time was Ionesco's *Rhinoceros*. This masterpiece of the Theater of the Absurd was set in a French provincial town in which all the inhabitants except for Bérenger, the part played by Olivier, one by one turn into rhinoceroses. Either one found this funny and curiously disturbing or concluded that it had no point at all. Noël Coward was in the second camp. "The beginning was brilliant and Larry, as usual, superb, but then it began to drag," he wrote in his diary. He burst into the dressing room after the final curtain with a small man in tow. "What a perfectly bloody play," he exclaimed, then introduced his companion as Eugène Ionesco. "He doesn't speak a word of English," he added. Olivier seems to have been inclined to agree with Coward. One evening a tumult broke out in the dressing rooms after the performance and Olivier was heard to shout: "I've shat better plays than this." If this was his considered view it is hard to see why he took it on: presumably the main reason was that he wanted to go back to the Royal Court and Ionesco's play had a good part in it for Joan Plowright.[7]

Another reason may have been that it was directed by Orson Welles. According to Welles, he was told that Olivier would not play the part unless he, Welles, was directing it; meanwhile Olivier was told that Welles refused to direct unless he, Olivier was acting in it. The fact that Welles was directing would have been an attraction for Olivier. The two were old friends. A few years before, Olivier had written Welles a letter that even by his own standards was strikingly gushing: "Darling boy, I have wanted to pick you up and hug you and swing you round and dance you up and down on my knee and even go birds-nesting with you to show you in some tiny measure how adorably sweet and generous was your dear thought . . ." The image conjured up by these raptures is bizarre and mildly disturbing; the more so because the "dear thought" which had provoked this outburst was the loan of a refrigerator. The enthusiasm endured, however. Olivier looked forward to acting under Welles's direction. He had implicit faith in Welles, he said; he might sometimes be arrogant and difficult but "fuck all that, he's a genius."[8] Genius or not, Welles's recollections of trying to direct Olivier, as related by the actor, Peter Sallis, do not suggest that he was given an easy ride. It was Gielgud and *Twelfth Night* over again. Olivier decided that Welles's direction was muddled and confusing. "I don't know if they had a row," Sallis recalled, "one day Orson simply didn't turn up and Larry said: 'I've sent him away. I've told him this is extremely difficult stuff. We've got to rehearse a set piece; we can't change it on a day-to-day basis.'" Welles's banishment only lasted a week—he was back before the first night—but he seems to have accepted Olivier's *diktat* as meekly as Gielgud had five years before. Welles never forgave the affront: "He told me to stay home, and I *did*! I was so humiliated and sick about it that you can't imagine . . . He *had* to destroy me in some way . . . He doesn't want anybody else up there. He's like Chaplin, you know. He's a real fighting star." (The comparison with Chaplin is interesting. The young Peter Hall once found himself at lunch with Olivier and Chaplin. He gazed at them in awe and admiration. "They then proceeded to out-boast each other about their possessions, lifestyles, houses, coming projects and conquests. They were like a couple of competitive schoolboys.")[9]

It was during the run of *Rhinoceros* that the uneasy maneuvering between Olivier, Vivien Leigh and Joan Plowright escalated into crisis. Over the previous two years Leigh had become convinced that she wanted to preserve her marriage. Some eighteen months before, she had told Noël Coward that her husband had asked her for a legal separation. The shock had been tremendous. "She had always assumed that, whatever might go wrong between them, they would stay together. She knew there was love and respect there . . . She could never love anyone else as she had loved Larry." But Olivier was as convinced that he could never love anyone else as he loved Joan Plowright. "The glow that emanated from him was blinding," wrote Lauren Bacall. "He dropped twenty years . . . He could have a life, he had something to look forward to." "I am in touch with the real beauty of happiness at last," Olivier told Tarquin. His friends urged him to give his marriage another try. "Can you really be happy, Larry, knowing that you're making someone you love absolutely miserable?" asked Stewart Granger. Rachel Kempson, too, argued that Olivier could never be really happy if that happiness was bought at the price of somebody else's misery. Vivien Leigh had changed, she said. She realized how much she had made Olivier suffer and had learned her lesson—"Viv would accept any terms at all." Put off any final rupture, they pleaded: keep up the façade of marriage and one day the reality might be restored. "What sort of a life do they think I can live?" demanded Olivier. "I could never act off the stage anyway."[10]

Olivier was indeed disturbed by the thought of the pain he would be inflicting on his wife, but as well as his wish to be with Joan Plowright he was convinced that his marriage could only get worse and that it would eventually destroy both the parties to it. When Michael Blakemore asked him why he had decided to leave Vivien Leigh, Olivier replied, bluntly and honestly, "Because there was no room on the raft." His life had become intolerable, he told Lauren Bacall. "He couldn't think, he couldn't sleep." He could never return to his wife.[11]

But though he was clear in his own mind that his marriage was at an end he had no fixed idea as to how to bring that end about. He shrank from the squalor and sordid publicity of a contested divorce and yet saw no way in which it could be avoided. Then, on May 22, 1960, Vivien Leigh, inexplicably and without warning, announced to the world that her husband had asked her for a divorce in order that he might marry Joan Plowright and that she proposed to accede to his wishes. This abrupt declaration was, of course, welcome to Olivier, but it also posed some serious problems. Leigh's statement that she would fall in with her husband's wishes could be interpreted as collusion and, in the state of the law at the time, this might make divorce impossible. It seems unlikely that any consideration of this kind was in her mind—she claimed herself that she had no recollection of even issuing the declaration and, given her mental condition, this seems entirely possible—but the danger could not be ignored. The immediate consequence was a hurricane of gossip; journalists and the idly curious besieged Joan Plowright's home and, even more, Olivier's apartment in Eaton Square. Plowright pulled out of her part in *Rhinoceros*, to be replaced by the rising star, Maggie Smith. Some people thought that Olivier would do the same and the understudy had been brushing up his lines, but when the evening arrived Olivier appeared at the usual time and carried on as if nothing had happened to ruffle his serenity. "I watched him very carefully and you would not have thought that anything was wrong at all," Peter Sallis recalled. "He didn't, from a theatrical point of view, bat an eyelid." The crowds outside the stage door were denser and more turbulent than usual, but even when they were at their most importunate he remained unshaken. "I think it says volumes for him," wrote Virginia Fairweather, who handled his publicity, "that never once did he lose his temper or alter his courteous attitude toward the scandal-seekers."[12]

Mrs. Fairweather had her work cut out over this period. She asked Olivier how she should deal with the divorce. "Darling, if anyone is going to come out looking like a shit, let it be me," Olivier replied. "Do your best not to let them persecute Joannie or Viv." He accepted that he was the guilty party when the divorce proceedings began; in fact, Vivien Leigh had been at least as guilty as he was but an unopposed action would avoid relentless mud-slinging and publicity. "Viv must have had a horrid time going through the divorce," he wrote to Tarquin, "but she did nobly and bravely and managed alright." He and Joan Plowright had had a horrid time too, but they knew that at the end of it there was stability and happiness. He had been passionately in love with Vivien Leigh, he still cared greatly for her, but he had no flicker of doubt that he had made the right, the only possible decision. "If only I can stop being agonized for V.'s suffering ," he told Jill Esmond, "I am in for the hell of a marvelous bloody time. This girl is so good, and so good for me . . . She makes me feel I am in a sort of idiot heaven." Richard Burton had been married to the relatively sedate Sybil Williams before moving on to the glamorous Elizabeth Taylor. "You have got it in the wrong order," Olivier told him. "I have gone about things the right way." Michael Denison said much the same thing. "Larry took whatever Vivien in her *extremis* threw at him with the most fantastic forbearance," Denison told Hugo Vickers, "and it was only when she had really gone that he turned to the total contrast—I mean from champagne to Guinness, from mink to macintosh—and to youth, of course, as well." Olivier had had a lifetime's worth of champagne and mink; it was time to give Guinness and macintosh a chance.[13]

His beloved Notley had been an incidental casualty of the breakup. He could not afford to keep it: "It is the first time we can feel thoroughly in line with the general run of English aristocracy," he told Garson Kanin. Parting with it was a wrench, but at least he was moving on to something different and more welcoming. For Vivien Leigh it was far more painful. "Notley is sold," she told Tarquin. "I can hardly even write the words. I walk from precious place to precious place and gaze at each beloved view with tears pouring down my face." She would never forget "the hundreds of times my beloved Larry and I have wandered here in wonder and grateful amazement at the beauty all around us." With her appearance and her fame Vivien Leigh was never going to be short of admirers. She had found a sort of solace in the company of Jack Merivale, a competent if undistinguished actor and a thoroughly nice man, who asked for nothing more than to be allowed to squire her around through life. But though she was fond of him and thankful for his existence it was Olivier she still loved. "Take care of your precious dearest self," she ended a letter to him when divorce proceedings were already under way. "My love, dear dear heart."[14]

It was at Notley that Olivier had made the most conscientious efforts to establish a proper relationship with his son Tarquin. He always reproached himself with having opted out of the duties of a father almost from the moment of Tarquin's birth, but his efforts to reinstate himself were erratic and not always successful. When his brother Dickie died in 1958 Olivier wrote to Tarquin to say how painful he was going to find the loss. "As time goes on you will no doubt fill that gap for me, as indeed you will many another one for me, and you will give me such gifts of ever-increasing pride, ever-closening devotion and joy in you and in your life." That all sounded very fine, but as time went on Olivier made little effort to fit his son into that or any other gap. When he did take steps to assert his presence he sometimes hit the wrong note. He expressed doubts, for instance, about Tarquin's plan not to settle down to a steady job but instead to embark on an ambitious and adventurous journey around the world. Jill Esmond rounded on him. "You have forgotten what it is like to be young," she wrote. "Go on! Go home to the next play. That's all you understand and care about."[15]

Vivien Leigh and Tarquin got on well together and for as long as she was around the relationship between father and son improved, but as the marriage foundered so Tarquin found the atmosphere at Notley less congenial. When Tarquin began to write a book about his travels, Olivier was at first unenthusiastic about the project, then critical because work was not progressing rapidly enough. Finally he was told that the book had been accepted by a publisher. "I have never asked to see the book," Olivier told his son, "because something told me that my opinion would be qualified enough not to be anything but depressing to you . . . I don't want to read the book now because I simply haven't got time, that's all. I go into rehearsal in four weeks and I don't know how I'm going to get through all I have to. I've taken on too much, I know. I'm sorry, but I don't see what I can do about it . . . I haven't exactly encouraged you to come stay or anything because I wouldn't be able to give any proper time to you." As a model of how not to write to an affectionate but neglected son, this letter could hardly be bettered. Noël Coward, as so often, got it right. "Tarquin is really a bright and sweet boy," he wrote in his diary. "Jill . . . has been a wonderful mother to him and he quite genuinely adores her. Larry, as a father figure, has not come off quite so well."[16]

Olivier and Joan Plowright were in the United States when the decree absolute ending the divorce proceedings came through on March 3, 1961. A fortnight later they married. "If someone had told me, fifteen years ago, that I would one day be serving as best man for Larry Olivier, I'd have summoned him a bloody ambulance," Richard Burton remarked on the Dick Cavett show. In fact he overstated his role; the ceremony, such as it was, took place in the strictest privacy in Wilton, Connecticut. The couple rushed back to New York, however, and Burton gave a party for them after their respective shows had finished. "Joan is a very natural and splendidly earthy young woman," Olivier told Tarquin, "and if I am to make her happy and fulfilled she's simply got to have [children], that's all, she's that type." He addressed himself to his duties as a putative father with commendable alacrity.[17]

CHAPTER SIXTEEN

CHICHESTER

"I know nothing about Festivals or how they are run," Olivier told an inquirer in 1952. "I have no signposts to show you, and know of no pitfalls of which to warn you." A decade later his reply would have been very different. Between those dates a prosperous, energetic and stage-struck citizen of Chichester, Leslie Evershed-Martin, had conceived and brought almost to reality his dream of building a theater in his home town and holding an annual Festival. Well did he call his book on the subject *The Impossible Theater*; to persuade his fellow counselors that the project was worth pursuing was hard enough, to find a suitable site and raise the funds to buy and build upon it was an almost absurdly ambitious enterprise. Even then his troubles were only just beginning. He had to find someone to run it, who would be prepared to work enormously hard for little money and who would be able to attract to Chichester actors and actresses of the caliber necessary if the fledgling theater was to be established.[1]

His first idea was Tyrone Guthrie, who had recently supervised a similar undertaking in Stratford, Ontario, a Canadian town very similar in size to Chichester. Guthrie was no more ready to take on a second festival than he had been to engage with the National Theater. He was in favor of the project, however. He read with interest the list of possible candidates that Evershed-Martin had drawn up, then commented: "Leslie, you keep on about having only the best of everything at Chichester, so why don't you go for the best? Ask Laurence Olivier." Guthrie offered to approach Olivier himself and duly did so, stressing that nothing very extravagant was being contemplated: "Just an opener, so to speak—a Shakespeare and a Shaw for three or four weeks." Olivier, who was in America, did not immediately respond and Evershed-Martin followed up Guthrie's letter. Olivier was cautious: he had just seen two London theaters—the St. James's and the Stoll—pulled down in spite of his efforts to save them and, as he wryly noted, he was beginning to think "that my presence in a London theater would only be enviable to a member of the I.R.A." He suggested that Evershed-Martin get in touch with his agent, Cecil Tennant. Would he have full artistic control? he asked. And how much would he be paid? Yes, and £5,000 a year, were the answers. Too much, said Olivier. He would accept only £3,000—"he wanted to be all in all with us in the adventure." By the time Olivier first met Evershed-Martin on June 23, 1961, a deal had almost been done.[2]

Binkie Beaumont and the producer, Cecil Clarke, were amazed to hear Olivier was interested in so precarious a venture. "I've got it," said Clarke. "He wants to prepare himself for the National Theater." He was not wholly wrong. Olivier did have in mind that to launch a new theater in Chichester would strengthen his claim to take over the National when the moment came, give him useful experience in running a repertory company and enable him to launch productions and build up casts that would be available for the South Bank. But this was not the whole story. Olivier was in a mood to start his own company and Joan Plowright is convinced that he would have grasped at Chichester even though he had known that the National Theater would never happen or that he would not be asked to take it on. Chichester provided an irresistible challenge; he never doubted that he could make it work and rejoiced in the opportunity to prove it.[3]

There was another reason why the idea of Chichester was appealing. If it had been Cheltenham or Salisbury he might have hesitated, but Chichester, as the crow flies, was less than thirty miles from Brighton and it was in Brighton that he and Joan Plowright had decided to make their home. In 1961 they bought a handsome four-story Regency house with twelve rooms in Kemp Town's celebrated Royal Crescent; believed by its inhabitants to be the best address in Brighton and certainly offering stiff competition to any rival. It had used to boast a statue of the Prince Regent, put up by the developer in an effort to ingratiate himself with the occupant of the Royal Pavilion. Unfortunately it was not made of durable material and the nose and fingers fell away. It seems that the developer must similarly have economized on the houses themselves. Olivier had not even moved in before it became apparent that the front of the house was on the point of collapse and that it would cost a fortune to restore it. To compound his troubles, he insisted on making certain structural alterations that involved substantial building works. The result was that he found himself committed to spend more on rebuilding than he had spent on the house itself and was confronted by a vista of apparently endless construction works. When the Oliviers spent their first night in the building on December 16, 1961, it was in the knowledge that for months to come they would be sharing their house with a gang of laborers. Not content with this, as their family grew they concluded that they needed more room. Within a few years they had bought the house next door and the builders were back again turning the two houses into one.

But they were enormously happy. The Cassons had dinner with them shortly before the move into the Royal Crescent. Sybil Thorndike noticed a striking difference. "For the first time in years he is relaxed and like the dear old Larry that we've not seen for the last ten years," she wrote. "Joan is a darling. You couldn't have anyone more unlike poor Viv." As a married couple they were entirely satisfied with each other: in that happy honeymoon phase when each one is discovering new and delightful things about the other and every difference seems a reason for congratulation rather than a presage of potential trouble. As actors, the relationship was rather more complicated. "Marry him if you must, but do not act with him if you can help it," had been George Devine's advice. He meant, Plowright thinks, that she must avoid being thrust into parts that

Olivier thought would suit her or would complement parts he himself was playing but which in fact were wrong for her. Plowright could see the danger and anyway dreaded the "Actor-Manager and his Wife" syndrome, which would damage both their own reputations and the reputation of whatever institution they were working in. Olivier realized that he must tread carefully. Years later he insisted that his wife was "one of the finest actresses in the country. I didn't give her much of a leg-up toward that," he admitted. "I've been wrong so often about her, so often I've thought: 'I'm not quite sure Joannie can handle that part.' I've always been wrong. I didn't really appreciate the darling thing. I don't think it was anything to do with being married."[4]

Though she did not wish to act with him, at least on a regular basis, it did not follow that she had little respect for his mastery of his craft or would not listen with attention to his counsels. Olivier was never averse to giving advice, whether to his wife or to some fledgling, and usually the advice was sound. When she played Major Barbara he urged her to avoid any self-conscious emphasizing of the difference between her and those around her: "There is one word that describes what you should bring onto the stage with you in this part: RADIANCE. And don't be frightened of it, pet, and don't let self-mockery guy you out of it." When it was *The Entertainer*, he repeated the advice he had been given by Tyrone Guthrie nearly twenty years before: "You are a wonderfully gifted and beautifully disciplined actress," he told her. "Do not be shy of Dedication. Grasp hold of it . . . We must love Sergius, Iago or Caliban; we must even love Jean Rice. Ours not to reason why—ours but to apprehend and impart. We must never shirk that preparation in the wings, the practicing of the old self-hypnosis act to transform ourselves completely before we step onto the stage."[5]

Whatever her reservations about acting with her husband, Joan Plowright had parts in two out of the three plays that Chichester featured in its first season. When Olivier first saw the site proposed for the new theater he must have wondered whether there would even *be* a first season, or at least one starting in July 1962. All that was visible was an open field and six drainpipes stuck in the ground to mark the six points of the hexagon that was to be the shape of the new theater. The design, by English standards, was revolutionary. The traditional theater was a box, open at one end, in which the cast performed to an audience seated in an auditorium in front of them. At the other extreme, then as now rarely to be found, was the boxing ring, with the audience seated all round a circular stage. In between there could be any number of permutations, with the stage protruding different distances into the auditorium. Chichester was to be closer to the theater-in-the-round than any major British theater had previously attempted. The drawback was, of course, that at any given time the cast would have their backs to half the audience; the advantage was that many more people were seated close to the stage and, in the view of some at least, a greater intimacy and sense of participation was achieved. Olivier was willing, indeed anxious, to try out theater-in-the-round, but he was dismayed by the fact that the players, unless some way could be devised by which they could emerge through an opening in the stage, would have to enter by a gangway through the audience. This, he believed, weakened the dramatic effect of an entrance and impaired the illusion on which the theatrical experience was based. His conclusion, by the time Chichester's first season ended, was that he had achieved a happy compromise. New theaters should be built and, if practicable, old theaters modified, so that the stage protruded at least a few rows into the auditorium.

The first priority, though, was to ensure that there *was* a stage. Work proceeded with remarkable speed, but as the moment for the opening approached rehearsals were conducted against a background of construction noises and the occasional eruptions of workmen wielding tools and wearing hard hats. It was not ideal, but it lent a touch of adventure to the proceedings and Olivier exploited it to foster a sense of embattled endeavor in the enterprise. Whatever happened, everyone resolved, the theater would open on time and its productions would be as polished as if Chichester had been holding its Festival since the dawn of time.

Of course things went wrong and Olivier's temper sometimes grew frayed. Nobody had realized that, since the shape of the theater made the conventional curtains impossible, normal safety regulations could not apply. Feverish last-minute changes had to be made to accommodate the fire regulations. Incompetence! Olivier stormed; was there nobody but he who was capable of looking ahead? A hammer dropped by a workman narrowly missed his head. He exploded with rage. The rage was characteristic; so was the fact that when he cooled down he realized that he had had no business to be in that part of the theater. Next day, he publicly and handsomely apologized to the workman, thereby reinforcing the will of everyone involved with the building to get the job done on time.

One of the main reasons Evershed-Martin had been so anxious to enlist Olivier had been that he felt nobody else would be able to attract important stars to come to an untried theater in a provincial town. Olivier turned first to his old friends, then, when he had made sure of them, looked for actors who he felt would be sympathetic to the challenge. Joan Plowright was the first to be recruited. Sybil Thorndike and Lewis Casson were figures of immense eminence whose presence alone was enough to guarantee the respectability of the enterprise. Michael Redgrave, another old ally, was recruited particularly to play the title role in *Uncle Vanya*. A powerful group was assembled to make up numbers: Joan Greenwood, Fay Compton, Max Adrian, John Neville, Robert Lang, Rosemary Harris, Keith Michell—it is hard to believe that anybody else in Britain could have persuaded so distinguished a body to come aboard. Rosemary Harris was in the United States when she was asked to join the company. What are the parts? she asked. He was not prepared to tell her, Olivier replied. "I don't want anybody to know what plays I'm doing. These plays have been on library shelves for the last hundred years and it's a big secret what they are." Harris stuck to her guns and in the end was given the information she wanted. "I don't know how I had the gall," she remembered. "I would have gone barefoot to China to play for him." Olivier himself was omnipresent. Not merely did he mastermind the whole enterprise and concern himself with the smallest detail, but he acted in two of the three plays and directed all of them. Chichester was no Toad Hall, but the malicious could see a touch of Mr. Toad in Olivier's determination to feature prominently in every aspect of the Festival.[6]

Not everyone succumbed to his blandishments. Claire Bloom wanted a part in *Uncle Vanya*," but when told that Joan Greenwood and Joan Plowright had already been cast for the play refused to come to Chichester. "Olivier's face became stone-like, his basilisk eyes as impenetrable as granite. All he said at the time was: 'How wonderful of you to have been so honest with me!' What he meant was: 'You will never work for me again.' Laurence Olivier never forgave a slight." "Claire would have felt a wee bit dull," was his explanation to Michael Redgrave, but he did indeed bear her a grudge and got his own back in due course. The following year she wrote to say that she had heard *Othello* was being planned. Perhaps Desdemona had already been selected, "but, should the occasion arise your Barkis is willin." Desdemona was indeed already cast, Olivier answered with some satisfaction; "Of course, I'll remember you, my dear, as and when." "Cold and wounding," Bloom found this reply; it certainly was not fashioned to spare her feelings.[7]

For every one who refused to join, ten clamored for the privilege. A twenty-three-year-old Steven Berkoff wrote to protest that he had been denied an audition. "I demand it!" he wrote. "I would not make the demand as a poor actor or even as an average or competent one. I only make it because I *know* that I shall not disgrace myself before you." "I have no further room in the company for anyone of your age group," Olivier replied, "that is the truth and the long and the short and the tall of it." Unlike Claire Bloom, Berkoff forgave the rebuff. Fourteen years later he wrote to invite Olivier to act or direct for him at the Greenwich Theater: "It is my greatest regret that we have never worked together. However, you have taught me as much as if you had given me lessons in the same room."[8]

It was not only actors and actresses whom Olivier sought to draw to Chichester. He wrote to John Arden, Robert Bolt and Harold Pinter, asking them to write plays for the Festival. "Whether this idea entertains you or not," he told Pinter, "I am writing to beg you to come see the theater and the work." In one dramatist, however, he had lost interest. "I do think we go on a bit about Kit Fry," he told Harold Hobson. "I do think he may come back, but I don't think he's the most important author in the world."⁹

Even if these dramatists had been ready to oblige there would have been no possibility of their plays being ready in time for the first season. Olivier had to choose three plays from the existing repertoire. He was determined not to do the predictable—"*Peer Gynt* and *Charley's Aunt*" as he contemptuously put it—and so, as he had told Rosemary Harris, he turned to the library shelf. From it he extracted two obscure seventeenth-century plays, *The Chances* by the Duke of Buckingham and *The Broken Heart* by John Ford. *The Chances* would open the season. It was "a romp and to my mind still a very endearing and pleasant little romp," he wrote—suitable for an occasion when the attention of the critics and public would be focused almost entirely on the theater itself. The Ford was more of a heavyweight piece, but also more difficult to put over. Olivier was apprehensive about its reception. It had, however, been brought to his attention by Kenneth Tynan, "with what I thought was a certain enthusiastic expectation," so at least one good review could be anticipated.¹⁰

The first night passed off smoothly, the weather was excellent, the audience in a mood to enjoy itself. "Warmest greetings from the other Chichester," read a telegram from a well-wisher. "Thinking of you as I approach New York. Wishing you fair winds and happy landfalls. Hope you're in for as good a voyage as Francis Chichester." Sailing a yacht single-handed across the Atlantic might seem a hazardous occupation, but, as the unenthusiastic reviews appeared, Olivier may have thought that the other Chichester was in the better place. *The Chances* was not a failure, but it was far from the resounding success the Festival needed. Worse was to follow. *The Broken*

Heart earned the hostility of some and indifferent dismissal from all except one benevolent critic from the *Yorkshire Post*. Unkindest of all: "That bastard Tynan . . . suggested it to me, then he just sent it up sky high . . . son of a bitch." The son of a bitch compounded his offense by writing Olivier an open letter in the *Observer*, denouncing the style of the production and concluding: "Tomorrow *Uncle Vanya* opens. Within a fortnight you will have directed three plays and appeared in two leading parts. It is too much." If he moved on to the National Theater, Tynan suggested, Olivier should revert to the Old Vic triumvirate, sharing power with Ralph Richardson and John Burrell, and perhaps adding Peter Brook and Anthony Quayle as joint directors.[11]

It was soon evident that, at matinees at least, *The Broken Heart* would be playing to half-empty houses. The Festival threatened to be a failure. The only hope lay in *Uncle Vanya* and Olivier was profoundly doubtful about its chances. He did not believe that Chekhov was suitable for theater-in-the-round and became ever more skeptical as rehearsals progressed. He had originally proposed that Ralph Richardson should play the name part, but his tentative suggestion had not been followed up on either side: "You don't want to keep bothering people unless you really mean it," Olivier reflected, "and I wasn't absolutely sure how deeply I meant it. Did I really want to make another partnership with Ralph? I wasn't really convinced I did." Richardson's replacement, Michael Redgrave, was in the end to provide what Olivier pronounced to be "the best performance I've ever seen in anything. It was absolutely marvelous;" but he was a slow starter and tentative in rehearsals. Casson was inaudible: "For fuck's sake, Lewis, I can't hear a bloody word," Olivier exploded from the back of the stalls. By the first night he was resigned to abject failure, the collapse of the Festival, a perhaps fatal blow to his prospects at the National. "Here's to another flop," he pronounced just before the play began. "Nonsense!" said Sybil Thorndike, and slapped him in the face. Afterward Olivier said that that moment woke him up.[12]

What followed was one of those infinitely rare productions in which everything works, everyone is perfect, nobody stands out.

The company were better than the Berliner Ensemble, wrote Harold Hobson, than which he could conceive no higher praise. "Here is a living work of art," was T. C. Worsley's verdict, "so perfect in every conceivable shade of detail, that those who are lucky enough to get to see it are privileged." From the moment that he walked onto the stage Olivier knew that his fears had been chimeras; all was going to be exceeding well. As Astrov he gave a marvelously muted and mellow performance, but it was as the director that he took most pride. "I did it awfully well," he claimed many years later. "I must say I was very clever with it." He had reason to be proud. Opinions differed about Olivier's merits as a director, but for his work on Chekhov he gained nothing but praise, and merited praise at that.[13]

Thanks to *Uncle Vanya* Chichester's first season had achieved dramatic success. Socially, and in terms of public relations, it had already triumphed. Olivier's personal prestige and the quality of the performers he had drawn to Chichester had ensured that the Festival had become part of the social season's calendar: with Glyndebourne and Ascot it was a place where one should be seen. The "darling Duchess of Norfolk," as Olivier described her, expressed her undying gratitude: "You take our great, majestic guest off our hands for one glorious night"—in other words, the Queen fitted in a visit to the theater while staying at Arundel for the Goodwood race meeting. Evershed-Martin was ecstatic; the season made a modest financial profit; Olivier could look forward with pleasure to a second season in 1963.[14]

He was convinced that the acerbic response of the critics to the first two productions at Chichester had been caused in part at least by the leak of the news that he was to be the first Director of the new National Theater. "An enemy hath done this," he concluded—the enemy in his view being probably the twenty-nine-year-old whiz kid from Stratford, Peter Hall. As a result, he believed, the press did not treat the Chichester Festival as an interesting new experiment that deserved encouragement but as something that should be judged by the standards of a national institution. It was bad luck, in that the last details of his association with the National Theater had yet to be sorted out and no announcement had been intended for several months. Whether it really made much difference to the critics' attitude is questionable. It certainly did not deter them from indulging in a paean of praise when things at last went right.[15]

Olivier's story is that the suggestion that he should take charge of the National Theater was put to him casually by Lord Chandos and Kenneth Rae when they were visiting him at Notley. "Are you really proposing that I should be the first Director?" he asked incredulously. "Don't you realize what a cunt I am? Well, you'll find out now!" It seems improbable that he replied in such terms and still less likely that he was taken by surprise. Olivier was by now pretty sure that he would be offered the job and would have been outraged if it had been given to anyone else. There was little opposition. Whoever was chosen, Tyrone Guthrie suggested, would have to satisfy the Board that he was a traditionalist at heart, while convincing the more turbulent critics and avant-garde directors that he was truly radical. He reckoned that was no job for him. Glen Byam Shaw had only just taken over at Sadler's Wells. Among the actors, Ralph Richardson and John Gielgud had the stature to take it on, but it was not at all Richardson's sort of thing and while Gielgud had some experience as an actor-manager he lacked the temperament to take over a large and complex organization. The most convincing competitor was probably Peter Hall; but, though he had already done great things at Stratford, he was extremely young and had only just taken over supreme command. Precisely when a formal offer was made to Olivier is hard to establish. In October 1960, he told Tarquin that his main interest was now the National Theater. He had, he said, "been instrumental in its present possibilities." He had been one of the three Trustees for about two years and had "managed to cut out a lot of dead wood, force conciliations and form a small, efficient working committee of which Kenneth Clark is the Chairman." It does not sound from this as if the identity of the first Director had yet been settled. Two months later Clark wrote to tell him that he was "*absolutely* delighted by your suggestion. I had sometimes thought of asking you if you would consent to become first Director of the National Theater, but hardly dared to hope for it." If he would like to take it on it would make all the difference "both to the public and to actors. Everyone has confidence in you and will be admiring your genius." The most obvious interpretation of this is that Olivier had suggested to Clark that he should become Director—something incompatible with Olivier's version of events but not necessarily incorrect for that reason. Another perplexing feature is that Clark's message makes it sound as if it was he who would select the first Director while in fact Chandos and/or Esher enjoyed the decisive voice. Olivier described a lunch with Esher about this time. Olivier guessed that he was about to say something important because of the concentration with which he was eating. "Eventually he looked up, his mustache dropping soup, and said: 'Do you hate me?'" Olivier denied he did. "I was afraid you did," said Esher. Olivier still cherished a grudge against Esher for his abrupt dismissal from the Old Vic during the Australasian tour, but he knew that it was essential that they should work together if the National Theater was to get away to a smooth start. "I thought he was a stupid old fart," he said, "and he was, but I knew whatever those boys did was in the purity of conscience." Esher was far from being a stupid old fart, and Olivier was well aware of the fact. In an ideal world he would have preferred to deal with someone rather more amenable, but if Esher and Chandos controlled the future of the National Theater then he would accept the fact and get along with them as best he could.[16]

Whatever the exact timing, Olivier's appointment as Director had been decided in principle by the time the season started at Chichester. The announcement was made a few weeks later. The staff marked the occasion by sticking a Union Jack on his door with a placard reading "God Bless Sir." Olivier came to the door, not knowing anyone was watching him, put his hands together, bowed his head and said, "Please God, help!" Until that moment all Olivier's preparations for Chichester had been made with the consciousness that the potential needs of a future National Theater should be

In 1914. He maintained that he was an unattractive child but here looks notably cherubic.

Olivier's much-loved mother Agnes, and feared and detested father Gerard.

As Katherina (back, right) in *The Taming of the Shrew*—a performance improbably attended and praised by Ellen Terry, Sybil Thorndike, and Theodore Komisarjevsky.

Aged eighteen. "My mouth is like a tortoise's arse," he complained. "It's an absolute slit."

As Uncle Vanya in 1927. Almost incredibly, he was only nineteen at the time.

With Adrianne Allen, watching Noël Coward and Gertrude Lawrence slug it out in *Private Lives.* As the photograph suggests, his role was very much that of a looker-on.

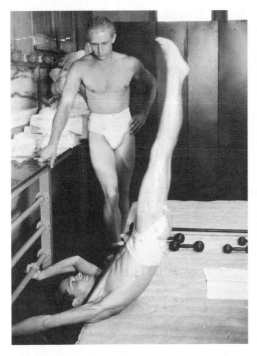

Working out in 1931. William Gaskill said that he had never met an actor so concerned about his physical appearance.

Arriving in New York in 1933 with his first wife, Jill Esmond. Olivier thought he was on his way to co-star with Greta Garbo in *Queen Christina.* He was to be disappointed.

Edith Evans as the Nurse in *Romeo and Juliet* seems notably ill at ease between Olivier (Romeo) and Gielgud (Mercutio).

As Romeo to Peggy Ashcroft's Juliet in 1935. He and John Gielgud alternated in the parts of Romeo and Mercutio.

Tarquin Olivier, showing early signs of the intrepidity that marked his life.

With Cherry Cottrell as Ophelia in *Hamlet*.

Olivier followed Hamlet with Toby Belch in *Twelfth Night*: a part, as he himself remarked "designed to demonstrate my staggering versatility."

As Henry V. "He's a scoutmaster," Ralph Richardson said. "But he raised scoutmastership to godlike proportions."

As Macbeth, conceived by Michel Saint-Denis. "Larry's make-up comes on," remarked Vivien Leigh, "then Banquo comes on, then Larry comes on."

With Vivien Leigh in *Romeo and Juliet*.

Sybil Thorndike as Volumnia to Olivier's Coriolanus at the Old Vic in 1938. She refused to play the part unless Olivier promised to act in "a natural, straightforward way."

OPPOSITE: In *Wuthering Heights*. "Thees actor es the ogliest actor in pictures," Sam Goldwyn protested.

With Greer Garson in *Pride and Prejudice*— "I thought darling Greer was as wrong as could be," Olivier remarked.

Planning *Rebecca* with Hitchcock and Joan Fontaine. Olivier disliked Fontaine from the start, deeming her "skinny and unattractive."

Making-up for *Lady Hamilton*. Olivier attached enormous importance to this operation and would spend hours in front of the mirror.

Olivier directed, produced and starred in *Henry V*. "He would play each part himself as he conceived it and expect the actors to copy it," said Dallas Bower.

"This day is called the Feast of Crispian"—the speech with which Olivier is above all identified and a recording of which was played at his memorial service.

With Ralph
Richardson in
Hamburg on an
E.N.S.A. tour
shortly after the
end of the war.

Vivien's Leigh's
dressing room in
Sydney, smothered
in flowers. Though
Olivier grumbled
about their reception
in Australia they
were, in fact, fêted
wherever they went.

Perched rather uncomfortably between his first wife, Jill Esmond, and his second, Vivien Leigh.

On the set of the film of *Hamlet* in 1948. Vivien Leigh had wanted to play Ophelia, but instead Jean Simmons, described by Olivier as a "ravishing sixteen-year-old," was given the part.

OVERLEAF: As Lear, in a production he also directed, with Alec Guinness as the Fool. "Frankly, Lear is an easy part . . ." Olivier proclaimed boldly. It isn't.

Olivier and Leigh as Caesar and Cleopatra in 1951. Already there were signs that their relationship was under strain.

Swashbuckling in *The Beggar's Opera*. "I hope and pray," Olivier wrote, "that my personal flop will be the worst that I will ever disenjoy."

Vivien Leigh and her soon-to-be lover, Peter Finch, flying off to Ceylon to film *Elephant Walk* in 1953. She was eventually replaced by Elizabeth Taylor, although she still appears in many long shots and with her back to the camera.

Malvolio to Vivien Leigh's Viola in the 1955 *Twelfth Night* at Stratford.

Olivier, Gielgud considered, was "the finest Macbeth I have ever seen." Leigh's performance was "almost the best thing I ever saw her do—but on a small scale."

With Claire Bloom as Lady Anne in *Richard III*. She was not merely seduced by Richard III on stage but by Olivier off it.

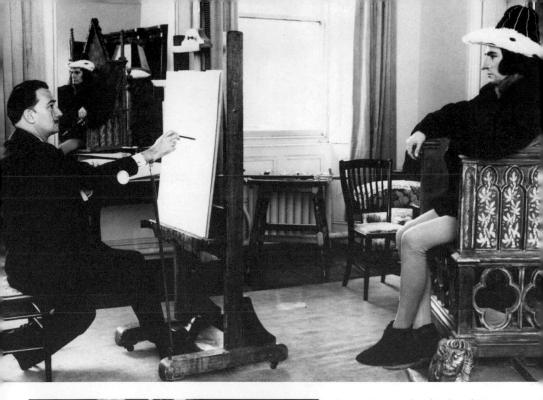

Dressed as Richard III
and being painted
by Salvador Dalí.
The portrait is now
in the Dalí Museum
in Catalonia.

The Oliviers with
Arthur Miller and
Marilyn Monroe
in 1956.

With Marilyn Monroe on the set of *The Sleeping Prince*. Olivier had expected to have an affair with Monroe but ended up hating her with consuming ferocity.

With Maggie Smith in Ionesco's *Rhinoceros*. "What a perfectly bloody play," protested Noël Coward, but others thought it a masterpiece of the theatre of the absurd.

With Joan Plowright in the film of *The Entertainer*. By this time Olivier's marriage with Vivien Leigh was all but over.

Peter O'Toole played Hamlet in the first production at the National Theater. Olivier directed—an experience not greatly relished by either party.

Olivier's Othello was one of his greatest roles. His interaction with Maggie Smith produced an unforgettable theatrical experience and much discomfort to both parties.

Olivier took three and a half hours to make up as Othello: blackening every part of his body, whether visible to the audience or not.

With the architect, Denys Lasdun, in 1967, inspecting a model of the new National Theater.

As James Tyrone in *Long Day's Journey into Night*—"a pretty well perfect play", Olivier judged it.

IAGO TEMPTS LORD OTHELLO OF BRIGHTON WITH
A LEWD PLAY BY A PERUVIAN MARXIST

With Lord Cottesloe, smoothing out the cement during the topping-out ceremony for the new National Theater in May 1973.

With Peter Hall in May 1973: the past and the future of the National Theatre.

As John Tagg in *The Party*: Olivier's last stage role and one of his most successful.

With Michael Caine in *Sleuth*—"He's young enough to be my son," said Olivier ruefully.

Opposite Sarah Miles's marvellously seductive schoolgirl in *Term of Trial* in 1962.

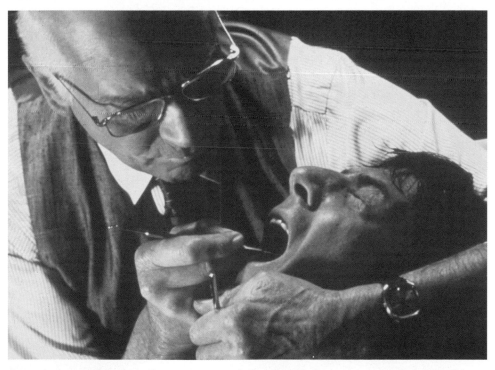

Operating on Dustin Hoffman. "I am awfully pleased about the *Marathon Man,*" Olivier wrote, "horrific as the story is."

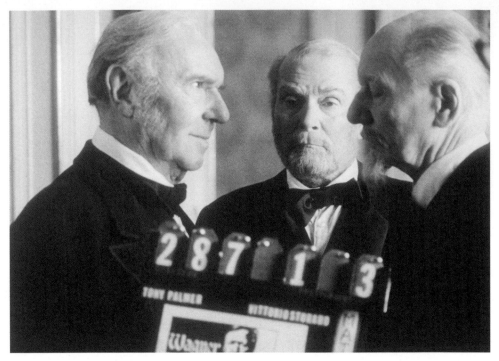

Reunited with Gielgud and Richardson in 1983 in a mini-series for television about Wagner.

As Lord Marchmain in *Brideshead Revisited* (1981) with Diana Quick as Julia Flyte.

Olivier with Joan Plowright.

The family at the time of Olivier's eightieth birthday. Tamsin, in the patterned dress on the left, Richard in the center and Julie-Kate on the right.

borne in mind, but with no direct association between one institution and the other. Once his appointment had been formalized, it was merely a question of how intimate the relationship should be. Olivier was anxious that—overtly at least—it should not appear too close: partly because he did not wish to fetter his freedom of action, partly because it was important that those at Chichester should not feel that they were of value only for the contribution they might make to the foundation of another theater. When the *Daily Mail* carried a story that the cast at Chichester would provide the nucleus of the National Theater Company, Olivier denied that this was so. Some had not yet been asked, some would never be asked, at the most it was the case that "certain members of the Chichester Company will, no doubt, be seen at the National Theater." "Oh dear, oh dear!" replied the editor of the *Daily Mail*; another story would be published putting things straight. As he no doubt suspected, the original story was closer to the truth than the correction. By the time the second season at Chichester opened every appointment made, every production undertaken, was planned with a view to its relevance to the National Theater.[17]

Evershed-Martin might have resented the subjection of his beloved theater to the needs of another organization, but he reckoned that, on the whole, greater glory would accrue to Chichester through its association with the National Theater than it could ever hope to earn as an independent body. He told Olivier that he could see "nothing but good" in the connection: "perhaps it would be best to call it 'in association with' rather than 'affiliated to,'" he suggested, so as to make it clear that Chichester kept its independence while both sides benefited from the exchange of "productions, casts, directors etc.." Olivier was almost as anxious as Evershed-Martin that the importance of Chichester as an independent Festival should not be underplayed. "I think it is putting it a little harshly," he wrote just before the second season started in 1963, "to call our efforts last year merely a dress rehearsal for something else. I know you don't mean this unkindly but it is, I think, not the kindest way in which they could be described." Olivier and Evershed-Martin were to have their differences, some of them pretty tempestuous, but on the central issue of Chichester's relationship to the National Theater they were as one.[18]

What sort of National Theater it was with which Chichester was to be associated was for some time in question. A resurgent Royal Shakespeare Company under Peter Hall, with its well-established power base at Stratford but already committed to an ambitious London season, could not be left out of the calculations. The Government worked on the preliminary assumption that there would be some sort of merger between Stratford and a new National Theater that would be based loosely on the Old Vic. So long as the details of the collaboration remained undefined the idea seemed in principle acceptable to all parties. "I don't believe there is enough talent in this country for two major classical theaters to be operating properly," Hall had concluded toward the end of 1959. "In other words, if there is a National Theater, it is essential that in some way this theater amalgamates with it." "Stratford could obviously not afford to operate in rivalry," agreed Olivier eighteen months later. "Unification is from every point of view both desirable and advantageous." But two strong-minded and ambitious individuals were involved, each reluctant to surrender any real authority to the other. Even if Hall had been willing to accept the disappearance of Stratford's independence he would not have been allowed to do so. Sir Fordham Flower, the assertive Chairman of the Royal Shakespeare Company and head of the brewing family that had conjured it into existence, would have regarded as intolerable the suppression of its identity in favor of some amorphous new organization based in London. Even Lord Goodman, that most persuasive and well-connected of fixers, was unable to negotiate the two parties into a viable partnership.[19]

In Olivier's view the breakdown of negotiations was almost entirely due to the intransigence and personal ambitions of Peter Hall. He viewed Hall with suspicion and alarm. The satirist John Wells wrote a skit in which Hall, as Director of the National Theater, was made to say that he planned to build a new theater on the

South Bank that would "probably be called the Peter Hall." "You mean, like the Albert Hall?" "Yes, only obviously rather larger!" To Olivier this seemed a fair comment. Hall claimed that Stratford had withdrawn from the negotiations only because they were trying to be constructive and because he thought the National would work better without them. "If your new empire is going to set out to kill Stratford and my Company . . . then what will have been achieved except the usual British waste?" Stratford was not being in the least constructive, retorted Olivier. "They withdrew entirely for their own reasons, entirely to do with their own *amour propre*. . . Your letter carries to me a slightly hysterical note (if I may say so without meaning to be in the tiniest bit offensive) which worries me and makes me feel you are not in a good state."[20]

The negotiations ended in acrimony. Hall's subsequent judgment was generous: "I doubt whether the National would ever have finally happened without Larry's power, prestige and glamour at that particular time." At that particular time, however, he was not disposed to be so charitable—Olivier was the enemy. It was a feeling that was not to make things any easier a decade or so later when Hall arrived in the National Theater.[21]

Olivier's appointment did not appeal to everyone. In the *Daily Mail* Bernard Levin wrote an article arguing that he was the wrong man for the job—mainly, it seems, because his choice of plays was not to Levin's taste. Olivier was convinced that the *Daily Mail* had waged a vendetta against him, ever since he had thrown a *Mail* journalist off the set during the filming of *The Prince and the Showgirl*. He wanted to sue them, was persuaded that there were no grounds, but sent a strong lawyer's letter threatening action. "Our Clients are most disturbed that your Client should think they are conducting any kind of personal campaign against him," came the dulcet reply. "Nothing could be further from the truth." Olivier was apt to scent persecution where none existed and the *Daily Mail* was not so unremittingly hostile as he imagined. Certainly there were others who shared its doubts. In the *Sunday Times* Harold Hobson had put forward seven names as potential Directors of the National Theater including Tyrone Guthrie, John Gielgud and Peter Hall, but did not suggest Olivier as a possibility. Noël Coward was opposed for a different reason. "I am sure everyone has been at you in one way or another," he wrote, "so I am going to pile Pelion on Ossa, Stoke on Trent and possibly Lee on Solent. *Don't* administer the National Theater. You have given us some of the greatest performances of the century. Administration is more frustrating and tiring than poncing about and shouting 'Ho, there!' or 'I'm fair Venice's lofty cunt.' What you need is a full year off duty."[22]

Olivier paid more attention to Coward than to most people, but no chorus of voices—however sage or experienced—could have changed his mind. As for "a full year off duty," even a week off duty caused him disquiet. He was a driven man. The National Theater had become his destiny and no discouragement was going to distract him from its pursuit.

One of the better features of Chichester was that, while the period of rehearsals and the Festival itself were intensely active, there was time to make films or act in plays at the beginning and end of the year. The first film that Olivier made when on leave from the Festival, *Term of Trial*, was as interesting for its cast as for its dramatic content. He was playing an alcoholic schoolmaster whose career has been blighted by his wartime pacifism. He is despised by his wife, played by the French actress Simone Signoret, but adored by one of his pupils who tries to seduce him and, when rejected, turns on him and accuses him of indecent assault. Olivier had vaguely assumed that he would have an affair with Simone Signoret whose husband, Yves Montand, was embroiled with Marilyn Monroe ("Spoiled, contaminated fat slug!" Olivier spat out, when Signoret complained to him about her husband's mistress). Instead he became infatuated by "a new little girl called Sarah Miles," a seductive twenty-year-old who was playing the delinquent schoolgirl. Miles claimed to have been in love with Olivier since seeing him in *Wuthering Heights*" when she was eleven years old. Her childish passion was quickly rekindled: "Seeing him in the flesh was an experience that way surpassed my Heathcliff on the screen. The smile, the wanton twinkle in his eyes, the friendly, springy gait, the determination in the set of his shoulder blades, the gentle stubbornness that continually won him his point of detail—all this reminded me so much of my father."[23]

Unlike the schoolmaster he was playing on the screen, Olivier saw no reason to reject this adoring admirer. Indeed, it proved to be one of the most serious of his casual affairs. According to Derek Granger he at one point even went so far as to consult his agent, Laurence Evans, about the possibility of securing a divorce so as to marry Miles. It does not seem likely that he did more than play with the idea and when Evans pointed out that it would seriously damage if not destroy his career, he quickly dropped it. Miles had charm and was almost indecently attractive, but he had no particular respect for her as an actress. He put her into Arthur Miller's *The Crucible* in 1965 but thought she "wasn't marvelously good," and when Noël Coward rejected her for *Hay Fever* he accepted the ruling without argument. "I had to fire her before the opening, it was awful for her," he remembered. Given their relationship it might have been expected to be awful for him too; the fact that he sent her packing without compunction illustrates well the order of his priorities. Sex was enjoyable and it was always satisfying to be loved and courted, but the demands of the theater came first. Sarah Miles was wrong for the part, Sarah Miles must go, and no amount of delicious dalliance could save her. Sarah Miles anyway denies that she was sacked: she retired hurt when a fishbone stuck in her throat and put her out of action for several weeks. Coward certainly wanted her gone, but it seems possible that Olivier, as was always his inclination, avoided the stark confrontation that his words suggest occurred.[24]

Semi-Detached, a first play by a talented young dramatist called David Turner, illustrates how even a producer/director as experienced as Olivier could misjudge a script. When he first read it, he thought that it sparkled with wit and that the author had brought off a brilliant success. By the time rehearsals had ended his confidence had dwindled; the reviews convinced him that he had made a monstrous error. "I was miserable doing it," he confessed. "They hated me—the critics, the audiences. I could feel it coming over me every night . . . it was thirteen weeks of sheer torture." Noël Coward read the reviews and hoped that they were unjustified. He went to see it and concluded that they were not. "It's a dreary, untidy little play with Larry good in spots," he wrote. "Oh, what a bad judge he is. To do this play was a major mistake."[25]

It was a painful experience in another sense. His diary entry for January 16, 1963, includes the sentence: "Gout started during Act I. Violent." Olivier had been suffering from occasional attacks of gout since 1947 but recently they had been coming more often and more intensely. "They are frequently provoked by stress," wrote the specialist who examined him, "and as stress of various sorts is obviously inseparable from his professional life one must fear that they may become, in time, even more frequent and extensive." Perhaps, he suggested, a mild tranquilizer might be permitted before particularly testing occasions such as first nights. Olivier had recourse to more arcane remedies. "Oh dear, Oh dear!" he wrote to his doctor. "I have allowed myself to be persuaded into trying one of those one-eyed, definitely un-B.M.A., absolutely quacky schemes that should work or otherwise in three weeks. I hope you don't mind. I shall no doubt be coming to you with my tail between my legs after that." He did, but neither the quacks nor the regular practitioners could do much to help. It was rare for Olivier to miss a complete evening, but he was quite often struck by agonizing pain in the middle of a performance. The discipline required to let no flicker of distress disturb his acting but rather to continue to appear light-hearted, thoughtful or whatever the part demanded, must have been one of the most testing experiences of his professional life.[26]

He had to turn down one invitation that would have cost him little effort and caused him some amusement. Bob Hope wrote to say that he and Bing Crosby were planning to enrich the next of their Road series—Road to Hong Kong—with a series of cameo parts in which major stars—Frank Sinatra, Dean Martin, David Niven and Sophia Loren among them—would appear unexpectedly, without billing, and utter a line or two. Hope would be a Chinese coolie pulling a rickshaw. He would turn to his passenger, Bing Crosby, and say: "I bet Laurence Olivier wouldn't play a part like this." Then the camera would cut to Olivier standing by a nearby lamp-post, who would say: "Nobody made me an offer." "Wouldn't it be thrilling," Hope concluded, "to do a scene without having to wait for Marilyn?" Olivier was tempted but could not find a slot in his crowded diary. He genuinely regretted it. He would gratefully have cut short the run of *Semi-Detached* so as to fit in a quick visit to Hollywood—or, for that matter, Hong Kong.[27]

On October 10, 1962, Olivier attended his first meeting of the National Theater Board as Director-designate. Before his arrival Chandos had told the meeting that Olivier's salary had been agreed at £5,000 a year: "The Board considered that Sir Laurence had acted in a very public-spirited way in accepting the financial terms, which were clearly far less generous than those that he could command elsewhere." Olivier was to be given a period of leave each year in which he could make films or do whatever else he wanted; a reasonable provision given the financial sacrifice he was making but one that caused Binkie Beaumont some alarm. It must, he insisted, be managed in a way that would not impair the running of the theater. Olivier then joined the meeting and, after a welter of mutual backslapping, it was minuted that "Sir Laurence should pursue the problem of the future relations between the National Theater and Stratford with Mr. Peter Hall on as broad a basis as he thought advisable." The following week Olivier visited Stratford and suggested that they should give up their efforts to maintain a London base and instead appear for three months of the year in some part of the new National Theater. In Hall's view, this was not a case of "as broad a basis as he thought advisable" so much as "as narrow a basis as he thought he could get away with." Fordham Flower agreed. This, he thought, was a fresh attempt on the part of Olivier to snuff out the Royal Shakespeare Company as a rival in London. Olivier, he believed, could not endure the thought of Stratford at the Aldwych and would stop at nothing to eliminate it. He was wrong, but not wholly wrong. There had been a time at which Olivier would have been ready to make sacrifices to patch up some compromise with Stratford; by the end of 1962 he asked for nothing better than to forget about Stratford and be left in peace to develop the National Theater as he thought best.[28]

He still had obligations to Chichester and, indeed, saw the Festival as playing an important part in its own right, but from the end of 1962 the National Theater was at the heart of all his planning. He identified himself wholly with its doings, committing to it the allegiance due to an institution that had taken over his life yet loving it with the fierce pride of an artist surveying his own creation. He was owned by the National Theater and yet he owned the National Theater. He did not agree with Peter Hall on many things, but when Hall said that the National was above all Olivier's creation, he would have endorsed the sentiment. In the not-so-small hours of the morning, after a heavy drinking session, Olivier announced in a stentorian voice: "There'd be no National Theater if it wasn't for me!" It was vainglorious, but it was nevertheless a case of *in vino veritas.* "Come on, Larry, it's time you went to bed," said Joan Plowright.[29]

CHAPTER SEVENTEEN

THE NATIONAL: ACT ONE

How he wished Tarquin was there, Olivier told his son in the autumn of 1962, to talk about anything except the National Theater, "because you can guess that every Jack who can use a typewriter is telling me how to run that." By the end of the year he was devoting all his energies to the Theater's affairs. He even made a resolution to give up alcohol for the whole of 1963. "I shall miss it dreadfully," he told Tyrone Guthrie, "but I have made an important discovery, and that is that if you don't drink there is nothing else to do but work, and that is the only way I can hope to get it done." Some might have thought his lack of alternatives a little dispiriting—could he not have read a book? Looked at pictures? Gone for a walk? Made love?—but even if his remark need not be taken too literally it demonstrates both the extent of the dedication he gave to his work and the importance he attached to drink. Acting and heavy drinking frequently go together. Olivier never drank before or during a performance but afterward, or if he was off duty, two or three whiskies and a fair amount of wine would have been the norm. Like most heavy drinkers, he thought that he had a strong head. Ralph Richardson disagreed. "Of course Laurence never had a head for drink," he said. "He came up to me one day and said: 'The trouble with you, Ralph, is that you can't hold your liquor.' And he fell flat on his face." There are enough accounts of Olivier the worse for wear to make it clear that Richardson was justified in his comments: he was never close to being an alcoholic, but he drank a great deal more than even the most liberal of doctors would have thought desirable. Drink was an important part of Olivier's life and to renounce it was an important sacrifice. He stuck by his word. He wrote triumphantly to Tarquin in December 1963 to announce that he was coming off the wagon on Christmas Eve: "I shall probably have a couple of drinks, be sick all over the kids and be carried screaming up to bed in disgrace."[1]

The burden of running the National was made the greater by his determination, from the very start, to concern himself with every aspect of its existence. "Delegation" was not a word that came easily to Olivier. Any significant policy decision would, he took for granted, be under his control. When the South Bank Board set up an Advisory Panel to supervise work on the new enterprise, Olivier wrote to the Chairman, Lord Cottesloe: "It is a little awkward for me to put to you what I want to, without sounding as if I thought no end of myself . . . It is that I do feel that I should run this Advisory Panel myself and I feel that, as Director of the theater, the idea need not be too unacceptable." But to be in charge of the broad sweep of policy while leaving the niggling details to others was not his style. When a long-serving doorman retired it was Olivier who decided that a party would be in order, vetted the guest list, approved the budget and in due course appeared and said a few words himself. He wrote petulant minutes about the low quality of the lavatory paper in the staff toilets and inquired whether it was necessary to have so many lights permanently burning in the entrance hall. "There were occasions when you thought: 'Will there ever be any peace?'" said Rupert Rhymes, the theater manager. No detail was too small to escape his attention. There had been much discussion about the exact color of the posters: from Canada he dispatched a postcard—"Lousy postcard, but this is the shade of yellow." Upset by the amount of coughing in the auditorium, he sent Rhymes round to a manufacturer of cough lozenges, instructing him to persuade them to supply sachets that could be handed out by the usherettes. His obsessive interest in detail could be irritating, sometimes even ridiculous, but no one doubted that it stemmed from his determination that the National Theater should be, in every way, as good as it could possibly be, and that the welfare of all those who worked in it was very much part of that consideration.[2]

Olivier had always maintained that it would be disastrous to build a theater and then look for a company to fill it; the company must come first, the building should follow a few years later when the company was well established. This meant that the National Theater would need a temporary home. For reasons both practical and sentimental the most proper place for it in those early years seemed to be the Old Vic. Olivier's glory days under the Old Vic banner had been while the company operating under that name was based in the West End, leaving its war-damaged headquarters in ruins just off the Waterloo Road on the South Bank. He had no particular affection for the now rebuilt theater, but it was serviceable enough and would act as a base while its permanent home was being built. His experiences at Chichester, however, had made him dissatisfied with the traditional hole-in-the-wall stage that the Old Vic then offered. He insisted that the stage should be thrust forward into the auditorium, a procedure that was both expensive to achieve and involved the sacrifice of a number of seats. Still worse, the change damaged the acoustics. "It was my fault," Olivier admitted. "I brought the stage forward one too many times. I ruined it. It used to have the best sound in the world."[3]

Even Olivier had to accept that he could not conduct the whole operation single-handed. For his principal support he hoped to enlist the driving force at the Royal Court, George Devine. Devine was only three years younger than Olivier; since his spectacular breakthrough with *Look Back in Anger* he had transformed the Royal Court into one of the most innovative and successful companies in the British theater; he felt no urge to embark on this new enterprise under the command of someone else. "We were like partners, we were never like rivals," protested Olivier. "I could have provided a formula that would have included him." Joan Plowright thinks that it could have worked, that the two men were sufficiently mature and respectful toward each other to have established a modus operandi. Olivier would have tried, but it is hard to see how the two men could for long have lasted in uneasy partnership. "He felt he couldn't work under Larry," said Devine's widow, and whatever arrangements might have been cobbled up, this in effect is what would have had to happen.[4]

Instead, according to Olivier with Devine's approval and certainly with his acquiescence, Olivier proceeded to poach the Royal Court's brilliant young directors: William Gaskill and John Dexter. Their appointment was a striking affirmation of the way he intended the National Theater to develop; it represented a rejection of the traditional ways of the old classical theater and an acceptance of the new world into which he himself had ventured with *The Entertainer*. Dexter accepted the invitation with alacrity; Gaskill took rather more persuading—he wanted assurances that the National would put an emphasis on modern work—but allowed himself to be convinced without too much difficulty. "We were tremendously excited and flattered," Gaskill remembered. At one point a formal relationship between the National Theater and the Royal Court was envisaged. The Drama Committee of the National Theater considered the issue and the Board was told that the Director "thought it would be advantageous if some link could be formed with an organization so intimately linked with the younger school of dramatists." A press release later that year announced that the two bodies would cooperate in certain fields, such as the training of young actors and the commissioning of new plays. In fact the traffic seems to have been mainly one way. As well as Gaskill and Dexter, the National was to recruit several of the Royal Court's most promising young actors as well as to invite dramatists who had first written for the Court to produce work for the National. Relations remained harmonious, though, and when something close to open warfare existed between the National Theater and the Royal Shakespeare Company it was reassuring to know that an ally was at hand in Sloane Square.[5]

In taking on Gaskill and Dexter Olivier was well aware that he was welcoming to the National two young directors who were not only used to working together but had ideas different from his own that they would not hesitate to promote. He accepted the incipient challenge with equanimity. "I was determined to surround myself with good actors and first-rate directors," he wrote. "I wanted people who were prepared to outgun me. I wanted the cream of the British theater, and I think I got it." So far as the directors were concerned this was true. Gaskill and Dexter were not given a free hand, but they enjoyed a high degree of independence and their views were canvassed and taken into account on most important issues. When it came to the actors it was not quite so clear-cut. Olivier did not relish competition. The British stage was littered with corpses of those who had tried to outgun Olivier and had perished for their pains. He was disinclined to give too much space to those few whom he saw as genuine or even potential rivals. But he was eager to bring forward young actors of promise who had a career to make, and he rejoiced in their success. He was resolved that the National Theater should provide the best dramatic performances in the world: for this he would need the best actors and to engage them was his resolve.[6]

He was determined that the National should not become a repository for actors who were past their prime or, at least, seemed to have little potential for new development left within them. To achieve this he was obliged to disappoint and sometimes offend many veterans who had served with him in the past. At least a hundred times he used a formula designed to keep petitioners at bay: "Even now plans long made persist in crumbling and fate will insist that we continue to find ourselves at Square One in a most aggravating and frustrating way." It seems unlikely that this meaningless mantra was of much consolation to the rejected, but Olivier convinced himself that it possessed almost mystic qualities and would appease even the most demanding applicant. It was soon apparent to him that the ability to say "No," whether gracefully or gracelessly, was going to be a most important weapon in his armory. Timothy Bateson, who had played quite important roles at Chichester, took it for granted that he would be invited to join the National. To his dismay he was passed over. "Obviously he [Olivier] had decided to associate himself with the contemporary Royal Court influence," he wrote sadly.

In spite of, or perhaps because of, his long association with Olivier, Roger Furse too was dropped. This "very much hurt him," thought Derek Granger, though, to judge by an amicable exchange of letters some years later, no lasting harm was done to the friendship. Some important actors were rejected too: John Mills, though an old and close friend, was told there would be no place for him at the National because—a not entirely convincing reason—the theater could not afford him; while Rex Harrison, much less of a friend, was turned down on the grounds that Olivier, "for the sake of the *amour propre* of the company," wished only very rarely to disturb a working ensemble by introducing stars from another sphere. Mills seems to have borne no grudge at his rejection; Harrison, either for this or for some other reason, saw Olivier as an enemy. "A stupid bastard, obsessed by *folie de grandeur*," he described him.[7]

Of the first group of actors Olivier picked, four, among them Joan Plowright and Robert Stephens, were associated with the Royal Court; two—Maggie Smith and Max Adrian—had established a name for themselves in revue, and two—Michael Redgrave and Diana Wynyard—were established stars. There was nothing strikingly innovative about this selection, nor about the bright young novices in their twenties—Anthony Hopkins, Michael Gambon, Derek Jacobi—whom Olivier picked from the plethora of talent that washed around the National Theater. As Michael Billington has pointed out, it would be extravagant to argue that Olivier, "with his instinctive patriotism and actor-manager paternalism," was in any way a revolutionary figure. But nevertheless he chose to reject not merely his own past but a large part of London's theatrical establishment. He ventured into terrain which, if not unexplored, was unfamiliar. And every appointment was *his* appointment. Anthony Hopkins, when his turn came to audition, was excited to find that Olivier was very much in charge of the operation and surprised how ordinary he looked, "very average in his horn-rimmed glasses and three-piece suit." Having seen Olivier playing Othello the night before he rather daringly offered the deathbed scene. "You've got a bloody nerve," remarked Olivier. He helped himself to a cigarette: "I'm terribly sorry," he said. "I'm so nervous in case you're better than me." This was, thought Hopkins, "his charming way of trying to relax me." Evidently it worked. After the piece was finished Olivier said: "Well done. I don't think I'll lose any sleep tonight, but I think you were awfully good. Would you like to join the Company?" By May 1963 the company had been selected prior to the opening in October. The Board was told that, as well as those mentioned above, a contract had been signed with Peter O'Toole. "It was agreed that the above, together with Sir Laurence himself, formed the nucleus of an excellent company."[8]

Of equal interest were the names of those who were not on the list. The only stars who could be mentioned in the same breath as Olivier were Michael Redgrave and Peter O'Toole. Where were John Gielgud, Ralph Richardson, Paul Scofield? It has often been claimed that Olivier willfully excluded from the National Theater those whom he considered to be his rivals. There is some truth in the allegation, but it is far from being the whole story. Ralph Richardson is the most interesting case. When he played John Gabriel Borkman at the National in 1975, after Olivier's departure, Harold Hobson wrote of his "angry grief that the Ibsen production, in all its splendor, should be Sir Ralph's first appearance in a National Theater that has already existed for more than a decade." The clear implication of this sentence was that Richardson had been kept out of a theater in which he would have loved to play. Yet the blame was not Olivier's alone. He could reasonably claim to have been discouraged by Richardson's response when he had been asked to play Lear at Chichester. "I am extremely grateful for your kind and magnanimous and too flattering thought," wrote Richardson. "Can I have time to think about this? You are so bold . . . Let your timorous friend turn this thought of yours over in his mind." The timorous friend duly did so and decided against the venture. When the action moved to the National, Richardson told his biographer, he was only offered dull roles—"odd dukes and the like." In fact he was offered Halvard Solness in *The Master Builder*, Claudius in *Hamlet* and Hobson in *Hobson's Choice*: not a dull duke among them and all subsequently played by Michael Redgrave. The reason for his refusal is to be found not in the dullness of the roles but in the relationship between the two men. "I was always happy with him on an equal basis," said Richardson, "but I wasn't very happy with him as the boss . . . he was schoolmastery, you know. 'Come to my office,' he'd say." The result was that Richardson not merely did not respond enthusiastically to any overtures but was discouraging in his attitude. Yet Olivier was by no means innocent. He admitted that he had not pressed his friend very hard. "I was a little shy of asking him because, obviously, if I was the Director, it put him in a slightly less right position in the public mind . . . I never went on about it very much. I said 'Would you like to play . . .' two or three things, I think, in the whole time I was there." The guilt, if guilt there was, seems to have been divided. As a result, the two men drifted apart. "I do wish I could see something of you," Olivier wrote a few years later. "My job seems to get more and more intricate and testing—I enjoy it, of course, but there is very little life apart." Ronald Harwood asked Richardson whether he still saw a lot of Olivier. "No, he only telephones me to ask for other people's numbers," was the terse reply.[9]

John Gielgud, too, said that he was "a bit hurt" at being offered so few important parts. Olivier admittedly was slow to approach him but when he did so he seems to have been at pains to dispel any feeling of rejection on Gielgud's part. In mid-1964 he wrote to stress "how overjoyed I would be . . . if you would ever like to consider working for us at the National." He should, he admitted, have made this clear much earlier, but if Gielgud had thought his silence indicated lack of interest it would be "not only tragic but utterly wrong. So please, dear Johnnie, if . . . you find yourself in possession of an idea you would like to present to us, I should be overjoyed to hear about it . . . To be perfectly frank with you, the National Theater earnestly needs your stature."[10]

John Dexter suggested Shylock. Gielgud replied that he had failed in the part in 1938 and saw no reason why he should do better now. "I remember thinking it was marvelous," retorted Olivier—and, anyway, he would hate to be judged by his own Macbeth of the same season. Gielgud was not convinced, nor was he any more enthusiastic about a suggestion that he should play Antony to Irene Worth's Cleopatra. "Johnnie feels, with good reason I think," Olivier told Worth, "that he does not wish to be hurried into something for any expedient reason, which means unless he feels dead right in the part . . . he does *not* want to be made to look or feel however slightly miscast." When finally Gielgud found something to his taste— Orgon, in Molière's *Tartuffe* and the Oedipus of Seneca—Olivier was, or at least professed to be, ecstatic: "I wish I could tell you how enraptured not only I, but all in the conclave, feel about your blessing the National with your presence." As with Richardson, it seems that the worst Olivier can be accused of is not pressing the point with sufficient urgency and vehemence. Even against this charge he has a good defense.[11]

So far as Paul Scofield's recruitment for the National was concerned, Olivier is even less guilty. "I am burningly desirous that you should be attached to the National Theater," Olivier told him. He would be welcome as a guest star, "but guest stars, nice as they are, are things that I don't feel altogether happy about in relation to the National." Would he not become a permanent member of the establishment? Scofield too was offered Antony and Shylock, and rejected both. In the end he was coaxed into the company as an associate director. Did Olivier believe that Scofield might eventually succeed him as Director? asked *The Times*. They had never discussed the matter, said Olivier, but he was sure "if it was a job Mr. Scofield wanted to do, he would do it well." The possibility, if it had ever existed, disappeared when Scofield flounced out with only two of his three designated plays performed. Olivier accepted the blame for the contretemps: "I know I cannot have been a v. satisfactory partner," he wrote. "If a man carries a load a bit too heavy for him, his condition perhaps makes him sparing of courtesies to his friends." Even then he stressed how much he hoped that the association would be renewed: "It would be ghastly if I really thought you could turn your back on us for good." He may indeed have been brusque or tactless but Scofield was at least as much to blame. Peter Hall, for one, is convinced that Scofield always found professional relationships hard to sustain and never gave his association with the National a reasonable chance. He was to do the same thing a few years later—walking out on Hall at the last minute with a cursory "Sorry to let you down."[12]

Letters do not tell the whole story: so much can be conveyed by timing, expression, tone of voice. Olivier can justifiably be accused of a certain lack of enthusiasm when it came to promoting the careers of those few people he looked upon as rivals. But he did not try to deny Richardson, Gielgud and Scofield access to the National Theater. On the contrary, he made more than token efforts to welcome them aboard. He was anxious for the National not only to succeed but to succeed spectacularly. His prestige as an actor might be somewhat diminished if one of his great contemporaries outshone him on the stage; the National Theater would be the more glorious. Olivier was no fool and he knew that in the end this would redound to his greater credit.

Gaskill and Dexter were another matter. Both were talented, strong-minded and capable, with ideas of their own. It was certain that they would clash with Olivier; the only questions were, how soon, and whether they would be able to work out a *modus operandi* that would satisfy both sides in the partnership. Gaskill was the more likely to fall out with his Director: he was a theorist, an ardent Brechtian, who longed to establish an acting team that would work together in total harmony, solving each problem by democratic discussion and shunning the vulgar appeal of the "star." In practice, of course, he was himself capable of imposing his will with the most autocratic rigor and had a shrewd idea of what would appeal to an audience, but he managed to invest all his activities with an aura of Brechtian purity. He urged the use of masks in rehearsal and encouraged improvisation in the early stages of a production. Olivier disliked what he held to be meretricious gimmickry, but he gritted his teeth and put up with it when Gaskill was the director and he the actor. He gallantly joined in the improvisation when Gaskill directed *The Recruiting Officer*: "I think he hated it," wrote Gaskill, "but he didn't show it." It was perhaps fortunate from the point of view of their relationship that George Devine died suddenly two years or so after the National Theater had started and Gaskill retreated to take over at the Royal Court. "I loved him [Olivier]," Gaskill told Derek Granger. "I can't understand why, for he was a sod really . . . The two years at the Old Vic were, I think, the happiest working period of my life."[13]

Dexter was more down-to-earth, less ruled by principle, but he shared the same ideals and ideas. He was rough, gruff and defiantly outrageous, with a sharp tongue and a ferocious wit. Less doctrinaire than Gaskill, he was no less effective as a director: he had a reputation for being sadistic and could be harsh and exacting, but the results were formidable. Olivier was one of the few people whom he respected, but even the Director was sometimes treated with less than deference. When rehearsing *Othello* on tour in Birmingham Dexter was enraged by what he thought a slovenly performance and berated the whole cast, Olivier included. Olivier drew him aside, "I won't have you speaking to my company like that," he said. "*Your* company?" Dexter retorted. "I thought this was the National Theater." The relationship survived that episode but grew progressively more edgy and in the end broke down altogether.[14]

There was another man in at the birth of the National Theater who was quite as influential as either of the two directors. Kenneth Tynan was acknowledged to be the leading theater critic of his day: brilliantly witty—sometimes too much so, since the temptation to indulge in a telling phrase from time to time got the better of his balanced judgment; well informed about the theater in half a dozen countries; with the ability to evoke the atmosphere of a play so that the reader almost felt that he had been in the stalls himself. His influence was enormous: a good review from him could make a play successful, a bad review do it irreparable harm. To Olivier he was above all the critic who had consistently ridiculed and belittled Vivien Leigh; the fact that he had also praised Olivier in the most lavish terms mitigated but did not altogether excuse his offense. He sometimes drew near the frontiers of absurdity—languid, affected, epicene—but he was nevertheless a figure of real importance: "When the history of the theater in the twentieth century comes to be written," said Jonathan Miller, "Tynan's role in giving back to the theater an image of its own importance, without in fact being self-important, will be recognized as both distinct and crucial."[15]

Tynan now proposed that he should join the National as "dramaturge"—an ill-defined role that would involve him in most aspects of the National's affairs but particularly in the selection of the plays that were to be put on. Olivier's first reaction was to reject the overture in the most offensive terms. Joan Plowright urged him to think again; to rebuff Tynan would be to turn him into an inveterate and dangerous enemy. To welcome him would be to affirm that the National Theater was going to be, not a conservative and traditional repository of outworn values but innovative, daring, striding boldly into the future. Besides, Olivier needed someone like Tynan, who would be a fount of new ideas and, with his encyclopedic knowledge of European theater, would open up a world that otherwise would remain closed or shrouded in mystery. Olivier reflected and was persuaded. "I think that your suggestion is an admirable one, a most welcome one, and—" stretching the limits of credulity rather further than even Tynan would have accepted—"one that I'd thought of myself already." At the bottom of his letter he scrawled in manuscript: "God—*anything* to get you off that *Observer*."[16]

Over the next ten years Olivier was from time to time to doubt the wisdom of his decision. Tynan combined prickly arrogance with oversensitivity. Olivier constantly found himself soothing injured feelings. "I felt conscious that I might have seemed to be leaving you out in the cold once or twice in my talks to the boys," he wrote—"the boys" being Gaskill and Dexter. "I am sorry for that. I *was* a bit too exhausted to manage things with proper smoothness." But Tynan himself was no respecter of the feelings of others. He was a mischief-maker and an intriguer, never happier than when stirring up trouble among his colleagues. He would express his opinions with alarming frankness and with indifference to other people's sensibilities. His progresses around the offices of the National Theater were marked by a series of vituperative rows. After one damaging escapade Olivier felt bound to write: "I like you. I like having you with me . . . But you can be too fucking tactless for words." He urged Tynan "to be a little quicker in letting me have your thoughts and a little slower in imparting them to others." But such rebukes were rare; on the whole he put up with Tynan's troublemaking with an equanimity that astonished those who had experienced his impatience and short temper.[17]

Not everyone felt Tynan was worthy of such indulgence. John Osborne, for instance, detected "a sort of intellectual spivery that Olivier mistakes for up-to-date awareness and flair. He's so afraid of being thought old hat that he's allowed himself to be sadly misguided by Tynan." Undoubtedly Tynan could be pretentious and sometimes silly, but on the whole his contribution was invaluable. Not merely was his knowledge enormous and his taste usually sound, he understood how a theater worked, he could see when a cut was needed or the pace was being allowed to flag, he could envisage not just a suitable choice of play but a package—play, director, designer, actors, and how to present it to the public. He was a versatile and skillful wordsmith who could formulate Olivier's inchoate concepts and put them into phrases that were both clear and telling. Olivier was right to take him on and, though the price was sometimes high, right to retain him when in due course the Board revolted against his rebarbative and gadfly presence.[18]

Osborne was correct, however, in thinking that Olivier was overawed by what he saw as Tynan's intellectual superiority. When Tynan was appointed, Cedric Hardwicke sent him a telegram of congratulation, ending: "Don't be too intellectual." "Is Larry an intellectual?" queried Tynan. "No, but he wants to be," was the reply. He did indeed want to be, but he considered that a university education was a prerequisite and that the chance was therefore lost forever. He had read little, and though he felt no urge to remedy the deficiency, he felt ill at ease in literary circles. When he was asked by a Miss Jepson to contribute to a collection of tributes to Max Beerbohm he confessed that the request filled him with shame. "It is true that I am a Maximilian, but it is also certain that I am by far the least qualified to be a member of that worthy throng . . . My knowledge and appreciation of his works is of the skimpiest and most unenlightened." When Miss Jepson responded by sending him a copy of Beerbohm's *Around Theaters* he appealed to his secretary to produce "a v. nice letter that I can copy out." It is unlikely that he ever opened the book. He did not always suffer intellectuals gladly, having the perception to realize that some of them were fools. He apologized to Tynan for having been off-hand with a visiting Italian: "There is nothing so depressing to a nonintellectual like me than his particular brand of mysterioso. I get terribly bored by . . . trying to look knowing when the reverse is true." But more often a reputation for being an intellectual inspired respect if not reverence. "You're so much cleverer than I am," he would say to his son Richard, meaning that Richard had been to university and so was supposedly better equipped to argue a case or to draw the right conclusion from some data.[19]

When intellectuals disagreed, Olivier had to choose between them. Gaskill and Dexter believed the Berliner Ensemble—the immensely influential company established by Bertolt Brecht in 1949—to represent the pinnacle of repertory theater. The Ensemble demanded a company without stars, or perhaps more correctly, a company containing nothing but stars, meshed together in practiced fluency. Of course, some people would have to play larger parts than others, but it was the team that counted. Tynan believed in stars, whether from within the company or from outside it: big names that would attract big audiences. Though the gulf between the two points of view might seem insuperable, in practice it usually made little difference: decisions were taken on the basis of the needs of the day and of the actors and actresses who happened to be available. It was all very well to urge the merits of a coherent ensemble that would operate as a permanent unit with no concern for the

ambitions of the individual—Joan Littlewood almost brought it off
in the Theater Workshop—but a company the size of the National
Theater could not be staffed by automata and few actors are without personal ambition. Gaskill complained that Maggie Smith, for
example, "kept going off to make films." She was not alone. "Gradually the company gets watered down to people who are less than
adequate. And that's the problem. You can never have a large-scale
true ensemble." The result, as Olivier had known it would be from
the start, was a compromise. Gaskill thought that too much was
lost as a result. It was "a spurious kind of ensemble" that didn't even
have "the glamour of old-fashioned actor-manager theater about it."
Olivier thought it worked and did not concern himself too much
about the issues of principle that lay behind it.[20]

He was emphatic in rejecting any form of a "house style." Again
with the Berliner Ensemble in mind Gaskill and Dexter hankered
after a uniformity of approach which, whatever the play, would make
the identity of the company instantly apparent. To the argument that
this required the genius of some superman like Stanislavsky, Gaskill
retorted that Stanislavskys did not spring fully-fashioned from their
mother's womb but grew with their job: only if the National Theater
adopted the true faith would a British Stanislavsky have the chance of
achieving greatness. Tynan argued that the National's repertoire was
too extensive and its staff too fluid to make any such rigidity conceivable, let along desirable. Here Olivier came down on Tynan's side. "I
wouldn't have allowed a house style," he declared. "You must find a
style for each play, I said, right from the beginning. There's not even
a National Theater Shakespearean style. I'm sure there is in almost all
other countries in Europe, but I have a prejudice against it."[21]

The key members of the personnel were designated or in place; the
venue had been chosen; the issues of principle had been aired if not
resolved: it remained to put on some plays.

CHAPTER EIGHTEEN

THE NATIONAL: ACT TWO

"I'm so glad you're still bossing Chichester," his sister Sybille told Olivier in July 1963. "This concentration thing is the very devil, I know. But you *have* it, alright." He needed every bit of it. The year 1963 was bad enough, with the first production at the National Theater scheduled to begin in October, but 1964 promised to be almost impossible. By 1963 he had given up any pretense that the Chichester Festival existed in its own right. "I quite deliberately created that second Chichester company for the National," he admitted. Evershed-Martin was, or professed to be, content with this arrangement but was put out when it seemed that, even if the average performance played to a house that was three-quarters full, there might be a loss of 9,000 on the season. That would cost the guarantors £1,000 each: "While some could well afford it others, like myself, could not." Olivier made soothing noises and in fact the season ended without a loss, but the goodwill that had reigned during the first season was wearing thin. It wore still thinner when the Chichester Board was offered only two seats for the opening night of the National Theater. "With the proposed close link between us and the National, I should have thought it would have been a common courtesy to have offered all members of our Board seats for the occasion," wrote an affronted James Battersby. The suggestion that the Board members should ballot for their seats was a sign of "unnecessary indifference." There were simply not enough seats to go round, pleaded a spokesman for the National; even members of the National Theater Board had had to ballot for tickets. Battersby was not appeased.[1]

So far it was a question of *amour propre*. When it became clear
that, in the 1964 season, Olivier was so preoccupied by his National
duties that he could devote relatively little time to Chichester,
Evershed-Martin took alarm. "I doubt if you could possibly realize
how much your actual presence during the last two seasons has created a feeling of trust and confidence in everybody that Chichester
was of importance in the theatrical world," he told Olivier. If Olivier
did not play in at least one of the productions it would have disastrous results for the box office and for the prestige of the whole Festival: "Please, Larry, this is terribly important to me and all of those
with me." He would do his best, Olivier promised; at the moment
the prospects looked good. In the event he managed to give them
a month of *Othello*. But even by his standards the burden was too
much. Early in 1965 he resigned, pleading the impossible pressure
of life at the National Theater. "The simple truth is that I have done
all that I can, and I can do no more," he wrote to Evershed-Martin.
"At least we have all got something on the map of English life, something that has been absolutely accepted into the landscape."[2]

The letter seemed to set the scene for a loving farewell, but things
went downhill in 1965. Olivier had recommended John Clements
as his successor, but Clements would not be available till the end of
the year. Olivier remained nominally in charge, but in fact acted in
nothing and paid little attention to what was going on. The company
became so worried by the lack of direction that they telephoned
John Dexter, who was in New York, and pleaded with him to come
back and take charge. To add injury to insult they used the phone
in Olivier's room at a cost of £62. Olivier was outraged. According to Robert Stephens, he gave them "the most terrible bollocking,
language you never thought existed . . . He played every single part
you've ever seen him play, from Heathcliff to Henry V, shouting
in that rasping tenor voice." Stephens admitted that it was he who
had called Dexter. "'You cunt!' Olivier screamed. 'You cunt!' I really
thought he was going to kill me. He was totally out of control."[3]

That final year soured Olivier's memories of Chichester and its
governing Board. "They are the stupidest bunch of people I ever

had to work with in my life," he said. "I was very unkind to them. I never asked the Board what I should do, I told them what I was going to do." He maligned both the Board and himself: for most of the time they worked in harmony. At the time of his resignation he told the General Manager, Pieter Rogers, that they could look at each other "with a special glow of parenthood in our eyes, for between us we have brought [a] child of some significance [into being], and at four years old it looks to be a very bonny one too." He never ceased to take a benevolent if distant interest in what he held to be his personal creation.[4]

When, several years later, Topol was enlisted to play in *The Caucasian Chalk Circle*, Olivier and Joan Plowright sent him a telegram: "Dear Hymie. Nobody ever died rich who played at Chichester. Loving wishes." Certainly Olivier did not grow rich at Chichester, nor did his salary at the National Theater enable him to support his growing family and considerable commitments. To supplement his income—and also because he enjoyed it—he slipped occasional films into his already bursting schedule. In the summer of 1965 he and Noël Coward together joined the cast of *Bunny Lake is Missing*, an inconsiderable thriller, directed by Otto Preminger, about a child who mysteriously disappears. Olivier was satisfied by his part—"it was perfectly alright"—but detested Preminger. "He's the most awful kind of German there can be," he once remarked. "He is a Nazi Jew; there can be nothing in the world more awful than that mixture." The comment is of some interest as being the nearest Olivier is recorded as having come to anti-Semitism. In general he was free of racial prejudice. If he discovered that a colleague was Jewish, or for that matter Bolivian or Bulgarian, he would have considered it a matter of mild interest but no great importance— not a reason for liking or disliking him. The only complaint he had about Jews was their readiness to take offense at an imagined slight. A Jewish friend complained that a line in *Caesar and Cleopatra* could be construed as anti-Semitic. "I have in my own heart nothing but fondness for the Jewish race," Olivier protested, "and have never been able to distinguish it in my thoughts from any other. All breeds of mankind have their faults and the only one that ever spurs me to a feeling of regret in the Jewish race is this kind of sensibility."[5]

Preminger had offended him by fawning on him and Coward and bullying the junior members of the cast. In fact, if anyone needed to be bullied, it was Olivier himself. He was not at his best. "Poor Larry had a dreadful time with his lines," noted Anna Massey. "They were full of details of bus times and probing *non sequiturs*. We ended up doing extremely short takes. He felt defeated." For Olivier to feel defeated was something so unusual as to cause real concern, to his fellow actors and, still more, to himself. Later the same year, when he filmed the Chichester/National Theater *Othello*, he admitted "it was a very tired performance. I was retreating a bit from the big moments and I shouldn't have." The pressure seemed to be telling to a point where it was undermining his acting.[6]

Yet always he had something in reserve. In the six months between, when he seemed to be close to succumbing to exhaustion, he contrived to produce on the stage at the Old Vic an *Othello* that was one of the highest spots in his anyway mountainous career.

As Evershed-Martin had realized, in Olivier's mind *everything* was subordinate to the National Theater. He had to produce from scratch, not just a company that would be capable of acting a vast range of contemporary and classical drama, but also an organization that would sustain that company, provide the theater and facilities, draw in the audiences, promote the productions. It was the work of the traditional actor-manager but conducted on an industrial scale. And on top of that, he had to play a primary role in the planning and building of the new theater to which the company would move in the distant but, it was hoped, not too distant future.

The Old Vic provided an adequate auditorium, but it did not have the office space required for such an enterprise. Nothing too lavish could be afforded for what would be only temporary occupation, but economy was carried almost to the point of absurdity. The headquarters of Britain's National Theater, in Aquinas Street, was a gaggle of squalid prefabricated huts ten minutes' walk from the theater through an unsavory and crowded slum. The ceilings were low, the windows tiny; it was too cold in winter, too hot in summer; the walls between the cramped rooms were so thin that when Olivier was in full cry his voice could be heard in all the nearby offices. To operate efficiently in such surroundings was a challenge; to sustain morale a testing problem; to create an atmosphere of passionate enthusiasm in which every difficulty was an incentive for greater effort rather than a reason for discouragement was something of a miracle. That miracle was Olivier's—not Olivier's alone, for no man could conduct such an operation single-handed, but one that could never have been brought about without his leadership and inspiration.[7]

"Leadership" is one of the most indefinable of qualities. It is to command loyalty, to make people feel that they belong, that they are part of a team, that they must do their best not just for their own good but for the sake of their colleagues who are also doing *their* best. In the armed services, where men must be expected to risk their lives in a common enterprise, it is above all essential, but it is also relatively easy to provide because soldiers, sailors and airmen have been taught from the moment they joined their service that they are part of an entity that is far greater than the sum of its parts. Actors, though they too have been trained to operate as a team, are the most individual of creatures. Every instinct tells them that they must assert themselves, make their own mark, establish their own public persona. The spirit of the hive depends for its potency on the docility and self-discipline of the bee; when every bee is different, every bee anxious to do its own thing, every bee quite ready to use its sting to protect its individual interests, the role of the queen becomes peculiarly difficult.

Olivier brought it off. "The way in which he led that little band in Aquinas Street is something I'll remember all my life," wrote Jonathan Miller. "He set a standard of leadership that no one can even *hope* to emulate." Ronald Pickup, another of the young men who rose to glory under Olivier, talks of the "incredible company spirit" which reigned at the Old Vic. One could cite a dozen such tributes. It was achieved by a conscious effort on Olivier's part; he could not have explained how he did it, but he knew he was doing it. In a way it was an act: Olivier the all-encompassing Director was as much a creation of his will and skill as Olivier playing Othello or Olivier playing Astrov. Yet it was an act that found its inspiration in his love for the Company, his pride in the Company, his conviction that the National Theater was, and must continue to be, the greatest company in the world. "It was the most beautiful thing, running a Company," he later said. His resolve to make this true was his inspiration, transformed him into another being, more intense, more passionate. When he was off duty, when there was nobody whom he needed to inspire, it was as if a light had been turned down; with other members of the company it blazed extravagantly.[8]

His success depended on his ability not just to communicate with the company as a whole, but to relate to every member of it. "His real quality is as a great leader," considered Edward Hardwicke. "He worked on a kind of instinctive thing; within seconds he seemed to be able to tell what people were going to do or not going to do. It's a very special quality; it's not something you acquire, you either have it or you don't." The ability to empathize was in fact not something with which Olivier was well endowed. He was himself so strong a personality that his instinct was to try to transform those with whom he had dealings rather than to understand and to work with them, seeking thus to divert them in the direction he wished them to go. His interest in the workings of other people's minds was limited. Tynan remembered trying to engage him in a conversation about his relationship with another member of the company. Olivier's eyes glazed over. When Tynan had finished, he said merely: "I wonder if I should get a new Daimler or a converted London taxi." Anything that involved emotional relationships, Tynan noticed, Olivier would shy away from. Gaskill felt the same. It wasn't that Olivier was cold or unemotional, he felt, but it was not realistic, just because he was a great actor, to expect him also to be "a man of great feeling and emotional depth. Not many actors are." But though there might be little emotional rapport, on a professional level the meeting of minds was total. Olivier understood what the young actor wanted as well as he knew it himself, and knew too how best that object could be achieved.[9]

The grander you are, the more your attentions are appreciated. A friendly nod from the Queen is worth half an hour's obsequious flattery from a court flunkey. Olivier was theatrical royalty and he did not have to do very much to win the hearts of the underlings at the National. What he did, though, he did with style and generosity. "He was always courteous to us understudies, walk-ons and one-liners," remembered Peter Jolley. "When I appeared for the rehearsals for *Eden End* he took the trouble to welcome me and introduce me to everyone." How far this sprang from a genuine interest in the young and how far it was done for the sake of public relations is a question that he never asked himself and could not have answered if he had. Simon Callow, who as well as being one of the most distinguished actors of his generation is also an intelligent and perceptive writer on the theater, can see both sides of the question. "Olivier surrounded himself with the very best of the younger generation," he wrote in one book, "he carefully modeled their careers, noting what challenges would most benefit them, giving advice and encouragement, teaching by example, leading from the front. They adored him, these young actors." "Olivier's National Theater was just that: organized by one man and what he stood for," was the verdict of the same author. "The company, as such, barely exists. The growth of the individual artist is not attended to in the least . . . Most of the company, far from slowly advancing through the ranks, decline in them, until finally they're out on the back doorstep with the rubbish."[10]

There is truth in both judgments. Olivier was Olympian, imposing his vision on the company with scant attention to the needs or feelings of individuals. He was also intensely human, liking to be liked, concerned about the needs of lesser mortals. "He was the perfect guide and mentor for all young actors," remembered Robert Stephens, "because while he was palpably *primus inter pares* he was also one of us . . . He rehearsed with us and he ate with us in the staff canteen . . . Larry knew and understood what made us tick, and helped you whenever he could. Which, usually, was always." Many are the junior members of the company who, while grabbing a rapid lunch in the canteen, were disconcerted and delighted to find a rather undistinguished-looking and bespectacled middle-aged man settle beside them and to realize that God had come down to earth.[11]

"You can't be too scrupulous," said Olivier when describing the problems of running a great theater. "You can't be too kind . . . You don't play for popularity." He *did* play for popularity, and when he had to be unkind he drowned the medicine under so thick a layer of treacle that the victim was left with a vague sense of gratitude for the trouble that had been taken. "Darling girl, I think we'll have to let you go," he told Billie Whitelaw. "We simply have nothing suitable to offer you, nothing that's worthy of you. I think you should now extend your career and expand your talent. It's been so marvelous working with you." She left, thinking how lucky she was to have so considerate a boss and how concerned he was about her career. Even when it was pointed out to her that she had just been fired she remained grateful. "He inspired hero-worship and genuine professional admiration in all of us."[12]

"Professional" is the most important word in that sentence. Olivier was above all determined that everything should be done to the highest professional standards, sloppy amateurism outraged him in anything to do with the theater and above all in any aspect of the National's activities. He felt it was essential that actors should be fit; he gave them full-time access to a gymnasium and set an example by himself working out with singular ferocity. He wanted the best acting voices in the world, so he employed a full-time voice coach available to all who needed her. He believed actors should eat, not lavishly, but well; the cafeteria was more likely to provide fruit, salad, cheese and milk than hamburgers and beer. The Liaison Committee at the National Theater dealt with issues of programming and training, but also such matters as the state of the cafeteria, the heating, whether men should clean the ladies' lavatory, whether table tennis should be played in the Old Vic rehearsal room. Olivier was more likely to attend its meetings than he was meetings of the Main Board. At the last meeting of the Liaison Committee that he attended it was minuted "that the Company wished him to know that they were currently a happy Company." He would have asked for no better farewell.[13]

"We were his other family," Ronald Pickup told Joan Plowright after Olivier's death, "and I know that is why people who were not part of the National Theater when he was the Guv'nor envy our blessed fortune and long to participate in glorious tales of the days of Olivier at the Old Vic." Nobody but he could have done it; Peter Hall, when in due course he took over, did not even try. In a sense Olivier was already past his time. "It is impossible for a catalog of reasons," wrote Richard Eyre, "that we will ever see again a great buccaneering actor-manager who is also a Hollywood film star, who is equally celebrated in the theater, and who is capable of remaking his life and his art so often and so judiciously." Olivier carried into the world of complex organizations, international financing, governmental subventions, health and safety, the spirit of the individual adventurer, the one-man band. It was not a one-man band in the sense that only one man counted, it was not even a one-man band in the sense that Olivier was autocratic, but it was a one-man band in the sense that it was Olivier's National Theater and bore the stamp of his personality in every facet of its being. When he boasted that, but for him, there would have been no National Theater, he pitched his claim too high. But what is certain is that, but for him, the National Theater that Peter Hall inherited would have been a lesser and very different place.[14]

CHAPTER NINETEEN

THE NATIONAL: ACT THREE

If one is launching a new theater company, should one ease it into existence by choosing something lightweight for its first production or go straight for the jackpot? If one is Olivier, it would be the jackpot every time. It was Peter O'Toole who first put the choice of *Hamlet* into his head. He called on Olivier and asked him to be the director of a production of *Hamlet* which he was planning. Olivier countered with the offer that *Hamlet*, with O'Toole playing the lead, should be the first production of the National Theater. If he had not committed himself in this way it is at least possible that he would have cast himself in the main part of whatever play was chosen: as it was he settled for director. But for the National Theater to feature in its first production an internationally famous film star, who had only recently achieved vast success in *Lawrence of Arabia*, called for some explanation. "This is a special engagement and rather outside our general policy," Olivier wrote apologetically to Tyrone Guthrie. "This policy concerns itself with a hoped-for permanent ensemble (the old, old yearning), such an ensemble not to have its nose put out of joint by the invitation of outside stars except on very rare occasions, the sales talk being that, in the beautiful future, to be a National Theater player is to be a star."[1]

Special engagement or not, it did not get the National off to an easy start. Olivier as director was at his most authoritarian. He told O'Toole, "I know my way about the map of *Hamlet* much more than you can possibly do," and proceeded to dictate not just the route that should be followed but the precise pace that should be set and every stopping place along the way. "He tried to make O'Toole act Hamlet as he, Olivier, would have done," remembered William Gaskill. During rehearsals—apart from the fact that the revolve, which had been installed at great expense, developed a personality of its own, refusing to budge when needed and, even more disconcertingly, revolving when it should have been stationary—all seemed to be going well. Olivier convinced himself that O'Toole was going to do everything that was asked of him.[2]

The final dress rehearsal provided what Olivier claimed was "the most perfect performance of *Hamlet* I think I shall ever see." And then, when the first night came, in Olivier's eyes at least, all went wrong. O'Toole was influenced by "silly and impractical ideas," Olivier recollected. He took too slowly scenes through which he should have galloped, he indulged his emotions extravagantly. "He stripped himself stark naked and said: 'Look, I've got nothing left at all.' I felt so ashamed for the poor chap." Not many shared his opinion. Noël Coward thought O'Toole's Hamlet was "wonderful" and, though some critics felt that his rendering was not princely enough, on the whole his performance was well received. Olivier, however, convinced himself that his advice had been ignored and that disaster had ensued. He made his feelings very evident and O'Toole took offense. They parted acrimoniously. It seems that the breach took some time to heal. "Please stop behaving like a pompous, ill-mannered, resentful, tuppence-ha'penny failed politician," O'Toole wrote to Olivier some years later. It was not till 1971 that O'Toole invited Olivier to "bury the hatchet in my head" by taking part in some "cinematic entertainment." "This end of any hatchet buried and forgotten long ago," Olivier responded; but he still turned the offer down.[3]

The choice of *Hamlet* as the first production was a resounding statement that the National Theater was not going to leave Shakespeare to Stratford and considered itself responsible for sustaining all that was noblest in classical British drama. This could not be its sole or even principal raison d'être, however. Olivier realized that his choice of plays over the first year or two was going to shape the public's perception of the theater. He had given William Gaskill the impression that he was going to concentrate on modern works; primarily British, though with American and European plays added for good measure. When it came to the point, however, there were two Shakespeares, a Shaw, a Sophocles, an Ibsen, a Chekhov, Brighouse's *Hobson's Choice*, Farquhar's *The Recruiting Officer* and, thrown in presumably to satisfy Tynan, Max Frisch's *Andorra* and Samuel Beckett's one-act *Play*. It was an eclectic list that displayed the range and versatility of the new company but did not do much for contemporary British drama. The choice of the Beckett was adventurous and Olivier did not regret it. "Would you be interested in writing a full-length play for the National Theater?" he asked Beckett in 1965. "If so, we'd be delighted to commission it." He did not claim to be at one with the avant-garde, but he had an instinctive perception of quality and, while not really knowing what *Play* was about, knew that it was good. It was much the same with Harold Pinter. "I enjoy, in fact love, every line of Pinter as it falls on my ears," he told Pamela Berry, "but at the end of the evening I always dread someone asking me what the play's been about."[4]

Tynan was keen that the National Theater should engage a resident playwright who would work with the company and be guaranteed a living wage. Young dramatists, he said, at the moment tended to offer their work to the Royal Court or to some West End producer like Michael Codron. If the National were to offer one of them a contract it would be a bold affirmation that they could now look south of the Thames to further their careers. Olivier was skeptical. How would the theater choose whom to take on? "It's a very, very vexed question and needs a lot of thought and discussion"—in other words, certainly not. He accepted Tynan's thesis that it was part of the National's remit to encourage young British dramatists—it would not be too long before writers like Peter Shaffer and Tom Stoppard were seeing their work appear in the Old Vic—but he was determined that the prestige of the fledgling theater should not be undermined by putting on work that was ephemeral or second-rate.

Better to be cautious and perhaps miss an opportunity or two than to be rash and damage the reputation of the theater.[5]

If it had been possible he would have liked to direct or play a leading role in every production in the Old Vic, but he knew it could not be done: partly to respect the susceptibilities of other members of the company, still more because the burden on him, already almost too heavy to bear, would become unsustainable. He must ration himself, pick out only those plays in which he could make an important contribution, play roles that would contribute both to his own reputation and to the reputation of the theater. When Tynan suggested that he should play Othello he at first demurred. Othello was a bass part—whatever Verdi may have thought about it—and, as Wolfit had pointed out when Olivier had played Lear, he was a natural tenor. Othello needed to be, or at least needed to seem to be, of massive build; Olivier over the years had enormously strengthened his physique, but he was still not a big man. Then the sheer excitement of the challenge overcame him. "One day I thought: I'm going to fucking well get the voice. Most things like that are a question of concentration and repetition and exercise. . . . One always regards one's limitations in the light of techniques rather than of not being right for a part. I would never admit that I was wrong for any part." For six months he worked on his voice with a voice teacher from R.A.D.A., roaring like a bull, forcing it lower so that in the end Sybil Thorndike asked incredulously what magic he had been practicing. For six months he worked on his physique, building up his muscles so that he could swagger around the stage as the full-blooded black man he had resolved to be: "I must say I looked perfectly dandy as Othello. I looked like Othello should look."[6]

And Othello should look, he concluded, like a burly immigrant from Central Africa, or perhaps Jamaica. He had no use for the concept of a coffee-colored Moor, as Othello was conventionally portrayed—"I had to *be* black. I had to feel black down to my soul. I had to look out from a black man's world." He maintained that this was what Shakespeare had intended and his audience had expected; what else could phrases such as "old black ram" and "sooty bosom" signify? Few were convinced by his arguments. "What he gives us is a Notting Hill Gate negro," said Jonathan Miller, "and his portrait is made up of all the ludicrous liberal cliché attitudes toward negroes: beautiful skin, marvelous sense of rhythm, wonderful way of walking etc. . . . Shakespeare's Othello was a Moor, an Arab, and to emphasize his being *black* makes nonsense of the play." It was above all the "wonderful way of walking" which seduced Olivier and led him into what most people felt to be a successful yet self-indulgent irrelevance: for hours he studied the way a black man moved, he practiced endlessly, as he walked from office to office in Aquinas Street his colleagues would notice his self-consciously rolling gait, his exaggerated gestures. As Sybil Thorndike observed, it was a fascinating study of a member of an oppressed race. But Othello, she went on, was not a member of an oppressed race: "He was a Moor, a proud man, bigger than any of the whites in the play."[7]

An extra reason for Olivier's modeling himself upon a black man was that it gave him unequaled opportunities to indulge his passion for making up. Before beginning his preparations he inquired what makeup the Black and White Minstrels used. Max Factor's "Negro No. 2," he was told; this was easy to apply and to take off and was guaranteed not to dry the skin. Whether it was easy or difficult to use was of secondary concern to Olivier; he would have made any effort to achieve perfection. It took him three and a half hours to apply the makeup, with two coats applied to every part of his body irrespective of whether or not it would be visible on the stage. Another hour and a half was needed to take it off. Even his devoted dresser, who normally viewed his master with unquestioning devotion, felt that the enterprise was misguided; other members of the cast found it slightly comic—"How now, brown cow?" asked Maggie Smith, as she put her head round the door while he was making up. Olivier was indifferent to such caviling. The distinguished actor-manager Mr. Vincent Crummles told Nicholas Nickleby that he had once had in his company a "first-tragedy man" who, when he played Othello, used to black himself all over: "But that's feeling a part and going into it as if you meant it; it isn't usual—more's the pity." No one went into a part as if he meant it more wholeheartedly than Laurence Olivier. But his transformation caused some confusion among the younger members of his family. His two-year-old daughter Tamsin visited him in his dressing room while he was removing his makeup. Fascinated, she watched him grow lighter under her eyes. Next day she saw a black girl in the playground of her infant school. Solicitously, she took out her handkerchief and set to work trying to rub her new friend clean.[8]

Olivier saw Othello as a "devil-worshipping savage," who in the first four acts of the play would alienate audiences by his arrogance and stupidity and then, at the very end, would "pull their emotions right back into loving him with an intensity they otherwise would never have felt." The image crystallized in his mind while the planning was still in the most preliminary stages; by the time of the first read-through it had been enriched and strengthened. Normally the first reading is a lackluster affair—a getting-to-know-you session with the players doing little more than mumble through their lines. Olivier, said Tynan, "delivered the works—a fantastic full-volume display that scorched one's ears, serving final notice on everyone present that the hero, storm-center and focal point of the tragedy was the man named in the title."[9]

The man *not* named in the title is Iago. Iago has more lines than Othello and can sometimes seem to have the more important part. When Olivier had played Iago to Richardson's Othello in 1938 he flattered himself that he had stolen the show. He did not intend that any Iago should steal *his* show. John Mills had suggested that it might be a role for him; Olivier did not relish the idea. Instead he chose Frank Finlay, a highly competent but not particularly charismatic actor who had only performed one Shakespearean role before and could be relied on to play second fiddle to Olivier's first violin. "He didn't want me or Albert Finney playing Iago," said Robert Stephens, "and he didn't want some cocky young fellow either; he wanted an ordinary actor . . . whom he could push out toward the corners, leaving the center of the stage for him." He wanted his Iago to be a noncommissioned officer: diligent, resourceful, but not an aspirant for glory. Partly this was to accommodate his own ambitions, partly because he felt that was the sort of man Iago was. During his wartime service he had seen many N.C.O.s hungry for promotion and resentful if somebody else was awarded the coveted extra stripe: any one of them, he believed, "could be guilty of Iago's offense if they hadn't enough sense."[10]

Maggie Smith's Desdemona more than made up for Finlay's drab rendering. According to John Dexter, as reported by his long-established boyfriend Riggs O'Hara, Olivier at first had doubts about Smith's suitability; he wanted the traditional simpering innocent and, anyway, was uncertain about her abilities as a classical actress. Olivier himself insists that he knew Maggie Smith was "a marvelous actress," and believed that the fact that she was celebrated for her roles in comedy was a recommendation rather than a handicap—"It would be a mistake to play a tragic role if you weren't a comedian." He took her to lunch at the Ivy and told her what he planned. "Oh, sir," she said. "You must be out of your mind." "You'll be out of *your* mind if you turn it down," Olivier retorted. Maggie Smith herself admits she was startled by the proposal. "I was very nervous of Sir Laurence," she told Bryan Forbes. "It's unfair on him, but it's bound to happen. You are in awe of him, very much so."[11]

Neither the awe nor the nervousness were apparent on the stage. Maggie Smith was one of the few players who stood up to Olivier in the theater. She had the courage to assert her presence and the skills to hold her own once she had done so. She complained vociferously when she thought she was being misused. "Me and Frank at the front," she complained. "We can't even see each other it's so dark; then *he* comes on, the lights go up, and we're blinded. We can't see each other because of the lights." Olivier seemed intent on keeping as far away from her as possible. "I've come all the way from Venice to see you," she protested. "You've won the war. I'm pleased to see you. What do you want me to do? Back away in fucking horror?" In one performance, Olivier became so enraged by her refusal to accept what seemed to him his sensible suggestions that, instead of slapping her across the face with the piece of parchment that had been sent to him by Lodovico, he punched her on the jaw. She fell heavily and for a moment seemed to lose consciousness, leaving the horrified stagehands wondering whether or not to bring down the curtain. They were only to act together on one other occasion and Smith never wholly forgave him. You must admit, Derek Granger told her, "that he is a great *monstre sacré.*" "*Monstre,* yes," she replied.[12]

Whether or not Maggie Smith's presence stimulated him to greater efforts, Olivier's Othello was one of overwhelming passion. In the course of his career he acted with greater subtlety, he showed greater psychological penetration, but nothing could excel the potency of this performance. "I knew by the trembling of my body as I left the theater," wrote an awed Christopher Fry, "that I had heard 'the hum of mighty workings.' The rage was elemental, the pain so private that it seemed an intrusion to overhear it." Some thought it vulgar—unspeakably so, judged John Osborne, adding that no other actor would have had the courage to do it that way—but no one doubted that they had experienced something titanic that was unlikely ever to be repeated. Billie Whitelaw took over the role of Desdemona from Maggie Smith. "It was like being on stage with a Force Ten gale," she said. He himself realized that he was achieving something altogether extraordinary, which he could scarcely comprehend. One night, when he had given a particularly spectacular performance, the cast applauded him at curtain call. He retreated in silence to his dressing room. "What's the matter, Larry?" asked another actor. "Don't you know you were brilliant?" "Of course I fucking know it," Olivier replied, "but I don't know *why!*"[13]

The price he paid was mental and physical exhaustion more complete than anything he had experienced before. When *Othello* opened in Chichester he had rationed the number of performances he would do because he suspected it would be exceptionally demanding; it proved to be far worse than he had believed possible. He refused to go to the premiere of the film *Khartoum*, even though he was one of the leading actors and it was to be graced by the presence of Princess Margaret, because he had a matinee of *Othello* that day, "after which, I shall, I am afraid, be quite exhausted. The only way I seem able to cope with this exercise . . . is by going straight home and having something on a tray in my bed." His colleagues in the National knew that it was best not to approach him if he had played Othello the night before—"I really felt I was useless in the office; as if I had been run over by a bus."[14]

Exhaustion was bad enough, but at least he knew that twenty-four hours off would restore him. It was when he was acting Othello that he experienced for the first time the far more threatening stage fright. "It is an animal," Olivier wrote in *On Acting*, "a monster that hides in its far corner without revealing itself, but you know that it is there and that it may come forward at any moment." Before *Othello* Olivier had known that stage fright existed but had assumed that it was something that happened to other people. Now it had happened to him, for no apparent reason, without warning. He forgot his lines, lost touch with the progress of the plot, developed an irrational audience shyness, "against my will I would find myself turning away from them to show them the back of my head." Some people he knew had never recovered from this paralyzing malady and had retired prematurely from the stage. Olivier refused to follow their example; mainly, he claims, because he thought he had an obligation to his colleagues—particularly the more elderly among them: "If I, who was acknowledged more or less the top, if *I* failed, how were those poor fuckers going to face up to the rest of their lives?" So he battled on, every evening a potential crisis. There were lulls in which it seemed impossible to believe that he had ever been affected, there were weeks of concentrated agony; it was to be five years before the affliction disappeared, as suddenly and inexplicably as it had started. Olivier's composure can hardly have been helped by the exploit of Anthony Hopkins. Hopkins for the first time was playing the humble role of the messenger from Cyprus who, in Act One, Scene Three of *Othello*, announces the arrival of the Turkish fleet. He lost his head and instead delivered Iago's opening speech from early on in Scene One. Nobody in the audience seemed to notice and the play resumed its normal course. "Oh, dear heart, my ears were flapping," Olivier told him. "I thought you were going to start the whole play over again." If Hopkins had been a more experienced actor or if the offense had been repeated, Olivier would have been unforgiving. As it was, he made a joke of it and the matter was never referred to again.[15]

The occasional critical reservation made no difference to the success that *Othello* enjoyed with the public. It was the play that anyone who claimed any familiarity with the theater *had* to see. Queues for the tickets available on the day stretched sometimes hundreds of yards, far beyond the point at which would-be purchasers could hope to be successful. Because people were allowed to stand at the back, it played to a phenomenal 102 percent capacity, breaking all records at the Old Vic. Franco Zeffirelli was an Italian director of enormous renown who knew the London stage better even than the continental. Olivier's performance, he said, was "an anthology of everything that has been discovered about acting in the last three centuries. It is grand and majestic, but it is also modern and realistic. I would call it a lesson for us all." It was a lesson for Olivier; it taught him that there was a limit to the burden he could impose on his physique, his voice, his nerves. He never acquired the gift of moderation, but he did learn some of the perils of excess. He was to play many more demanding roles, but never again would he engage in something so compelling and all-absorbing as the Othello he played in 1964 and 1965.[16]

But *Othello* had not long completed its run at Chichester before he found himself flung into another major part. Michael Redgrave had been engaged to play Solness in Ibsen's *The Master Builder*. It was a part for which he was well suited, but after a few months it became obvious that he was incapable of playing: he floundered, forgot his lines, dragged down the performances of his fellow actors. The production, the most expensive that the National Theater had so far mounted, threatened to be an out-and-out disaster. Subsequent history suggests that Redgrave was in the early stages of Parkinson's disease; Olivier attributed the failure to drink.

Probably the two worked together: Redgrave was anyway known to be a heavy drinker and the terror induced by the onset of that odious and—to him—inexplicable disease may well have driven him to excess. Knowing nothing of this, Olivier was unsympathetic: "I did have a scene with him one day and gave him a very long lecture." Redgrave felt that Olivier had lost confidence in him. Worse still he had lost confidence in himself. He abandoned the part and left the company. If he had known the full facts, Olivier might have handled him more gently, but the result was the right one. Redgrave was unfit to play the part. After only four or five days of rehearsal, Olivier took over.[17]

Once more he found himself pitted against Maggie Smith. According to Robert Stephens, who was to marry Smith two years later, Olivier was offended by a review that said that she had acted him off the stage. He turned on her: "If I may say so, darling angel, heart of my life, in the second act you nearly bored me off the stage, you were so slow." Incensed in her turn, she tore through her scenes so fast that he could barely get his lines in. "She made him look a complete monkey," wrote Stephens, "and not many people did that to Larry and lived to tell the tale . . . Larry swore never to work with her again." This must be a somewhat exaggerated account of the confrontation. Olivier and Smith were both highly professional and conscientious actors and neither would have contemplated destroying a performance so as to score points against the other. But it was not a comfortable occasion for either actor. The audience were the ones who gained. William Gaskill doubted whether Olivier much enjoyed acting with Smith, but he says that their partnership generated an electricity that almost set the theater alight. The fact remains that Olivier never did act with her again.[18]

What Olivier did not enjoy about his performance in *The Master Builder* was a recurrence of the panic that had afflicted him in *Othello*. He had just had to rush to Manchester to deal with a furious Noël Coward. Coward was directing a revival of his play *Hay Fever*, which was touring in the provinces before moving to the Old Vic. He claimed that the production was being destroyed by the inadequacy of the elderly Edith Evans who seemed quite incapable of remembering her lines. Evans must be dismissed, he insisted. Olivier found himself physically and emotionally drained by this imbroglio, but still dashed back to London in time for the evening performance of *The Master Builder*. "There I was, when I had despised Edith so much for not knowing her lines, playing the part that should have been played by Michael, whom I had despised so much for not knowing *his* lines, in the dressing room where of rights *he* should have been dressing, and I suddenly thought: 'Christ, I believe I'm too tired to remember my lines!'" He plucked up his courage, took to the stage, and for ten minutes all went well. Then in an instant, "I never felt so ill in my life." He began to eye the exits: "I could only dream of one thing: run, out of the theater, straight into the station, buy a ticket for anywhere at all, sit in a railway carriage and never be seen again." The worst of the panic passed, probably it only lasted a few seconds, but for the rest of the evening Olivier was on autopilot, coasting along with no real knowledge of where he had come from or to where he was going. Years later he told Anthony Shaffer that he had suffered an identity crisis so severe that he did not know who he was. "You mean, you did not know what part you were playing?" asked Shaffer. "No, I didn't know who *I* was."[19]

Olivier had warned Coward before the tour of *Hay Fever* started that Edith Evans was always slow in learning her lines and that there was no point in worrying about it. When he saw her in Newcastle, however, he was horrified by her performance—she was "no good at all. She nearly killed it . . . I took against her very strongly, but thought it was worth sticking with her at least until the play reached London." He was proved right when she finally turned in a performance that, if not exceptional, was at least workmanlike. Coward too came round to her; he thought that the only weak link in a cast that otherwise "could have played the Albanian telephone directory" was Sarah Miles, and she, fortunately, retired hurt after the first day's rehearsal and was never seen on the set again. Success was more than usually important, since *Hay Fever* was the first play written by a living British dramatist to be performed at the National Theater. Dexter and Gaskill thought that this lightweight comedy was hardly worthy of so exalted a status. They demurred still more when Olivier insisted on bringing in Coward himself to direct it. "Why import a director from outside?" they wanted to know. The existing staff at the National was capable of looking after its own requirements. Olivier overruled them. "It was obviously the box-office thing to do," he reflected. Also he believed that the importation of the occasional star director from outside, unlike a star actor, was compatible with the concept of the ensemble. They would bring in new ideas, challenge accepted conventions, revivify what might otherwise become a stagnant institution.[20] He had to overcome the doubts of the putative director as well as his own colleagues. Coward was at first reluctant to take on the task and only agreed in the end because Olivier was "in a frizz" about having to take over in *The Master Builder*. "He was very clear and persuasive and said how important it would be to the company." Neither Olivier nor Coward had reason to regret their decision; *Hay Fever* had a rapturous reception on its first night and was second only to *Othello* in its drawing power. "Bravo to my beloved one and only prettiest and best," telegraphed an ecstatic Olivier. "What a frigid, ungenerous little telegram," replied Coward. "I love you if possible more than ever." If that amorous exchange fell into the hands of the police, Joan Plowright observed drily, the two men would be arrested.[21]

The first two years at the National Theater had been an almost unqualified success. They had been fun as well as supremely testing. "I was taking a tremendous amount of things in my stride," Olivier remembered with some satisfaction. "I was showing a lot of power, a lot of guts, a lot of strength, a lot of reserve and a lot of stamina." But the price he paid was a high one. Whether his stage fright was in part caused by his exhaustion, or his exhaustion was exacerbated by his stage fright, the burden sometimes seemed too great to bear. Not only was he producing, directing and acting in a range of testing plays; he was running a complex organization. Nor could he do this without any outside interference; at every stage he had to carry with him a Board of Directors who could thwart his efforts if they were so minded. He was to find that Olivier as the servant of the Board had a task quite as testing as any other of the functions he performed in the National Theater.[22]

Peter Hall professed dismay at the terms of Olivier's contract. "The Board can require him to do anything they want," he told his agent. "More horrendous, they can appoint, after consultation with him (although he has no right of approval), any associate directors they see fit. I would not sign a contract like this." There was something in what he said, but in practice it mattered little. The Board had no doubts about the status of their Director. Technically he was their servant, but they would not have dreamt of treating him as such. Olivier, as they minuted after a discussion of the National Theater's relations with the press, was "a great world star." No journalist would have much interest in talking to anybody else who professed to speak for the National Theater, whether he came from within the organization or as a member of the Board. They were well aware that, if he were driven to resignation, the effect on the National would be catastrophic. It followed that his influence, if not his power, was infinite. When he came to Board meetings, said John Mortimer, he would treat its members "with mock humility, behaving like Othello before the Senate, calling us his 'very notable and approv'd good masters.' Naturally, he didn't mean a word of it." They would never have contemplated imposing an associate director on him without knowing that he wished it; almost always any such appointment was made at his initiative. If they did express an opinion—as when, according to Olivier, they "indicated strongly" that he should confine his relationship with the press to occasions on which he was speaking formally on behalf of the National Theater—it was almost certainly because this was a ruling that he wanted himself and had put into the Board's mouth.[23]

Nevertheless, the members of the Board were men of stature and independent minds. They would accept the preeminence of their Director and defer to his opinion, but they knew their rights and felt there were issues on which they were not merely entitled but obligated to express their views. Olivier had agreed with Lord Chandos that he would only discuss the choice of plays with the Board if "there would be cause to worry on political or the other main grounds for censorship—profanity, obscenity or libel." This made sense provided Olivier and Chandos agreed in their definition of these words and drew the same conclusions about the consequences. Nearly always they did, but there were differences of opinion, and with polemicists like Tynan eager to stir up outrage over any attempted restriction on the freedom of the artist, the possibility of acrimonious argument never disappeared. In the early years at least, Olivier's relationship with the Board was reasonably trouble-free, but it was still a preoccupation and one that made demands upon his time and energies.[24]

Censorship was, of course, not an issue that involved Olivier and the Board alone; the Lord Chamberlain was still the arbiter of what should or should not be shown upon a stage, and when Olivier debated with his Board the potential hazards of a piece, it was the likely reaction of this remote panjandrum that concerned them both. Olivier's own views on the issue, as he confessed, were "deliciously though probably maddeningly vague." On the whole he thought the Lord Chamberlain was not the appropriate person to judge the propriety of a play, but he was by no means in favor of abandoning censorship altogether. Somebody would have to make the decision, but who that man should be, it was hard to decide. The trouble, as Olivier saw it, was that any change to the current system "might carry with it worse disadvantages." To Tynan this seemed pitifully pusillanimous. He was forever urging on Olivier into an outright row with the Lord Chamberlain. When the Lord Chamberlain excised "Balls," "Bugger" and "You can take a crap" from *Mother Courage*, Tynan argued that the National Theater was a special case and should be exempt from such restrictions. Nobody had greater respect for the National than the Lord Chamberlain, his office responded blandly, but he had no discretion to distinguish between one theater and another. He was, however, prepared to accept "You're all wetting your pants" as a substitute for "You're all shitting in your pants." A group of similarly trivial excisions from *Andorra* stung Tynan to still greater indignation. He proposed that a list of the censored phrases should be included in the program so that the audience should not be robbed of its fair share of obscenities. Olivier had never much liked the play anyway and privately thought that the Lord Chamberlain had a good point. "I am sorry to be po-faced about this," he wrote, "but the value or nonvalue of the Lord Chamberlain's office is something about which my mind maintains a stubborn duality. In any event, I am against this form of attack, which has a petulant feeling about it."[25]

As well as running one theater Olivier was time-consumingly involved in the development of another. The South Bank Board was responsible for the design and construction of what is now the National Theater—a task which it was at one time thought might be completed by the end of 1964 but which slipped further and further behind schedule at every step. Olivier was the only actor on the Board and so felt his contribution to be particularly significant. In his view he was thwarted and frustrated at every turn. "No one listened to what I wanted," he told Sarah Miles. "My way was the only way it could work." His colleagues saw things differently: all of them, wrote Richard Eyre, agreed on one thing: "It was Larry's baby . . . It embodies him as he was—grand, grandiose even, bold, ambitious, difficult, exasperating even, but often thrilling and occasionally unique." Unquestionably his was the loudest and most persuasive voice, but he did not have things altogether his own way. His original plan had been for a building with a single theater seating not more than a thousand people— the largest number, he was convinced, on which it was possible for an actor to impose himself. But should that theater be in the round, a compromise as in the remodeled Old Vic, or of a traditional proscenium design?[26]

Olivier seems to have been as "deliciously and probably maddeningly vague" over this as he was over censorship. He was never certain as to what was the ideal solution. In 1969 a new theater was being opened in Sheffield. Bernard Miles was asked to sponsor the enterprise. He refused indignantly. It was worse than Chichester, he protested: "They have even got forty or fifty seats at the back. All that is now required is a glass stage [through which] to look up the girls' skirts!" He sent a copy of the brochure to Olivier. "Here's another FUCKER! Worst of the lot to date. Acting is largely a frontal job, *as you well know.*" Olivier was not sure how well he knew or, indeed, what he knew. It all depended what one meant by "largely." He wrote to the director of the Sheffield theater to say that he was "a little bit anxious about the extreme design," but he was not prepared to join Miles in his out-and-out condemnation of the project. When Miles denounced the enterprise in the newspapers and cited Olivier as being on his side, Olivier took him to task—"Do learn to manage the opening of your pretty mouth with a little more discretion, dear boy." "That was a real shitty little note you wrote," Miles replied. "After all, I'm only doing it for you and your doubtless gifted progeny, who will one day be faced with the problems of this stupid, bookish theory."[27]

It was easy enough to see both sides of the argument when somebody else's project was in question. Olivier was faced with the problem here and now in the National Theater. He was not prepared to dispense altogether with the traditional proscenium stage—how else could he invite the Comédie Française to act in London? he asked—but was determined that this should not be the only, or even the most usual configuration. What he wanted was a single theater that could be adapted to a variety of shapes, something that was eventually achieved on a small scale in the Cottlesloe Theater, but which he accepted was impossible in a larger auditorium. So two theaters evolved: the traditionally designed model, to be called the Lyttelton, and the Olivier with its thrust-forward stage. Nobody really wanted the Lyttelton, said Peter Hall; he, George Devine, Peter Brook, Michel Saint-Denis, all opposed it. They were overruled, "because Larry was the boss man, and that was it." The charge is not wholly accurate, but the contemporary National Theater, with its weaknesses and far greater strengths, is more the creation of Laurence Olivier than of any other individual involved.[28]

He was no less influential in the choice of architect. It was he who conceived the idea of getting the Royal Institute of British Architects to nominate twenty individuals competent to undertake the task and then for each one to be interviewed by an advisory panel who would recommend a name or names to the South Bank Board. Olivier was, of course, prominent on the advisory panel and it was largely his doing that, in the event, only one name was recommended to the Board, that of Denys Lasdun. All the interviewers, said Olivier, had been "impressed by his spirit of cooperation and his sense of dedication, as well as by evidence of his work." There were to be times over the next few years when he wondered whether the panel had made the right decision, but at the end of the day he had no doubt that his opinion had been justified.[29]

As he had predicted from the start, one of the most difficult problems facing the National Theater was finding the best actors and actresses and retaining them, even though suitable parts would not always be available. Olivier urged Christopher Plummer to be ready to accept a minor role; if he did so, he would "look a jolly good sport by mucking in with the company." The trouble about this was that Plummer, like almost every other actor, was more concerned about his career than whether he appeared a "jolly good sport." Ian McKellen refused to sign a three-year contract. "The crux of my decision," he admitted, "is ambition. My ambition to achieve recognition as an actor . . . I think there is more chance of establishing my ability publicly elsewhere." He was to come back to the National, but only after he had achieved his object of making his name elsewhere.[30]

Nor, even when they could be prevailed upon to stay, were many actors prepared to make the sort of financial sacrifice that Olivier was ready—and much more able—to accept. Artists' fees were costing the theater much more than he had expected, he told the Board: actors were not "inclined to regard work at the National Theater as a charitable duty." When Peter O'Toole held out for a

higher salary, Tynan declared loftily that, if an actor was not prepared to accept a lower wage in exchange for the honor of playing
in the National Theater, then "he was not the sort of actor the theater wants." Olivier agreed that this was an admirable sentiment,
but "it's not an entirely workable principle these days." He knew
that his success or failure as Director would be judged by the Board
as much by the financial returns as by the quality of the productions. This in its turn put an additional burden on him. Box-office
receipts slumped when he was not himself acting in a play. He
therefore saw it as his duty to act whenever his schedule made it
possible—a duty that fortunately for him coincided with his pre-
dilection for playing a leading part in every production if he could
get away with doing so.[31]

The relationship with Stratford, too, made constant demands
on Olivier's energies and patience. By the end of 1963 Peter Hall
had convinced himself that the Royal Shakespeare Company was
in peril, that it could not survive the unfairly subsidized competition of the National Theater. "We are now at the end of the road,"
he told Joan Plowright. "Unless persons in high places can help we
shall be finished at the beginning of 1965 and Stratford will have
a new Director." The person in a high place to whom this appeal
was implicitly addressed was Olivier himself. On the whole he
responded generously. He told his Board that a Coordinating Committee was being set up to consider how the National could help
Stratford in its fight for survival. He stressed the importance of its
outpost in London at the Aldwych Theater and "pointed out that the
disappearance of Stratford's London branch would reflect adversely
upon the National Theater." But soon the exchanges became acrimonious. In February 1964 the *Sunday Times* carried a story about
the rivalry between the two theaters and reported that Hall proposed to denounce the National if it didn't offer its rival some tan-
gible support. Plowright felt certain that Hall himself was the origin
of the story, and wrote to remonstrate. Three days later Olivier fired
the second barrel. It was Stratford that had sabotaged the negotiations for some sort of merger; it was the National that had been

responsible for Stratford getting "its bloody dough . . . all of which history seems to me to be pretty bloody immaculate, and I think it is now time somebody said so, and I think that somebody is you . . . Sorry, cock, over to you." No such public avowal was forthcoming and resentment lingered on both sides, but it was soon apparent that Hall had overstated the desperation of Stratford's plight and that there was plenty of room for the two companies to survive in healthy competition.[32]

Tynan, it is hardly necessary to say, was zealous in fomenting the hostility between the National and Stratford and more specifically between Olivier and Hall. He was no less energetic when it came to making trouble within the National itself. Dexter, in particular, was his target. "At the moment I expect he would quite like to assassinate me," he told Olivier. Were not three directors more than the National Theater needed? He reported that he had asked the Director of the Prague National Theater how it was that his theater ran so smoothly. "It's simple," he had been told. "I decide on the repertoire with the dramaturge and then we tell the other directors what they are going to do. Is there any other way?" Was there not a lesson there for the National Theater? asked Tynan. Olivier did not think there was and urged Tynan both to curb his tongue and to moderate his aspirations. He had no intention of dispensing with his services, though, and a large part of his already overstretched energies had to be devoted to repairing the damage that his irrepressible dramaturge had done. There was little on which Tynan did not feel qualified and entitled to express an opinion. When a filmed version was made of the National Theater *Othello*—not a film in its own right, but a photographed record of what was happening on the stage—Tynan insisted on being present and clamored for more close-ups of Olivier. If one took close-ups of what Olivier was doing on the stage, explained the film's producer, Anthony Havelock-Allan, the audience would be in "gales of laughter because he's spitting, his face is contorted. It's an overblown performance for a big theatrical performance; the antithesis of what you can do on film." The trouble was that

Olivier, never totally reconciled to the demands of the screen, was more than half inclined to agree with Tynan. He gave a stage performance, and made little attempt to curb his gestures or expressions to suit the different medium. The result was an uneasy compromise: much better than nothing, but still only a distorted shadow of its majestic original.[33]

Tynan made so much noisy mischief that it is easy to overlook the good work he did. He was particularly efficacious in opening Olivier's eyes to Europe. Without Tynan he would never have invited the Berliner Ensemble to act in London. Even this got him into trouble with Peter Daubeny, who had brought the Ensemble to London some ten years before and appears to have thought that he had a monopoly on the importation of foreign companies. "It seems to me a betrayal of the good faith on which relations between people and great theaters are customarily based," he complained. Olivier replied that he was baffled: "Really, dear Peter, you have invited the Moscow Art Theater, the Comédie Française, the Habbima etc., with nothing but my blessing . . . Must you begrudge us our East Berliners?"[34]

Less controversially, it was Tynan who advocated the visit to Russia that the National Theater made in 1965. Olivier proposed that the Company should tour with three productions: Miller's *The Crucible*, *Othello* and Congreve's *Love for Love*. *The Crucible* had already played in Moscow and had been a flop: would not two productions be enough? asked Humphrey Trevelyan, the Ambassador. If they confined themselves to *Othello* and *Love for Love*, he would be involved in every performance, replied Olivier, and would be exhausted before the tour was over. *Hobson's Choice* was substituted for *The Crucible*: whether the Muscovites were likely to make much of this peculiarly homespun comedy was an open question, but at least it would be a novelty. *Love for Love* was played by the company for the first time in Moscow. It was "a smasharoo," Olivier told Tarquin. It did not escape some adverse comment, however. One leading critic complained about the salacious content of the plot. "They are terribly easily shocked, the Russians," observed Olivier. "It's a lovely comedy, delicious, it's not yoff-yoff laughing, it just purrs over your ears."[35]

But it was *Othello* that made the greatest mark. It was the first production of the tour; the Russians were known to revere it above all other plays by Shakespeare; Madame Furtseva, the powerful Minister of Culture, was in the audience; there was all to play for. The effort of getting the company to Moscow and onto the stage had been stressful; Olivier had had no time to go to the gym; he had had to cut to a few minutes the leisurely and ritualistic build-up that usually preceded every performance. Out of his exhaustion he conjured what was perhaps the greatest performance of his life. He was staggering, Billie Whitelaw said. "He was able to show what in my view had always been missing: Othello's vulnerability." The Russians were ecstatic. When he opened his curtain speech with the word "*Tovarishchi*," "Comrades," it seemed that their applause would never stop. Olivier drank too much in the celebrations that followed, was put to bed by Joan Plowright and was so hungover the following morning that he missed a pompous luncheon given in honor of the National Theater. It did not diminish his triumph: half a century later people in Moscow still speak of Olivier's Othello with bated breath.[36]

The National Theater goes very well, Olivier told Tarquin, at the beginning of 1966, "but the brain-teasing miasma of permutations never seems to lessen or grow simpler." The National had indeed got off to a sensationally successful start; it remained to be seen whether the burden on Olivier would grow any lighter now that it was established.[37]

CHAPTER TWENTY

PROBLEMS

Tarquin Olivier had dinner with his father and Joan Plowright in the summer of 1962. "They were still happy and in love with their young family," he wrote. Their relationship may have lacked some of the hungry passion that had fired Olivier's relationship with Vivien Leigh, but it was more mature, more equable, more likely to endure. Many people remarked on the conspicuous success of their marriage, the pleasure they took in each other's company. Rosemary Harris was impressed when Olivier, having smashed a particularly precious Dresden china cake stand three tiers high, was stricken with guilt. "Oh well, dear, never mind," said Plowright. "Get on with your supper while I fetch a dustpan and brush."[1]

But they were also two ambitious and professional actors who were conscious always of the demands of their individual careers. Plowright was quoted as saying that, of course, she loved her family, "but the theater is my life." If the words had been attributed to Olivier they would have been no more than the truth; coming from Plowright they must either have been misquoted or taken out of context. During the years that she was bearing children and seeing them through their infancy her theatrical life unequivocally took second place to her responsibilities as a mother. It was fortunate both for her and for Olivier that those years coincided with the early days of the National Theater at the Old Vic. Olivier longed to promote the interests of his wife and knew that she was qualified to undertake most of the leading female roles; equally, as Director of the National Theater, he had to consider the needs of the Company as a whole and to keep all his leading ladies happy. Maggie Smith and Geraldine McEwan, to mention only the two most prominent, would have been quick to protest if they had thought that Plowright was getting preferential treatment. As he told Tammy Grimes when she asked him to find her a part, he was already having "hell's own job keeping these girls happy"; to add another prominent figure would make the task impossible. Plowright was given some splendid parts, but she might have been offered more if she had not been the wife of the Director. In other circumstances she might have resented this; coming when it did she felt only relief. When Billie Whitelaw was brought in to replace her in *Hobson's Choice* because she "had gone to have Olivier's baby," Plowright may have felt a pang of regret, but she had no doubt that she had chosen the better course.[2]

This was their third child. Richard, the first, had been born at the end of 1961. Having been scarcely aware of Tarquin as a baby, Olivier was startled by the exultation that his new son's birth caused him. Fabia Drake came to inspect Richard when he was only a few days old. "Oh, Fabby," said Olivier. "I am *so* happy!' More temperately he told Tarquin that the baby looked like the squashed lemon in the advertisements for the soft drink Idris, but he was improving: "You never saw anyone as happy as Joannie (or me for that matter)."[3]

Richard proved a restless child. Once Olivier volunteered to sleep next door to his bedroom when the nanny had a night off. When Plowright joined them for breakfast next morning there was cereal and apple sauce all over the carpet and down the front of her husband's silk dressing gown. "I'd rather play Othello eight times a week than do this again," Olivier grumbled. Richard was convinced a man-eating crocodile lived at the end of the corridor in which he had his room and, on the evenings that the nanny was out, would call upon his parents for reassurance. Nanny insisted that the proper thing to do was to let him cry himself out and then go back to sleep. With some reluctance the Oliviers agreed to give this tactic a try. Sure enough, Richard ran out of breath, said feebly "How can I keep on crying if no one is going to care?" and made his way back to bed. The crocodile, similarly discomfited, never reappeared. It was a triumph for stern parenting, but not one that was often repeated. Olivier was an indulgent if distrait father and was even less likely to treat his daughters severely than he was his son.[4]

Their two daughters, Tamsin and Julie-Kate, followed in 1965 and 1966. Julie-Kate almost finished off her mother. Joan Plowright had suffered a debilitating miscarriage at the end of 1964 and was still undergoing surgery. The doctors claimed there was no possibility of her conceiving but were proved wrong. Julie-Kate was born by Cesarean and, according to her father, would undoubtedly have been dead if there had been even a few hours' delay. He was present at the birth. Plowright wanted him to be there, Olivier remembered; he was able to "hold her hand and stroke her head and bring comfort to her while they were attending to things down below." No doubt she did want him there, but he would have taken some keeping away. Even if he was himself the victim, Olivier was always anxious to know what was going on and, if possible, to watch it. This operation was almost too much for him, however: "My God, there was a lot of blood. The floor was inches thick in it. That really began to make me feel a tiny bit queasy." He gave Tarquin a gory account of the occasion. "I don't know if surgical detail interests you," he wrote. "I'm afraid it always fascinates me."[5]

The three children never doubted that their father loved them and wished them well; they also knew that, by the standards of most of their friends, he was a remote and evasive figure. In retrospect it seemed to them almost as if he were pretending to be a father, acting the part conscientiously and with skill but shedding it when he left the stage. He thanked Ralph Richardson for agreeing to reshuffle the order of appearance in a charity performance so that he could catch the last train home to Brighton—"taking my little ones to school is almost my only chance of seeing them these days, and has a special place in the day for me"—but often even this limited duty proved unfeasible. His visits to Brighton, he told the journalist David Lewin, were "bounded at one end by flinging myself into bed to an exhausted and sound sleep, and at the other by a lunatic scramble for the train." The children literally lived next door, in the neighboring house in the Royal Crescent that had now been integrated with their parents' rather smarter house. "I know exactly how you must feel about not having enough time with your babies," wrote his sister Sybille: "But truly the more important time for them to be with you will be when they are a little older." Olivier may have drawn consolation from this advice, but he was deluding himself if he imagined that in five or ten years he would manage to spend very much more time with his children. Even when they were together they were apart. Richard remembers staying with his father at Franco Zeffirelli's house in Italy. In theory it was a family holiday; in practice his father was learning a twenty-minute monologue for a forthcoming play: "He was constantly at it and could not be approached while it was on."[6]

He was still less effective when it came to maintaining a relationship with his elder son, Tarquin. "How wrong you have got me, or more probably we have got each other," he wrote. He was dismayed to find that Tarquin felt he had been putting on "a stern father act"; on the contrary he had been trying to do the very opposite, to "take you as I found you." The trouble was, he hardly ever found him, at all events not often enough to form any clear impression of what he was really like. Tarquin got married at the beginning of 1965. Olivier announced that his duties were so demanding that he could not afford to do more than attend the ceremony. His new daughter-in-law's parents tried to organize a meeting; he refused their invitations and did not even offer them tickets for the National. On the way from the church to the reception the bride's mother berated him for his bad manners. Placatingly, he expressed the hope that they would meet again. "*That* won't be necessary," she answered.[7]

The ghost of Vivien Leigh could not altogether be exorcised. It had taken her separation from Olivier to convince her how desperately she loved and needed him; when she was acting his photograph was always on her dressing table. He, for his part, felt a residual loyalty toward her. In 1963 he heard that Marlon Brando was to play Macbeth in New York. He wrote to Binkie Beaumont asking if there was "some subtle and tactful way" by which it could be suggested to Brando that Vivien Leigh would be the perfect Lady Macbeth for him. "Of course, the last thing in the world I would want is for it ever to be known by anybody that the suggestion came from me, as it would be completely misunderstood." The idea came to nothing—it is unlikely, anyway, that Leigh's health would have allowed her to undertake such a role. A few months later she was convalescing at her country home from yet another breakdown. Olivier arrived to visit her. You must go down to meet him, said her nurse. "She said, 'Oh, no, I can't!' . . . and then this voice came up the stairs: 'Vivien, are you coming down or am I coming up?' She just took off like a little schoolgirl, you know, meeting her boy-friend—oh, it was beautiful, and they walked by the lake together."[8]

It seems that this is the last time they met, at any rate for more than a casual exchange. At intervals Leigh tried to arrange a meet-ing, the last time being at the end of 1966. Her doctor advised Oliv-ier not to accept the invitation. If he once acceded to her request she would be importunate in her demands and would never take no for an answer. "I am quite sure that emotional contacts of this kind would in the long run not be good for Vivien as it would be likely to push the state of elation and all its other aspects into a more disturbing state of mind." Six months later Olivier was him-self in the hospital. Douglas Fairbanks was visiting him when the news came that Leigh had died. "There was a long, sad moment and then he said, 'Poor, dear, little Vivien.' It seemed to me that their life together was running like a film through his mind." Olivier insisted on leaving the hospital to visit the apartment in Eaton Square where her body was still lying. He stood in silence by her bedside and, he said, "prayed for forgiveness for all the evils that had sprung up between us." He did not have much with which to reproach himself. He might have been a little more sympathetic, a little more under-standing, but on the whole he had showed exemplary patience and had tried to the best of his ability to grapple with problems that were not only beyond his comprehension but beyond the grasp of any of the psychologists of the day. By chance, as he was leaving the memorial service, he found himself standing next to Jill Esmond.

"I put my hand on his as he left the pew, and he put his other hand on top of mine and gave it three little squeezes. I thought he looked gray right through."[9]

By singular ill-fortune, Cecil Tennant, Olivier's agent and most trusted friend, was killed in a car crash while driving back from Vivien Leigh's funeral. "He wasn't supposed to die, you know," Olivier told Lord Chandos. "He was supposed to live forever and look after me." This reaction might seem a little solipsistic, but can perhaps be excused on the grounds that Olivier had many reasons to feel self-pity in 1967 and 1968. It was unsurprising that Jill Esmond described him as looking "gray right through" since, against the urging of his doctor, he had emerged from the hospital to attend the service. Some weeks before, while directing rehearsals of *The Three Sisters*, he had experienced sharp pains and was overcome by exhaustion so complete that he could hardly breathe, let alone give instructions. As he prepared to leave the theater he remarked to Joan Plowright how terrified the other members of the cast had seemed. "They thought you were about to die," she retorted. "So did I. Go to the hospital, or you'll be dead in the morning." Prostate cancer was diagnosed—"the best kind of cancer," he noted, "so I was lucky in that." This did not make the treatment any more agreeable: it involved being interred in an opaque coffin, reduced almost to freezing point and then bombarded with radium-soaked cobalt. He endured this with striking fortitude; the only indication of the strain that was imposed on him was his reluctance to be left alone until the very last moment before the treatment. Noël Coward visited him in the hospital and found him "writhing on his bed" but rejoicing in the fact that the cancer was reported to be responding to treatment. "I hope to God this is true."[10]

It *was* true, but it was far from being the end of the story. Olivier emerged from the hospital and almost immediately contracted pneumonia: it was back to the hospital again, from which he emerged, against the advice of his doctors, to attend Vivien Leigh's memorial service and then to read a lesson at Cecil Tennant's—"That's the kind of man he was," said Tennant's widow Irina. His plight got much attention in the press and he was bombarded by well-meaning but generally fatuous suggestions as to how he might restore himself. Most of them recommended a vegetable diet, but he was also urged to visit various gurus all over Europe and the United States, as well as Agra, Benares and Calcutta. All such letters got a reply; a large number of them signed by Olivier himself.[11]

"My disease is at its worst just now," he told Chandos after Cecil Tennant's death. "They told me the convalescent period was the worst, and 'they' are bloody well right. But I shall get over all that and get a whole chapter written on 'the things I've done for England,' by getting to Canada and (what is more) coming back." The National Theater was due to visit Canada in October and November 1967. Nobody would have reproached him if he had opted out, but he knew how much the success of the tour depended on his presence and was determined to be there if it were physically possible. The only concession he made was that *Othello* should be removed from the repertoire because of the strain involved: even so he was going to play a part in all the forty-two performances that the company gave in Montreal and Toronto. And then, early in 1967, while playing *The Dance of Death* in Edinburgh, he developed agonizing stomach pains. Appendicitis was diagnosed, he was rushed back to London and operated on the following day. "Just in time," said the surgeon. "The appendix was about to explode." Once again pneumonia followed. It must have seemed to Olivier as if his problems would never end. In fact, in the short term, the worst was over, but he was never really a fit man again. He lived every day in the knowledge that he was vulnerable and in the fear, if not the expectation, that something would go wrong.[12]

His mood cannot have been lightened by the publication early in 1969 of Virginia Fairweather's biography of him, *Cry God for Larry*. Fairweather had been for a long time in charge of publicity at the National Theater and before that at Chichester, but she was abruptly dismissed for reasons that are obscure but are rumored to have involved some flagrant misbehavior. When her book was about to appear she appealed to Olivier to attend a Foyle's literary lunch that was to be given in its honor. Reluctantly Olivier agreed. In a letter to Fairweather's husband, undated and perhaps never sent, he said that he had not yet read the whole book. He had been shown some excerpts to which he might object but "as the whole enterprise is clearly meant to be generous, and at times generous beyond all justice in my direction, I can't very well take exception to details." Then came serialization in the *Sunday Times*. As so often, newspaper serialization featured all the more salacious and sensational elements and gave a false impression of the book as a whole. Olivier reacted violently. He wrote to the *Sunday Times* denouncing "this distressful tissue of overstatements and other digressions under the terms of gossip" and complained of Fairweather's "lifelong addiction to the overdramatic" which was apparent throughout the excerpts. He in particular disliked a passage that described a quarrel he had had with Leslie Evershed-Martin and gave the impression that it was this that had led to his departure from Chichester. There had been one such exchange, he told the editor of the local paper, the *Chichester Observer*, "for which, she is correct in saying, I was entirely and regrettably to blame," but it had been another three years before pressure of work at the National Theater forced him to give up the Festival. Fairweather's words, he complained, had been neither kind nor helpful.[13]

In fact Olivier's first impression had been fairer to the book than his considered opinion. *Cry God for Larry* was almost entirely innocuous, and gave an impression of Olivier and his activities which, though from time to time mildly critical, was on the whole generous almost to a fault. As with Crawfie's saccharine reminiscences about the royal princesses who had been in her charge, *The Little Princesses*, the fault was not so much with the content as with the fact that it was written at all. Olivier and Joan Plowright saw it as an invasion of their privacy, unpardonable when coming from somebody who had once been a trusted insider. There were to be many more books on Olivier—any biographer of him must be appalled by the acreage of print already devoted to his theme—but none caused quite such offense to its subject.

The National Theater had gotten off to a triumphant start. The success of the Company was firmly established, Chandos declared at a Board meeting in October 1966, and it was "thanks first of all, and it *is* thanks, to Sir Laurence Olivier. Quite apart from his own marvelous performances, he has been the mainspring of all our activities." Two months later the Board offered Olivier an extension of his contract to July 1973, with a view to him still being Director when the new theater on the South Bank was finally opened. Superficially all was tranquil, but behind the scenes the harmony—or perhaps constructive disharmony—which had bound Olivier, Gaskill, Dexter and Tynan together was wearing thin. This meant that Olivier's daily round became still more stressful. When, in the spring of 1966, he was pressed to star in a film adapted from Somerset Maugham's short story *Rain*, he refused to make any commitment: "The one thing one is certain of is that much less is going to be possible than one ever caters for, as much more is the load than one ever imagines. (Quite poetic that, don't you think?)"[14]

His first serious confrontation was with John Dexter. The relationship had been edgy for some time, but it was exacerbated by the all-male production of *As You Like It*. Olivier—or more probably Tynan—had read Professor Jan Kott's essay on the subject, in which he argued that the verbal impact would be different if the female roles were played by men, and put it to the Board that it would be interesting to try the idea out in practice. The Drama Committee adopted the suggestion with enthusiasm and Dexter was chosen to direct it. It soon became obvious that his ideas were different from Olivier's. He argued that, as would have been case in the late sixteenth century, the female roles should be played by boys, or at least the nearest approach to young and androgynous actors that the National Theater could assemble. Olivier thought that this approach would lead to the production being a dismal flop. "He didn't understand why we didn't wear red fingernails and pad our bosoms out," said Charles Kay, who played Celia. "He just didn't dig it." Olivier was convinced that Dexter, who was an unabashed homosexual, was "making an exhibition of himself." Shakespearean boys, he believed, would have used every device at their disposal to look like mature women: "Ronald Pickup had no tits. They thought that was very clever and I didn't. That's all." Being Olivier, he intervened energetically to assert his point of view. Pickup may not have got his tits, but Olivier burst into the dressing room, painted his mouth blood-red, penciled his eyebrows and put mascara on his eyelashes. It was typical of his hands-on approach, thought Pickup; also, in Pickup's view, it made him "look like the worst kind of drag queen." There are suggestions that the row with Dexter may have had a nastier element. Olivier believed that Dexter had tried to seduce a young man who was applying for a part in *As You Like It*. "I nearly killed him," Olivier recalled. "I said 'I'll fire you and I'll give to the press why. I'll show you no mercy at all if you dare do that again.'" Dexter for his part complained about "the covert undermining of the production, and the betrayal of trust." Olivier had professed to worry that the production was going over budget. "Over the top, yes," protested Dexter. "Budget, no!"[15]

Whatever the facts of the case, a draft letter from Olivier to Dexter written a little later makes it clear how far the relationship had deteriorated. "Right from the beginning, almost," Olivier began, "I felt that neither friendship nor artistic partnership was going to flourish very happily." Dexter was not cut out to be an assistant, least of all to Olivier: "My authority over you (no matter how slight) irritates you to a frenzy." This had come to a head over *As You Like It*. Dexter's behavior could have only two explanations: "Either it is a dare to test the strength of your position or you can feel no consideration at all for me or my job." Olivier said that he had put up with a lot in recognition of Dexter's real abilities, but "I can recognize the end of the road when I see it and it is here and now."[16]

But it was *not* the end of the road. Dexter resigned and went off to America, but in his calmer moments Olivier knew that he had made an important contribution and that, with Gaskill gone, the National Theater was the weaker for his absence. "He had a lot of very good ideas," he said reflectively some years later. "He was much more helpful to me than I've ever had the decency to give him credit for." Dexter for his part recognized that the National Theater under Olivier was a place where he had been happy to work. He was never to return as a full-time associate, but two or three years later he wrote to say how much he was looking forward to working with Olivier again. "Believe one thing, no matter how violently I disagreed, I admire and respect you more than anyone I have ever known in the theater, with the exception only of George [Devine], and there I'd say the billing is equal. My ambition is to make the National Theater as you would want it." Given the circumstances it was a generous tribute and one that Olivier must have appreciated if not wholly reciprocated.[17]

Gaskill lasted till 1965, when he returned to the Royal Court to take over after the death of George Devine. Possibly he would have stayed longer at the National if he had not fallen out with Tynan. They were together in Olivier's house and Tynan reverted to his often-advanced thesis that what the National Theater needed was more stars from outside. Exasperated, Gaskill said that, while he accepted Tynan must have a big voice in the selection of plays, he should not, in any circumstances, be involved when it came to deciding on the actors. According to Gaskill, Olivier left the room, went upstairs, and then reappeared half an hour later to say that he wished Tynan to have a voice in *all* such deliberations. Olivier denied that he needed any time to make up his mind, but agreed that he insisted Tynan's voice should be heard in every debate. For Gaskill, who disliked as well as distrusted Tynan, this was too much. "It was at that point I knew it was no good going on." Olivier regretted his departure. His relationship with Gaskill had not always been easy. Gaskill, for instance, preached the concept of a democratic company in which everyone must be allowed to have a voice. Olivier thought that this was nonsense and said as much. When it was a matter of academic argument this mattered little—Olivier usually managed to do what he thought best and leave the theorizing to others. Sometimes, however, Gaskill's views led to confrontation. Once, for instance, Olivier wanted to replace an actor playing a small part in *The Master Builder* with Derek Jacobi. Gaskill consulted the other members of the cast and reported that they were opposed to the idea. Olivier was outraged and refused to budge. "Speak to the management and not the actors," he ordered. But though his autocratic soul rejected such libertarian ideas, he knew that Gaskill and Dexter had qualities he could ill spare. "They were the two most gifted directors in Britain at that time," he admitted.[18]

To Gaskill and Dexter Olivier sometimes appeared almost intolerably conservative, opposed to any kind of radical departure. To the Board, on the other hand, he seemed dangerously progressive. Kenneth Clark told Chandos that he dreaded meetings of the Drama Committee because "three-quarters of the ideas they propose seem to me fashionable nonsense." He deplored Olivier's "obsessive fear of being thought old-fashioned . . . I am deeply worried that Larry has got so far out of touch with the Board and with me." Neither the associate directors nor Kenneth Clark were wholly wrong. Olivier's tastes did indeed lie in the direction of the traditional and well-established, but part of him hankered after modernity and he longed to be considered, if not one of the avant-garde, then at least a champion of progress. To achieve this he was prepared from time to time to take on projects that he did not understand or which, insofar as he did understand them, he disliked. One had to be prepared to run the risk of being wrong, he said. It was this urge to countenance modernity that led him to yield to Tynan's importunities and accept Adrian Mitchell's *Tyger*, even though he privately considered it "the most God-awful piece of work I've remembered seeing in my life."[19]

No play illustrated more clearly that, though Olivier's authority within the National Theater was absolute when he so wished it, he allowed limits to be imposed on it when he thought his reputation as an innovator was at stake. Having accepted *Tyger* against his better judgment he became alarmed by the stream of obscenities of which it largely consisted. When Binkie Beaumont told him that it was seditious into the bargain he resolved that something must be done. John Dexter and Kenneth Tynan made common cause in thwarting him. Olivier appealed to the author, claiming that he would be in trouble with his Board and that the subsidies on which the National Theater depended might well be cut if the play was put on unexpurgated. Tynan took it upon himself to stiffen Mitchell's resolve: "Of course *all* the disputed lines are not necessary," he admitted, "but 'Reason not the need'—they are Adrian's, they are part of his play, and they must be included." Olivier took particular exception to the line, "God damn the Queen." Mitchell had strong republican sympathies, Tynan argued, he had a right to express his views. "Why doesn't he go and live in a republic then?" asked an exasperated Olivier. He gained a few excisions, but not nearly as many as he would have liked. "How one longs to reveal," concluded Tynan, "that if *Tyger* succeeds it will be in the teeth of panic-stricken opposition from this obtuse, lick-spittle Laurence Olivier, who would rather insult a poet than cause moments of dismay to Her Majesty."[20]

Sure enough, the Board was horrified by the extravagances of *Tyger*. Victor Mishcon, an eminent solicitor and Socialist county counselor, thought it "cheap and vulgar." Binkie Beaumont darkly remarked that he had the impression that "some element had more or less insisted upon the play being mounted"—presumably a reference to what the Board felt to be the malign influence of Tynan. For the Director merely to give the titles of the plays he proposed to put on was not enough, argued Mishcon: "Where matters of policy were concerned . . . the entire Board must be alerted and a frank report submitted." For the first time the Board braced itself for a confrontation with its all-powerful Director. Olivier was summoned to attend the next meeting. "If I am to be given a wigging on account of *Tyger* and Lord knows what else, I shall take my beating like a man," Olivier told Kenneth Rae—but he stipulated that he would rather the representatives of the Arts Council, the Treasury and the G.L.C. were not present to witness his humiliation. In the event the wigging was mild—the Board was quite as nervous of offending Olivier as he was of offending them—but he found it galling to be called upon to defend a play that he himself had disliked and had done his best to sanitize.[21]

Fortunately the Board had no jurisdiction over Joan Little-wood's irreverent and mocking satire on the First World War, *Oh! What a Lovely War*. They would have deplored it if they had been given the opportunity. Richard Attenborough had been asked to direct the film and tried to raise money in the United States. Who's going to be in it? asked the putative sponsors. Oh, Laurence Olivier, John Gielgud, Ralph Richardson, Michael Redgrave, said Atten-borough. At this point he had approached nobody. Impressed, the sponsor agreed to put up the money. Attenborough now turned to Olivier. Knowing that he was robustly patriotic and might well disapprove of a film that set out to mock the traditional heroics of First World War historiography, Attenborough was uncertain how Olivier would respond to the appeal. Fortunately he had enjoyed the musical and agreed to play Field Marshal French. Attenbor-ough admitted that he had already promised that Gielgud and Richardson would also be in the cast. "Make sure you tell both of them, particularly Ralphie, that I've already agreed to appear for Equity minimum rates, and they must do the same," said Oliv-ier. Attenborough was convinced that, if Olivier had refused to appear, his fellow theatrical knights would have followed suit and the whole project would have foundered.[22]

The Board would have looked more kindly on another film that Olivier made in 1969. To play in the same year a caricature of Field Marshal French and a soberly heroic Air Marshal Dowding, head of Fighter Command during the Battle of Britain, was a remark-able exercise in flexibility. Olivier played Dowding with deliberate sobriety; a still center of calm responsibility contrasted with the maelstrom of violence in the skies above him. He grew a mustache in the hope of looking like his hero, but he admitted that he was still wide of the mark. "Dowding had a more definite type of face than mine," he said. He tried to imitate Dowding's voice, but "there was nothing very remarkable about it." Many years later he said that he would have liked to have met Dowding if he had been alive: "I do like to meet them provided I know that they are acceptable to the idea." His memory betrayed him. Dowding was very much alive and Olivier almost certainly met him. It is said that the Air Marshal saw *The Battle of Britain* and "wept at the beauty of the interpretation."[23]

Cinematic excursions of this kind were very much an extra, undertaken to make some money and supplement the inconsiderable wage paid him by the National Theater. The National itself continued to absorb almost all his energies. Though he was frequently called on to act as both producer and director, Olivier understood and shared the fears and aspirations of the actor. This, however, did not make it any easier to supply their needs. Sometimes, indeed, it seemed to him that his principal function was to frustrate them. Derek Jacobi, for instance, professed his loyalty to the Company but concluded that he no longer felt he was "developing as an actor along the path that makes me an individual performer." If he was to progress he had to be offered roles that would "make demands on me emotionally and give me an opportunity to use fully the potential that I believe I have." He had begun to think of himself as a "competent—adequate—professional—supporting—actor who can be relied on to turn in an acceptable piece of work—and I think that that is a very dangerous state to be in." It was a state that Olivier could never have borne to be in himself and he sympathized with Jacobi's feelings. It has been alleged that Olivier resented and sought to curb the success of any young actor who he felt might challenge his preeminence. He may have been guilty, from time to time, of avoiding appearing with younger actors whose performance might, he felt, distract attention from his own. But except in such rare cases he rejoiced in the success of the up-and-coming members of the National staff. He did not view Jacobi as his rival, on the contrary he felt that the younger man's success reflected credit on him, Olivier, for having brought Jacobi forward. But that did not mean that he could always, or even often, find the parts to satisfy the hungry young would-be stars. The fact was that, in a repertory company where acting of the highest standard was the norm, there were not enough good parts to go around. Should Olivier promote Jacobi at the expense of Alan Bates, who appealed for a "yonking big classic part"? Or Alan Adams, to whom Olivier apologized for giving only inadequate roles: "You must understand that it is only on very rare occasions that a Theater like this . . . can find useful opportunities for showing a person in the process of development."[24]

The women were no less exigent. Maggie Smith was ready to play Hedda in *Hedda Gabler* but wanted Olivier to be Judge Brack. He would love to do it if it were feasible, he said, but "will you be kind enough please to remember that I have to cast from within the Company, and that strive to please you as I might I would hope that you would be prepared to find my final decision acceptable." He accused her agent, Peter Dunlop—"*Agent Provocateur*," he described Dunlop in a letter to Smith—of trying to play him along so that they would be able to dictate all sorts of conditions as the price of her acceptance—"and that, my friend, is a situation I do not intend to find myself in." Eventually Maggie Smith agreed to go to America in *The Three Sisters*, but it was not with "a free and happy mind," reported Michael Hallifax, the company manager. Smith felt that she had been led up the garden path; her agent reported that it was most unlikely that she would want to stay with the National Theater after the end of the current season. There was still worse trouble when Smith, playing Masha in *The Three Sisters*, received a letter from Olivier making various points about her playing of the role. He addressed her letter to "My darling Mageen"; her reply was signed coldly "Margaret." Could he not have spoken to her? she asked: "The written word is always very black and really rather unhelpful, also it is sad that you have *nothing* to tell me about what is *right* (if indeed anything is) about my performance."[25]

Trying to persuade a recalcitrant actress to do what he wanted was bad enough, but at least in the case of Maggie Smith he knew that she was a skillful player who was worth saving for the National Theater if it could possibly be done. What was more painful was dismissing players who were not up to the required quality. Angela Baddeley was a distinguished classical actress, today best remembered for her role as the irascible cook in *Upstairs, Downstairs*. She proved unsuitable for her role in *The Dance of Death* and Olivier dismissed her to make way for Geraldine McEwan. Her husband, his old friend Glen Byam Shaw, rounded on him and accused him of being cruel, hard and a cold snake. "Only a character of truly Saint-like qualities could be a manager in this line of business without the slightest characteristic of business growing upon him," Olivier pleaded. "Yes, I do try to take a cool attitude and not let my emotions influence my judgment . . . When I took on this job, I said that in 5 years I would not have a friend left in the world . . ." He had two fewer now. It was episodes of this kind that made Olivier wonder whether he had done well to take on the National Theater; but if he was honest with himself he would have concluded that, whatever, the price, there was no job on earth he would more willingly be doing.[26]

CHAPTER TWENTY-ONE

CHALLENGES

With the departure of Gaskill and Dexter a proliferation of outside directors was brought in to handle a single production
each, or perhaps two or three. The number of arrivals and depar-
tures, as Michael Billington has remarked, was more what one would
expect in Waterloo Station than in a theater in the Waterloo Road.
Out of five productions in the repertoire in the autumn of 1969, four
were the responsibility of outside directors. The casual-labor policy
was convenient and, Olivier thought or claimed to think, was a useful way of keeping the regular members of the cast on their toes.
It could not be the complete answer, though, and Olivier was constantly looking for someone who could provide long-term support
and might even one day prove a worthy successor.[1]

One of the few who seemed a real possibility was Michael Blakemore. Blakemore had toured with Olivier, playing minor parts in
the Stratford tour of Europe in 1957, but since then had veered
toward direction. He joined the National Theater in 1969 and
became an associate director two years later. He felt in awe of his
imposing superior. He told Olivier that he felt he must address him
as Larry—"I won't be able to express an opinion at all properly if
I have to call you Sir Laurence." "Yes, I always hoped you would,"
Olivier replied. Blakemore thought he said this rather grudgingly—
but in fact Olivier welcomed an approach that was egalitarian and
informal in manner, even though deferential in substance. A subordinate who would call him Larry but would do as he was told
was the ideal. Blakemore did not always do as he was told and the

two men had occasional rows, but he won Olivier's confidence to a greater extent than any other of the directors who from time to time worked in the National Theater.[2]

In October 1967 the Board had also authorized the employment of Frank Dunlop as an associate director. With Dunlop and Blakemore installed, and Robert Stephens doing some directing, it seemed that the burden on Olivier would at last be relieved. Within a few months, however, Dunlop began to devote most of his energies to the Young Vic. This concept had been inspired by Olivier. He had pleaded the case for a subsidiary company that would train up potential recruits for the National with Jennie Lee, the Minister for the Arts. She was impressed, both by the cogency of his arguments and his benevolence in advancing them: "I was conscious that great actors can be concerned only for themselves, but here was Laurence Olivier pleading for the talented young," she claimed. Olivier for his part was characteristically extravagant in his gratitude. "My dear Minister," he wrote, "*our* dear Minister, dear kind wonderful Minister. We shall never live long enough or grow eloquent enough to thank you even halfway properly for all that you have done and we pray may long continue to do for us." He had nevertheless done himself out of a large part of Dunlop's services; the pressures on him were as great five years after he had taken over as they had ever been.[3]

Those pressures were augmented by the turbulent presence of Kenneth Tynan. He bombarded Olivier with suggestions—many of which were excellent, some of which were crass—and was endlessly inventive in his ideas for introducing novelty into the traditional repertoire. He asked Paul McCartney to write the music for some Shakespearean songs. He didn't really like words by Shakespeare, McCartney replied. "Maybe I could write the National Theater stomp sometime. Or the ballad of Larry O." Few weeks passed without Tynan being embroiled in some fearful row, usually contriving to involve Olivier in it as well. In 1965 George Devine was added to the list of his enemies. Devine had been brought in to direct Samuel Beckett's *Play*. Egged on by the author, who was in close attendance,

Devine took what was anyway an extremely short play at breakneck speed. Tynan was horrified; "It's beautiful poetry," he argued, "and I want to be able to hear it." He wrote Devine one of his most tactless letters, complaining that the dialogue was inaudible and that Beckett was "trying to treat English as if it was French." Devine responded with predictable fury. Tynan's letter was "impertinent and ignorant"; even if the dramaturge had any business to interfere in this way—which Devine doubted—his manner of expression was "presumptuous." Tynan had compounded his offense in Devine's eyes by suggesting that members of the Board were disturbed and that the whole future of the project was in peril. Given Tynan's record, to find him invoking the Board as an ally in his effort to encroach on the independence of a director is comical. Devine felt it to be unacceptable: "I find your suggestion that a visiting director should be menaced with conservative members of the National Theater Board preposterous."[4]

Worst of all, Tynan had claimed to speak "on behalf of the National Theater" and had invoked Olivier as an ally in the cause. As it happened, in this particular case Olivier did think that Tynan was right, but he was appalled by his dramaturge's methods. He had known Devine all his life and very intimately, he said: "he is overweeningly proud but wonderfully valuable." Anyone of any sense could have seen that Tynan was going about it in the wrong way. Would he please in the future learn to curb his tongue?[5]

He might have been sharper still if he had known that this was a sighting shot for Tynan's most explosive venture. The Hochhuth affair disturbed Olivier so deeply that he devoted twenty-eight pages to it in his memoirs. Rolf Hochhuth was a German dramatist whose new play, *Soldiers*, was submitted to the National Theater at a moment when Tynan's craving for the sensational was at its most virulent. "I'm worried," he had told Olivier at the beginning of 1966. "Nothing really specific: just a general feeling that we are losing our lead . . . We are doing nothing to remind [the public] that the theater is an independent force at the heart of the country's life—a sleeping tiger that can and should be roused whenever the national (or international) conscience needs nudging." When a play came along that condemned Churchill for authorizing the bombing of Dresden and accused him of complicity in the "murder" of the Polish leader, General Sikorski, Tynan's delight knew no bounds. That the author was German made it even better—"only a damn Boche would have had the crust to attempt it," wrote Air Marshal Arthur "Bomber" Harris: a reaction that would have enchanted Tynan if he had known of it. Hochhuth may not be Euripides, Tynan handsomely admitted, nor *Soldiers The Trojan Women*, "but it is in the same tradition. Hochhuth is the test of our maturity, the test of our willingness to take a central position in the limelight of public affairs. If the play goes on under our banner, we shall be a genuinely national theater, and, even as the stink-bombs fly, I shall be very proud of us."[6]

Olivier had his doubts. Unlike Tynan, he disliked rows; he was an ardent patriot and worshipper of Churchill; he did not even think it was a good play—"I dislike the bloody thing," he told Joan Plowright. He may have seen some attractions in Tynan's insistence that he was the only man to play Churchill: "My God, how like you the old bastard is! The passionate maddening love of detail, the concentration that can wither other people by simply ignoring their presence, the sudden changes of subject, the sudden focusing on apparent irrelevances, the love of anecdote and quotation, the brutally realistic assessment of human motives, the terrible stubbornness, the impatience and the patience." More than this, though, Olivier was attracted by the idea of espousing a cause that seemed both daring and controversial, and which would put the National Theater in the forefront of progressive thinking. He assumed that there would be trouble and was ready to accept, even welcome it: if he had realized how severe that trouble was going to be he would have been more cautious, but by the time it became apparent it was too late.[7]

Please reassure the author that there are no political problems over mounting his play, Tynan told Hochhuth's English agent. "We are subject to no political pressures of any kind." He quickly discovered how wrong he was. The Board took strong exception to the play and were unconvinced by Tynan's assurance that Hochhuth possessed documentary evidence to support his thesis and that eminent historians considered that it might be correct. Olivier, for his part, took strong exception to Chandos's argument that he could not support a play that criticized Churchill so vociferously when he himself had been a member of Churchill's wartime Government. Until that moment, he said later, he had been "completely on the Chairman's side in my heart," but he found this argument "so appallingly dangerous that I turned against him." The Board debated, dithered, debated some more and concluded that it must ban the production of the play. Olivier protested. The Board took note of his protest. Olivier insisted that the fact that he was unhappy about the ruling should be recorded in the minutes. "I don't think that's necessary," said the Chairman. Olivier stuck to his guns. "Oh, let him be unhappy if he wants it," cut in Kenneth Clark.[8]

As far as Olivier was concerned the matter was now closed and the National Theater could move on. Tynan was made of sterner stuff. He hinted that he and Olivier were about to resign—an idea that Olivier insisted he had never contemplated; he announced that he and Olivier hoped soon to mount a production of *Soldiers* in the West End—"I was never partner to this hope," Olivier noted drily; he wrote to John Arden and other prominent dramatists suggesting that they should refuse to allow their plays to be produced by the National Theater if the ban on Hochhuth was not rescinded. When Tynan eventually got *Soldiers* put on in the West End, Olivier refused to come to the first night, dreading the awkward questions that the press would put to him. Tynan pleaded that his absence would cause unfavorable comment; if he would come he could hide in Tynan's box and, at the end, be smuggled out unmolested. "I can't quite make sense of your wishfully comfortable assurance that I needn't be seen," Olivier complained, "as this isn't consistent with your real reason for wanting me there." When Churchill's grandson, Winston Churchill junior, urged Olivier to state publicly what he had told him in private—that he did not accept Hochhuth's claim to historical authenticity—Olivier agreed but then agonized for weeks, discarding draft after draft before he finally wrote to *The Times* to say that he had never been convinced by any of Hochhuth's allegations about the death of Sikorski.[9]

The most significant victim of the imbroglio was Olivier's relationship with his Chairman. Formally, all was as it had been, but harsh enough words had been exchanged between Chandos and Olivier to mean that complete confidence in each other would never be restored. Chandos realized how much this had been the work of Tynan and deplored the influence the dramaturge exercised over his Director: "there are now a number of libel actions about," he warned Olivier, "and I beg you to be careful, because Tynan as a controversialist is a piece of cake to his enemies, and a disaster to his friends. He is both dishonest and untruthful, and if you recognize this fact it will save you a lot of tears in the future." Over the next few years a disproportionately large amount of Olivier's time and energy was to be devoted to defending his dramaturge against the indignation of his Board and its Chairman.[10]

The Dance of Death, the rehearsals of which had been interrupted by Olivier's appendicitis, was Strindberg's partly autobiographical portrait of a doomed marriage. "I like old Strindberg," Olivier told Ralph Richardson, "he gives you a nice clear field to work on." The field in this case was a field of battle, waged between Olivier, playing a manic Prussian army captain, and his dejected wife. It provided a horrifyingly realist portrait of a marriage that was sustained by tedious rituals and enlivened only by explosions of mindless violence. "I love it," Olivier told Robert Stephens. "This is the best part I've ever played, apart from Archie Rice. This is me. I'm the Captain." He refused to accept that the tortured bleakness of the marriage was in any way exaggerated; he told the translator, Michael Meyer, that there was not a line in his part that he had not, at one time or another, addressed to one of his three wives. Tynan agreed. "Larry and I regard the play as a wholly realistic study of marriage, red in tooth and claw," he told Alan Dent. "In fact there are whole passages that take me back to dear old Notley."[11]

Olivier claimed he took the play on above all because it offered a good part for Geraldine McEwan: "I didn't give a damn if I made a success, I really didn't; it was her success I was after." The concept of Olivier not giving a damn whether he made a success of a part strains the reader's credulity, but he may well have seen the play primarily as an opportunity for McEwan. If so, he was disappointed. "I have been fantastically lucky with the notices," he told Richardson, "at the expense, I am afraid, of my partners, whose work has been very grossly underestimated." "It was one of Olivier's greatest performances, perhaps his greatest," judged Penelope Mortimer, and his physical transformation—"a close-cropped Prussian head, hooded stony eyes, aggressively jutting jaw, a choleric red face that went purple in his fits"—was among the most realized of his career.[12]

A Mr. Andrew Main wrote to Olivier to condole with him on what he felt was the inappropriate laughter that his performance had from time to time provoked. Olivier's reply illustrates his conviction that even *Hamlet* or *Macbeth* were the more effective for a little humor. *The Dance of Death*, he said, was in his view not a tragedy. "Even if the play were to be a tragedy I would not object to laughter . . . I personally feel that the difference between tragedy and comedy is far more thin than by most is imagined, and it is my aim in life to make that more and more so. I wish, you see, to leave the audience in the position of the gods, to whom, after all, our most searing tragedies must be things of comedy."[13]

The Dance of Death was for him the most taxing of the plays the National Theater took to Canada in the autumn of 1967. Having decided not to tour in *Othello* Olivier felt bound to appear in all three plays and took over the tiny but significant role of the butler in Feydeau's farce, *A Flea in Her Ear*. He had not played so small a part for years and, perhaps for that reason, found it peculiarly difficult to remember his lines. He kept a copy of his script on a music-stand in the wings, with his spectacles beside them, so that he could go offstage, refresh his memory as to what came next and then come back on to resume the action. "Darling girl," he said to Jane Lapotaire, who had just joined the company and was playing the French maid, Antoinette, "if I should dry, you will help me out, won't you? For example, if a line begins with 'I,' just point toward your eye." Lapotaire thought this was the most preposterous thing she had ever heard; but then Olivier did dry. "He just spun round 360 degrees, slapping his hands that had got white-buttoned gloves . . . The audience thought it was the funniest thing they'd ever seen." Lapotaire asked Geraldine McEwan what it was like to have Olivier join the cast. "Well," said McEwan, "it used to be a play about a woman who thinks her husband is unfaithful to her; now it's a play about a butler who works for a woman who thinks her husband is unfaithful to her." Being Olivier, he could not resist behaving like the director if the real director was absent or even, now and again, if he was present. Once, he saw Lapotaire was having trouble working out how she ought to play her role. "Now, darling Jane," said Olivier, "the maid should be like this." He took an imaginary feather duster, bent over and stuck his bottom out, glanced around him with the wickedest, most sexually alluring look and said, "You see, she's like that." "And within about ten seconds," remembered Lapotaire gratefully, "there was my Antoinette."[14]

Everyone who knew him well realized that, medically speaking, he should not have been on the tour at all. He remained ebullient, contriving to get a great deal of fun out of his activities and to make it fun for other people. In Montreal he saw some actors from the company getting ready to go to hear a group of black singers called The Supremes. He asked if he could join them. "Who are The Supremes?" he inquired in the taxi on the way to the concert. He was given a few facts. The Supremes heard that he was in the auditorium and, before the concert started, the lead singer announced how privileged they were to have "the greatest actor the world has ever known" in their midst. Olivier promptly went on stage and delivered an eloquent eulogy to The Supremes and their achievements. "And he'd never even heard of them half an hour before!" said one of his party in wonder. "God!" said Olivier afterward. "I've fallen in love." He invited The Supremes to the next day's matinee and, in his curtain speech, made them stand up and introduced them to the audience. They then went back stage and had a riotous time. "It was such fun," said Edward Hardwicke. "Can you imagine Peter Hall doing it?"[15]*

But he himself felt that he was beginning to lose his grip on things. Back in London, he found that he was facing what seemed to him a critical challenge. He had invited Peter Brook to direct Seneca's *Oedipus*. His relationship with Brook had never recovered from the near-debacle of *The Beggar's Opera* and it may have been the recollection of that contretemps that led Brook to introduce into the production some features that he knew Olivier would find offensive. At the end of the play the cast were to dance up and down the aisles to the tune of a jazzed-up version of "God Save the Queen"; meanwhile a vast phallus was to be displayed on the stage, first wrapped in swaddling clothes, then displayed to the world in proud erection. Olivier believed these to be vulgar and pointless extravagances that would destroy the effect of an otherwise impressive production. Brook refused to give way: John Gielgud, who was playing Oedipus, agreed with Olivier—"I understand why Larry was so upset; he thought they'd close the theater." He felt it was not his place to intervene, however, and when a fearful row broke out in his dressing room after the dress rehearsal, he fled the scene. He returned to find that the full-length mirror had been shattered—"I never discovered which of them had thrown the ashtray." In fact, according to Frank Dunlop, who was also there, it was not an ashtray but Peter Brook himself, who tried to storm out and, in his rage, walked into the mirror instead.[16]

---

* Rather similar is the occasion when the actor Jack Hedley was dining in a restaurant with Olivier and a group of friends. The Goodies came in, causing something of a stir. Olivier asked who they were and what they did. Later, he went to the lavatory, stopped at their table and said how enormously he admired their work. "But you'd never even heard of them," protested Hedley. "Yes, but they'll never forget it," Olivier replied.

A compromise was eventually reached: the jazzed-up national anthem was dropped, but only on condition that "God Save the Queen" was not played at all; the phallus was retained. Tynan and Dunlop both took Brook's side: Tynan relished the offending elements; Dunlop was less enthusiastic, but thought the director's wishes should prevail. Olivier believed that he had been defeated: "I felt weak; I was weak; and weakly I gave in." In Dunlop's view he got the whole thing out of proportion; nobody paid any attention to the phallus and the bacchanalian riot amounted to very little. Olivier, though, felt that a crushing blow had been dealt to his authority. His relationship with Brook remained sour. A few months later he invited him back to direct *Antony and Cleopatra*. Possibly with some relish, he explained that the pay would have to be less than it had been in the case of *Oedipus*; the National Theater was short of money. Brook took offense and accused Olivier of making him an insulting offer with the intention that it should be rejected. "Oh God, Peter," Olivier replied. "I sometimes think you take a delight . . . in missing no opportunity of reminding me of the wretched level I hold in your estimation. It is hard to have to keep having to pluck up the courage to make continual efforts to settle our quarrel against a wall so obviously determined to keep things in this unhappy state." In the end a reconciliation was achieved, but Brook never worked with Olivier again.[17]

What caused Olivier the greatest chagrin at this period, however, was not a production that did not turn out to his satisfaction but one that did not take place at all. He had set his heart on doing the American musical *Guys and Dolls*, reserving for himself the role of the crap-game impresario, Nathan Detroit. He believed *Guys and Dolls* to be a masterpiece, an Everest towering above the foothills of traditional musicals; he also longed to show that the National Theater was up to any challenge. Nothing is taboo, he pronounced: "There may be some types of play that it is felt need to be represented with varying degrees of frequency or infrequency, but there is nothing against our producing a musical." Robert Stephens did not agree. He canvassed opinion among the actors—"which perhaps I should not have done," he later admitted—and reported that the general view was that, if the National put on *Guys and Dolls* without professional American singers and dancers, the production would be no better than the work of "some local amateur operatic society." Worse still, he infected the Board with his doubts. Chandos in particular was skeptical. He thought it would cost too much, he questioned whether *Guys and Dolls* could be considered a classic, he even doubted whether it came within "the terms of reference for which they received public subsidies." The Board always preferred to leave the choice of plays to the Director, but, said Chandos, they would be shirking their duty if they did not consider these points. They duly considered these points and Olivier's eloquence won the day; everyone except the Chairman either supported the project or felt that the decision should be left to the Director. "After great battle won Board meeting this morning," Olivier cabled triumphantly to Garson Kanin, the American whom he planned should direct the musical. To Noël Coward he stressed how important for the *amour propre* of the company it was that they should show themselves capable of mounting such a production out of their own resources. "Of course we're not going to do musicals every bloody year. This escapade is just to freshen up our dreary old image a bit."[18]

Victory proved fleeting. Olivier's health broke down and the Board ruled that, without him, it would be folly to press on. Don't be so precipitant, urged Olivier. "Surely you wouldn't turn down Paul Scofield, Richard Attenborough or Johnnie Mills, if I could get them?" He couldn't get them, though, and the day seemed lost; but by the end of 1970 he had made an unexpectedly complete recovery. He returned to the charge and thought that he had once more prevailed; the long-term forecast that he prepared for Chandos envisaged the opening of *Guys and Dolls* in November 1971. "They proceed apace with *Guys,*" he told Kanin. "I shall start my own private preliminary dancing course in a couple of months." Quite what happened next is obscure, but it seems that Paddy Donnell, the company manager, took fright at the expense of the production and threatened to resign unless it was abandoned. Olivier could not afford the resignation of someone of such stature on the business side, and so gave way. "I was really betrayed by that," Olivier remembered some years later. "This man was really responsible for my quitting the job, because when that happened, I thought, if I'm going to have to put up with treachery from my partners, I'm going."[19]

While the battle over *Guys and Dolls* was still raging, Olivier played one of his last great Shakespearean roles. This *Merchant of Venice* was to be set in the late nineteenth century. Olivier claimed to have conceived the idea himself and to have sold it to the talented young director, Jonathan Miller. Rather more credibly, Miller says that it was his idea and that Olivier only agreed to take on the part of Shylock himself when he had been convinced that Miller's approach would provide a new and challenging experience. The production is of particular interest as being one of the few in which Olivier accepted direction from somebody far younger and less experienced than himself. "I'm awfully snooty with directors, I'm afraid," he once admitted, but Miller impressed and intrigued him. Olivier had conceived his Shylock as being a traditional Fagin-like creature with hooked nose, ringlets, protruding teeth and rich Jewish accent. Miller convinced him that Jews did not have to be like that and that, if he imposed this vision on the kind of production that was envisaged, he would end up looking like "a ridiculous pantomime dame" in the midst of a rather ordinary nineteenth-century set. Even more daringly, he challenged Olivier on his verse-speaking. As Olivier had found Gielgud declamatory and "poetic" a quarter of a century before, so now Miller accused Olivier of being preoccupied by the sound rather than the sense and intoning melodiously when he should have been realistic. "I'd made a mountain out of mannerisms and had ended up impersonating myself," Olivier admitted. "Jonathan decided that nobody would have the nerve to tell me things about myself if it wasn't he . . . I took no offense at all . . . it was bloody plucky of him and I admired him." The false nose went, the ringlets went, the mannerisms were curbed: all that was left were the dentures; these had cost Olivier so much money that Miller did not have the heart to suggest they too should be discarded.[20]

Olivier knew that, if the doctors had their way, he would not have been on the stage at all. Jane Lapotaire, who played Jessica, was horrified by his condition and doubted whether he would survive the first night. "They've come to see whether I'm going to die on stage," Olivier told her grimly. To add to his woes, he suffered stage fright more agonizing than anything he had so far experienced; he begged the other actors not to look him in the face: "For some reason this made me feel that there was not quite so much loaded against me." Somehow he got through the performance on the first night, gained rapturous applause at the end, and felt such relief at having survived that the stage fright almost miraculously receded. By the end of the London run it had gone forever. Gielgud refused to watch Olivier as Shylock: "Larry with false teeth and fur coat à la Rothschild," he told Irene Worth. "I don't think anyone really likes it much, though of course the new look intrigued the critics." He must have been selective in the people with whom he discussed the performance; most people seem to have felt that Olivier's Shylock was a brave and intelligent representation of what is one of Shakespeare's most testing parts. "One of the most astonishing things you have ever done," Tynan considered. "You show us Shylock turning into a Jew before our eyes." Shylock started as a businessman who happened to be a Jew, his daughter's flight with a Christian reminded him what it was to be Jewish, by the end of the trial "he knows it through and through—so indelibly that no one in the theater will ever forget it."[21]

The Merchant of Venice was still running when Olivier was reminded that the problems of the Director of the National Theater were by no means confined to the plays in which he himself was involved. He had taken on, more or less unseen, a version of *Coriolanus*, reworked by Brecht, which Tynan had assured him was "desperately exciting." The play came as a package, with directors from the Berliner Ensemble thrown in. "I fell for the argument that here was the great modern production," Olivier admitted. "I always had wide-open flapping ears for anything to do with modern work." Constance Cummings, who had been invited to play Volumnia, asked whether the production would be Brechtian, "for she wasn't very keen on Brecht." Either Tynan had misled him or Olivier deceived himself. He assured Cummings that it was essentially Shakespeare's *Coriolanus* that would be played. Brecht might have made some minor adjustments, but nothing of significance. Scofield had originally been intended to play Coriolanus but had defected from the National Theater. Christopher Plummer took his place. Plummer was an excellent actor but one with certain pretensions: he arrived each day in a Rolls-Royce and insisted on being personally called when due to go on stage rather than accepting the summons by loudspeaker that Olivier and everybody else found adequate. Not surprisingly, the rest of the cast resented him; a circumstance that caused him little disquiet since he dismissed all but two or three of them as "a bunch of unwelcoming humorless malcontents whose socialist leanings not only were far left of Lenin but made Harold Wilson look like King Farouk."[22]

When the German directors and the Brechtian script arrived it was discovered that Shakespeare's text had been treated with scant respect and that Plummer's part, in particular, had been cut ferociously. The director spoke almost no English: after a tirade in German lasting several minutes the translator would interpret his words as: "He say: 'You stand there.'" When Plummer demanded that his lines be restored, the Germans said that Brecht's widow insisted that there should be no deviation from the sacred text. In the end they agreed to some of the cuts being put back, but not enough to satisfy Plummer, who insisted that either they or he must go. A cast meeting was held, and it was decided unanimously that it was Plummer who should be the loser. "The whole episode [was] a splendid vindication of the new collective leadership at the N.T.," wrote Tynan in his diary. Olivier did not see it quite like that. He would far rather have kept Plummer and lost the German directors, and would have ignored the views of the company if he had had the chance. The fact was, however, that he was committed by contract to the Brechtian package and would have been involved in expensive lawsuits if he had tried to escape his obligations. Like it not: Plummer must go and the German directors stay.[23]

There was yet more trouble to come. Plummer's place was taken by Anthony Hopkins. As a result Hopkins was replaced by Plummer in what he considered to be a more important role in *Danton's Death*. He was furious and demanded to see Olivier. "I know you're very, very angry," said Olivier. "Yes." "Punch me on the jaw," suggested Olivier. The proposition did not appeal to Hopkins. "Just give me a bloody explanation," he asked. "Why did you do it?" "I'll tell you why. Because Chris is a big star and you're not." This somewhat brutal statement of the truth did not seem calculated to appease Hopkins's susceptibilities. Nor was Olivier much more conciliatory when it came to Hopkins's performance. "Highly lauded and welcomed" as Hopkins's Coriolanus had been, he wrote after the play had been running for a few weeks, "there really is a very general complaint about incomprehensibility, because the audience cannot understand what you are saying . . . I *must* draw this to your attention . . . a general complaint such as this could well sink us." There followed a few lines of unctuous flattery about Hopkins's brilliance and the "stellar proportions" of his success, but the opening rebuke must have been hard to swallow.[24]

Coriolanus was not a success and Tynan can be blamed for it. On the other hand, he must be praised for inducing Olivier to take on a role that he would otherwise have shunned. Eugene O'Neill's *Long Day's Journey into Night* is the story of a defunct actor, once modestly celebrated, never great, moldering in obscurity with his alcoholic sons and drug-addict wife. It is bleakly, blackly depressing and one of the greatest, if not *the* greatest play of the twentieth century. It terrified Olivier. He had seen Fredric March act it in New York in 1956 and had thought: "I wouldn't play this bloody part for anything and, what's more, I'll never play any actor now I've seen this." Whoever played James Tyrone would have to bring off that most difficult trick: to be a great actor pretending to be a bad actor, or at least a second-rate actor. Yet he knew that it was a magnificent part in "a pretty well perfect play." When Tynan told him that he had more or less committed him to mount the play at the National Theater at the end of 1971 and to play Tyrone himself, he professed outrage. "I feel a bit incredulous," he wrote, "that you should be quite so prepared to land me in for studying a huge part and sweating out performances for possibly many months . . . feeling nothing but cold dislike for the part, the play and the whole occasion."[25]

And yet he knew that it was a part he had to play and even while he groaned in public a bit of him rejoiced. For several months *Long Day's Journey* took over his life. Learning a part was no longer the matter of routine it had once been: for twelve weeks, he told Tynan, he had "devoted every single second of my thinking, learning and reading life to it—*sans* alcohol too." The demands the part made on him were second only to those of Othello, and physically he was far less able to resist them. Denis Quilley remembered that during the one-minute break between Acts One and Two he would slump into a chair in the wings and go to sleep: "I'd have to tap him gently on the shoulder and remind him which stage of the play we'd reached, and he'd go on as vigorously as ever. He loved hard graft."[26]

The graft was almost too hard. Derek Granger at some point asked him whether he was not enjoying the part. "Crazy wife, drunken old ham actor, don't you think it's just a little near the bone?" Olivier replied. "Some of us have lived a little, boysie." In fact Olivier never for an instant identified with Tyrone, but he introduced some of his own actorly tricks and techniques into his performance, he knew that he was playing what he might have been, he walked a tightrope between self-parody and self-revelation. It was "a performance of intense technical and personal fascination," wrote Irving Wardle. "The dejection that settles on Olivier's frame from the start—his body hunched and his mouth cracked into a small, crooked line— expresses a sense of defeat that encompasses his whole life."[27]

For all that he knew that *Long Day's Journey* was destined to be one of Olivier's greatest roles, Tynan was nevertheless disturbed about the future of the National Theater. Olivier, he felt, through ill health and inattention, had let the organization crumble. The whole place was going to rack and ruin, the repertoire was fusty and unadventurous, there was hardly an actor in the permanent company who was more than a competent journeyman, attendances were down, no thought was being given to what would happen when Olivier retired. He set out all his fears in a long, angry letter and had it delivered to Olivier's dressing room shortly before the curtain went up on the first night of *Long Day's Journey*. His assistant, Rozina Adler, was dismayed. "I begged him not to," she remembered. "You just don't do things like that when someone is going to appear in the first performance of anything, let alone this show, which came when it did and when 'Sir' himself was so worried . . . The situation at the National was terribly serious, but it was a terrible thing to do." There is no evidence that Olivier read Tynan's protest before the curtain rose. If he had, it did not affect the quality of his performance. Nor was the situation at the National as "terribly serious" as Rozina Adler maintained. But all was not going well and Olivier, as he scoured the ecstatic reviews that his acting had earned him, was conscious of the fact that something needed to be done and that he was not sure what it should be or how he should set about it.[28]

CHAPTER TWENTY-TWO

WHO WILL TAKE OVER?

"The National Theater," said John Osborne, in atrabilious mood, "has, I think combined the worst aspects of the commercial theater with those of an institution—a stuffy institution. I also think Olivier's the least suitable person to run a national theater. He always wanted to be an actor-manager, but that is something quite different from being the administrator of a theatrical institution . . . On the one hand he wants to be trendy, or to keep up with public taste, or get beyond it; and on the other he is also . . . very orthodox and conservative."[1]

Not many people would have seen things as starkly as that, but Tynan, a man whom Osborne loathed and despised, would have echoed every word of it and disquiet was general. At the end of 1970, instigated by Robert Stephens, there was something of a palace revolution. A meeting was held, at which doubts about the Company's future were voiced, and reports leaked into the newspapers. "Difficult phase at the N.T.," was the headline in the *Evening Standard*. In the face of such publicity, the Company closed ranks and professed its total loyalty to its Director, but the Board, too, was concerned. Average attendances had dropped from 85 percent to 78 percent and were at one point to sink to a miserable 67 percent. The Board concluded that "one or two recent productions had not been very exciting, that new faces in the Company would help renew interest and that new impetus would be given if Sir Laurence were to appear again in a major role."[2]

The last point at least had been met by the production of *Long Day's Journey*, but the need for new faces was something with which Tynan would have concurred. "I think the Company is at present so weak that it could not succeed in *any* program of plays," he told Olivier. "There isn't anyone at the Vic (except possibly Pickup) to whose next appearance one looks forward with real excitement." The charge came ill from someone who had himself contributed signally to the National Theater's malaise. Only a few months before he had been responsible for Arrabal's arcane and anarchic *The Architect and the Emperor of Assyria*. The critical response had been one of cautious interest; in terms of attracting audiences it was disastrous. Nor could it even retain the audiences it got. Olivier stood with Tynan to watch the mass defection at the end of the first act. "'Such a good idea of yours to put this play on, Ken,'" he said, "with the crisply projected diction that could be heard well down the Cut." But though the primary blame was Tynan's, Olivier could not avoid all responsibility. "This is a piece of shit, baby," he had told Anthony Hopkins. "But Ken loves it and says that it will be ecstasy. So let us see." If he really thought the play was a piece of shit, why did he put it on? Had his experiences with *Tyger* taught him nothing? As Director he had no need to pander to the whims of his dramaturge. To be brainwashed into seeing merit in something that was daringly avant-garde is explicable; to take it on while seeing no merit in it cannot be condoned. Olivier was abrogating the responsibilities of his office; a piece of weakness that was not unique but was strongly at variance with his authoritarian nature.[3]

It was the odder because he did not hesitate to put Tynan down when he thought his dramaturge had gone too far. Tynan had followed his denunciation of the acting ability of the present company with his proposal for improving the situation. His remedy was that the company should be cut back to a hard core of fifteen, "at the most. There may not be another chance of rising from the ashes." "I'm sure your own thoughts must be running along similar lines," he concluded optimistically. Olivier's thoughts were taking no such course. Tynan was talking nonsense, he retorted. He urged him to be more sensible and discreet. "To let a wish to get something off your chest guide you to an action is obviously going to lead you into prejudicial statements and consequently erratic judgment."[4]

He was writing with especial feeling because he was having to devote a large amount of his time and energy to defending his dramaturge against a rampant Board. Chandos in particular had been convinced by the Hochhuth affair that Tynan was a malign nuisance who should never have been employed and had far outstayed his welcome. As early as 1967 he was urging that Olivier dispense with Tynan's services: "He is a man completely lacking in probity and loyalty and is unscrupulous and untruthful." Tynan was well aware that Chandos thought little of him and returned the hostility with interest, but he would have been disconcerted if he had known that his stock stood quite so low. To his mind, he was a model of reason and propriety. Germaine Greer used the word "fuck" in a program note for a production of Shaw's *Mrs. Warren's Profession*. Olivier asked Tynan to get it changed. He couldn't possibly do so, protested Tynan. He had already persuaded Greer to cut out "two other uses of the word 'fuck,' the word 'cunt,' a reference to the anal practices of prostitutes and the amount of semen in a prostitute's vagina." How could he now ask for more? Olivier then himself telephoned Greer and got her to substitute "sexual intercourse" for "fucking." "I blamed myself, Kennie," he told Tynan. "I told her you had shouted at me. I said it was my fault." If Chandos had heard about this exchange he would have known very well whose fault it was and would have notched up another score in his tally of Tynan's offenses.[5]

For Olivier's sake—"out of friendship and out of gratitude"— Chandos agreed that Tynan could stay on. When Tynan applied for six months' leave of absence, however, he saw a chance to get rid of him altogether. John Mortimer, a Board member, went to see Olivier in the hospital and found he was as loyal to his dramaturge as ever. He was "dependent on and indebted to Mr. Tynan's work," Mortimer told the Board. If Tynan were removed, Olivier felt it would "enormously increase the heavy burden that he has to bear." He did not think any adequate replacement could be found. Once more Chandos stayed his hand, but he insisted that Derek Granger, from London Weekend Television, should be brought in as fellow dramaturge. Worse still from Tynan's point of view, he was no longer to be Literary Manager but only Literary Consultant. The salary was the same and the significance of the change in title might seem inconsiderable, but it mattered greatly to both Chandos and Tynan. "He will no longer be able to speak as an officer of the National Theater," Chandos told Olivier, "and pontificate on theatrical matters as if he was speaking with our voice."[6]

Tynan was outraged, feeling that he played a far more significant role in the National Theater than Granger could ever hope to do. "I am not by temperament a credit-grabber," he assured Olivier, possibly with his tongue in his cheek but more probably in self-delusion, "but honestly, my dear heart, I am getting a tiny bit fed up with sharing equal billing with Derek." He thought it was high time he was reinstated as Literary Manager, leaving the consultancy to Granger, "whom the word accurately describes." Olivier knew well that Tynan was lucky still to have a job in the National Theater at all. It was only by claiming that Tynan should be a "consultant," and that a consultancy was within his gift and not an appointment by the Board, that he had been able to keep Tynan on the strength. In part Tynan must have realized how much he owed to Olivier's championship, but he continued to feel that he had been misused and that the Director had failed to defend him as vigorously as he had deserved. Olivier, for his part, continued to extol Tynan's qualities with a generosity that was ill rewarded by Tynan's malice. Mrs. Green spoke for many members of the public when she wrote to say that Tynan should be dismissed from the National Theater because he had been responsible for the nude review *Oh! Calcutta!* He was not prepared to pass judgment on Tynan as an impresario, Olivier replied, "but he is still, in my opinion, one of the finest theatrical intelligences in this or any country. It is this that qualifies him as one of the two Consultants to the National Theater."[7]

In the summer of 1970 the financial problems of the National were more severe than ever. They were contemplating a deficit of £73,000: "most disturbing," considered Chandos. Olivier had to say that he was "very sorry and deeply concerned" about the unexpected gap between his budgeted surplus and what had actually happened. What was more: it seemed that things were sure to get worse before they could get better. It was not a happy situation and one that was made worse by the Director's uncertain health.[8]

The Board might have reservations about his management, but his public reputation stood as high as ever. In the little group of theatrical knights he was unquestionably the most prominent. He had enjoyed his knighthood and would have felt bitter chagrin if it had been denied him. It still caused him mild disquiet, however. Privately he might know that he was different from other people, but he did not want to have the fact bruited abroad in any pompous or establishment manner. When Laurence Evans, who had become his agent, asked him if he would like the "Sir" to be left out in any advertising, he replied "Yes, yes, yes, *Please!*" He suggested that a joint approach should be worked out with John Gielgud: "I don't want us to be different, but personally I don't like using it at all in billing matters—makes me feel like Cedric Hardwicke or Aubrey Smith, or even Lady Tree."[9]

This cautious coyness was redoubled when, early in 1968, he received a letter from the prime minister, Harold Wilson, asking him to accept a peerage. "Kind and giddy-making," he called the invitation, but on reflection he turned it down. He was a workman certainly, he told Wilson, "an artist hopefully; but I should be a Lord only very uneasily." If he had to attend in the House of Lords he would be distracted from what he believed was his proper work: "I would have to give up acting altogether, with no time to learn or give due study to my roles." Wilson was quick to point out that it would mean nothing of the sort: a few appearances and perhaps one or two speeches a year would be the most required of him—"those occasions would be all the richer for your presence." It was the most

egregious flattery, and Olivier loved it, but he stuck by his guns—
the honor was again rejected.[10]

Quite why, it is hard to say. According to Richard Burton, he had
said two or three years before that it was his ambition to be the first
theatrical peer. Many years later he admitted that he thought the
invention of the life peerage had been an excellent idea: "My darling
Joan will be a baroness till she dies, I think that's nice, and my nip-
pers are little honorables, which is also nice; and, we hope, keeps
them up to the mark." He cannot have believed that his duties in the
House of Lords would prevent him from acting. He told his friends
that "there was something about the title that really did, and still
does, and probably always will, make me feel a bit awkward. Perhaps
there is still enough of the urchin in me to feel a little mockingly
about it." Not enough of the urchin remained, however, to prevent
him from accepting when Wilson renewed the offer two years later.
Perhaps it had always been a question of timing. When the offer
had first been made the funding of the National Theater was still in
question: his acceptance of a peerage might have been interpreted
as meaning that he had been bought off or awarded the honor as a
consolation prize. Joan Plowright suspects that he would never have
rejected the peerage in the first place if he had not felt reasonably
sure that the offer would be repeated. He himself claims that he gave
way the second time round because Wilson persuaded him that
it was his duty as a member of society to make his special contribution in the House of Lords: "Thus was my conscience—habitually
and quite properly a guilty one—quite cunningly appealed to."[11]

The next battle came over the choice of title. He would be Lord
Olivier, that was clear; he had played too many parts in his life
already to wish to reemerge under a new name. But Garter King of
Arms ruled that, as his uncle, the colonial governor, had been Lord
Olivier within the last thirty years, he would have to add some ter-
ritorial appendage to his title so as to distinguish himself from the
late proconsul. For some reason Olivier took strong exception to
this. Possibly he felt that, in the eyes of the world, there could only
be one Lord Olivier worth remembering, possibly he felt that to

be Lord Olivier of somewhere-or-other would add an unnecessary touch of pomposity to something that he feared some of his theatrical acquaintances were anyway going to find ridiculous. Anyway, he told Garter that he was "distressed more than you can perhaps understand . . . I so much infinitely prefer the simple title to the more ponderous 'of somewhere.'" Garter was unmoved; Olivier did not press the point; it was as Lord Olivier of Brighton that he renewed life in the birthday honors of June 1970.[12]

He did not make his maiden speech for more than a year. Since he reproduced it in his memoirs one must assume that he took some pride in it: his delivery, indeed, may have been impeccable, but the speech itself was pompous, contrived and grovelingly sycophantic. He never spoke again. "I wish I'd been a little more courageous about it now," he admitted some years later. "It's an ordeal by fire, you know. If they sense that you are speaking on a subject just a little outside your province, they will shoot you down in flames." Olivier knew a great deal about his province, but little about anything outside it and debates that related to the theater were few and far between. He was intimidated by what he imagined to be the superior learning and wisdom of their lordships, he hardly ever visited the House and was silent when he did so: "I was going to get up late one night, then I thought, in the first place, do I know what I really feel, and the second, am I going to phrase it properly?" But he liked being a lord. Formally, he was a committed egalitarian. He would urge people to call him Larry or, at least, Sir Laurence; he complained when Harold Hobson referred to him in a review as Lord Olivier; but he still had occasional flickers of *folie de grandeur*. Joan Plowright remembers him remarking that he thought the staff ought to refer to him as "The Baron" and that the children should be known as "Master Richard" or "Miss Tamsin." It did not take much to laugh him out of such pretensions, but if his family had been more inclined to ostentation he might have ended up a very lordly lord.[13]

Lord Chandos retired as Chairman of the National Theater Board in July 1971. Olivier made all the appropriate noises. "It was unlikely," he told the Board, "that anyone would ever again be able to do so much for the British Theater." Not only had Chandos done more than anyone else to transform the National Theater from a vision to a reality, he had continued the battle so that the new buildings were now at last under construction. "For that building London, Great Britain and the theatrical profession would be eternally grateful." This was not hypocrisy—Olivier appreciated the importance of Chandos's contribution—but in many ways he was glad to see Chandos go. Their relationship had never recovered from the imbroglio over Hochhuth. Recently things had got even worse. According to Max Rayne, Chandos's successor, Olivier had suggested to Chandos that Joan Plowright should succeed him as Director, either as an individual or as part of a governing consortium. Chandos is said to have treated this recommendation "with such contempt that Olivier refused to speak to him." There cannot be much truth in this. For one thing, Chandos liked and respected Joan Plowright. When Olivier put forward the need for employing another associate director, the Chairman replied: "Why pay another £5,000? You've got Joannie." He might well have doubted whether it would be wise to appoint a woman Director, let alone one who was the wife of the present incumbent, but he would never have dismissed the idea with offensive scorn. Possibly he was reluctant to discuss the issue, feeling it should be left to his successor, and Olivier took offense at what he saw as an attempt to exclude him from the debate. At all events, Olivier saw Chandos go with little regret.[14]

About Chandos's successor, Olivier was cautiously optimistic. Max Rayne was a Jewish entrepreneur who had made a vast fortune out of property development and was notably benevolent toward the arts. He did not know very much about the theater, but acquaintanceship with the minutiae of theatrical life was not a necessity for the Chairman of the National Theater Board; indeed, might almost be a handicap. He was shrewd, clear-headed, tactful, and quite prepared to accept unpopularity if he felt it was the price of doing what was right. He was also discreet and preferred to keep his own counsel until he felt the right time had come to reveal it.

Olivier offered his resignation to the incoming Chairman. He knew that it was highly unlikely to be accepted and would have been outraged if it had been. Rayne insisted that he should stay on at least until his contract ran out in 1973 and hoped that he would in some way continue to be associated with the National Theater long after that date. Like everybody else, Rayne assumed that Olivier would be very much present, if not in charge, when the Company moved into the new building.

At the time Chandos retired it still seemed likely that the first production in the new building would take place within the period of Olivier's contract or, at least, very shortly afterward. Even by the standards of institutional architecture, however, progress was sluggish. Nobody could decide quite what was wanted, nor exactly where it was going to be. Denys Lasdun had ceased to be the universally acceptable figure Olivier had once imagined him. Every member of the Building Committee had his own ideas about the way plans should develop, Lasdun resolved the problem by sticking to his own solution. The Committee was becoming frustrated by what they saw as Lasdun's intractability, Olivier told Cottesloe: "What we all hoped for all along were many more designs from Lasdun . . . but it always does seem to come back to the same thing." The final design satisfied nobody completely, but it was not so far removed from anybody's conception as to be unacceptable. By the time the foundations had been laid and serious building begun, most people were so relieved that *something* was at last going up that they were ready to accept it. Olivier could tell himself, without too much self-deception, that *his* concept had won the day and that it was *his* National Theater that would be opened.[15]

The question of who would run it now began to preoccupy him. Even if he himself were still in charge when the new theater opened he knew that this could not last for long. His contract would soon run out, and even if the Board was anxious to renew it he would be well into his sixties, his health was not at all what it had been, he was tired and even slightly bored, he wanted to make some money to support his young family: it would be time to move on. He must leave his beloved National Theater in safe hands. Joan Plowright was only one of many ideas that occurred to him. It was not a good one; mainly because she had no wish to do the job. She loved acting, she was determined to devote time to her children: "There is no way I could have given every working moment to running a place like that." "Suggesting me was a sort of frenzy," Plowright told Tynan. It was a way of carrying on himself in spite of the fact that he had retired.[16]

There were plenty more ideas. "I was quite determined that it should be an actor if possible," Olivier stated. Albert Finney was one of those whom he recommended. He was the right sort of age, Olivier told Arnold Goodman, who as Chairman of the Arts Council was bound to be involved in the selection process, he had the right sort of following, the right sort of promise, the trust of his colleagues. Finney was in his early thirties, he was relatively inexperienced, and even if Chandos had not been irritated by the fact that Olivier had chosen to make an oblique approach by way of Lord Goodman rather than directly to the Chairman, he would have dismissed the idea out of hand. Anthony Quayle was another possibility, though Olivier doubted whether he was "quite of the right generation" (a curious observation given that Quayle at the time was almost exactly the age that Olivier had been when he had taken over the National Theater). If neither of these appealed, then how about Richard Attenborough, an actor and director of serious distinction in spite of having been the star in the early days of Agatha Christie's *The Mousetrap*?[17]

Olivier had other, still more exotic ideas. At what seems to have been an exceptionally drunken dinner he more or less offered the Directorship to Richard Burton. Burton seems to have taken the offer seriously and an embarrassed Joan Plowright had to persuade her husband to write to him explaining that the job was not in his gift. "He must have been very drunk the last time we talked to him," wrote Burton in his notebook, "as nobody could have turned down the job with more firmness." He wrote to say that he thought he had already made it clear that Olivier should drop any idea that he might do the job: "I didn't think I had the administrative ability and certainly not the experience." Privately Burton considered that the job would be intolerable on the terms under which Olivier held it: "I couldn't see myself being overruled by a Board of Governors." Olivier should have resigned over Hochhuth, even though the play "was a travesty and badly written . . . Those old Etonians, etc., would drive me mad in five months." He also thought that Olivier had let the National Theater subside to a level of depressing competence. Robert Stephens and Maggie Smith were all very well, but they lacked grandeur. What the National needed were "the towering oaks of the profession: Scofield, Guinness, Redgrave . . ." and, by implication, Burton. "I love Larry," he concluded, "but he really is a shallow little man with a mediocre intelligence."[18]

His stock of eligible actors exhausted, Olivier looked nearer home. He had been gaining increasing confidence in Michael Blakemore, especially since Blakemore had made an excellent job of directing him in the *Long Day's Journey*. Tynan supported Blakemore as Olivier's successor, no doubt in part because he believed that Blakemore as Director would keep him on and that his influence would not be noticeably diminished. Olivier was impressed by the idea and tried it on Lord Rayne. Rayne, it turned out, had never even met Blakemore: he was too junior, he ruled, he did not carry the guns required in a Director. "They were confoundedly stupid about any of my suggestions," Olivier recalled. "All they were concerned about was the stature of the man concerned, which I tried to point out was the wrong way round."[19]

One name that he did not put forward, a name that it seems did not even occur to him, was that of Peter Hall. His relationship with Hall had varied over the previous years. In August 1966, when it had seemed that Hall might be washing his hands of any responsibility for the design of the new theater, Olivier wrote to urge that it was "really terribly, terribly important" that he remained part of the operation. "It isn't our theater, it's yours . . . It is a National Theater, and you are every bit as much a national figure as I am, probably more." He knew that this was not true and did not expect Hall to believe he really meant it, but his anxiety to keep Hall on board was sincere. Yet it never occurred to him that Hall should one day succeed him. On the contrary, Hall was Stratford; Hall was, if not the enemy, then at least a member of another and rival family. Within a few weeks of his urging Hall to remain involved with the planning of the National Theater he was complaining that the Royal Shakespeare Company was trespassing on the National's territory. "You must not think that I am questioning your right to put on any plays whatever . . . it is merely that we find ourselves a wee bit caught unawares by the rapidity with which our work seems to be coinciding. I wake up one morning and find you in bed beside me—charming, of course, but surprising."[20]

At the beginning of 1968 Hall gave up the job at Stratford. Olivier wrote in warm tones to praise this decision; he felt he should similarly move on from the National Theater, but he didn't know what else to do. He praised the "dazzling brilliance" with which Hall had run the Shakespeare Company. "Our relationship has been one that others might have found difficult," he wrote, "but you have always made me believe that the *great liking* (somehow true and more trustworthy than 'love' . . .) was, together with the undoubtedly wholehearted admiration—somehow reciprocated." Hall was touched and responded in equally ardent terms. "I not only admire you inordinately," he wrote, "but ever since we met first to work with each other, I have *liked* you, and trusted you, and felt you my friend."[21]

When they worked *with* each other, that was no doubt true; but in the nature of things they more often than not found themselves working against each other. In the autumn of 1969 war was declared. Peter Shaffer had written a new play, *The Battle of Shrivings*, which Olivier considered had been commissioned by the National Theater, or at any rate was morally theirs. Shaffer told Olivier that he wanted Peter Hall to direct it. No, no, protested Olivier, what the play needed was for him and John Gielgud to act in it, "kindly, charitably, directed by Glen Byam Shaw, and the three of us must be strong enough to cut your text, which is terribly overlong." Whether it was the threat of extensive cuts or a conviction that Hall was essential as part of the package, Shaffer now spoke directly to Hall about the production. Olivier was disconcerted. "Please don't think I do not share your enthusiasm for Peter," Olivier told Shaffer, "because I do, and have particular good reason to, as I have seldom enjoyed working with a director more than I did with him on *Coriolanus* some ten years ago, but I would never have thought of *Shrivings* as a Director's piece—by which I mean that a star director's signature needed to be written across it . . . I must say it was a little bit of a jolt to learn that you should have talked to him without my knowledge and I could not help wondering if this was the beginning of a big freeze-off."[22]

It was: the next thing Olivier knew was that Shaffer had offered the play to Binkie Beaumont, who took it over as private management and mounted a production with Hall as director. "I was absolutely ashen with disappointment," Olivier remarked. "He just went right ahead and snatched the fucking thing away from me. I didn't know people of that ilk behaved like that, that Peter Hall could do it in order to pinch the play for himself. I guess he thought 'This is a nice turn-up. Thanks, Larry!' I've never been able to wish any of them well ever since." No doubt the facts of the affair would have sounded very different if recapitulated by any of the other parties; the result was, however, that when the matter became urgent, Olivier thought ill of Hall and would not have viewed him as a possible successor at the National even if a former director from Stratford had been the sort of person whom he felt right for the job.[23]

It therefore came as an unpleasant shock when on March 24, 1972, he met Max Rayne to discuss the succession and was told that Peter Hall was the Board's favored candidate.

CHAPTER TWENTY-THREE

The Coming of Hall

Laurence Olivier, age sixty-five, was a man acutely aware of his limitations. For most of his life he had believed that anything was possible; now he accepted that it was not and that what powers he had left were fast diminishing.

He had been the most physical of actors. Simon Callow wrote of John Dexter that his conception of acting was at heart athletic, it was a skill requiring physical address as well as mental stamina: "It was a bad day for the rest of us when he met Olivier, who is that sort of actor supreme." For decades Olivier had been pushing his body to the limit; sometimes, as his multifarious breaks and strains attested, beyond the limit. He knew that this could not go on indefinitely. In 1968 he had refused to act in Robert Lowell's version of *Prometheus Bound*; "I don't feel quite up to such a brutally physical effort." In fact the play did not appeal to him for other reasons as well, but this was not an excuse that would have occurred to him ten years before. When he first played *Long Day's Journey* he introduced a feat of startling physical virtuosity, clambering onto a table so as to light a lamp and then stepping backward into space and landing on his feet. By the time that the run was over, this piece of business had been dropped and James Tyrone made a more decorous descent. There may have been other reasons, but it seems most likely that Olivier realized he no longer had the flexibility, the agility, to make his backward leap an acceptable maneuver.[1]

His eyesight had long been failing. He preferred not to be seen wearing spectacles in public, but he found them increasingly hard to escape. Things became worse in 1973 when he came back to the house in Brighton, went upstairs and was hit by a burglar whom he disturbed at work. The eye specialist assured him that his vision would not be affected, but it was later discovered that damage had indeed been done to the optic nerve and that only the constant administration of eye drops could save what was left of his sight. His hearing too was not what it had been; it did not get badly worse until the 1980s but he found it difficult to follow the dialogue if he was watching a play or to pick up the cues if he was acting in one. His voice—those reverberant, clarion tones that had dominated the stage for more than forty years; the lung power, which Vivien Leigh said had only been surpassed by Kirsten Flagstad—was still remarkable by any standards, but did not come so naturally as had once been the case. In the past he had effortlessly imposed himself, now he had to strive to achieve the same effect. Most difficult of all for an actor, his memory was not what it had been. Ralph Richardson had once marveled at the incredible facility with which Olivier could learn long and complex parts; now he was subject to human frailties. The last role he played on the stage included a twenty-minute monologue. He took four months to learn it, adding another twelve or fifteen lines a day: "I was never able to confront it without fear of making mistakes and ultimately being forced to dry up." He viewed each challenge with increasing nervousness. "I think it only honest to advise you," he had warned a young actor as long ago as 1949, "that nerves are things that do not get better; they get very much worse as time goes on. I myself am now an extremely anxious actor; when I started I had not a nerve in my body." It was above all his nervous fears about his memory that led him to confine himself to cinema and television in his last acting decade, yet even here the problem existed. Michael Caine, who acted with Olivier in *Sleuth*, felt at the outset that he would be costarring with a titanic figure whom he could view only with awe. "But there he was coming to me with the problems *he* had. And you quickly realize this was someone with human frailties, and as he began to worry endlessly about the script and his problem remembering lines, I found myself in the position of being the one who listened to him and giving my advice!"[2]

His powers of concentration, once so unwavering, were diminished. He fell asleep at inappropriate moments. When Tynan wanted him to take on Tom Stoppard's *Jumpers* it happened that no clean script was available. Stoppard was told to read it aloud to a select group, including Olivier. Long before he had finished it was embarrassingly clear that the Director, eyes gazing up toward the ceiling, was unaware of what was going on. When Stoppard finished, Olivier stirred uneasily. "Ken," he asked. "Where *did* we get those lights?"[3]

Decrepitude is relative. Olivier at sixty-five still enjoyed the memory, the energy, the versatility of many actors half his age. Though he might somewhat curb his physical activities, he had no intention of giving in. Derek Granger remembers being with a drunk Olivier who was making a bad job of backing his car into a restricted space. Give it up, urged Granger, there was man at the garage door who would be happy to put the car away. "You don't understand, baby," said Olivier, "that some of us have got to do things like this and conquer them." His powers might be fading, but he still intended to confront each challenge as it arose and to overcome it. Yet there was a difference, and he knew it. "Most actors," Beverley Baxter had written in 1949 of Olivier's performance in *The School for Scandal*, "are like electric bulbs. The speaking of a line switches them on and the ending of a line switches them off. Not so Olivier. With him the light dims or rises but is never extinguished." Even now it was never put out, if only because the weight of public expectation Olivier's mere presence on a stage inspired was still a potent source of energy, but compared with what it had once been the light was burning low.[4]

It is hard to imagine why Olivier was so surprised when Rayne put forward the name of Peter Hall as the next Director. To most people Hall seemed the obvious candidate, a man who had proved himself by running with conspicuous success the only theatrical organization that, in its stature and its complexity, could be compared to the National Theater. It was not as if the idea was new to him. John Dexter had warned Joan Plowright that he had heard Hall was being mooted as Olivier's successor. Plowright passed on the warning; Olivier smiled knowingly and said: "You mustn't believe every rumor." Now the rumor had become reality; what was more, it was clear that Rayne was not trying out a new idea on Olivier but that matters were far advanced: the Board was behind the choice, Hall had been consulted and had given his provisional agreement. The provision was, of course, that Olivier should pronounce himself happy with Hall's succession. "We do not wish to go ahead with the idea unless you are wholeheartedly in favor of it," Rayne told Olivier. Hall had been emphatic that he would not think of taking on the job except with Olivier's blessing. In theory it was in Olivier's power to block the appointment. In practice it would have been almost impossible. All his other suggestions had been discussed and turned down; he could not argue that Hall did not have the proper qualifications; to veto the Board's decision would be to reject somebody whom everybody else thought suitable on no grounds except those of personal distaste and a vague feeling that Hall was not right for the job. Olivier accepted the inevitable, made polite noises about Hall's outstanding qualities and retired to brood over the way in which he had been misused.[5]

He *had* been misused. It was months since Rayne had first asked Hall whether, in principle, he would be willing to become Director. Hall had replied that he would, but only if Olivier wanted to retire and approved of his proposed successor. He felt that Olivier should at once have been brought into the discussions. Rayne disagreed. He said that it was not fair to trouble Olivier over such an issue while he was playing so grueling a role as James Tyrone in *Long Day's Journey*. This cannot be the whole explanation. It seems more likely that Rayne feared Olivier would object to the proposal and wanted to present him with something close to a fait accompli. Hall was told that he was not to say anything to Olivier about the matter; when he went to see *Long Day's Journey* he felt that he could not go backstage after the performance in case the matter of the succession came up and he was forced to lie or at least to equivocate intolerably. The secret was well kept, few people seem to have known what was in the wind, but by the time Olivier was told, Hall had discussed the proposal with a variety of friends including Peggy Ashcroft, Peter Brook and Trevor Nunn.[6]

Olivier was the more aggrieved because, when his own suggestions had been dismissed, he had put forward the idea of establishing a Consultative Committee that would consider the various possibilities and make recommendations to the Board. Rayne had never approved this idea, but nor had he rejected it. Olivier thought it would be the way forward. In fact it might have been difficult to find suitable members for such a Board who did not consider that they were eligible for the job themselves, but it was a workable proposition and would have given Olivier a chance to revisit and perhaps promote candidates whom he had considered in the past but who had been rejected. Rayne, no doubt, viewed such a prospect with some dread and decided to take a short cut, even at the price of Olivier's feelings. Olivier considered that he had been, at the best, sidelined, at the worst, misled. He had been maneuvered into an impossible position. "It is, I think," he told Max Rayne, "pretty good humbug for anybody to say that if I had had any reservations on the choice I should have voiced them, since I could not possibly have done so without creating an appalling scandal." He had no aversion to Peter Hall—"apart from my admiration for him he does also happen to be my friend"—but he did feel that he had been given no chance to argue his case. Rayne disagreed. He claimed that there would have been no scandal if Olivier had vetoed Hall; "The only embarrassment the Board would have had . . . would have been finding another candidate as good." The Board might not have been embarrassed, but Olivier would; his grievance was real and justified. It rankled, and poisoned the atmosphere during what would anyway have been a difficult and painful period.[7]

The pity is that, if the matter had been presented to him in a more civil manner, he would probably have come round to the

Board's view without too much hesitation. "When we talked to each other about it," wrote Joan Plowright, "we had to admit that Peter was the only properly qualified candidate at the time." Tynan reproached her for not having put up a stouter fight against Hall's selection. She replied that, if she had done so, she would not have known "what I would be fighting FOR. Hence the rather fatalistic acceptance on my part and, I suspect, many others." She had no great faith in any of Olivier's suggestions—nor, if he was being honest with himself, did Olivier himself feel committed to them. Hall might be *faute de mieux*; but if there was really no rival candidate as good or better, then *faute de mieux* became a conclusive argument.[8]

Olivier rather curiously made the central plank of his grievance the fact that, from the start of his time at the National Theater, he had believed it to be part of his duties to seek out and to groom his eventual successor. To that end he had imported a series of outside directors in the hope that one of them would establish himself as a potential Director. This was done, he maintained, at great personal sacrifice to himself. "I could easily have directed three times as many plays," he claimed. "I could have directed thirty-seven instead of seven and made myself into a sort of Stanislavsky, which was my ambition . . . So when finally it turned out that they'd known perfectly well they were going have Peter Hall all the time, I realized the sacrifice I'd made was for *nothing*. . . That's what made me sick; that's the only thing that really did turn me badly in remorsefulness about my own history at the National."[9]

This is, of course, absurd. The Board had not "known perfectly well they were going to have Peter Hall all the time"; they had scarcely given a thought to the succession until a few months before Olivier's contract was due to run out. Nor could Olivier have added the direction of another thirty plays to his monstrous workload; he could already be criticized for putting too much on himself, to have done still more would have been disastrous both for himself and for the National Theater. Olivier had good grounds for feeling aggrieved without dragging in this extravagant red herring. He convinced himself that it was true, however, and never abandoned the belief that he had been cheated out of his birthright.

Olivier's first act on leaving Rayne was to send Peter Hall a generous message of welcome and congratulation. The two men met a few days later and talked for several hours. Hall found Olivier in a confused and volatile frame of mind. Part of him wanted to retire as Director and be rid of the place as soon as possible, part of him did not want to retire at all. One part was pleased that Hall was to be his successor, another hated the idea: "I am Royal Shakespeare, not National," Hall reflected. "I have not been Larry's man, ever." The conversation covered many subjects. Olivier still had his heroic energy, judged Hall, "but he strays from the subject, forgets names, muddles up attitudes." On the whole the talk went well and Hall was relieved, "although I don't kid myself that life will be simple . . . The interregnum period will be very difficult, and even thereafter, Larry will never be an easy man to have around."[10]

Just how difficult it was going to be was illustrated when Olivier addressed a meeting of the Company to break the news of his impending departure. Hall was in New York but was telephoned by a friend who told him that Olivier had become emotional and had given his colleagues the impression that he had not been consulted about the succession and that he intended to "fight on" so as to ensure that he was still in charge when the move came to the new building. "Who is he fighting?" Hall asked himself. Nobody, was the answer. Even when at his most indignant, Olivier had no intention of trying to reverse Hall's appointment or even to make his accession to power more difficult. But in the excitement of a public meeting, urged on by the sympathy and support he felt around him, he went further than he had intended in expressing his feeling that he had been betrayed. "You must have known that the company were too tongue-tied to say what was in all their hearts," Maureen Lipman told him. "Just—they are (and me) so sorry you are going and so glad you will still be here."[11]

But how long would he still be there and how would the inter-regnum be handled? If Tynan had had his way, Olivier would have fought to retain his position and to make life as difficult as possible for his replacement. In the same way as Hall had been prevented from telling Olivier what was planned, so, for several weeks, Olivier felt unable to warn Tynan, Blakemore and the others of his forth-coming departure and the identity of his successor. Tynan knew that Hall disliked and distrusted him and that he would not sur-vive under the new regime. The fact that Olivier had kept him in the dark added an edge of fury to his outrage. By failing to nomi-nate a successor from among his colleagues, Olivier, Tynan felt, had "passed a vote of no confidence in us all . . . He had hired us, stolen our kudos, and now shows no compunction about discarding us!" Tynan made it his business to envenom and, so far as it was possible, protract the period of the handover. He told Hall that feelings were now so inflamed at the National Theater—"by him, no doubt," Hall added in his diary—that a cooling-off period in which no decisions were taken was the safest course. "I made no comment," wrote Hall. Two days later Hall recorded apprehensively that the "scandal" was growing so large that "Tynan may achieve what I guess is his objec-tive and either get a mass resignation from the company, or one from Olivier, or both." According to Tynan, Blakemore and Dexter were equally indignant; Blakemore, he wrote in his diary, was "out-raged at the lack of consultation and feels betrayed by L.O." So far did Tynan go in suggesting that the staff of the National Theater was against change that Dexter felt bound to dissociate himself from his turbulent colleague. He thought the manner of the announcement had been unfortunate, he told the Board, but he agreed that Hall "by his previous work and reputation" was the best man to take over as Director.[12]

In essence this was also the position of Olivier, but occasional fits of pique reminded the world how badly he thought he had been treated. On April 13 Hall attended his first Board meeting. It was most important that Olivier should be present too and he had indicated that he would be coming. Instead, with no warning or explanation, he went home to Brighton. Rayne wrote to remonstrate. "The discussion continued in a most interesting and agreeable way until well after 8:00 p.m.," he told Olivier. The next meeting would take place in four days. "Clearly it is most essential that you should be present at that meeting and, as with last evening's meeting, the time is being arranged to suit your convenience." This time Olivier turned up and the text of the formal press release was agreed. On April 18, 1972, the world learned that Olivier would be retiring as Director of the National Theater and that Peter Hall would be replacing him. "Apart from weeding out Larry's purple prose (why is it that actors are addicted to over-writing?)," noted Hall in his diary, the announcement was intended to be as unspecific as possible. Hall would be joining the National Theater in the next few months; he would take over as Director sometime after that when the Company had moved into the new building: all was for the best in the best of all possible worlds.[13]

Not everyone swallowed this bland presentation of what had been and was still proving a fractious process. At a meeting of the Arts and Recreation Committee of the Greater London Council (one of the National Theater's main financial sponsors) Illtyd Harrington accused the Board of being "ham-fisted, heavy-handed and blundering" and said that Olivier had been treated "very shabbily indeed." T. C. Worsley, the critic, told Olivier that he had not believed "that things were being done in so unmannerly, so huggermugger a fashion" but was now convinced that the Board had indeed ensured "as ungracious an exit as they could contrive." Tynan was far from being alone in his efforts to persuade Olivier that he had been misused. From the point of view of the National Theater and of Olivier's own reputation, it was fortunate that he was not left with much time on his hands in which to brood on his misfortunes. One of his regrets while at the National had been that he was left with little time in which to make films. "Full-length films are practically impossible for me these days," he had written a year or so before. "My job at the National Theater really is a full-time one and my escapes are few and far between." From time to time, however, he was able, for two or three months at least, to divest himself of most of his duties as Director and get back to the cinema. Within a few days of his learning that Hall was to succeed him, one of those precious breaks began.[14]

Olivier had seen Anthony Shaffer's play *Sleuth* when it was on its provincial tour at Brighton. He caused some offense to the author. Anthony Quayle, who was playing the part of the mystery writer Andrew Wyke, asked him what he thought of the play. "The first Act is a bit of fun," said Olivier, "but it's piss, isn't it?" This had been forgotten, by Olivier if not by Shaffer, when the play, which had proved enormously successful, was turned into a film and Olivier was invited to take over Quayle's part. He would be playing opposite Michael Caine, already an established star but, as Olivier ruefully noted, "young enough to be my son."[15]

Their relationship got off to an edgy start. Olivier remarked that Caine reminded him of Leslie Howard. The resemblance was only skin deep, Caine replied; adding rather enviously that, though Howard looked as if butter wouldn't melt in his mouth, he had notoriously slept with all his leading ladies. "Not, I believe, in *Gone With the Wind*," said Olivier sweetly. Horrified by his gaffe, Caine stammered that, of course, Vivien Leigh had been an exception. Olivier was amused rather than annoyed. After that all went well. Caine was initially intimidated by Olivier's grandeur, Olivier by Caine's youth. Each thought the other was carrying the day: "He overwhelmed me," remembered Caine. "It was frightening the way he bore down on me—and just kept coming." Olivier thought that he lacked the authority to establish Wyke as the dominant figure in the first half of the film: "I had developed a habit of being an audience to Michael, a foil for him." Both resolved to correct the imbalance, both found that in fact there was no imbalance and that once they had got used to each other they acted in complete harmony. Characteristically, Olivier solved his problem by sticking on a Ronald Colman–style mustache: "I've discovered something," he told Caine. "I can't act with my own face. I have to be disguised." It was hardly a new discovery—indeed, Olivier had recently shown signs of abandoning a lifetime's addiction to disguise and rejoicing in his own unvarnished appearance—but in moments of stress he still found it reassuring to take refuge behind a false mustache, a wig, a plastic nose.[16]

And in *Sleuth* he found that there were many moments of stress. It was a two-actor film and Wyke's speeches were numerous and elaborate. He was in the middle of "a great mountain-load of work," he told Ralph Richardson, "it's a v. long part indeed and v. hard to learn." How did Richardson write out his parts, he wondered: all of it at once or only the bits he was going to need immediately? (Richardson replied that he typed the whole thing, but in different colors, cues in red and text in black.) It was, indeed, a singularly testing role but Olivier would not have made nearly such heavy weather of it a decade before. Joe Mankiewicz, the director, was disconcerted to find that this great actor, famed for his ability to master long parts at short notice, was subject to "mortifying lapses, he repeatedly stopped takes with an 'Oh, shit!' or 'Sorry, Joe,' when he knew he had erred or dried up." There was more to this than the ravages of age. Olivier had been combating the stress he was under at the National Theater by taking what were for him unusually large doses of tranquilizers. A side effect of this seems to have been that his memory was affected. It did not last. Olivier never regained the prodigious powers of his youth, but, once the pills were abandoned, his capacity to master a script came back to him. Within a couple of years of making *Sleuth* he would be tackling a long and taxing stage role, with difficulty, but with notable aplomb.[17]

Caine never ceased to hold Olivier in a certain awe, but he also felt solicitous about the older man's patent frailty. Olivier for his part, though under pressure, by no means resigned himself to letting Caine carry the film. He "had no hesitation in placing himself center stage in every scene," Caine remembered, "and whenever I had a line that cut across a move he wanted to do, he rather grandly ordered Joe to cut it." The two men still got on well. "It was obviously a marvelous relief when we each discovered that it could be perfectly easy to act together," wrote Caine in his memoirs. "He was marvelous in it. He's a lovely fellow." On screen their partnership worked to perfection. It is not a great film, but it is a fine example of how two important and ambitious actors can mesh together in total symmetry. Nobody watching the film could detect a trace of the pressure under which Olivier was working; something that reflects great credit on his supreme professionalism, but also on his costar and his director.[18]

If Harold Pinter had had his way Olivier would have switched directly from Andrew Wyke to Proust's Baron Charlus in Pinter's screenplay of *À la Recherche du Temps Perdu*. Olivier did not take to the idea. He confessed that he could see nothing in Charlus beyond "a plain dilettante" or a "*filthy* old snob." He went on pay tribute to the quality of the script, and to the glories of the original novel: "Quite simply, can you see and hear a shirt rustling with the same evocative reaction as when Proust describes it?" This was, Joan Plowright surmises, a characteristic piece of bluff. Olivier had never read a line of Proust and had probably no more than glanced through Pinter's script. Reading of any kind, except for the study of possible scripts, hardly entered his life; the exquisite longueurs and subtleties of Proust were alien to his temperament. The film was never made.[19]

The new building of the National Theater was topped out on May 2, 1973. There was still much to be done—the probable date for opening had by now slipped to 1975 and was expected to go later still—but at least the topping-out ceremony seemed to add a certain inevitability to the process. But would Olivier be part of the organization when the move was made? The arguments for a quick departure grew stronger by the day. He in no way lost interest in the future of the institution. He still expressed his views on every problem that arose. When it was proposed that the move to the new building should coincide with a change of name to "Royal National Theater" he argued that this would be too "suggestive of pomp and circumstance." To call it "The National Theater of *Great* Britain" might offend the Welsh and Scots. "The National Theater of Britain" would be "both vague and unambitious." "The National Theater of England" sounded too isolated. Let it just be "The National Theater." Whether or not one accepts his reasoning, the reality of his concern was obvious. Yet it was a detached concern. He asked Roger Furse whether he thought he should stay on to see in the new theater. "It seems to me you've done the real job in preparing and building up the company," Furse replied. "You have built a great reputation, almost a tradition, which has had its downs, as anything of that kind must, but has had far more ups. Anyway, what could be more important than your children, particularly now at their present ages?" Little by little Olivier became convinced that Furse was right.[20]

Hall joined the National early in 1973. On the whole his first months went smoothly. There were moments of friction, but on most issues Olivier and Hall were more or less in accord. Both, for instance, agreed that Barbra Streisand's proposal that she should play a Shakespearean role at the National should be politely but firmly rejected. "I admire the lady greatly," wrote Hall, "but I would prefer to watch her do Shakespeare somewhere else." Their views on plays usually coincided. Olivier told Hall that left to himself he would have rejected a play by the American dramatist Michael Weller, which Tynan had recommended. He found it "frankly disgusting," which he suspected was the main reason for Tynan liking it. He felt, however, that in the circumstances, Hall should make the final decision. Hall found it "very perceptive and original," but agreed it was not one for the National Theater.[21]

Hall's original title when he joined the National had been Director Designate. It was Olivier who proposed that, from April 1973, they should appear with equal billing as Co-Directors. At the end of October, he went on, Hall should become Director and Olivier Associated Director, with or without the honorific title of President: "This would create a good impression of continuity, of friendliness and cooperation." After March 1974 he would like to take six months' sabbatical, after which he would return "to take such part as might be required of me for the opening of the new theater." Rayne was relieved by this proposal. He had foreseen ugly squabbles between Olivier and Hall, now all seemed set fair. Olivier's proposals, he said, were "eminently reasonable and immensely helpful."[22]

But even when he put forward these obliging propositions Olivier had doubts about whether he was going to adhere to them. Several months earlier Joan Plowright had told Dexter that her husband was changing his mind from day to day. At one time he would conclude that he should withdraw immediately, "and let P.H. sort it all out"; twenty-four hours later he would say that he must see it through. "Even so," she went on, "he's not sure he's going to stay on in the capacity they (including Peter) all hope for." More and more he sought to withdraw from the everyday running of the theater. Early in 1973 he asked Tynan and Dexter to dinner in his apartment in Roebuck House and told them that he was going to resign in October: he was bored by the administrative chores, felt no artistic excitement in the job and wanted to escape as soon as possible. They urged him not to retire prematurely and he found that, when it came to the point, it was painful as well as difficult to disengage.[23]

If 1973 was an uncomfortable year for Olivier, he made sure that it was almost equally awkward for his successor. Overtly he seemed to be anxious to work closely with Hall. "He tries to talk to me most days now," wrote Hall in his diary: "I can't quite make out what is going on . . . If I could be with him at lunch and dinner and sit up drinking with him all night he would be happy. But I can't do that." Olivier was at least as confused as Hall. He wished to give the impression that he was doing all he could to help his successor, part of him genuinely wanted to be cooperative, but he still found Hall's presence a constant irritant, a reminder that this was no longer his personal empire, would, indeed, soon not be his empire at all. He knew that it would be damaging to his reputation if he seemed uncooperative and yet he could not resist flickers of resentment. In March, with some ostentation, he announced that he proposed to vacate his office so as to make room for the Director Designate. Olivier could do what he liked, Hall retorted, but *he* wasn't moving in to the Director's office until he took over in November.[24]

In fact, Hall was more than happy to take over the management of the National. He would have preferred his predecessor to linger on in some titular role so as to emphasize the "continuity, friendliness and cooperation" which Olivier had extolled a few months before, but provided there was no overt falling out he could accept Olivier's resignation without too many qualms. What mattered most to him was that Olivier should continue to act in the Old Vic and, in due course, in the new theater as well. He was anxious not to be cast as the man who had driven Laurence Olivier from the stage of the National, if only because any production that included Olivier in the cast list was likely to attract 10–15 percent more ticket sales than plays that featured any other actor. When Olivier at the last minute had to drop out of a performance of Trevor Griffiths's *The Party*, Hall recorded, "the disappointment of people coming into the theater . . . was almost unbearable. Many of them looked and behaved like heartbreakingly deprived children." When it came to committing himself to regular appearances, however, Olivier proved disquietingly evasive.[25]

What Hall wanted above all was to ensure that Olivier would play Lear: preferably in the forthcoming season in the Old Vic. Olivier prevaricated, seemed to say that he would, then hesitated. Once he told Hall that he had tried to telephone to confirm his readiness to play but had failed to get through and had now changed his mind. Undiscomfited, Hall battled on. At least if Olivier was not ready now, let him promise to make his Lear the first production in the new theater. "You know I want you to do this more than anything in the world." Of course he would be honored to direct the play himself, but "I think you should do it in any way you want and with whoever you want, but please don't direct it yourself unaided. It is too much." Olivier's first reaction seems to have been to accept, but soon doubts crept in. In a letter starting "My very dear Peter," undated and probably never sent but providing the basis for a conversation, Olivier explained that "there does seem to exist very strongly in my mind and my being a feeling of unhappiness at committing myself to this extent . . . Something tells me that we both of us—more particularly you than me—may be glad not to cope with my reentry when it is at present planned." He asked Hall to avoid making any announcement that included "plans that involve us in commitments that we both may well and truly wish we had not undertaken."[26]

For Hall, who was not merely prepared but anxious to commit himself in this way, this must have been a disquieting message. He fared no better when he tried to persuade Olivier to undertake *The Tempest*. In the past Olivier had dismissed Prospero as an unrewarding part; now he seemed interested and at once began to talk about his costume and makeup—"I love the fact that actors always go straight to their appearance," remarked Hall. But wasn't the old sorcerer abjuring his magic and breaking his staff almost too obvious a theme for what was likely to be Olivier's Shakespearean swansong? Joan Plowright thought so. "I don't think Larry *will* play Prospero," Hall concluded. "I believe he will open the National with *King Lear* directed by Michael Blakemore. I shall let him do exactly what he wants."[27]

What he did want was unexpected. Trevor Griffiths was a politically conscious left-wing dramatist who was compared with Shaw for his combination of wit with reasoned argument. His new play, *The Party*, featured Tagg, a disillusioned Communist who bemoaned the fate that had overcome his beloved Party. Olivier told Tynan that he had never understood Marxism before he read *The Party*. It does not seem, though, that it was the political content that drew him to the play. Mainly he was impelled by a wish to disconcert those of his admirers who took it for granted that he would bow out with something obvious like Lear or Prospero. As well as this, he was attracted by what he must also have found most daunting. *The Party* opened with a monologue lasting twenty minutes and consisting of a dense and dialectic exercise in political analysis. To retain an audience's attention through this overture would be a testing challenge, and Olivier in 1974 was no more ready to resist a challenge than he had been forty years before. Finally, and most curiously, he disconcerted the author by telling him that he was anxious to play the part because he had never played a Scotsman before (presumably Macbeth, being royal, did not count). To master a new accent was another, and still more beguiling challenge.[28]

It was a brave decision, though. The long speech was not just at risk of boring any nonpolitically minded audience to distraction, but it was also hard to learn. Olivier found it very testing. "I used to spend the whole first half of the evening knowing that when you start you couldn't help hearing a little voice saying: 'Cheer up. You'll be finished in twenty minutes.' My memory faculty was beginning to go." Diana Boddington had to stand by with a stopwatch and let him know whether he had been quicker or slower than the night before: "I don't know how he did it," she wondered. Tynan initially doubted whether he was the right man for the part. Whoever played Tagg, he felt, must possess "a core of burning revolutionary zeal: a passionate and caring political intensity." Olivier would never have laid claim to such attributes, but he was an actor and he believed that he could counterfeit Tagg's idealism quite as convincingly as Hamlet's doubts or Othello's consuming jealousy.[29]

From the first reading Tynan's reservations were proved unfounded. Olivier delivered his speech without even glancing at the text and won a round of applause from the rest of the cast. It would be "the most inspiring call to revolution ever heard on the English stage," wrote Tynan in his diary: "How ironic—and splendid, that it should be delivered by Larry from the stage of the National Theater." Olivier took his evangelical fervor from his father's pulpit manner; his aged green tweed suit came from Joan Plowright's father; his hairstyle was borrowed from the socialist pioneer, James Maxton: the rest was genius. John Dexter said that, within the profession, Olivier's Tagg was held to be one of his finest pieces of acting: "I don't think any other actor in the world could have held me totally absorbed with the long political speech," Eileen Atkins told him. "That is magic. And your *granite* silence!' Olivier himself said that he was a bit disappointed by the reception—"Maybe they were horrified at my being a Communist." Neither the reviews nor the takings at the box office suggested that his doubts had any basis.

Tagg may not have been his greatest role, but in the challenges it posed and in the courage and skill with which he overcame them, it was a worthy end to his career.[30]

There had been no announcement that he would never act on the stage again, probably he had not finally decided it himself, but on the last night there was a feeling in the theater that an era was ending. Olivier made an emotional curtain-speech, then knelt down and kissed the stage. "This may sound schmaltzy, but it was not," Gawn Grainger remembers. "He was bowing to the roots of his theatrical soul. The King was abdicating." And then the cast went up to the rehearsal room at the top of the Old Vic and had a party: "Denis Quilley played the piano and we sang and danced and behaved like four-year-olds. And Larry was part of our gang."[31]

"Part of our gang": it was an epitaph that Olivier would have relished. Peter Hall would never have been part of "our gang"—nor would he have wanted to be. Perhaps the spirit of the gang could never have survived the transfer to the clinical wasteland of the new building. But at the Old Vic it was Olivier's singular achievement to start with nothing and to end with a proud and passionately united body, taking great pride in its achievements, resolved to correct and build upon its failures, committed in loyalty to the man whom it had accepted as its leader. Perhaps it was anachronistic; people have claimed that Olivier's National Theater was the last proud flourish of the actor-manager rather than the first manifestation of the big-business, depersonalized institution that would be needed as the twentieth century wore toward its end. It might be fairest to see it as a halfway house. Olivier's National Theater could not have survived in the form in which he had fashioned it, but nor could the National Theater of today have existed but for the passionate exuberance, the dynamic energy, of Olivier's creation. It is true to say that there would be some sort of National Theater today even had there been no Olivier, but if there had been no Olivier the triumphant impetus that carried it into the new millennium would have been lacking. The debt owed to him by the British theater is inestimable.

CHAPTER TWENTY-FOUR

OLIVIER'S OCCUPATION GONE?

"Farewell the plumed troop and the big wars, that makes ambition virtue . . ." Was it indeed a case of Olivier's occupation gone? For the previous ten years the National Theater had been at the center of his life; in his thoughts every waking hour and sometimes sleeping hour as well. For nearly fifty years acting on the stage had been his first preoccupation: he had made many and important films but for him, in the last analysis, the theater was what really mattered. Now his role in the National Theater had been diminished, if not yet extinguished; his career as an actor on the stage was over. The cinema and television might expand to occupy a greater part of his still considerable energies, but would they be enough? Had he the intellectual resources, the range of interests, to fill his life in a way that he would find satisfying? Could his family play a large enough part to compensate for the dwindling of his professional activities? However those questions would be answered it was sure that he was venturing into unknown waters and that the process of adjustment would be difficult and might well be painful as well.

Meanwhile he had to disengage himself from the National Theater. This process would not be easy for anyone involved. The scene was set early in 1973 when Hall in his diary recorded that Olivier had been "in a devilish mood and was changing ground on anything

that had been said previously." He told Hall that he had been recon-
sidering and now was by no means sure that he meant to hand over
power at the end of the year. "I said it was his decision and he must
do what he wanted; I would stand by in any way that was necessary."
How far Rayne would have tolerated an Olivier determined to cling
on to power after his allotted span must be uncertain; in fact Olivier
had no serious intention of staying on and was doing no more than
voicing his pique and getting some satisfaction out of causing Hall
disquiet. His attitude continued to sway, day by day, from an almost
exaggerated helpfulness to a campaign of willful noncooperation
that sometimes amounted to sabotage.[1]

The situation changed in November, when Hall took over as
Director and Olivier was demoted to Associate Director. It was little less difficult for Hall, however. He was the boss, but it was still
Olivier's theater, almost all the personnel were Olivier's appoint-
ments, now working for Hall but owing allegiance to Olivier. The
powers and duties of the Associate Director were ill defined. If
he had chosen to, Hall could have left Olivier out of the decision-
making process altogether. He did not, partly because he admired
Olivier and valued his opinion, partly because he did not wish to
provoke a revolt and a spate of resignations among the Olivier loy-
alists of his staff. Olivier missed no opportunity to demonstrate his
independence, as, for instance, by failing to turn up at a press conference though well aware that his absence would raise embarrassing questions. He relished the occasional opportunity to criticize
Hall's decisions. In July 1974 Hall mentioned that he was thinking
of appointing a Deputy Director: Olivier at once challenged him,
doubting the wisdom of such an action. The company were already
restless, he said; they never saw Hall, they did not know what they
were supposed to be doing. They wanted to work with Hall, not
with some deputy: Hall was the boss, he must be seen to be the boss,
and he must do some bossing. Hall ruefully admitted that there was
some truth in these strictures. But it was not easy to be the boss with
the potent shadow of the former boss still very much on the premises. It was as if President Pompidou had had to govern France with

General de Gaulle not lowering balefully in Colombey-les-Deux-Églises but still in residence in the Élysée.[2]

Joan Plowright contributed to Hall's uneasiness by telling him that there were widespread doubts in the National about the future of the theater and the threat posed to it by growing institutionalization and bureaucracy. She told Jonathan Miller that she felt the company was becoming unhappy and fragmented. She and Robin Phillips, the artistic director at Stratford, planned to form a new company that would try to rekindle the spirit of the old National Theater. Would Miller be prepared to direct for it if they did? Nothing much happened, but the possibility cannot have made Hall sleep more soundly.[3]

It was not only Hall who was disquieted by Olivier's presence. John Gielgud took on the role in *The Tempest* which Olivier had turned down. Olivier asked if he could attend the rehearsals and then joined Gielgud and Hall in the latter's office. "He sat and chatted, making Gielgud feel uneasy," Hall noted. "It is extraordinary to watch these two giants. Gielgud obviously is disturbed by Larry, and Larry knows it." When Richardson joined forces with Gielgud in Pinter's *No Man's Land* Olivier went backstage after the performance to tell them that he had not been able to hear a word either of them had said and that he had gone to sleep. Richardson was very upset, Hall recorded, asking: "Why is Larry so harsh?" Yet when Hall later criticized Olivier's attitude, Richardson admitted the justice of what he said but added gently that "as soon as he saw him, the charisma, the size of the man, took over, and he loved him again." "I know what he means," Hall commented. Olivier for his part seems to have been resentful of the fact that Richardson and Gielgud, perhaps feeling some irritation at being, if not rejected by the National, then at least insufficiently appreciated by it, had struck up a working relationship as well as a friendship that was producing some spectacular performances. In an embarrassing tribute broadcast on Richardson's seventieth birthday, Olivier declared: "Ralphie, Ralphie boy, my dear old cocky, I'm probably your oldest friend. I know I'm not your best friend, but I believe I am the one who loves you best." Constantly he reiterated the fact that he and Richardson had been close friends long before Gielgud had known either of them; a fact that was true, but one that did not necessarily redound to the credit of the man who asserted it.[4]

His growing detachment from the day-to-day running of the National left him with more time than he had previously enjoyed to indulge in public life, at any rate so far as it impinged upon the theater. Almost always he exercised his influence in the interests of traditional and right-wing values. When it seemed that Vanessa Redgrave and other elements of the extreme left were on the point of capturing the actors' trade union, Equity, Olivier rallied to its defense. "Obviously the freedoms that you and I and those like us require are going to cost us something," he told a friend, "and I am awfully sorry but that means the effort of turning up and raising a hand at the right moment. It is a perfectly frightful sacrifice to give up a Sunday . . . but it does need sensible people to make a few sacrifices." He wrote an article in *The Times*, or at least put his name to an article in *The Times*, warning of the dangers facing the acting profession if Equity fell into the hands of the militants. His reward was to be pilloried in *The Stage and Television Today* as an antiquated grotesque "redolent of the Garrick Club and astrakhan collars rather than the jeans and T-shirts that are the garb of the contemporary actor." Viewed from the perspective of the far left the charge was justified. Olivier was an authoritarian figure with little sympathy for the vagaries of youth or any kind of libertarian excess. When Keith Joseph, in 1974, was under fierce attack for a speech suggesting that Britain's breeding stock was threatened by the number of working-class mothers unfitted to bring up children, Olivier sent him a congratulatory telegram. Viewed from nearer the middle of the road he seemed a man of liberal instinct and a generous disposition, not interested in politics as such, but conservative with a small "c" and sturdily patriotic. He liked and was attracted by Edna O'Brien, a close friend of his wife, but when Joan Plowright first suggested inviting her for the weekend he replied that he wasn't having anybody in the house who supported the I.R.A.[5]

When the Russian dancers Valery and Galina Panov fell afoul of the Communist regime, being refused permission to visit Israel and expelled from the Kirov ballet company, Olivier demonstrated outside the Russian Embassy, sent Panov a personal telegram and took part in an N.B.C. documentary on the subject. With Harold Pinter and Peggy Ashcroft he took the lead in organizing a boycott of a visit by the Kirov to London in protest against the Panovs' victimization. Part of him relished the attention that his activities gained him: the limelight was where he belonged and he felt uneasy if exiled from it. His sympathy for the Panovs was sincerely felt, however. Nor did he wish to be given more credit than was his due. He was genuinely put out when the newspapers made too much of his contribution and said nothing of Rosemary Winckley and others who had devoted far more time and effort to the cause. "I do so want you and whoever else may be hurt or upset by this sort of inference to understand that I never consciously let this be thought," he wrote to Miss Winckley. "They always want you to be boastful and that is the way they will have it." "You ask us to forgive, but for what?" Winckley replied. "We are indebted to you for *always*. . . It is a wonderful thing to know that someone you've profoundly admired for years is as great a human."[6]

That he had energy to spare for such diversions is the more remarkable because in 1974 and 1975 his health suffered a series of destructive and, finally, almost fatal blows. As if cancer, thrombosis and appendicitis were not enough, in the autumn of 1974 Olivier developed a rare and ruinous disease called dermatopolymyositis that attacked the muscles, leaving him almost speechless, unable to keep his eyelids open, dependent for survival on heavy doses of steroids that in turn fostered wild delusions or all-consuming lethargy. "I shall be quite a few weeks in this place," he told Peter Hall from the hospital in November 1974. At least it meant that he would be spared having to play Father Christmas; always one of his least successful roles. "I know *you*. You're not Daddy Christmas, you're just

Daddy," was a reception he had grown used to over the years. This was not much compensation, however, for several weeks of extreme pain in which he was in imminent danger of death, and several months of slow and painful convalescence. Only a man of singular strength, both physical and psychological, could have survived. "It shrinks, it eats one up, it's one of those things when the body is at war with itself," he remembered with horror. "I had enormous quantities of steroids until I went a bit mad. Poor Joan got really frightened. I said: 'It's all round here, Joan. I can feel it going round and round; this madness is going round and round in my ears.' It was incredible." It destroyed his looks: an unkind trick of fate for a man whose professional life depended in large part on his appearance. Worse still, it attacked his voice. Peggy Ashcroft visited him at Brighton when he had just emerged from the hospital. She was dismayed by his appearance but still more by the difficulty he found in speaking: it was dreadful, wrote Peter Hall, that "a man who has spent all his life getting the last note out of his voice should now find that his vocal chords are affected."[7]

Inch by inch he fought his way back. He had to teach himself to walk, to teach himself to write, to strengthen his muscles by remorseless training in the gym, to strengthen his voice by endless hours of practice. He never altogether recovered. John Gielgud saw him at a lunch for Lauren Bacall early in 1979 and was dismayed to find him "so changed and withered, but he talked gallantly, made a speech—a bit rambling—and even said he might be tempted to try and act in the theater again." It was not Peter Hall's fault that he did not do so. From the moment that Olivier had recovered to the point where his appearance on a stage did not seem inconceivable, Hall had been bombarding him with invitations to direct or play whatever took his fancy. Would he like to direct *Romeo and Juliet*? Or *The Wild Duck*? Or a Chekhov? Or act in a new play by Howard Brenton—"It has an amazing part!"? Or give a master class on Shakespeare? "I am letting the ideas tumble out in an attempt to show you the strength of my feelings and our need to have you here." If Olivier had replied that he wanted above all to play Dick

Whittington, or even his Cat, the idea would have been greeted with delight. As it was, he replied discouragingly: "I just cannot think of anything I particularly want to do." He had just visited the new theater that at last was somewhere near completion. A "marvelous place," he found it, though "I cannot honestly swear . . . that the impression given by the O[livier] Theater is overridingly one of intimacy. The Lyttelton is also a perfect gem." But fine though the new theaters might be, he held out little hope that he would ever act in them.[8]

One reason why he fought shy of too conspicuous a relationship with the National Theater was that he had residual doubts about what he suspected might become a takeover of the National by Stratford. One of his objections to Peter Hall as Director had been that he was too closely associated with the Shakespeare Memorial Theater. He complained to Hall that actors, when they came to see the Director, would not know whether they were seeking a job at the National or at Stratford. Hall retorted that he had resigned as a director at Stratford sometime before. "He was delighted," Hall recorded. Delighted, perhaps, but not convinced. When tentative plans were revived for what would in effect have been a merger between the National and Stratford, Olivier at first professed himself enthusiastic but soon recanted. He sabotaged the negotiations by imposing what Hall and the Director at Stratford, Trevor Nunn, felt to be unreasonable restrictions on the time that the Stratford company would be allowed to perform on the South Bank. Since nobody takes his "contortions very seriously, not much harm done," wrote Hall. "It's very difficult to know what motivates Larry's vacillations. Certainly in some cases—and this is one of them—a Machiavellian love of intrigue." A delight in thwarting Hall would have been more accurate: that, and a genuine belief that the last decade had shown that Stratford and the National could coexist in amicable competition and that the theater in Britain would be the stronger for their continued independence. Hall was deluding himself if he really believed that nobody took Olivier's attitude "very seriously" and that he could be ignored. Lord Goodman, that master power broker, knew better. He told Hall that opinion was turning against the merger. Olivier was the only person who could reverse the trend, "and that he was not about to do."[9]

The new building opened at last in October 1976. "I really thought it was *his* National Theater and it was *his* building," Hall recalled. He urged Olivier to take the center of the stage at the opening: "You have to open *your* building." Olivier prevaricated. He was frightened of being at the center of anything, he said. "I think I can possibly undertake to get away with not more than a few ill-chosen words to start the thing going." His qualms were not entirely fictitious—he was far from restored in health—but he must also have been getting some satisfaction from keeping Hall in doubt. His pleasure was the greater because Tynan, eager as ever to make mischief, had gleefully reported that an exhibition mounted to mark the opening of the National Theater contained fifty-seven items relating to Barry Jackson's Birmingham Rep., only five relating to Olivier's time at the National and "room after room devoted to Hall's Stratford." "We didn't really understand Peter Hall," Olivier said, or is quoted by Tynan as saying. "I've never known a man more dedicated to self-glorification." Hall sensed and deplored Olivier's hostility. "It was one of the nastiest periods of my life," he told Richard Eyre. "The friendship went because I was the next generation— I was the future. And I understood it all, none of us likes giving up. And Larry wasn't just the king, he was the emperor."[10]

In fact Olivier can never have doubted that he was going to speak at the first night in the new theater, in the presence of the Queen and with everyone who was anyone in the audience. Peter Hall heard that he had been sneaking into the theater at 8:00 a.m. and practicing his speech behind locked doors. "I have to admire his professionalism," he remarked. Olivier returned the compliment, though somewhat grudgingly. He rejected Joan Plowright's advice and learned his speech by heart. "I knew that slimy bastard wouldn't be using notes," he told Tynan, "and I was damned if I was going to let him outdo me." The effort was worthwhile. The play that Hall had selected for the first night proved to be a disaster. "The one undoubted success of the entire opening ceremony," Hall generously admitted, "was Larry who . . . made an elegant, though over-written speech. The audience gave him a standing ovation. So they should have done. But it was difficult for a play to follow that." It is hard to be sure whether Olivier would have derived more satisfaction from the success of his speech or the failure of Hall's opening play.[11]

"For a year after I retired I was Associate Director," Olivier told Mark Amory, "to look like a good sport and not let people think I was sulking." In fact it was more like four years between the time that Hall took over as Director and Olivier's final resignation as Consultant Director. His role, however, became more and more nominal over the years. He told Rayne in June 1977 that he was fed up with being asked what was going on at the National when he had virtually nothing to do with it. When he had made similar noises in 1975 Hall had begged him to stay on and to accept the Life Presidency. When in the end he left it seemed no more than the public affirmation of what was already an accomplished fact. The Board had proposed that they should commission a portrait by David Hockney to commemorate the occasion; Olivier rather ungraciously replied that he disliked having his portrait painted and that, while he did not know Hockney's portraits, he found his landscapes hard to understand. He countered with the proposal that the Board should commission a group picture of his children by "some artist of a more formal type." The Board did not feel that this would quite meet the needs of the occasion. In one of his last letters to Peter Hall Olivier said: "If there is anything for which I am really required advice-wise or any such thing as that, you have only to call; but I shan't be even the tiniest bit surprised if you never do." They never did.[12]

There was little point in taking the story beyond 1975, Olivier told George Weidenfeld when considering the shape of his autobiography, "because, since then, the only remarkable thing I can boast of doing is to recover from a frightening illness. The jobs I have done have been some half-dozen pictures and a year's work producing a T.V. series for Granada—none of it really worthy of any cock-crowing." There were indeed no supreme achievements yet to come, but by the standards of most mortals he did much that was memorable. In particular, he came to terms with television. The film that did most to reconcile Olivier to the medium was *Love Among the Ruins*, a dated but enjoyable romantic comedy, directed by George Cukor and costarring Katharine Hepburn. Olivier said in his memoirs that he was devoted to both of them. The three had often idly discussed the possibility of doing something together; now it had happened. "It was an unforgettable six weeks," wrote Olivier. "It passed like a lovely pink shooting star, so memorable but quickly gone." The film was not as memorable as the filming; with such a director and such stars, however, it could hardly fail to succeed. The producer, Allan Davis, remembered it with affection. He found Olivier "most cooperative," ready to work on a Sunday and, by so doing, inspiring Hepburn to do the same. She was acting in a play by Enid Bagnold at the time. Olivier took Davis backstage to meet her. His lead-up to the meeting was not quite so affectionate as his memoirs might lead one to expect. "Don't get too excited, boysie," he told Davis. "She can be the most awful fucking bitch in the world and she might be like that tonight."[13]

The T.V. series that he had told George Weidenfeld he was making for Granada was a much more onerous affair. When Olivier emerged from the hospital after his bout of myositis he was emaciated, exhausted and cautious about taking on any new commitment. His brother-in-law David Plowright, who was controller of programs for Granada Television, decided that the best cure would be immediate and demanding work. He signed up Olivier to select and produce a series of six plays, each of which had first appeared in the last seventy-five years and each of which was deemed "the best play" for its particular year. "This series saved my life," Olivier remarked. "I was dying. I know I was. I didn't want to live any longer. I had nothing to live for and I felt that it was cruel of me to put Joannie through agony any longer . . . and then my dear brother-in-law gave me my life back." "I had nothing to live for" is a curious declaration coming from a man who had a wife and three children under the age of fifteen. Probably Olivier would have rephrased it if he had been challenged. It contained an essential truth, however. Olivier loved his family and would have been distraught if ill had come upon them, but work was his life-blood. Nothing could replace it. He accepted the new challenge with gluttonous zest. In his memoirs Olivier said that he "reluctantly" played in five out of the six films. There was no reluctance about it, said Derek Granger, who coproduced the series; he would have been outraged if anyone had tried to stop him. "As you know," Granger told Tynan, "he is fanatically and obsessively interested in all processes and mechanical gadgets, so that the whole technical business of television was fascinating for him. In all this, he masterminded every detail. He designed his own titles, he worked out the billings . . . he worked with the composers on the incidental music. He virtually did the adaptations himself."[14]

David Plowright was right; the scent of battle rekindled Olivier's appetite for work, and therefore for life. Peter Sallis and Alan Bridges joined him for dinner while the six plays were being filmed. Bridges remarked that he was just about to embark on a feature film. Olivier immediately wanted to know if there were parts for him and his wife. It was "the energy of the man" that amazed Sallis. "There he was, finding out what else he could cram into his life. There was a restless urge to keep working." But could the urge be gratified? However willing the spirit, the body was frail, and it was the body that concerned the producers who stood to lose large sums of money if a star had to abandon work when a film was still unfinished. It was the custom to insure against such a risk. In the case of the Granada series it proved impossible to get cover except for a premium that was ruinously expensive. The money at stake in a television series of this kind could be kept within limits; Granada took the risk and got away with it. The problem was far more intractable when a full-length feature film was involved.[15]

In the autumn of 1975 John Schlesinger conceived the idea of casting Olivier as Dr. Christian Szell, a Nazi arch-villain, in a

splendidly black and over-the-top thriller called *Marathon Man*.
The Marathon Man himself was to be played by Dustin Hoffman,
the cost of the film would be enormous, the stakes were very high.
Olivier went to lunch with Schlesinger to discuss the possibility. At
first he was unenthusiastic and Schlesinger in his mind wrote him
off as a potential Szell: "His voice was terribly high, his muscles had
weakened, he said he did not want any lunch." Schlesinger began to
expound the plot. "This is when you run after him," he explained.
"Can't run, dear boy, can't run," observed Olivier. "I can walk fast,
though," he added helpfully. Schlesinger became more and more
convinced that this would not do. Then Olivier became enthused
by the plot, particularly a lurid scene in which Szell tortures the
unfortunate Hoffman by drilling holes in his teeth. As the afternoon
wore on Olivier recovered his strength and seemed to shed years
off his age. "I would so love to play this, such a monstrous part," he
said; adding cautiously, "if Paramount will pay my exorbitant fee."[16]

Paramount was more than happy to do so. The next problem
was that Dr. Szell was supposed to be bald. Was it fair to expect
an old, sick man of Olivier's stature to submit to this humiliation?
Schlesinger braced himself to introduce the topic, but before he had
time to do so, Olivier suggested that he should be shaved immediately: "I think it might be best to get it done." It had never occurred
to him to ask for changes to the script that would have spared his
hair: he was proud of his appearance, but the demands of the part
must come first.[17]

Olivier got on well with Schlesinger from the start and concluded
that he was a director to be trusted. Nevertheless, he found it necessary to ask Derek Granger whether he thought that Schlesinger was
gay. "Why do you want to know?" asked Granger. "Because when
some of us actors are under the thumb of a director, we like all the
information we can get," Olivier answered darkly. Whatever information he may have gleaned he found no cause to use it. Schlesinger
thought that Olivier was overacting in certain scenes and suggested
that he might make it "more intimate." "You mean, cut the ham
fat?" asked Olivier. "You know, a lot of people don't tell me these

things because I have this reputation of being so perfect I don't need direction—but I do, I do, just like the next man." Schlesinger would have been ill advised to push his luck too far, but he had won Olivier's confidence and anything he said would be treated with respect if not invariable deference.[18]

"I am awfully pleased about The *Marathon Man*," Olivier told George Cukor, "horrific as the story is, and look forward madly to Justin Hoffman and John Schlesinger." In spite of a certain vagueness about his Christian name, Olivier on the whole liked and got on well with Dustin Hoffman, but he complained that, though "a wonderful actor," he was "too concerned with the bloody 'Method.'" Hoffman was eager to improvise certain scenes. Olivier would have none of it. "I've got lines to learn," he protested. "I'm perfectly happy to do it any way you want, but once I've learned the lines be very careful, or I'll forget them." Olivier's story is that on one occasion Hoffman held up the action while he was trying to establish the right motivation for taking off his shirt. "Why don't you try acting, dear boy?" Olivier asked in irritation. Schlesinger said it was not quite like that: the remark was made to him and not to Hoffman, provoked by Hoffman's habit of drinking quantities of red wine so as to achieve an "out-of-it" sensation. Whatever the details, a certain tension built up between the two stars. It is perhaps significant that, at a surprise party for Olivier when the filming was over, Hoffman proposed a toast to "a great soldier, a great warrior" but not to "a great actor."[19]

William Devane, playing the head of a secret American agency, was particularly effective in an early rehearsal. He was congratulated on his showing. "This is rehearsal," said Devane. "It's nothing. When the camera starts to roll Olivier will give me a little of this, he'll give me a little of that, and you'll never know I'm in the movie. No one's going to be watching me—that's Olivier, man." He was proved right. Hoffman gave a more than competent showing, but it is Olivier who most people remember. Mercifully the ham fat was not entirely eliminated; Olivier's role cried out for it. "A very theatrical demon king performance," Peter Hall found it, which "in a way

makes the horror easier to take." What was certain was that, however ignoble the vehicle, Olivier would tackle his role with the same
fury and dedication as he would have given to a Lear or an Othello.
Some people criticized him for taking on parts unworthy of his talents. He needed the money, he frankly admitted, and, anyway "they
were all rattling good 'entertainment' pictures, expertly made, with
touches of the innovative." *Marathon Man* was outstandingly good,
he thought; so was *The Boys from Brazil*, in which he played a Jewish Nazi hunter, based on Simon Wiesenthal, who is tracking down
the fiendish Dr. Josef Mengele, a part given to a distinctly out-of-
character Gregory Peck.[20] Olivier was nominated for an Oscar for
his part in *The Boys from Brazil*—the eleventh time he had enjoyed
that distinction. He was tipped as favorite and had already prepared
his acceptance speech when he was told that he was also to be given
a special award for a lifetime's achievement. At once he remembered the time he thought he had been cheated out of the Oscar for
Henry V. Was this also a device to rob him of the award that was
rightfully his? He told the Academy that he would far rather stand
his chance in the open field and renounce the special award. There
was no link between the two, he was assured; his chances of winning an Oscar would in no way be diminished. "Please don't ask us
to withdraw your name because it will look very bad and people
will think you've refused it." Olivier agreed and, sure enough, the
real Oscar went elsewhere. It was a sad disappointment.[21]

Honors, though, were not slow in coming in these years of semi-
retirement. In February 1982 he won the jackpot with the award of
the Order of Merit. The O.M. is an honor awarded personally by the
monarch of the day, limited in number to twenty-four at any given
time and regarded as the supreme accolade to be bestowed on the
most distinguished service officers, statesmen, scientists, artists or
writers. No actor had ever won it before and no award could have
given him greater satisfaction. Perhaps after that the honor that
pleased him most was to have a locomotive of British Rail named
after him. With the O.M. he found himself ranked with Graham
Greene, Benjamin Britten, Earl Mountbatten of Burma. British

Rail's roll of honor featured Winston Churchill, Francis Drake and William Shakespeare. In either company he felt thoroughly at home.

Olivier was prepared to defend *Marathon Man* and *The Boys from Brazil*, but sometimes he found himself abashed by the depths to which he sank. "Larry has to keep on doing any film that will pay the price he needs," wrote William Walton. "He has to keep the children at school and it costs the earth. He's now doing *Dracula* and loathing the thought of it." "DRACULA . . . God, the shame of it," Olivier told Tarquin. But $750,000 for a few weeks' work was irresistible. Sometimes he drew the line. He was offered $500,000 to play the distinguished physician Sir William Gull in a film about Jack the Ripper. He expressed cautious interest, but said that the money was not what he was accustomed to. "Offer him anything!" said the producer, Andy Braunsberg, but "anything" was not enough; Jack the Ripper is a favorite theme for the cinema, but this version, it seems, was never made. Sometimes he asked too much. He was suggested for Lord Ames in *The Missionary*, playing opposite Maggie Smith. There were doubts about his health and suitability for the role, but the producer persisted; then, Michael Palin records, "Olivier has asked for a million dollars to play Lord Ames. Which makes a decision very easy. Not Olivier." In the event Trevor Howard played the part for a more modest fee. Olivier was not worried: there were plenty more where that came from.[22]

In the late 1970s and early 1980s Olivier was earning more money than he had ever done in the past. He was convinced that he needed every penny. He was not altogether wrong.

CHAPTER TWENTY-FIVE

OLD AGE

"If it puts your mind at ease at all," Olivier wrote to a well-wisher in September 1979, "I would say that I feel better now than I have done for at least four years." For the sake of *his* peace of mind it was as well that he felt ready to face the world again. He had the capacity to earn huge sums of money with little investment in time and effort, but his earnings from films were erratic and uncertain. He had convinced himself that his resources were limited and the demands likely to be made upon his pocket were unlimited. "When you are ill you become very anxious for your wife and family," he explained; when you are better—especially if you are over seventy years old and uncertain how temporary your recovery will be—the need to do something to help that wife and family can seem very pressing.[1]

By now Richard, his second son, was eighteen. The first time Richard realized that his father was anything out of the ordinary was when a contemporary at Bedales refused to accept that he could be the son of "*the* Laurence Olivier." Since then he had grown accustomed to the idea and had assumed—against the strong urging of his father—that his career, in some unspecified way, would be theatrical. Now he was through with school, but it would be some time before he could hope to be financially independent. In the immediate future he was destined for the University of California to study film and drama. Tamsin and Julie-Kate were still at Bedales, though Tamsin was entering the world of boyfriends. She found her father well-disposed toward her suitors but disconcertingly

vague about their identities. "Darling Djadja," she wrote reproach-
fully, "you really must get Carl's name right. It isn't good enough
to keep calling him Mark." It was symptomatic of his performance
as a parent. Olivier convinced himself that he was the most dutiful
of fathers and he was indeed a loving one, but he was distracted by
other issues that seemed more urgent. It was still a matter of playing at being a father. The performance was enthusiastic enough to
convince himself that it was the real thing, but it was not always
good enough to take in his wife and children. He could never have
been accused of meanness, however. He was prone to sudden bouts
of economy-mindedness in which he would storm around the
house—turning off lights, turning down fires, complaining about
dripping taps—but he was the most generous of men and rarely
failed to treat his children with indulgence.[2]

The alimony that he was still paying Jill Esmond was an expense
that he particularly resented. Derek Granger visited him in the hospital while he was recovering from having his kidney removed. He
was sitting up in bed working out how much he had paid her since
their divorce: "She's cost me £75,000 a fuck!" he announced. Otherwise he barely thought of her. For Esmond it was very different.
"I hear Daddy is not well . . ." she wrote to Tarquin. "I hope you will
make a special effort to see him . . . I haven't seen him much in the
last forty years. It's funny after all that time how *I* can still love him
so much."[3]

The alimony and the cost of the children's education were only
part of the expenses that convinced Olivier he could not afford to
stop work for more than a few days at a time. His style of life was
lavish. The Rolls-Royce had given way to a Daimler, but it still called
for a full-time chauffeur. His secretary was another, in his mind
unavoidable expense. By now they had acquired a house in St. Leonard's Terrace, one of Chelsea's most agreeable and therefore expensive streets. The Malt House was another drain on their resources.
This was a pleasant Elizabethan farmhouse extended in the 1960s,
with none of the pretensions to grandeur of Notley but still more
spacious than it appeared at first glance. Its chief attraction was its

setting on the River Adur near Steyning, with a fine view of the South Downs. It had been bought as a house for Joan Plowright's parents, but its strategic position between Brighton and Chichester meant that it evolved into being, first their weekend retreat, then their main home.

For Olivier the greatest attraction was the acre of land, lying almost wild when they started but destined to become a garden of some elaboration. As always, Olivier proved incapable of doing anything halfheartedly or to less than professional standards. He found an old gardener called Reg who did some of the spade work, but he devoted to it every spare minute that he could contrive: digging, planting, fencing, creating a series of small gardens, "each separate like a small stage set, the main feature being a curved 'where'er you walk' tunnel of trained lime trees, redolent of Notley." He took delight in his achievement. It was not even a vicarage garden, he told Peter Hiley, with what must have been affected humility, no more than a curate's garden—"a poor thing, in fact, but mine own . . . I feel proud of it for the pleasure it gives me." For good measure he added a tennis court and a swimming pool, in the second of which he swam sixty-six lengths, half a mile, every morning regardless of the weather. "Monotonous, but worth it," he observed. "To be fit should be one of an actor's first priorities."[4]

At least he did not have an expensive wife to maintain. Joan Plowright was a great actress at the height of her powers. If it had been required of her she could have supported the family single-handed. Olivier would have denied it if he had been told that he was jealous of his wife's achievements. "Joannie seems to be a more splendid actress every time I see her," he told his old friend, Fabia Drake. "Much, much better since her work has been entirely independent of mine. I know you will believe me when I say this with gladness." Up to a point she had reason to believe him, but at the same time he resented the fact that Plowright was still able to shine in a forum that once he had dominated but which now was barred to him. When she received an effusive fan letter he at once announced that it was time he returned to the stage himself. He knew there was no real possibility of his doing so, but could not bring himself finally to rule it out.[5]

What put their marriage under still greater strain was that he sought to compensate for his own inactivity by managing his wife's professional life. "As I've got no career of my own left, I shall have to live through you . . ." Joan Plowright remembers him saying, "I must direct all your performances, stage or screen." He must have known this was impossible, but he still felt possessive toward his wife's career. She knew that he was unable to play the role to which he seemed to be aspiring, knew too that only one person was going to control her acting life, and that was Joan Plowright. Things came to a head when Peter Hall asked her to return to the National to act in Edward Albee's *Who's Afraid of Virginia Woolf?* It was a sumptuous part and she was resolved to play it. "You're not going back to that bloody theater unless *I* direct you," Olivier decreed. Even if Hall had agreed, Plowright did not think her husband had the intellectual or physical stamina to undertake the task. She ignored Olivier's ultimatum and told Hall she would be happy to play the part. Olivier seemed to have acquiesced; then suddenly a lawyer's letter arrived threatening divorce. It was only then that she realized how far her husband's grasp on reality was fading. When he returned to their house in St. Leonard's Terrace, apparently in the best of moods, she told him that she would be replying to the letter through her lawyer. He looked bewildered, and it soon became clear that he had no recollection of having instructed his lawyer to send the letter nor any idea what it contained. He was horrified at the very idea that there could be any talk of separation. The incident passed; it could be forgiven, but it was not forgotten. In self-defense Plowright began to withdraw from the marriage. Formally their relationship remained unstrained; a good face was put on it by all. In practice they grew further and further apart and Olivier felt himself isolated in the heart of his own family.[6]

Another irritant in their relationship was Olivier's resolute philandering at an age when Plowright might have thought such adventures were beyond him. Olivier loved women. "One of the prides of my life has been my women friends," he announced in the early 1980s. "I've got two, or three, or four now whose company I really delight in. I've always loved having women friends . . . When a woman is a friend to a man, an absolute loving friend, I think they're simply marvelous." An "absolute loving friend" covers a multitude of sins or, for that matter, virtues. In the case of Olivier the sins were the more apparent. He enjoyed making love and felt that the fact he could persuade some much younger woman to go to bed with him was a comforting reaffirmation of his virility. According to Marcella Markham, an actress who coached Olivier in his Viennese accent for *The Boys from Brazil*, he conceived a maudlin passion for her. When the production moved to London he arrived at her home with a gardenia and a diamond-studded ring. She told him she was on the point of becoming engaged and he was "visibly angry." "Well," he said, "it'll be over in a few years—sex, the relationship, everything. It doesn't last. Why do you bother?"[7]

Miss Markham was forgotten within a few days; Sarah Miles was more long-lasting. She came back into Olivier's life in Hollywood in 1976. He took her to a party and after that they made love. It does not sound a wholly satisfactory occasion. Olivier was much preoccupied by his recent illness. "See here," said Olivier, turning on the light, "that's why I wouldn't hold your hand." He showed Miles the grayish, watery substance oozing from his fingertips. In spite of this they kept the affair going when they got back to London. According to Miles he was at his most vulnerable emotionally and claimed he was anxious to divorce Joan Plowright and marry her: "How easy it would have been then, in his lonely and tormented state, to have him fall—albeit a slightly overripe fruit—plop, into my lap." One suspects that, when it came to the point, she would have found the apple clung rather more tenaciously to the tree than she had anticipated. He told Miles's parents that there was nothing he wanted more than to marry their daughter but that his wife had made him realize that "the scandal would be too much for the children to bear." Miles was hurt that her lover had elected to make this revelation to her parents rather than to her, but the affair flickered on.[8]

His light still burned in the National Theater where the existence of the Olivier Theater made it doubly certain that his name would never be forgotten. As the Company evolved in the new building it seemed to him that all the values he had fostered were being eroded and that the theatrical edifice that Peter Hall was creating had less and less to do with the National Theater of which he had once dreamed. "His hatred of Hall is now incredible and borders at times on paranoia," Joan Plowright told Tynan. "He now passionately regrets ever having given his backing to P. Hall as his successor." To his mingled dismay and satisfaction things were going badly wrong on the South Bank: there was a strike backstage, pickets outside the theater, plays acted on stages bereft of scenery. It would never have happened in my day, Olivier may have thought; and with some justification, for the loyalty he commanded among those who worked for him would almost certainly have frustrated the efforts of any unionist seeking to stir up resentment of the management. Though he never said as much, it gave him much satisfaction that what was considered to be the best auditorium in the National Theater bore his name. Douglas Fairbanks wrote triumphantly to point out that he was not the only man to have a theater called after him. There was now a Douglas Fairbanks Theater in New York. True, the theater was off Broadway and only seated 199, but that did not affect the principle of the thing. More serious, perhaps, was that nobody seemed sure whether it was named in honor of Douglas Fairbanks *père* or Douglas Fairbanks *fils*. Perhaps the solution, Fairbanks reflected, would be to call it the "Both Douglas Fairbanks' Theater."[9]

As Olivier approached the age of seventy-five it became evident to everyone—even evident to him—that he was every day finding it more difficult to undertake any demanding role. His memory deteriorated by the day. Toby Stephens, son of Robert Stephens and Maggie Smith, remembered how kind Olivier had been to him when he met him with his parents, "but later he was struggling and couldn't remember who anyone was." The names of people he had known well for years began to escape him. Who was that man, he asked, with whom he had been conducting a long conversation about cricket? It was Harold Pinter. "Sometimes the forgetfulness was feigned. Once he saw Maggie Smith in the garden at the Malt House. "Who is that woman?" he asked one of his children. "Daddy, you must recognize Maggie Smith." "Oh, *another* of your mother's friends!" He must have been in an exceptionally cantankerous mood. Maggie Smith had always been one of Joan Plowright's closest friends and any acrimony that had existed between her and Olivier had long disappeared. But over the years he had become crotchety and unable to control his tongue. Hugh Whitemore opened a play in Brighton. At the last moment Olivier announced he wanted to go. The play starred Glenda Jackson and was booked up, but Whitemore managed to secure two tickets. "We've got people staying," Olivier said. "I need six seats." Again Whitemore obliged. The following day the two men met. "Didn't think much of your play," said Olivier. "He *may* have been joking," says Whitemore, doubtfully. And the need to earn more bulked ever larger in his mind. Still, he never rated money above the pleasure of living as and where he wanted. People would ask him why he did not follow the example of Noël Coward and decamp to some tax-free exile. "I don't care what the taxes are or how ghastly the people are—and God knows they *are*!" he declared. "I will not be told I may not return to my own country. That would drive me absolutely mad."[10]

Though his memory grew weaker and his physical powers diminished by the day, he continued to play important roles. Each time his fellow actors would ask themselves if he could carry it off, each time when the challenge came Olivier rose to it and showed that he could still conjure a commanding performance from what had seemed to be the ashes of his career. Some of the material was pretty ghastly. Olivier's own bête noire was *The Jazz Singer*. "I've never had such a horrid time," he protested. "The sickening, absolutely molasses-like Jewish sentimentality of it! It made me feel ill . . . it oozes sentiment like pus. I never saw anything, heard anything, read anything so absolutely awful." Still, if one was earning $1 million for a few weeks' work, feeling ill seemed a small price to pay.[11]

Almost as awful was *Inchon*, in which he played General Douglas MacArthur. Gregory Peck, who had played MacArthur in another film a few years before, wrote to reassure him that he felt no pique at Olivier usurping his role: "I shall look forward to seeing what you do with the old boy." Don't, he advised, let the producer do what happened to him: put him on the bridge of a battle cruiser during the assault on Inchon when the film company had been too stingy to portray the assault itself. Olivier would happily have settled for such a misfortune: instead he had to cope with a monsoon, a typhoon, a director on the edge of a nervous breakdown and makeup that took an hour and a half to put on. It left him most impressively disguised, but his new persona did not "look a scrap like MacArthur either." It was a disaster, Olivier concluded; "it was one of those occasions when one says: 'I'm doing my best. You didn't *have* to ask me to play.'" Once again his feelings were solaced by a payout of $1 million. *Newsweek* called it the worst movie ever made, but as it was never shown in Britain Olivier was at least spared the humiliation of being exposed before his native audience.[12]

This was his "last chance to make big money," he considered. Even while these films were being shot Olivier was engaged off and on in the aesthetically far more rewarding yet financially less well-rewarded task of playing Lord Marchmain in a television series based on Evelyn Waugh's novel *Brideshead Revisited*. "It's a masterpiece of a book," he announced. Some people consider that it was far from being Waugh's masterpiece, being marred by sentimentality and odious snobbery, but it made magnificent television. In Olivier's hands Lord Marchmain's protracted and picturesque death bed, already an important scene in the novel, became the most memorable feature of the series. Olivier himself was upset because John Gielgud had been given the role of Edward Ryder, the narrator's splendidly eccentric father. "Why did you give Johnnie the best and funniest part?" he asked the producer, Derek Granger. "Why didn't I get it?" In fact the director had thought that Gielgud was the better choice for Ryder, but Granger assured Olivier that Lord Marchmain was a far more glamorous role. Olivier was just being mischievous, thought the director; given half a chance he would have played both parts and others as well. Olivier was right for Marchmain: it is hard to believe that the aged aristocrat fighting to retain his independence and his dignity even as death closed in could have been more convincingly or movingly portrayed. "You are a clever old one," wrote Robert Flemyng. "After all those triumphs in the theater and on film, to complete the hat-trick on television too."[13]

It was television that occupied most of his energies in the declining years of his career. His small part in a drawn-out and unsuccessful series about the life of Wagner was memorable only because he appeared on the screen with John Gielgud and Ralph Richardson, the first time they had acted together since *Richard III* a quarter of a century before. The director, Tony Palmer, remembered that "each tried, in a gentlemanly way, to upstage the other two." Richardson, he felt, managed to be the most successful. Richard Burton was playing Wagner. He gave a dinner party for the three veterans, drank too much and chose the occasion to abuse his guests. Olivier, he said, was "all technique and no emotion," Richardson had lost his memory, Gielgud's offense was being a homosexual.[14]

In 1983 Olivier was asked to play Lear for Granada Television. The doctors told him the effort was beyond him; Joan Plowright refused to discourage him, if he felt he could do it he must try. Several years before, Peter Sallis had suggested that he should make a film of *King Lear*. "Oh no, dear boy," Olivier had replied. "There's no way I'd do that." Now the possibility was there, all inhibitions were forgotten. He would stumble onto the set looking so tired and decrepit that it seemed he would not even be able to stand upright while the shooting was on; then, as if at the click of a switch, he would come alive and blast his way into one of the most exacting roles ever written for the theater. John Hurt, who was playing the Fool, felt that Olivier was all the time conscious that he was battling against failing powers. "He hated it, but Larry would never capitulate . . . He'd get edgy, basically with himself. If people tried to help him too much he would say 'Oh, just leave me alone.'" Hurt was afraid that Olivier might resent him, as being a young upstart with a career before him. On the contrary, he found that he was treated with respect and as an equal. Olivier was always ready to offer advice if it was asked for, but he would never thrust himself forward. Indeed, he could sometimes be irritatingly evasive. His Cordelia, Anna Calder-Marshall, once asked him: "Please, tell me anything I should know." "Ah, do you know where babies come from?" asked Olivier. "Yes, I've just had one." "Oh blast, I wanted to be the first to tell you."[15]

"It was the most moving performance he had ever given," wrote Joan Plowright. Moving, perhaps, not so much in the quality of the performance as in the courage and the resolution that he displayed. Olivier advised Christopher Plummer not to see it. "I'm not very good in it, you know," he said. "I was so bloody weak they had to lift me onto my horse." Plummer saw it nevertheless and had to agree with Olivier's verdict: "He was indeed very frail and his voice was pitched unusually high—he no longer owned those wondrous ringing tones . . ." George Hall acted as his voice coach. Very little coaching was needed since Olivier understood and controlled his voice with a completeness that Hall had not found in any other actor. But though the technique was still perfect, some of the power had gone. He tired quickly, and not only where his voice was concerned. Hall noticed that even though Anna Calder-Marshall was far from substantial Olivier tottered perceptibly when carrying her around the stage. Lear, of course, is an old man's part, but it is a part that demands authority and grandeur. Olivier still enjoyed all the technical skills that had allowed him effortlessly to dominate so many stages, but the fury had dwindled, the force was no longer with him. He was to act in seven or eight more films for the cinema or television, in several of which he played substantial roles, but after *Lear* he knew that he was on the way out. He had put his foot flat down on the accelerator and the surge of power had failed to come. He would not yet get out from behind the wheel but he knew that his racing days were done.[16]

It remained to ensure that a proper record of his life was left for posterity to marvel at. There had already been a dozen or so biographies, some substantial, some trivial, none approaching the definitive. Olivier professed to have read none of them. A joint biography of Olivier and Vivien Leigh by Felix Barker was the only one that could claim any sort of endorsement by its subjects; it had been published in 1953 and so had long been overtaken by events. Olivier had at that point no intention of undertaking anything himself and felt little enthusiasm for the idea that he might feed the necessary information to some trusted confidant. "My peculiar dislike of interviews," he told an aspirant for this role, "my inability to do them well, my horror at the result and my consequent reluctant decision to avoid this means of expression, are things that are going to make you find me not the most cooperative person in the world."[17]

Then Kenneth Tynan, early in 1977, announced that the *New Yorker* had asked him to write a profile of Olivier. Tynan was different: Olivier trusted him; he was already conversant with much of the background; however malevolent his treatment of Vivien Leigh in the past, his reverence for Olivier as an actor had never been in question. Olivier gave the project his blessing and, still more important, gave Tynan permission to quote from their correspondence. Probably Tynan from the start had intended to develop the article into a book; at all events, at the end of 1978, he announced that it had grown beyond the bounds—already generous—laid down by the *New Yorker* and that, as soon as the magazine had finished with it, he proposed to publish it, "in expanded form, of course." Olivier made no direct response to this and Tynan therefore assumed that he would have no objection and proceeded to do lucrative deals with British and American publishers. It was not going to be a full biography, he explained to Olivier, it would concentrate on Olivier's postwar career, particularly his time at the National Theater. The response was a blunt statement that Olivier did not propose to cooperate with the project in any way and, what was even worse, that he would recommend all his friends and associates to take the same line.[18]

The reasons for this volte-face are obscure. Olivier much later told Kathleen Tynan that he had decided he wished to do his own

book, "which was why he had been so tough on Ken." This cannot be the whole story. Olivier was not to sign a contract to write
his own memoirs for another eighteen months and even then took
much persuading: it was the demise of Tynan's project that led Olivier into undertaking his own book, not the other way round. Sarah
Miles among others had been trying to persuade him to take on
the task, but he had proved most resistant: "'I can't write my own
book,' he grumbled, like a fifth-former over Latin prep." A series
of gossipy articles in the *Daily Mail* had perhaps contributed to his
reluctance to authorize Tynan's book. These professed to be based
on interviews, but were in fact culled from the tape recordings of an
American journalist who had encouraged Olivier into indiscretions
during a drunken dinner in Venice and secretly recorded them. No
doubt these articles gave their victim a jaundiced view of any sort
of publicity, but Tynan had no possible connection with them and
their effect on Olivier's attitude can have been no more than peripheral. The factor that seems to have been most immediately responsible was a piece in the *Evening News* in which Tynan's wife, Kathleen,
was quoted as saying that Olivier wanted "the whole truth" to be
told about his relationship with Vivien Leigh. Worse still, the article
implied that Tynan's biography would be official, written with the
authority and at the request of its subject. "The New York cocktail
circuit is buzzing with rumors of the revelations Kenneth Tynan is
going to make in his book on Larry," recorded Peter Hall. A journalist interviewing Olivier at this time made the mistake of mention-
ing Tynan: "Olivier tightened up and was very frightening." It took
a few weeks before Tynan accepted that the cause was lost—"The
Tynan work is, I think, at the moment, still waffling in the melting
pot of altercation," was Olivier's characteristically opaque exposi-
tion of the affair when in May 1979 he turned down an offer to ghost
his memoirs—but within a few weeks the altercation was over; the
way was clear for Olivier to do the job himself if he felt so inclined.[19]

He had, in fact, envisaged the possibility some years before.
Hamish Hamilton had written him a loving letter urging him to
write a memoir for his "old and trusted friend." If he failed to do so,

Hamilton pointed out, then "vulgar opportunists like Weidenfeld" would go on putting out "undesirable quickies." Olivier seems to have taken this to heart and even to have started work. "The difficulty I am up against," he told Jill Esmond, "is that I am absolutely determined that every single word in it as far as I myself am concerned shall be the absolute and utter truth." Perhaps this daunting prospect proved too much for him; there is no reason to believe that anything was written. In due course Tynan took up the baton. He then dropped it, or had it forcibly removed. The next thing an outraged Hamilton heard was that the "vulgar opportunist" George Weidenfeld had successfully signed up Olivier to write his memoirs for an advance of £100,000. "George wants you to feel absolutely free of any pressure and to write as much or as little as you feel inclined," Olivier's agent, Laurence Evans, assured him. The contract, though, was for a book of 80,000–90,000 words. Ten percent of the advance was to go to Mark Amory, a young and talented writer, whose exact role was undefined but who was, in effect, expected to ghost write the autobiography.[20]

Weidenfeld seems to have wooed Olivier with lofty talk of Kenneth Clark's *Civilisation*, suggesting that his autobiography would be an important contribution to Britain's cultural history. Olivier took the bait and, when Amory began his long series of interviews, he was disconcerted to find that his subject seemed concerned mainly to talk of Irving and Kean. He knew that this was not at all what Weidenfeld required. Joan Plowright saw what was going on and reassured him: "You're having difficulty persuading Larry to talk about himself? I don't think you need worry." Sure enough, when Olivier warmed up he began to talk with alarming candor: the fifty or so hours on tape revealing what he really thought, rather than the emasculated version that appeared in his autobiography, *Confessions of an Actor*, are as rich a source as any biographer could ask for. Olivier later remarked that "he liked Mark Amory a lot but couldn't relax with him; he wasn't one of the boys." By this he presumably meant that Amory had no theatrical background and therefore could not join in the anecdotal ramblings in which Olivier rejoiced. He nevertheless conducted the interviews with great skill: if Olivier did indeed not feel relaxed then the imagination boggles at the thought of the indiscretions that he might have perpetrated if he had felt more at ease. Only once did he ask Amory to turn off the recorder: it was to protect his revelation that: "Joannie was no good at accents."[21]

Then Olivier went on holiday and returned announcing that he proposed to write the book himself. Amory's role became that of sub-editor, to point out omissions or suggest minor changes. The latter were rarely accepted. Something was "preciously valuable," wrote Olivier. Did the word "preciously" really add anything? asked Amory. Olivier rolled the phrase around his mouth. "I like it," he concluded. Once he had committed himself to the project he undertook it with characteristic enthusiasm and energy. "I am able to do absolutely nothing until the end of May but work on That Book," he told Fabia Drake. "I shall not meet my deadline date if I think of anything else, so I don't." He reaffirmed his determination to tell the whole truth and nothing but the truth. The book, he told Drake, would be "as 'wide-open' as anyone could wish, self-revelatory, with no holds barred, and I tried to be more sparing of all the other characters that came into my book than I am of myself."[22]

When he submitted his text he was disconcerted to be told that Weidenfeld, supported by the American publisher, thought it was too long. Worse still, at certain points in the book Olivier had told the story by quotations from letters and other papers. One of these was the section on Hochhuth, which the editor considered was anyway too long and should be rewritten in narrative form. "Disagree!" wrote Olivier in the margin. The same was true of the passages relating to his retirement from the National Theater. "Violently disagree!" wrote Olivier. Weidenfeld sent Olivier a version of his book edited in a way that he felt would have greater appeal for the general reader. "I am not willing that this latest edition of the book should be published under my name," stormed Olivier. "Your editors are clearly antipathetic to me, my life, my career and my story." Weidenfeld's response does not survive, but it must have been placatory.

Olivier thanked him for his "infinitely kind reply to my queru-
lous petulance," but on the essentials he gave little ground. "Whatever criticism my writing deserves, it is at least mine, and comes
straight from my mind and heart . . . I cannot and do not pretend
to be a writer of distinction, only one of personal and individual
images." He had reworked the text with Mark Amory and this was
his last word.[23]

It was not the lack of distinction to which Weidenfeld's editors
objected but the wordiness, the convoluted sentences, the vapid
rhetorical flourishes. The final version, published in the autumn
of 1982, was a good deal better than what had first been submitted, but it could have been much improved by further editing. It
was, however, in its way a remarkable book. Olivier kept his word
about being harder on himself than on any other character. He was
quite as ready to describe what had gone wrong in his career as to
extol his triumphs: "One thing that does come out is the essential
modesty of the man," wrote Michael Billington. "There is steel and
iron in this man, yet there is an extraordinary humility as well."
He wrote about his personal relationships with sometimes startling
frankness: it was "a most courageous book," Ronald Pickup told
him. "For those of us who know how truly you protect and value
your privacy, I think the courageousness is particularly telling." It
also caused considerable offense to those who felt that Olivier, in
his determination to expose himself, had not hesitated to expose
other people at the same time. His elder son, Tarquin, felt that there
was much in it that was untrue. In particular his picture of his first
marriage was distorted. Olivier suggested that he had never loved
Jill Esmond nor she him, something that Tarquin believed to be
wholly misleading, at least so far as his mother was concerned. John
Gielgud was offended by what he felt to be the coarse and over-
candid revelations about Olivier's life with Vivien Leigh. This was
not the woman he had known, he complained. Max Rayne was so
shocked by what he thought to be Olivier's misrepresentation of
his last years at the National Theater that he wrote to the *Sunday
Telegraph* to protest. Everything, he said, had been done in a way

considerate of Olivier's susceptibilities and to suit his convenience: anything else would have been incompatible with "our relationship, not to mention the enormous respect and admiration I have always had for that great man."[24]

Several critics commented on the curious artificiality of Olivier's descriptive writing. He "*acts* writing," wrote Craig Raine, "an uneasy mixture of the chatty and the bellelettrist flourish." John Carey made the same point: "His abject penitential routine belongs, you feel, to a stage voice—another acting role for the great impersonator to lose himself in." But it was Olivier's style that most offended Carey: "His sentences ramble and flounder, and he has a fondness for deeply thought platitudes that come thudding out like stuffed bison." As for the jokes: "They stud the pages like wet washing." He didn't blame Olivier for having no sense of humor, he wrote, "but if you're without one it's best to avoid jocularity."[25]

What Olivier lacked was not so much a sense of humor as the ability to project it on paper. A host of witnesses pay tribute to his wit and gaiety. Roger Furse spoke of "his wonderful sense of humor, fun and nonsense that have so often broken up tense or unhappy situations." "I've never laughed with a man so much. I miss him. I miss the laughs," remembered John Mills. "He had a wonderful sense of the ludicrous, a touch of Monty Python or the Goons," said Anthony Havelock-Allan. His humor was the richer for being understated. "One has to be careful with Larry," wrote Richard Burton. "He is a great deadpan leg-puller and one is never quite sure whether he is probing very subtly for weak spots or majestically sending one up." To be a good raconteur and to laugh much and loudly is not necessarily proof of a sense of humor, but Olivier had a fine feeling for the ridiculous and was more likely to mock himself than anyone else. In a letter to Ralph Richardson in 1945 he described his performance in *Henry IV, Part One* one evening when he knew John Mills was in the audience. It was, he wrote, "one of the most self-conscious performances of Hotspur on record—either in such good taste and underacting it can't be heard, or else 'Look at my red hair and flashing eyes—aren't I *different!*' 'No' keeps coming back from the blackness . . . The man sitting next to Johnnie said, as the curtains parted on that most carefully arranged careless posture, white tights, garter just-so, light through window hitting one at just that angle, and all things that go to make up my startling and awe-inspiring second appearance, 'Oh, here's old Ginger again!' Christ!" The humor is, perhaps, not of the most sophisticated, but it was written by a man who was prepared to find himself absurd and to expose himself to others for being so. His memoirs would have been vastly improved if he had banished his inhibitions and let such irreverent fantasies run loose.[26]

What were almost but not quite his last words could also never have come from a man devoid of humor. The young male nurse, trying to give Olivier some liquid refreshment in the middle of the night, cut an orange in half, put it in a gauze and tried to squeeze some juice into his mouth. Olivier moved uneasily, the juice splashed onto his cheek and a dribble ran down into his ear. Memories stirred of a royal Dane sleeping in his garden and a murderous brother leaning over him. "It's not fucking *Hamlet*, you know," said Olivier.[27]

CHAPTER TWENTY-SIX

DEATH

The months and years leading up to those almost-final words were singularly unpleasant. There are no absolutes about old age. Some people in their late seventies or early eighties are fortunate enough still to be energetic: walking vigorously, gardening, finishing the crossword puzzle, even writing biographies. Others withdraw from life, cease to take an interest in other people, switch off the light or let it burn very dim. Physical health plays a part in this: it is harder to engage fully with life if one feels perpetually debilitated. Olivier had had more than his fair share of illness: his spirit was undaunted, but his body and, in some ways, his mind were sadly handicapped. Something vital had been extinguished. "I hated the last few years, because it wasn't Larry," said John Mills. "It didn't look like Larry." It didn't sound like Larry, either. Almost, one could say, it wasn't Larry.[1]

He made valiant efforts to convince others, indeed to convince himself, that business was as usual. John Gielgud wrote to congratulate Cecil Beaton on rising above his miseries: "Larry and Michael Redgrave are both equally to be admired for their courage and determination. There must be something about the theater . . . which manages to drive one, against all reason, to continue to be lively and interested and to refuse to lie down." Olivier did refuse to lie down, but the opportunities for standing up became ever more infrequent and more erratic. His last and most bizarre performance in a theater was in 1986 when he appeared in hologram as a disembodied head emerging from an extraterrestrial egg above the stage

of the Dominion Theater at the start of a new Cliff Richard musical. "I am Akash," the head proclaimed. "All your questions will
be answered." "Unfortunately they are not," commented Sheridan
Morley. "My questions would include, how does the greatest actor
of our century come to be entering his eightieth year involved, even
if only in facsimile, with what may well prove to be one of the worst
musicals of this century?" Olivier's reply would have been that he
needed the money. He may have believed that this was the case but
it was not the most important motive; he took on such ignoble tasks
because he needed to convince himself that he was still relevant, still
in demand, still capable of commanding an audience. Each time he
showed more clearly that it was in fact beyond his powers. The last
commission in which he was engaged when his final illness forced
him to withdraw, was to read poetry on television. Kenneth Williams watched aghast as Patrick Garland handed sheets of paper "to
the ancient lord for him to read aloud. It was a dreadful exhibition
of senility. He quavered his way through bits and pieces like some
poor old sod being made to audition."[2]

Emboldened by the friendly reception that his autobiography had
received, Olivier decided to write another book. *On Acting* was to
be the repository of a lifetime's experience, the wisdom and under-
standing that he had gleaned and that he was uniquely qualified to
pass on to the world. For many hours he talked to Gawn Grainger,
a young actor who had become Olivier's confidant and close friend,
and who was expected to do most of the work of putting Olivier's
thoughts on paper. There was to be no repetition of the moment
when Olivier thrust Mark Amory aside and took on the business
of writing his autobiography himself. He knew that the task was
beyond him. *On Acting* was interesting and modestly instructive,
it was better written than it would have been if its originator had
undertaken the task himself, but Olivier did not put one word of the
main text on paper. He wrote in his preface that, when he finished
Confessions of an Actor, he thought that he had done with writing
forever, but now, here he was, "sitting with my nose buried into the
blank page again," suffering all the agonies of authorship. "I typed

the bit about the writing of his book with my teeth clenched," Olivier's secretary told Gawn Grainger. "However, you and I know, don't we? As long as there's two of you it doesn't make it quite so bad." At least, in his will, Olivier left the royalties for *On Acting* to "Gawn Grainger, who wrote the book with me."[3]

David Niven wrote to tell Olivier that he had been diagnosed with motor neuron disease. The end result could be quite horrid, he said: inability to move one's limbs or to talk but with the brain still clear. "I'm afraid, dearest friend," he went on, "that I have discovered that I am made of different stuff from you. Your shining example of blazing courage in the face of one vicious piece of bad luck after another *should* have inspired me; but alas! I know myself for what I have always suspected—I am a gibbering coward!" Olivier's courage still blazed but with every month that passed it seemed that there was less and less for it to feed on. Olivier was bored. He lacked the intellectual hinterland that would have provided a profitable resource: he had lost the habit of listening to music; he read few books; he found abstract discussion tedious if not impossible—he knew how to act and to direct other people in their acting, that was all. At home, at the Malt House, he would fitfully revive when old friends came who would gossip with him about the theater; then he would sink back into a stupor, not actively unhappy but getting little joy from life. Much of the time he was alone. Joan Plowright's career meant that frequently she was in London. His children had full lives of their own. When people did come he sometimes tended to be contentious and bad tempered. Matthew Burton stayed with the family as a teenager. He remembered how Olivier enjoyed outraging his wife and daughters. "Women are no bloody use in a film set when they've got the Curse," he would complain; then, not yet satisfied that he had been sufficiently annoying, would continue: "They are *incapable* of work one week every four!"

"Being cantankerous was both sport and revenge for him," said Burton. "He was regimented, medicated, exercised and mollycoddled and, although he needed help, he hated being thought incapable."[4]

It was the powerlessness that most distressed him. For years his son Richard had been taking over responsibility for his affairs and estate, proceeding more and more without reference to Olivier himself. He remembered "the flashes of bitter resentment" that would cross his father's face when he saw his wife and son busily making plans for him and admitted to deriving some sadistic pleasure from speaking softly so that Olivier was excluded: "I reveled in the opportunity to punish him, for being away, for being ill, for taking mother away to work, whatever it was." At first Olivier would revolt, protest indignantly, storm out of the room in injured dignity; gradually he became apathetic, accepted his exclusion with sullen resentment. His memory got worse and worse. The *Daily Mirror* reported that he was using a teleprompter for his television roles; Olivier was offended but he knew that it was true. When at home, he found that he was constantly uncertain what he was supposed to be doing next. Was he going to London that afternoon? Or tomorrow morning? "I daren't keep asking because I know I've asked at least three times . . . I daren't ask Joan; Dickie gets impatient; Oh God, it's so awful!"[5]

His memory, though faltering, was not yet defunct. When Tom Stoppard arrived at one of the parties given to celebrate Olivier's eightieth birthday, he was greeted with: "I remember you. You're the one with big teeth." The birthday was at least a landmark in his ever less eventful life, even if it reminded him of something he would far rather not have known. They had laid on a spectacular jamboree in his honor in the Olivier Theater: John Mortimer devised the entertainment; Geraldine McEwan, Peggy Ashcroft and Albert Finney took part; Peter Hall appeared as Shakespeare. When Olivier arrived, wrote Hall's successor as Director, Richard Eyre, "there was a wail from the crowd of almost Iranian intensity, and out of the car stepped Olivier, smaller, almost unrecognizably so, a very, very frail man supported by Joan Plowright." At the climax of the evening a large white birthday cake was carried in, out of which erupted his daughter, Julie-Kate, to wish her father a happy birthday and to start the singing. The audience turned to Olivier and launched into a standing ovation that seemed as if it would never end: "He smiled, an enchanting childlike smile of pure pleasure. He was a man for whom applause was almost better than life itself." And then it was back to seclusion at the Malt House and wondering what, if anything, was going to happen next.[6]

Richard Olivier, worried about his father's deepening depression, persuaded him to see a Jungian analyst, Desmond Biddulph. Olivier welcomed his visits, clearly viewing him as an audience for his anecdotes rather than a physician. Biddulph found that he was always impeccably dressed and very much in control of himself. His short-term memory had almost gone, however, and he lived very much in the past. He reverted constantly to his life with Vivien Leigh and reproached himself for not having played a more active role at the time of her first serious breakdown. He took modest pride in the achievements of his children, but seemed to view them, as indeed everything else, with uneasy detachment. His closest relationship, Biddulph judged, was with his ginger cat.[7]

His relationship with Joan Plowright was tenuous. They had been living largely separate lives for the last ten years. He was convinced that he was being excluded from the inner family. Once, when Plowright was talking to Derek Granger at one end of the dining table, Olivier asked what they were discussing, then got angrily to his feet, demanded "Does anyone know where an unwanted old man can go to find a home?" and stalked from the room. He allowed himself to be coaxed back by one of his daughters, but made no attempt to conceal his resentment. Plowright accepted her responsibility for his welfare and preserved the proprieties. To an outsider it seemed a united ménage. "I was so moved by your spirit and tenderness to him," wrote a friend after his death. "What a sadness to lose him, and what patience and love you showed during his time of illness." Patience certainly; love, perhaps less. "I still loved him," Plowright insists. "The love was a bit squashed and battered, but it was still there." But there is a limit to the amount of squashing and battering that even the strongest love can survive. For years before he entered the final phase, he must have been difficult to live with. He became obsessed with the idea of suicide. He did not go to Joan Plowright's first night in "Who's Afraid of Virginia Woolf?" but instead interrupted the dinner party after the performance with a telephone call. How should he kill himself? he asked. Gas? Stones in the pocket and a plunge into the river? He reverted to the question at dinner at home and insisted on conducting a discussion on the subject. Plowright once told him that she could not endure this sort of life much longer. He launched into a bitter analysis of his own shortcomings: "The fact is that I don't know who I am . . . I've played all these parts and I don't know who I am. I'm a hollow man." The worst thing was that to a great extent she agreed with him. In the last few years of Olivier's life Plowright was increasingly asking herself whether she was sharing her life with a real human being.[8]

It seemed for a moment as if religion might provide part at least of his needs. At the end of 1983, when Olivier was in the hospital recovering from the removal of kidney, Alec Guinness called on him, armed with a handsome jar of caviar. He had intended just to leave the caviar with a suitable message, but to his surprise—"After all, I was not an intimate chum"—Olivier insisted on seeing him. He was most affectionate in his greeting. "Thank God you've come! I've been thinking of you so much. Help me! Help me! I want to become a Catholic." Guinness dithered, but eventually suggested that Olivier should see Father Nugent from Farm Street or some other sophisticated priest. "I have an idea he thinks it was all just a question of acknowledging the Pope's supremacy. He said a couple of times: 'I believe in transubstantiation, you know.' He was very sweet and I felt easier with him than I have in forty-eight years." A few days later he wrote to suggest another man whom Olivier might like to consult. "I'm a pretty lousy Catholic," he admitted, "though I love the Church (in spite of some of its ghastly supermarket modern ways) but if you want me to call on you for half an hour or so when you are out of the hospital, I'd be only too happy to visit you and chat."[9]

Olivier does not seem to have taken up the invitation. Nor was there much further evidence of his newfound quest for faith. He had told Denys Blakelock as long ago as 1931 that he felt he could "no longer throw in his lot with any organized religion" and from that time he had done little more than conform to the social shibboleths of the Church of England. At some point during the war Vivien Leigh told Cyril Cusack that "Larry was going through a religious phase." "But I'll soon get him out of that," she added. She seems to have succeeded. Max Adrian, for one, noted that he was certain Olivier had "found great solace in religion when he has been troubled emotionally." But it does not seem that this amounted to much. The prevailing picture is of one who was not prepared categorically to deny the existence of a deity but who gave the matter little thought. The Rev. John Hencher had once been an actor, then had joined the Church, but in 1963 wanted to revert to the stage. Olivier advised him to think twice and then think again. "I am deeply sympathetic to your problem, but I feel that, if one is called to the Church, one can assume it has been from the right quarter, whereas this is by no means certain with the stage." It was hardly a clarion call to rally to the faith, but nor was it the counsel of a confirmed disbeliever. Richard Olivier for one felt that his father, to the end, sat on the religious fence. There is no reason to believe that he was consciously insincere when he spoke to Guinness or Adrian but always he sought to adapt his personality to suit the person with whom he happened to be talking. Guinness and Adrian wanted to find him spiritually aware; then spiritually aware he would be.[10]

During his closing years Olivier was preoccupied by approaching death. "I wish my body to be cremated," he wrote, then changed his mind and substituted the word "buried." From time to time he tinkered with his will; in the final version his eldest son, Tarquin, was to get 10 percent of his estate, or £25,000, whichever was the smaller, the Malt House was to be Joan Plowright's for life; as to the residue, 40 percent was for Plowright, 60 percent divided among their three children. One portrait of him was left to the Garrick Club, another to the National Theater. A few friends—Peggy

Ashcroft, John Mills, Mu Richardson, Rachel Kempson and other intimates—were invited to choose from a collection of "smaller objects" which were specified in his will. John Gielgud was left "my early edition of the play *Hamlet*." He lived with the thought of his death. Alan Webb called on him by appointment and was kept waiting. Eventually a rather disheveled Olivier appeared. He apologized and said that he had been lying down imagining he was lying in state in Westminster Abbey.[11]

But he did not go gentle into that good night. Diana Quick said that when, in *The Dance of Death*, Olivier got to the line "I don't want to die," his voice always faltered. The world was a stage, the stage was a place where he had always gloried, the thought of an empty stage, a world without him, was intolerable. Gawn Grainger once asked him what it was like to know that he would end up in the Abbey. "After a long, thoughtful pause he said: 'Westminster Abbey will be just as cold as the village graveyard. I don't want to die.'" While the body weakened, the will to live remained as strong as ever. Gielgud saw him only a few days before he died. Traditionally, Gielgud was credited with disastrous tactlessness. This occasion proved to be no exception. "My God, Larry, I thought you were dead," he exclaimed. "I mean, dying. I mean, getting better." Like everyone in his circle Olivier relished Gielgud's gaffes; this example may not have been so welcome.[12]

The family organized an eighty-second birthday party, knowing that it would be his last, not even certain whether he would survive to enjoy it or would be able to recognize the few old friends who were invited. Richard Olivier described the final stages in the days that followed: "that gray face, rasping away for three days when lesser mortals would have given up the ghost." He was intermittently conscious, muttering when he was very near the end: "I don't want this." Did he mean he did not want painful life or impending death? his son wondered. Probably the latter. The last words Edna O'Brien heard him say were: "Oh sun, oh bloody sun, shine on me." Were they a semiconscious echo of Oswald Alving's last awful appeal at the end of Ibsen's *Ghosts*: "Mother, give me the sun"?

In any case, they do not suggest the mood of someone who sees the darkness approaching and who accepts it gladly.[13]

Laurence Olivier died on July 11, 1989. He had been ill, off and on, for more than twenty years, his dying had been protracted—but his death still left an immense gap in the world of anyone connected with the theater. "When he died, it was to me such a division," said Rosemary Harris. "It was like during Larry and after Larry . . . When he died, suddenly, the pinnacle wasn't there, there wasn't anybody at the top." Something had gone that could never be replaced. "When the realization has sunk in I might manage a tear," John Dexter wrote in his diary; "at the moment I feel a gigantic space that no one can occupy."[14]

The funeral was held in the tiny twelfth-century church of St. James's in the Sussex village of Ashurst. It was to be strictly private: family, a very few neighbors and close friends. "Private" can mean a multitude of things. When the few close friends include Douglas Fairbanks, Alec Guinness, Maggie Smith, John Mills, Franco Zeffirelli, it is inevitable that the event will attract attention. The press were there in force, outnumbering the congregation, but they behaved with rare decorum: the paparazzi, who had so often mobbed Olivier during his life, left him at peace in death.

If Olivier's funeral was, by his standards, a modest and domestic affair, all the stops were out when it came to the memorial service. First there was some indecorous jostling between Westminster Abbey and St. Paul's. The Abbey was delighted to hold a memorial service, but regretted that there could be no question of deeming him worthy of interment in Poets' Corner until at least ten years after his death. The family made some hurried inquiries and announced that fortunately St. Paul's was able to provide both a memorial service and a burial site. It would be nice for Olivier to lie alongside Garrick and Irving, but if that could not be managed Nelson would do. Westminster Abbey reconsidered its position and decided that, in the circumstances, an exception could be made. It is a telling indication of Olivier's stature that the two greatest religious institutions in the land should have vied for the honor of housing his remains.

The service was fixed for October 20, leaving plenty of time to make the arrangements. Every minute was needed. It was conducted on the most lavish scale: with pomp and circumstance but without pomposity or ostentation, in a style that the Church of England manages with singular skill. If ostentation did creep in, it was when a cortège of Olivier's theatrical associates processed up the aisle to lay trophies representing his various achievements before the altar. Douglas Fairbanks carried the insignia of the Order of Merit; Michael Caine his Oscar for Lifetime Achievement; Maggie Smith a silver model of the theater in Chichester; Paul Scofield a similar model of the National Theater; Derek Jacobi the crown used in the film of *Richard III*; Peter O'Toole the script used in the film of *Hamlet*; Ian McKellen the laurel wreath worn in the Stratford *Coriolanus*; Dorothy Tutin the crown from Granada's *King Lear*; and Frank Finlay Kean's sword—the one that Gielgud had presented to Olivier. Ralph Richardson had died a few years before; John Gielgud himself was unfit to take part in the procession, but he sat by the High Altar viewing the proceedings, perhaps with a touch of disapproval. According to his biographer, he thought the service unduly ostentatious and left instructions that nothing of the sort should be attempted when he died. "Public celebrations are awfully embarrassing," he said, "they've become society functions." To Irene Worth he was more charitable. The service, he wrote, "was a tremendous affair, extremely well organized and hugely attended, of course." Peggy Ashcroft and he had read poems, Alec Guinness had made a "memorably clever and appropriate speech" and Joan Plowright had "behaved most dignifiedly and hosted a fine party at the National." One sharp comment he did allow himself: a friend who had watched it on television had remarked that it should have been held not in the Abbey but in Drury Lane.[15]

The Abbey is not well suited to intimate occasions. Whatever the event may be, its services verge on the theatrical; when a theatrical demigod is being honored it is bound to be doubly so. Yet there was nothing meretricious or flamboyant about the Dean's bidding prayer:

> On Friday, October 20, 1905, Sir Henry Irving was buried in Poets' Corner. Eighty-four years later to the day we come to honor the greatest actor of our time; and next year the ashes of Laurence Olivier will lie beside those of Irving and Garrick, beneath the bust of Shakespeare and within a stone's throw of the graves of Henry V and The Lady Anne, Queen to Richard III.
>
> Laurence Olivier received from God a unique and awesome talent which he used to the full. We come then to give thanks for his integrity and professionalism; for his magnetism; his powers of observation; his boldness and his sense of danger; for his breathtaking versatility and his combination of strength and grace; for his resilience and his incorrigible sense of humor; for his courage, both as an actor and in facing illness and pain; and for so long outfacing death; and for the joy he found at the end in his garden and in the love of his family.
>
> *Non Nobis Domine*: Not unto us, O Lord, but unto Thy name give the praise.

Biographer's Afterword

Nearly thirty years ago I completed a biography of Admiral of the Fleet Earl Mountbatten of Burma. Time and again as I worked on Laurence Olivier I was struck by the similarities between the two men, whose lives followed very different trajectories yet whose personalities were in so many ways the same.

Mountbatten and Olivier were natural leaders. In his film *In Which We Serve* Noël Coward, a close friend of both men, portrayed Mountbatten as Captain Kinross, in command of a destroyer in the Second World War. "I want my ship to be a happy ship," Kinross/Mountbatten famously declared. He wanted his ship to be a happy ship because happy ships were more likely to be efficient ships but also because he had a strong sense of belonging and mutual responsibility. The crew were like an extended family: he took it for granted that they would be loyal and would respect, admire, even love him. He felt the same for them. Olivier wanted the National Theater to be a happy theater: he knew everyone, took an interest in everyone, consciously fostered a sense of community. Both men were adored by the people who worked under them.

Both men were inordinately ambitious. Mountbatten was sixteen when he announced that he would one day follow his father as First Sea Lord, professional head of the British Navy; Olivier was only a few years older when he said that he intended to be the greatest actor in the world. To achieve their ends they both thrust upward, paying little heed to the victims of their progress. Mountbatten may have been adored by his men, but the contemporaries over whose heads he jumped were decidedly less enthusiastic about his qualities. Richardson, Gielgud, Redgrave, Scofield, all paid tribute to Olivier's transcendent skills, but disparaging comments were not infrequent when it came to discussion of his personality.

Both were obsessed by detail. Nobody would deny that Mountbatten was capable of viewing the picture as a whole; the creative force behind the National Theater could hardly be accused of taking the narrow view; but given half a chance they would each have accepted responsibility for every tiny technicality. Mountbatten had views on what equipment each infantryman should carry when he stormed the beaches of Normandy; Olivier would interfere in the choice of makeup worn by the humblest member of his casts. Nothing was so small that they found it unworthy of their attention.

In large part this was because neither man could bear not to be in complete control. Of course one cannot run a giant enterprise without accepting the need to delegate, but both men did it with reluctance, both preferred subordinates who did not have too many ideas of their own; who were content to carry out the policies dictated from on high; who were, in fact, wholly unlike Mountbatten and Olivier.

Both men were courageous, both physically and morally. At sea, Mountbatten took it for granted that he should take as many, if not more risks than any man aboard. The chapter of Olivier's accidents is grisly evidence that he never allowed considerations of pain or danger to deflect him from what he felt would be, theatrically, the most effective course. Both men loved to be loved, which meant that they did not lightly court unpopularity; but if they felt a course was necessary they would force it through regardless of the rancor they might stir up among those who were the victims of their decisions.

Both men were unscrupulous in profiting by and taking credit for the deeds and ideas of others. Olivier was, on the whole, more ready to give credit where credit was due, but both could quickly convince themselves that, though a contribution might have been made by others, the principal distinction was deserved by them.

Often, far more often than in the case of more ordinary mortals, their pretensions were justified. Sometimes they were not.

Both men were capable of petty jealousy. They were upset when they saw someone doing something better, or even as well as they themselves could do it. Mountbatten was put out when one of the generals under his command in South East Asia was acclaimed for some striking successes. Olivier admitted that he could not bear to watch somebody play a part that he had played himself in case they in some way surpassed his achievements. Both men could be generous in their judgments of others but were less happy when it came to direct comparisons with themselves.

Both men possessed extravagant charm. Mountbatten was the more skilled in the presentation of a case—he would have been a formidable barrister—but they were both likely to prevail even if they were in the wrong because of the force of their personalities and their capacity to please. Confronted with the full blast of their persuasive powers, only the most resolute could resist.

Olivier got greater pleasure from sex than Mountbatten did, but for neither was it a matter of overriding importance. Except perhaps for a brief period when he was extravagantly in love with Vivien Leigh, Olivier would never have allowed the demands of sex to interfere with his career. As for Mountbatten, he would have rated his polo playing almost as high as his sexual relationships and neither would have been allowed to mar his professional progress.

Neither had much in the way of cultural hinterland. Neither read books unless they were directly related to their other activities, neither looked at pictures; Olivier knew more about music, but it did not play a significant part in his life. Mountbatten was more involved with politics, but only because politicians were important in the success or failure of his career; neither man held any strong political convictions. Both men, if asked, would have said that they were practicing Christians and active members of the Church of England; for neither did religion hold any real significance.

Of course one can find ways in which they differed. Olivier, for instance, had the ability to turn down the power and become, almost literally, invisible. He could become Mr. Nobody from Nowhere-in-Particular and blend with the crowd. Mountbatten's power was permanently at full blast; his headlights never dipped, still less did he resort to sidelights. "Off" was the alternative position, and that could only be achieved by sleep or death.

But the resemblances are far more striking. Mountbatten and Olivier must have met each other: both were present, for instance, at Noël Coward's seventieth birthday party. There is no record, however, of any encounter of consequence. If there had been such a meeting they would have recognized themselves as birds of a feather and, since they had no conceivable reason to be jealous of each other, would probably have got on very well. The last sentence in my biography of Mountbatten reads: "He flared brilliantly across the face of the twentieth century; the meteor is extinguished but its glow lingers on in the mind's eye." The same words would serve well for Olivier. Perhaps, however, one might better leave him with the lines from Byron that he inscribed at the back of one of his prewar pocket diaries:

> Thy day without a cloud hath pass'd.
> And thou wert happy to the last;
> Extinguish'd, not decay'd;
> As stars that shoot along the sky
> Shine brightest as they fall from high.

Decay rather than sudden extinction was to be his lot, but the glow that lingered after his fall burns brilliantly to this day.

Note on Sources

By far the most important collection of manuscripts concerning Laurence Olivier is to be found in the British Library. This contains not only his voluminous personal correspondence and diaries and a remarkably comprehensive assembly of papers relating to his time at the National Theater but also notebooks covering his time at Chichester and the tour of Australasia, the draft of the biography by his sister Sybille that was suppressed on his instructions and the tapes of the interviews conducted by Gawn Grainger that provide the basis for his book *On Acting*.

Other collections of papers in the British Library that have proved invaluable for this book are those of John Gielgud, Ralph Richardson and Kenneth Tynan. Michael Redgrave's papers are in the Theater Museum. The most important of the holdings of the National Theater Archive are duplicated in Olivier's own papers but some more detailed material is available there.

As indicated in the Acknowledgments, Olivier's widow, Joan Plowright, retains a certain number of valuable papers while his eldest son Tarquin, his friend Derek Granger and Vivien Leigh's biographer, Hugo Vickers, all possess important collections of manuscript material. The papers of his close colleague, Peter Hiley, now in the possession of Hiley's son, include an extensive essay on Olivier's achievements and personality by his close friend and associate, Roger Furse.

The interviews that, for more than fifty hours, Mark Amory conducted with Laurence Olivier, provide one of the most important sources for this book. A few of these have been transcribed, the majority survive only on tape. Olivier spoke with total freedom and his personality emerges far more vividly than from his own writings or the recollections of other people.

Letters from and papers relating to Olivier are to be found in many other collections mentioned in the Notes to this book. A small but particularly interesting group is to be found in the Chandos papers in the Cambridge University Library.

There is an alarmingly large number of books about Olivier already in existence. Olivier's own books, *Confessions of an Actor* (1982) and *On Acting* (1986) are, of course, of the first importance. Among the others, Terry Coleman's *Olivier* (2005) is the most comprehensive. Felix Barker's *The Oliviers* (1953) is of interest as being written with the approval and cooperation of its subject. Donald Spoto's *Laurence Olivier* (1991) is sometimes quirkish in its judgments but contains much of interest. Books by members of the family—Joan Plowright's *And That's Not All* (2001), Tarquin Olivier's *My Father Laurence Olivier* (1992), and *So Who's Your Mother* (1012) and Richard Olivier's *Shadow of the Stone Heart* (1995)—must be of particular significance to the biographer. Virginia Fairweather's *Cry God For Larry* (1969) is written by someone who worked closely with Olivier for many years. Many other books are mentioned in the notes that follow.

Notes

Abbreviations

CHAPTER ONE

1 S.O.'s draft biography of L.O., Add Mss 80591, p. 3.

2 Thomas Kiernan, *Olivier: The Life of Laurence Olivier* (London: Sidgwick & Jackson, 1981), p. 5; Kenneth Tynan, *The Sound of Two Hands Clapping* (London: Cape, 1975), p. 130; M.A. tapes 18.

3 L.O., *Confessions of an Actor* (1982; London: Orion, 1994), p. 23; Kiernan, *Olivier*, pp. 4 and 24.

4 Robert Stephens, *Knight Errant: Memoirs of a Vagabond Actor* (London: Hodder & Stoughton, 1995), p. 60.

5 L.O., *On Acting* (London: Weidenfeld and Nicolson, 1986), p. 25; *Olivier at Work: Compiled by the Royal National Theater*, ed. Lyn Haill (London: Nick Hern Books, 1989), p. 66; S.O., biography, p. 39.

6 L.O. to "Ross," 11/8/62, P.H. papers.

7 Reports in Add Mss 79782; Dickie Olivier, in *Sunday Times*, 16/11/53.

8 S.O., biography, p. 35.

9 M.A. tapes 1; Michael Munn, *Lord Larry: The Secret Life of Laurence Olivier: A Personal and Intimate Portrait* (London: Robson, 2007), p. 14.

10 Bernard Quaritch Catalog, "From the Library of Lord Olivier" (2011), Item 162; Edith Craig, *Ellen Terry's Memoirs* (London: Gollancz, 1933), p. 318.

11 Craig, *Ellen Terry's Memoirs*, p. 318; Sidney Dark, *Mackay of All Saints* (London: Centenary Press, 1937), p. 121; Thorndike in *Olivier*, ed. Logan Gourlay (London: Weidenfeld and Nicolson, 1973), p. 24; S.O., biography, p. 37.

12 M.A. tapes 1 and 53.

13 M.A. tapes 53.

14 Reports in Add Mss 79782; John Cottrell, *Laurence Olivier* (London: Coronet, 1977), p. 27; Kiernan, *Olivier*, pp. 16–20.

15 M.A. tapes 18.

16 D.G. tapes, interview with Benjamin Whitrow, 27/1/99; M.A. tapes 18; Cottrell, *Olivier*, p. 32.

17 L.O. to J.E., 21/4/61, T.O. papers; Quaritch Catalog, Item 111.

18 L.O., *On Acting*, p. 25; *St. Edward's School Chronicle* (March 1924); A. H. Packe to D.G., 1/3/99, D.G. papers.

19 M.A. tapes 18; S.O., biography, p. 53.

20 Terry Coleman, *Olivier: The Authorized Biography* (London: Bloomsbury, 2005), p. 21.

21 *Confessions*, p. 42.

22 Donald Spoto, *Laurence Olivier: A Biography* (London: HarperCollins, 1991), pp. 24–5; Elizabeth Sprigge, *Sybil Thorndike Casson* (London: Gollancz, 1971), pp. 225–6.

23 Hugo Vickers, *Vivien Leigh* (London: Hamilton, 1988), p. 65; *Confessions*, pp. 42–3.

24 Interview for Melvyn Bragg, "Laurence Olivier: A Life" (1986); *Peter Hall's Diaries: The Story of a Dramatic Battle*, ed. John Goodwin (London: Hamish Hamilton, 1983), p. 53; Roger Lewis, *The Real Life of Laurence Olivier* (London: Century, 1996), p. 81.

CHAPTER TWO

1 L.O. to Warren Mangi, 8/1/77, Add Mss 79935.

2 *Confessions*, p. 45; M.A. tapes 53; *Confessions*, p. 51.

3 Cottrell, *Laurence Olivier*, p. 43.

4 M.A. tapes 1.

5 Thorndike in *Olivier*, ed. Gourlay, pp. 9 and 25–6.

6 Felix Barker, *The Oliviers: A Biography* (London: Hamilton, 1953), p. 27; Bache Matthews, *A History of the Birmingham Repertory Theater* (London, 1924), p. 34.

7 Denys Blakelock, *Round the Next Corner: A Life Story* (London: Gollancz, 1967), p. 56; Tarquin Olivier, *My Father Laurence Olivier* (London: Headline, 1992), p. 56; M.A. tapes 45; Interview with William Gaskill.

8 M.A. tapes 6; *Confessions*, p. 57.

9 M.A. tapes 16 and 6.

10 Garry O'Connor, *Ralph Richardson: An Actor's Life* (London: Hodder and Stoughton, 1982), p. 58; Meriel Forbes to L.O., undated, Add Mss 79771; Sarah Miles, *Serves Me Right* (London: Macmillan, 1994), pp. 71–2; M.A. tapes 13 and 18; L.O. to Meriel Forbes, 29/9/45, Add Mss 82045.

11 Beldon, *Observer*, 12/3/62; Lewis, *Olivier*, p. 92.

12 *Confessions*, p. 59; L.O. diary, Add Mss 79794; S.O., biography, p. 69; Meriel Forbes to L.O., undated, Add Mss 79771.

13 *Lewisham Borough News*, 29/9/26; M.A. tapes 22; *Birmingham Post*, 4/4/27; L.O. to N. Pogodin, 3/10/59, Add Mss 79897.

14 *Evening News*, 30/8/46; Jonathan Croall, *Gielgud: A Theatrical Life* (London: Methuen, 2000), p. 102.

15 Kiernan, *Olivier*, p. 49; Richardson, *Evening Standard*, 7/6/70.

16 G. W. Bishop, *Barry Jackson and the London Theater* (London: Arthur Baker, 1933), pp. 88–9.

17 S.O., biography, p. 76; *Confessions*, p. 65; L.O. to T.O., 21/2/52, Add Mss 88951/1/2.

18 *Olivier: In Celebration*, ed. Gary O'Connor (London: Hodder & Stoughton, 1987), p. 23; M.A. tapes 36; *Confessions*, p. 74–5; Miles, *Serves Me Right*, p. 143.

19 R. C. Sherriff, *No Leading Lady* (London: Gollancz, 1968), pp. 50–1; Kiernan, *Olivier*, p. 61.

20 Cottrell, *Olivier*, p. 52; M.A. tapes 9 and 58.

21 Virginia Fairweather, *Cry God for Larry: An Intimate Memoir of Sir Laurence Olivier* (London: Calder & Boyars, 1969), p. 43.

CHAPTER THREE

1 M.A. tapes 59.

2 Lewis, *Olivier*, p. 104; M.A. tapes 4.

3 J.E. to L.O., 23/12/29, T.O. papers; M.A. tapes 4 and 24; Interview with T.O.

4 *The Letters of Noël Coward*, ed. Barry Day (London: Methuen Drama, 2007), p. 212; M.A. tapes 31; John Mills, *Up In the Clouds, Gentlemen Please* (London: Weidenfeld and Nicolson, 1980), p. 92.

5 Stephens, *Knight Errant*, p. 105.

6 Douglas Fairbanks Jr., *The Salad Days* (London: Collins, 1988), p. 174; M.A. tapes, J.E.

7 *Confessions*, p. 92; Sheridan Morley, *Tales from the Hollywood Raj: The British Film Colony On Screen and Off* (London: Weidenfeld and Nicolson, 1983), p. 80; Kiernan, *Olivier*, p. 83; David Selznick to B. P. Schulberg, 25/2/31, *Memo from David O. Selznick*, ed. Rudy Behlmer (New York: Viking, 1972), p. 32.

8 Fabia Drake, *Blind Fortune* (London: Kimber, 1978), p. 95.

9 M.A. tapes, J.E.; David Thomson, *Showman: The Life of David O. Selznick*, (London: André; Deutsch, 1993), pp. 133–4.

10 Interview with T.O.; M.A. tapes, J.E.

11 S.O., biography, p. 104; *On Acting*, p. 177.

12 M.A. tapes 22; J. B. Priestley to L.O., 21/8/37, Add Mss 79777.

13 L.O. to Devine, 18/4/36, Add Mss 79935; Orson Welles and Peter Bogdanovich, *This Is Orson Welles*, ed. Jonathan Rosenbaum (London: HarperCollins, 1993), p. 15.

14 *Confessions*, pp. 99–100; Cottrell, *Olivier*, p. 89.

15 Jan Herman, *A Talent for Trouble: The Life of Hollywood's Most Acclaimed Director, William Wyler* (New York: Da Capo, 1995), p. 185; *Confessions*, p. 100; M.A. tapes 20; Kiernan, *Olivier*, p. 100.

16 M.A. tapes 16; Quaritch Catalog, Item 50.

17 Michael Meyer, *Not Prince Hamlet: Literary and Theatrical Memoirs* (London: Secker & Warburg, 1989), p. 16; *Confessions*, p. 156; O'Connor, *Richardson*, pp. 57–8.

18 Kiernan, *Olivier*, pp. 105–6; Croall, *Gielgud*, pp. 203–4; M.A. tapes 39; Interview with Ronald Harwood; M.A. tapes 1.

19 Kenneth Tynan, *He That Plays The King: A View of the Theater* (London: Longmans, Green, 1950), p. 39; M.A. tapes 12.

20 M.A. tapes 12; James Agate, *Ego 3: Being Still More of the Autobiography of J. Agate* (London: Harrap, 1938), p. 138.

CHAPTER FOUR

1 *Evening Standard*, 18/10/35; *Sunday Times*, 20/10/35; *Confessions*, p. 105; *Observer*, 20/10/35; Gyles Brandreth, *John Gielgud: An Actor's Life* (Stroud: Sutton Publishing, 2000), p. 56.

2 John Gielgud, *Early Stages* (London: Falcon Press, 1953), p. 231; Croall, *Gielgud*, p. 209; M.A. tapes 18; Interview with Patrick Garland.

3 O'Connor, *Richardson*, p. 79; Barker, *Oliviers*, p. 70; Croall, *Gielgud*, pp. 210–11.

4 Sofka Zinovieff, *Red Princess: A Revolutionary Life* (London: Granta, 2007), p. 190.

5 M.A. tapes 29; *Spectator*, 5/3/37.

6 H.V., *Leigh*, p. 67; Jean-Pierre Aumont, *Sun and Shadow: An Autobiography* (New York: Norton, 1977), p. 429.

7 Add Mss 79802.

8 M.A. tapes 29; Barker, *Oliviers*, p. 111.

9 M.A. tapes 12; *Confessions*, p. 109.

10 M.A. tapes 14; tapes of interview with Gawn Grainger for *On Acting*; *On Acting*, p. 57.

11 *Confessions*, p. 64; Interview in *New York Times*, 3/2/60; Peter Daubeny, *My World of Theater* (London: Cape, 1971), pp. 40–1.

12 Barker, *Oliviers*, p. 121; Redgrave and Guinness in *Olivier*, ed. Gourlay, pp. 56 and 68; *cit.* S.O., biography, p. 120.

13 Agate, *Ego 9: Concluding the Autobiography of James Agate* (London: Harrap, 1948), p. 230; Michael Redgrave, *In My Mind's Eye: An Autobiography* (London: Weidenfeld and Nicolson, 1983), p. 107.

14 *Confessions*, p. 109; Ashcroft to L.O., undated, Add Mss 79766; *On Acting*, p. 58.

15 Munn, *Lord Larry*, pp. 78–9; Coleman, *Olivier*, p. 98; *Confessions*, p. 111; Agate, *Ego 9*, p. 230; M.A. tapes 13.

16 Note by Furse, P.H. papers; M.A. tapes 14; Agate, *Ego 9*, pp. 248–9; M.A. tapes 13.

17 Jonathan Croall, *Sybil Thorndike: A Star of Life* (London: Haus, 2008), p. 289; L.O. to Rathbone, 14/3/49, Percy to L.O., 11/5/38, Add Mss 79777.

18 Interview with T.O.; M.A. tapes, J.E.; Interview in *Life*, 18/10/48.

19 H.V., *Leigh*, p. 69; Jesse Lasky, *Love Scene: The Story of Laurence Olivier and Vivien Leigh* (Brighton: Angus and Robertson, 1978), p. 39; Kiernan, *Olivier*, p. 138; M.A. tapes, J.E.

20 Tyrone Guthrie, *A Life in the Theater* (London: Hamilton, 1960), p. 174 and Guthrie, *In Various Directions: A View of the Theater* (London: Joseph, 1965), pp. 66–7.

21 M.A. tapes 57; Spoto, *Olivier*, p. 98; M.A. tapes, J.E.; Add Mss 79803.

22 *Confessions*, p. 108; Add Mss 79868.

CHAPTER FIVE

1 M.A. tapes 9; A. Scott Berg, *Goldwyn: A Biography* (London: Sphere, 1989), p. 322.

2 *Confessions*, p. 114.

3 S.O., biography, p. 148; M.A. tapes 10; Wyler in *Olivier*, ed. Gourlay, pp. 84–5; Alexander Knox in *Olivier*, ed. Gourlay, p. 89; Spoto, *Olivier*, p. 112.

4 Michael Munn, *David Niven: The Man behind the Balloon* (London: JR Books, 2009), pp. 85–6.

5 M.A. tapes 10; Susana Walton, *William Walton: Behind the Façade* (Oxford: Oxford University Press, 1988), p. 138; Munn, *Niven*, pp. 85–6.

6 Wyler in *Olivier*, ed. Gourlay, p. 87; M.A. tapes 9.

7 Graham Greene, *The Pleasure-Dome: The Collected Film Criticism 1935–40* (London: Secker and Warburg, 1972), p. 220; Herman, *Wyler*, p. 460.

8 There are several differing accounts of this episode. Probably the most reliable is that of Irene Mayer Selznick in *A Private View* (New York: Alfred A. Knopf, 1983), p. 215.

9 M.A. tapes 29; Lasky, *Love Scene*, pp. 116 and 73–4; Fairbanks, *Salad Days*, p. 344.

10 M.A. tapes 9 and 29.

11 Tad Mosel, *Leading Lady: The World and Theater of Katharine Cornell* (New York: Little, Brown, 1978), p. 155; M.A. tapes 29; Interview with Derek Granger.

12 S.O. to L.O., 7/5/39, Add Mss 79891; M.A. tapes 29; Gerald Olivier to L.O., 18/2/37, Add Mss 79890A.

13 S.O. to L.O., 7/5/39, Add Mss 79891; J.E. to L.O., 1/5/39, Add Mss 79879.

14 M.A. tapes 37; *Memo from David O. Selznick*, pp. 144 and 264.

15 M.A. tapes 37; Charlotte Chandler, *It's Only a Movie: Alfred Hitchcock: A Personal Biography* (London: Simon & Schuster, 2005), pp. 126–7; *Memo from David O. Selznick*, p. 264.

16 Chandler, *Hitchcock*, pp. 124–6; *Sunday Times*, 3/11/63.

17 Korda to L.O., and L.O. to Korda, 22/6/39, Add Mss 80461A.

18 *Memo from David O. Selznick*, p. 274; Douglas Fairbanks Jr., *A Hell of a War* (London: Robson Books, 1995), p. 56.

CHAPTER SIX

1 H.V., *Leigh*, p. 94.

2 M.A. tapes 10 and 43.

3 Munn, *Niven*, p. 92; *Confessions*, p. 123.

4 Munn, *Lord Larry*, pp. 111–18.

5 Cottrell, *Olivier*, pp. 176–7; Coward, *Letters*, pp. 408–9; Jesse, *Love Scene*, p. 126; J.E. to Mrs. Esmond, 28/12/40, Add Mss 88951/2/1.

6 M.A. tapes 10.

7 V.L. to Leigh Holman, 9/8/40, *cit.* Alan Dent, *Vivien Leigh: A Bouquet* (London: Hamilton, 1969), p. 34; Michael Korda, *Charmed Lives: A Family Romance* (London: Allen Lane, 1980), p. 151.

8　Michael Powell, *A Life in Movies: An Autobiography* (London: Heine-mann, 1986), p. 363.

9　M.A. tapes 19; Reader Bullard, "The birthday party that changed the war," *Password* 34 (December 2012); *Tatler and Bystander*, 6/8/41.

10　S.O., biography, p. 158.

11　James Carson, *Modern Screen* (June 1940); H.V., *Leigh*, p. 132.

12　V.L. to Leigh Holman, 30/4/40, *cit.* Dent, *Leigh*, p. 34; Barker, *Oliviers*, p. 171.

13　Kiernan, *Olivier*, p. 191; *Confessions*, p. 121; *New York Times*, 10/5/40.

14　Barker, *Oliviers*, p. 174; Jesse, *Love Scene*, p. 123; S.O., biography, pp. 162–3.

15　Spoto, *Olivier*, p. 131; *On Acting*, p. 15.

16　J.E. to Mrs. Esmond, 22/7/40, 9/8/40 and 30/10/40, Add Mss 88951/4.

17　J.E. to Mrs. Esmond, 26/10/41, Add Mss 88951/4.

18　T.O., *My Father*, p. 86.

19　Barker, *Oliviers*, pp. 182–3.

20　Coward, *Letters*, pp. 408–9.

CHAPTER SEVEN

1　Bernstein to L.O., 27/1/41, Add Mss 79766; M.A. tapes 18.

2　M.A. tapes 18; O'Connor, *Richardson*, pp. 104–5.

3　L.O. to J.E., undated, Add Mss 88951/1/1; D.G. tapes, interview with Jack Hedley; M.A. tapes 38.

4　*The Noël Coward Diaries*, ed. Graham Payn and Sheridan Morley (Boston, Mass.: Little, Brown, 1982), p. 8.

5　*Confessions*, p. 128; Richard Huggett, *Binkie Beaumont: Eminence Grise of the West End Theater* (London: Hodder & Stoughton, 1989), p. 275.

6　M.A. tapes 18.

7　Diaries, Add Mss 79795; M.A. tapes 26.

8　*Confessions*, p. 131; Asquith to L.O., 24/11/43, Add Mss 79766; *Olivier: The Films and Faces of Laurence Olivier*, ed. Margaret Morley (Godalming: LSP Books, 1978), p. 95.

9　Powell, *Life in Movies*, p. 402.

10　J.E. to L.O., 26/4/42 and 25/9/42, Add Mss 79879.

11 Gielgud to Mrs. Gielgud, 10/9/41, Add Mss 81308; Vickers, *Leigh*, p. 138; Herman, *Wyler*, p. 253; Thomson, *Selznick*, p. 479; L.O. to "Trudie," 25/9/42, H.V. papers.

12 *Confessions*, p. 130; Powell, *Life in Movies*, pp. 401–2; Interview with T.O.

13 Spoto, *Olivier*, pp. 142–3; Powell, *Life in Movies*, p. 602; Note by Furse, P.H. papers.

14 L.O. to Young, undated, Add Mss 79780.

15 D.G. tapes, interview with Dallas Bower; L.O. to T.O., 1/8/43, Add Mss 88951/1/2.

16 John Gielgud, *Shakespeare: Hit or Miss?* (London: Sidgwick & Jackson, 1991), p. 50; Esmond Knight, *Seeking the Bubble* (London: Hutchinson, 1943), p. 95; M.A. tapes 39.

17 L.O. to Muriel Smith, undated, Add Mss 80087; Walton, *Walton*, pp. 94–5.

18 M.A. tapes 13; D.G. tapes, interview with Dallas Bower; Andrews in *Olivier*, ed. Gourlay, p. 77.

19 L.O. to Young, undated, Add Mss 79780; Spoto, *Olivier*, p. 147; M.A. tapes 14.

20 James Agate, *Ego 7: Even More of the Autobiography of James Agate* (London: Harrap, 1945), p. 311; Melvyn Bragg, *Laurence Olivier* (London: Hutchinson, 1984), p. 73.

21 D.G. tapes, interview with Dallas Bower.

22 *Confessions*, pp. 135–7; T.O., *My Father*, p. 128; V.L. to L.O., 2/8/43, Add Mss 80719

23 Lasky, *Love Scene*, p. 151; Note by Furse, P.H. papers.

24 Barker, *Oliviers*, p. 204; D.G. papers, interview with Stephen Greif.

25 M.A. tapes 39.

CHAPTER EIGHT

1 *Cit.* Richard Eyre, *Utopia and Other Places* (London: Bloomsbury, 1993), p. 119.

2 M.A. tapes 9; Radie Harris, *Radie's World* (London: W.H. Allen, 1975), p. 95.

3 Dominic Shellard, *Kenneth Tynan: A Life* (New Haven; London: Yale University Press, 2003), p. 84; Kenneth Tynan, *The Sound of Two Hands Clapping* (London: Cape, 1975), p. 127; Mortimer, in *Olivier at Work*, p. 9.

4 Interview with Michael Redington; Guthrie, *In Various Directions*, pp. 157–8; Simon Callow, *Charles Laughton: A Difficult Actor* (London: Methuen, 1987), p. 249.

5 Kiernan, *Olivier*, p. 143.

6 Peter Brook, *The Empty Space* (London: MacGibbon & Kee, 1968), p. 138; Ronald Hayman, *Playback* (London: Davis-Poynter, 1973), p. 161; Interview with Ronald Pickup.

7 William Gaskill, *A Sense of Direction* (London: Faber, 1988), pp. 45–6; L.O. to Stanley Hall, 29/4/51, Dover Wilson to L.O., 22/5/51, Add Mss 80049.

8 Christopher Plummer, *In Spite of Myself* (London: JR Books, 2010), p. 518; Milton to L.O., 31/7/51, Add Mss 80050; L.O. to Peter Fetterman, 11/1/74, Add Mss 80505.

9 L.O. to Freddie Pyne, 7/2/69, Add Mss 80398; Antony Sher, *Beside Myself: An Autobiography* (London: Hutchinson, 2001), pp. 99–100; Michael Billington, *The Modern Actor* (London: Hamilton, 1973), p. 210.

10 L.O. to Lewis Beck, 27/6/44, Add Mss 79785.

11 Gielgud to Mrs. Gielgud, 8/2/46, Add Mss 81308; Garry O'Connor, *The Secret Woman: A Life of Peggy Ashcroft* (London: Weidenfeld & Nicolson, 1997), p. 90; Croall, *Gielgud*, p. 313; Gielgud, B.B.C. Radio 4 interview, broadcast 3/6/00; *Gielgud's Letters*, ed. Richard Mangan (London: Weidenfeld & Nicolson, 2004), p. 95.

12 Sheridan Morley, *John G: The Authorized Biography of John Gielgud* (London: Hodder & Stoughton, 2001), p. 300; Brandreth, *Gielgud*, p. 10; Interview with Laurence Harbottle.

13 L.O. to Asherson, 19/4/44, Add Mss 79975.

14 L.O. to Jeans, 23/5/44, Add Mss 79975.

15 Michael Billington, *State of the Nation: British Theater since 1945* (London: Faber, 2007), p. 32.

16 L.O. to Wanbon, undated, Add Mss 79976.

17 O'Connor, *Richardson*, p. 114; M.A. tapes 7.

18 M.A. tapes 7 and 26.

19 *Confessions*, p. 146.

20 Coward, *Diaries*, p. 24; Ronald Harwood, *Sir Donald Wolfit, C.B.E.: His Life and Work in the Unfashionable Theater* (London: Secker and Warburg, 1971), p. 237.

21 M.A. tapes 12; L.O. diary, 1/3/44, Add Mss 79795; Mills, *Up In the Clouds*, p. 193; D.G. tapes, interview with John Mills.

22 Mills, *Up In the Clouds*, p. 193; J. C. Trewin, *The Theater since 1900* (London: Andrew Dakers, 1951), p. 271; Gielgud, *Letters*, pp. 77–8; Coward, *Diaries*, p. 24; Quaritch Catalog, Item 31; Stephens, *Knight Errant*, p. 179; Alec McCowen, *Double Bill* (London: Elm Tree Books, 1980), p. 58; *On Acting*, p. 82; Bragg, *Olivier*, p. 77.

23 Interview with Roger Braban; Kathleen Tynan, *The Life of Kenneth Tynan* (London: Phoenix, 1995), p. 38; *On Acting*, p. 82; Dominic Shellard, *Harold Hobson: Witness and Judge: The Theater Criticism* (Keele: Keele University Press, 1995), p. 83; Agate, *Ego 7*, p. 244; L.O. to Alan Dent, 4/4/45, Add Mss 79975.

24 M.A. tapes 7; Boyle to Cooper, 2/4/45, Add Mss 79975; Edith Olivier, *From Her Journals, 1924–48*, ed. Penelope Middelboe (London: Weidenfeld & Nicolson, 1989), p. 295.

25 Gielgud to Mrs. Gielgud, undated, Add Mss 81308; Dent to L.O., March 1945, Add Mss 79975.

26 M.A. tapes 42; Interview with Roger Braban.

27 Huggett, *Beaumont*, p. 409; Barker, *Oliviers*, pp. 227–8.

CHAPTER NINE

1 L.O. to J.E., October 1944, Add Mss 88951/1/1.

2 M.A. tapes 16; *Sunday Times*, 21/10/45; Bryan Forbes, *That Despicable Race: A History of the British Acting Tradition* (London: Elm Tree, 1980), p. 61.

3 M.A. tapes 16; *Confessions*, p. 155; *Henry Root's World of Knowledge* (1982), cit. Lewis, *Olivier*, p. 8; Kenneth Tynan, *He That Plays the King*, p. 46.

4 Tynan, *He That Plays the King*, p. 47; Coward, *Diaries*, p. 42; Dent, *Glamour* (January 1947); *Confessions*, p. 156.

5 *On Acting*, p. 93; Adrian in *Olivier*, ed. Gourlay, p. 34; Gielgud to Mrs. Gielgud, *Letters*, p. 95; Harwood, *Wolfit*, p. 237.

6 Leighton in *Olivier*, ed. Gourlay, p. 112; Langner to L.O., 30/1/47, Add Mss 79977.

7 L.O. to Spencer, 30/8/46, Add Mss 79976.

8 Barker, *Oliviers*, p. 240; *Confessions*, p. 175.

9 *On Acting*, pp. 144–5; Coleman, *Olivier*, pp. 181–2; Interview with D.G.; Munn, *Olivier*, p. 140.

10 Bartley to L.O., 16/12/48, Add Mss 79770; L.O. to Rattigan, 5/4/46, Add Mss 79777.

11 *The Film Hamlet: A Record of its Production*, ed. Brenda Cross (London: Saturn Press, 1948), p. 50.

12 Interview with Ronald Harwood; Hayman, *Playback*, p. 164; Barker, *Oliviers*, p. 262.

13 M.A. tapes 6 and 14.

14 *Confessions*, p. 161.

15 *Film Hamlet*, p. 50; Kiernan, *Olivier*, p. 231; Laurie, *Film Comment* (April 1982).

16 Interview with Knight, H.V. papers; D.G. tapes, interview with Morgan; *Confessions*, pp. 163–4.

17 *Film Hamlet*, p. 30; M.A. tapes 41; L.O. to Kenneth Warner, 27/6/47, Add Mss 79935.

18 *Film Hamlet*, p. 15; Guthrie, *In Various Directions*, pp. 76–8; Tynan, *He That Plays the King*, pp. 134–5.

19 Jerry Vermilye, *The Complete Films of Laurence Olivier* (New York: Carol Publishing, 1992), p. 415; L.O. to Rank, 9/5/47, Add Mss 80479; Mathieson to L.O., undated, Add Mss 79776.

CHAPTER TEN

1 M.A. tapes 26.

2 L.O. to Richardson, 26/10/46, Add Mss 79786; L.O. to Alan Moore, 25/2/50, Add Mss 79908; L.O. to Jane Smith, 7/11/51, James Jackson to L.O., undated, Add Mss 79932.

3 M.A. tapes 20; L.O. to Coward, in Coward, *Letters*, p. 531; Gielgud, *Letters*, p. 105.

4 Beyer to Stephen Thomas, 23/2/48, Add Mss 79978.

5 D.G. tapes, interview with Alec McCowen; Cushing, *Olivier*, ed. Gourlay, p. 124; Garry O'Connor, *Darlings of the Gods: One Year in the Lives of Laurence Olivier and Vivien Leigh* (London: Hodder and Stoughton, 1984), p. 82; Cushing to L.O., 20/3/48, Add Mss 79768; V.L. to Mu Richardson, 15/5/48, Add Mss 82044.

6 M.A. tapes 20; Barker, *Oliviers*, p. 278.

7 M.A. tapes 20; O'Connor, *Darlings of the Gods*, p. 94.

8 L.O. to Burrell, 20/3/48, *cit.* O'Connor, *Richardson*, p. 147; Cushing, *Olivier*, ed. Gourlay, p. 124; D.G. tapes, interview with Georgina Dumel.

9 L.O's Notebook, 5/4/48, Add Mss 79980.

10 Beyer report of 16/4/48, Add Mss 79975; V.L. to Mu Richardson, 15/4/48, Add Mss 82044; Redington to H. J. Keates, 5/10/48, Redington papers; Barker, *Oliviers*, p. 282; Freyberg to L.O., 15/10/48, Add Mss 79978.

11 L.O. to Tennant, 14/7/48, Add Mss 79981; Tennant to L.O., 13/7/48, Add Mss 79978.

12 L.O. to S.O., quoted in L.O. to Tennant, 5/8/48, Add Mss 80594.

13 *Confessions*, p. 168; L.O. to Tennant, 19/6/48, Add Mss 79977.

14 *Confessions*, p. 165.

15 George Chamberlain to Tennant, 24/7/47, Add Mss 79977; L.O. to Tennant, 14/7/48, Add Mss 79981.

16 Harold Hobson, *Theater in Britain: A Personal View* (Oxford: Phaidon, 1984), pp. 138–9.

17 Guthrie, *A Life in the Theater*, p. 203; John Elsom and Nicholas Tomalin, *The History of the National Theater* (London: Cape, 1978), pp. 96–7; M.A. tapes 26.

18 O'Connor, *Richardson*, pp. 134–5.

19 Hamilton to L.O., 16/12/48, Chamberlain to L.O., 19/7/48, Richardson to L.O., 22/9/48, Add Mss 79777.

20 *Confessions*, p. 168; Elaine Dundy, *Finch, Bloody Finch: A Biography of Peter Finch* (London: Joseph, 1980), pp. 127–9; L.O. to Tennant, 31/8/48, D.G. papers.

21 H.V., *Leigh*, pp. 179–80; O'Connor, *Darlings of the Gods*, p. 3.

22 O'Connor, *Darlings of the Gods*, p. 122; L.O. to Stephen Watts, 13/2/46, Add Mss 80619.

23 H.V. papers, interview with Emma Brash; *Confessions*, p. 170.

CHAPTER ELEVEN

1 M.A. tapes 26.

2 M.A. tapes 26; Hunt to L.O., 23/12/48, 2/5/50, 22/12/50, Add Mss 79977.

3 L.O. to Beaton, 15/10/48, H.V. papers; Cecil Beaton, *The Strenuous Years: Diaries 1948–55* (London: Weidenfeld and Nicolson, 1973), pp. 19–20.

4 Esher to L.O., June 1949, Add Mss 79977.

5 L.O. to Thorndike, 23/10/52, Add Mss 79779.

6 Selznick, *Private View*, p. 321.

7 L.O. to L. F. Pickin, 18/10/49, Add Mss 80034; Selznick, *Private View*, p. 324; L.O. to Kanin, 6/10/49, Add Mss 79773; M.A. tapes 35.

8 M.A. tapes 57.

9 L.O. to J. B. Priestley, 9 and 21/11/49, Add Mss 79777.

10 Add Mss 79766; Stefan Kanfer, *Somebody. The Reckless Life and Remarkable Career of Marlon Brando* (New York: Alfred A. Knopf, 2008), p. 99; *Confessions*, p. 92; Simon Callow, *My Life in Pieces: An Alternative Autobiography* (London: Nick Hern Books, 2010), p. 198.

11 Gielgud, *Letters*, p. 483; Interview with T.O.; Rattigan to L.O., undated, Add Ms. 79777; Beaton, Diary, H.V. papers; Adrian Woodhouse, *Angus McBean: Facemaker* (London: Alma, 2006), p. 148; *The Kenneth Williams Diaries*, ed. Russell Davies (London: HarperCollins, 1993), p. 238.

12 D.G. tapes, interview with Rosemary Harris; Bloom to L.O., undated, Add Mss 79766; Graham Lord, *Niv: The Authorized Biography of David Niven* (London: Orion, 2003), p. 308.

13 L.O. to T.O., 20/7/51, Add Mss 88951/1/2; J.E. to L.O., 1/1/52, Add Mss 79897; L.O. to T.O., 4/12/53, Add Mss 88951/1/2.

14 L.O. to J.E., 8/4/49, Add Mss 79879; The records of the various L.O.P. meetings are at Add Mss 79987; Banks to L.O., 3/4/50, Add Mss 79766.

15 Guthrie, *A Life in the Theater*, p. 120.

16 Hobson, *Sunday Times*, 27/3/49.

17 Barker, *Oliviers*, p. 293; D.G. tapes, interview with Christopher Fry; L.O. to Kanin, 27/1/50, Add Mss 79773; Elliott to L.O., 7/8/50, Add Mss 79770.

18 Rex Harrison, *Rex: An Autobiography* (London: Macmillan, 1974), p. 127; Patrick Garland, *The Incomparable Rex: A Memoir of Rex Harrison in the 1980s* (London, Macmillan, 1998), pp. 30–1; L.O. to Harrison, 23/5/63, Add Mss 80396.

19 Coward, *Diaries*, p. 146; Mills, *Up In the Clouds*, pp. 211–12; *Confessions*, p. 179; M.A. tapes 56; L.O. to Banks, 3/4/50, Add Mss 39766.

20 *The Letters of Evelyn Waugh*, ed. Mark Amory (London: Weidenfeld & Nicolson, 1980), p. 282; Waugh to Bushell, 16/8/48, Add Mss 79767.

21 L.O. to Nancy Halliwell-Hobbes, 2/1/51, Add Mss 79773.

CHAPTER TWELVE

1 H.V. papers, interviews with Anne Norwich and Athene Seyler.

2 M.A. tapes 13.

3 House Agent's report, Add Mss 79849; M.A. tapes 13; Kenneth Clark, *The Other Half: A Self Portrait* (London: John Murray, 1977), p. 60.

4 H.V., *Leigh*, p. 173; Godfrey Winn, *The Positive Hour* (London: Joseph, 1970), p. 388.

5 T.O., *My Father*, p. 141; D.G. tapes, interview with John Mills.

6 Lewis, *Olivier*, p. 182; Spoto, *Olivier*, p. 180; *Confessions*, p. 172; Richard Olivier, *Shadow of the Stone Heart: A Search for Manhood* (London: Pan, 1995), p. 87.

7 *Confessions*, p. 173; M.A. tapes 21 and 34.

8 M.A. tapes 56; Dundy, *Finch*, p. 182; Kiernan, *Olivier*, p. 249.

9 *Confessions*, p. 201; M.A. tapes 56.

10 M.A. tapes 56.

11 Gielgud to Mrs. Gielgud, 20/12/50, Add Mss 81310; Gielgud, *Letters*, p. 140.

12 *Confessions*, p. 181; M.A. tapes 21; John Mason Brown, *As They Appear* (London: Hamilton, 1953), p. 91; Olivier to Wilson, 28/2/51, Add Mss 80049.

13 Byam Shaw to L.O., 9/3/51, Add Mss 79778.

14 H.V., *Leigh*, p. 202.

15 M.A. tapes 42; L.O. to Miss Huflet, 24/7/70, Add Mss 80050.

16 Tynan, *Evening Standard*, 11/7/51; Harold Nicolson, *Diaries and Letters 1945–1962*, ed. Nigel Nicolson (London: Collins, 1968), p. 208.

17 Tennessee Williams, *Five O'Clock Angel: Letters of Tennessee Williams to Maria St. Just, 1948–1982* (London: Deutsch, 1991), p. 51; M.A. tapes 21; L.O. to Dent, 4/1/52, Add Mss 79770; L.O. to J.E., 6/3/52, Add Mss 88951/1/1.

18 *Confessions*, pp. 186–9; M.A. tapes 20.

19 Interview with J.P.; L.O. to del Giudice, 18/2/52, Add Mss 79769; L.O. to Lord Mayor, undated, Add Mss 79866.

20 Correspondence on Add Mss 79914 and 79830.

21 O'Brian to Churchill, 18/6/51, CHUR 2/531; L.O. to Aylmer, 16/3/50, Add Mss 79910.

22 Thompson to L.O., 25/2/49 and L.O. to Thompson, undated, Add Mss 80367; Tennant to editor *Evening News*, 2/6/51, Add Mss 80367.

23 L.O. to editor *This Month*, 15/11/45, L.O. to Metcalfe, 16/10/46, Add Mss 79895; Dent to Tennant, 29/7/48, Add Mss 79981.

24 L.O. to Barker, 18/7/53, Add Mss 80367; M.A. tapes 16; *Memo from David O. Selznick*, p. 144.

25 Herman, *Wyler*, pp. 328–9.

26 J. C. Trewin, *Peter Brook: A Biography* (London: Macdonald and Co., 1971), p. 69; *Confessions*, pp. 194–5; Peter Brook, *Threads of Time: A Memoir* (London: Methuen Drama, 1998), pp. 99–100.

27 Brook, *Threads of Time*, pp. 99–100; *Confessions*, p. 195.

CHAPTER THIRTEEN

1 R.O., *Stone Heart*, p. 4; Meyer, *Not Prince Hamlet*, pp. 260–1; Tynan, *Tynan*, p. 222.

2 Lewenstein to J.P., 12/7/89, Add Mss 79875; Bragg, *Olivier*, p. 10.

3 Billie Whitelaw, *Billie Whitelaw—Who He?: An Autobiography* (London: Hodder & Stoughton, 1995), p. 89; M.A. tapes 1.

4 22/2/52, Add Mss 79896.

5 L.O.P. Board Meeting of 29/1/53, Add Mss 79987; *Confessions*, p. 207; Gourlay, *Olivier*, p. 132.

6 Michael Darlow, *Terence Rattigan: The Man and His Work* (London: Quartet Books, 2010), pp. 304–5; Gourlay, *Olivier*, p. 133; Tynan, *Daily Sketch*, 6/11/53.

7 Fairweather, *Cry God For Larry*, p. 22.

8 V.L. to Mu Richardson, undated, Add Mss 82044.

9 Baddeley, *Daily Sketch*, 11/12/53; Kiernan, *Olivier*, p. 252; M.A. tapes 19.

10 M.A. tapes 9; Croall, *Gielgud*, p. 389.

11 Nicolson, *Diaries and Letters*, p. 292; Williams, *Diaries*, p. 118; M.A. tapes 19.

12 John Gielgud, *An Actor and His Time* (London: Sidgwick and Jackson, 1979), p. 176.

13 Interview with Trader Faulkner; Croall, *Gielgud*, p. 391; Gielgud, *An Actor and His Time*, p. 184; Spoto, *Olivier*, p. 220; Gielgud, *Letters*, p. 180.

14 Coward, *Diaries*, p. 266; Gielgud to L.O., 12/4/55, Add Mss 80299; Gielgud, *Letters*, p. 180; M.A. tapes 21.

15 Byam Shaw to L.O., 24/6/58, Add Mss 80299; M.A. tapes 21; Winn, *Positive Hour*, p. 383; D.G. tapes, interview with Fry; Kennneth Tynan, *Curtains: Selections from the Drama Criticism and Related Writings* (New York: Atheneum, 1961), p. 98; Gielgud, *Letters*, p. 180.

16 M.A. tapes 21; Hobson, *Sunday Times*, 12/6/55; M.A. tapes 13; Interview with Patrick Garland.

17 M.A. tapes 16.

18 Eliot, *cit.* J. C. Trewin, *The Night Has Been Unruly* (London: Robert Hale, 1957), p. 260; L.O. to Rathbone, 14/3/49, Add Mss 79777; L.O. to Blakely, 29/2/72, Add Mss 80394; Brook, *Threads of Time*, pp. 102–3; *Confessions*, p. 215; Brook to L.O., Aug 1955, Add Mss 79766.

19 Tynan, *Observer*, 21/8/55; Gielgud, *Letters*, p. 188; M.A. tapes 21.

20 Gielgud, *Letters*, p. 188; Coward, *Diaries*, pp. 279–80.

21 L.O. to Mu Richardson, 14/9/55, Add Mss 82045; H.V., *Leigh*, p. 230; Faulkner, *Finch*, pp. 159 and 162; Dundy, *Finch*, pp. 202–3; Walton, *Walton*, p. 202.

22 Coward, *Diaries*, p. 308; Coward, *Letters*, pp. 614–18.

23 *Daily Sketch*, 13/7/56; T.O., *My Father*, p. 183.

24 L.O. to T.O., 13/7/56, T.O. papers.

25 L.O. to Walton, 5/12/57, Add Mss 79777.

CHAPTER FOURTEEN

1 M.A. tapes 42; Note by Furse, P.H. papers; Munn, *Niven*, p. 155.

2 Screenplay, Quaritch Catalog, Item 161; Davis to Cecil Tennant, 6/11/57, P.H. papers.

3 Correspondence on Add Mss 80508; *The Selected Letters of William Walton*, ed. Malcolm Hayes (London: Faber, 2002), p. 309; Note by Furse, P.H. papers.

4 L.O. to Walton, 29/7/58, Add Mss 79779; T.O., *My Father*, pp. 221–2; Furse to L.O., 14/7/58, Add Mss 79771.

5 L.O. to Saint-Denis, 17/3/55, Add Mss 79778; Eliot to L.O., 23 and 24/11/56, Add Mss 79770; L.O. to Mankiewicz, 8/1/56, Mankiewicz to L.O., 13/1/56, Cecil Tennant to Lew Wasserman, 25/4/56, P.H. papers.

6 L.O. to Kubrick, 23/11/59, P.H. papers; Miles, *Serves Me Right*, p. 30.

7 Meyer, *Not Prince Hamlet*, p. 161.

8 Nicolson, *Diaries and Letters 1945–62*, p. 269.

9 L.O. to T.O., 29/4/56 and 1/11/53, T.O. papers.

10 *Confessions*, pp. 218–19.

11 Geoffrey Wansell, *Terence Rattigan* (London: Fourth Estate, 1995), p. 288.

12 Colin Clark, *The Prince, the Showgirl and Me: The Colin Clark Diaries* (London: HarperCollins, 1995), p. 40; Coward, *Letters*, p. 619.

13 Kanin to L.O., 12/7/56, Add Mss 79773; Clark, *The Prince, the Showgirl*, p. 162.

14 H.V., *Leigh*, p. 240.

15 Croall, *Sybil Thorndike*, p. 415; Clark, *The Prince, the Showgirl*, p. 158; Arthur Miller, *Timebends: A Life* (London: Methuen, 1988), pp. 418–20.

16 M.A. tapes 22.

17 Coward, *Letters*, p. 619; Michael Blakemore, *Arguments With England: A Memoir* (London: Faber, 2004), pp. 155, 156–7, 159.

18 M.A. tapes 16; Interview with Lord Norwich.

19 Blakemore, *Arguments With England*, pp. 162–3; M.A. tapes 21; L.O., Diary, 3/6/57, Add Mss 79797.

20 M.A. tapes 36; Barrault to L.O., 25/3/54, Add Mss 79766.

21 *At the Royal Court: 25 Years of the English Stage Company*, ed. Richard Findlater (Ambergate: Amber Lane, 1981), p. 40.

22 See, in particular, Billington, *State of the Nation,* pp. 93–4; Gaskill, *Sense of Direction,* p. 13; Hobson, *Theater in Britain,* p. 183.

23 Miller, *Timebends,* pp. 416–17; *Confessions,* pp. 232–3; John Osborne, *Almost a Gentleman: An Autobiography: Volume II* (London: Faber, 1991), p. 28.

24 Gourlay, *Olivier,* pp. 146–9; Gaskill, *Sense of Direction,* p. 82.

25 L.O. to John Cummock, 13/11/57, Add Mss 80087; M.A. tapes 36 and 58; D.G. tapes, interview with Jocelyn Herbert.

26 Gaskill to L.O., 14/3/66, Add Mss 79908; Osborne, *Almost a Gentleman,* p. 35; Hobson, *Sunday Times,* 14/4/57; Joan Plowright, *And That's Not All* (London: Weidenfeld and Nicolson, 2001), p. 50; Osborne to L.O., 10/4/57, Add Mss 79776.

27 M.A. tapes 7; Osborne, *Almost a Gentleman,* p. 81.

28 Parton to L.O., 24/10/57, Add Mss 80087.

29 Osborne, *Almost a Gentleman,* p. 41; *TV Times,* Vol. 137, No. 52.

30 Coward, *Diaries,* p. 431.

CHAPTER FIFTEEN

1 Elsom and Tomalin, *National Theater,* p. 112; M.A. tapes 16.

2 Rae to L.O., 2/6/58, Add Mss 80367.

3 Wolfit to L.O., 31/3/57, Add Mss 79780; Harwood, *Wolfit,* p. 237; L.O. to Tynan, 5/4/47, Add Mss 79779; Wolfit to L.O., 24/7/57, Add Mss 79780; Tynan papers, Add Mss 87804.

4 *Confessions,* p. 240; M.A. tapes 14.

5 M.A. tapes 14; L.O. to Cecil Tennant, 25/3/58, P.H. papers; L.O. to T.O., 26/1/59, Add Mss 80951/1/2.

6 Charlton Heston, *The Actor's Life: Journals, 1956–1976,* ed. Hollis Alpert (New York: Dutton, 1978), pp. 81 and 84–9.

7 Coward, *Diaries,* p. 436; D.G. tapes, interview with Peter Sallis; Peter Allen to Granger, 16/4/96, D.G. papers.

8 D.G. tapes, interview with Sallis; L.O. to Welles, 13/11/52, Add Mss 80064; M.A. tapes 42.

9   D.G. tapes, interview with Sallis; Barbara Leaming, *Orson Welles: A Biography* (London: Weidenfeld and Nicolson, 1985), pp. 456–7, and see Simon Callow, *My Life in Pieces*, p. 284; Peter Hall, *Making an Exhibition of Myself* (London: Sinclair-Stevenson, 1993), p. 125.

10 Coward, *Letters*, pp. 648–9; Lauren Bacall, *Now* (London: Century, 1994), p. 162; L.O. to T.O., 28/8/60, Add Mss 88951/1/2; Stewart Granger, *Sparks Fly Upward* (London: Granada, 1981), p. 400; Kempson to L.O., 30/3/60, Add Mss 80619; J.P., *And That's Not All*, p. 65.

11 D.G. tapes, interview with Blakemore; Bacall, *Now,* p. 161.

12 D.G. tapes, interview with Sallis; Fairweather, *Cry God for Larry*, p. 35.

13 Fairweather, *Cry God for Larry*, pp. 27–8; L.O. to T.O., 28/8/60, Add Mss 88951/1/2; L.O. to J.E., 4/10/60, Add Mss 88951/1/1; Denison, H.V. papers.

14 L.O. to Kanin, undated, Add Mss 79773; V.L. to T.O., 19/2/60, Add Mss 88951/3; V.L. to L.O., 20/6/60, Add Mss 80618.

15 L.O. to T.O., 13/12/58, T.O. papers; Interview with T.O.

16 L.O. to T.O., undated, T.O. papers; Coward, *Diaries*, p. 494.

17 T.O., *My Father*, p. 239.

CHAPTER SIXTEEN

1   L.O. to H. T. Patterson, 18/2/52, Add Mss 79935.

2   Leslie Evershed-Martin, *The Impossible Theater: The Chichester Festival Theater Adventure* (Chichester: Phillimore, 1971), pp. 176, viii and 77–8.

3   Evershed-Martin, *Impossible Theater*, p. 79; Interview with J.P.

4   Croall, *Thorndike*, p. 451; Interview with J.P.; M.A. tapes 43.

5   L.O. to J.P., undated, Add Mss 80306.

6   D.G. tapes, interview with Rosemary Harris.

7   Claire Bloom, *Leaving a Doll's House: A Memoir* (London: Virago, 1996), p. 125; L.O. to Redgrave, undated, Redgrave papers, THM/31/3/5; Bloom to L.O., 4/6/63, L.O. to Bloom, 11/6/63, Add Mss 80400.

8   Berkoff to L.O., undated, L.O. to Berkoff, 3/4/62, Berkoff to L.O., 30/4/76, Add Mss 80394.

9   L.O. to Pinter, 2/8/62, Add Mss 80303; L.O. to Hobson, undated, Add Mss 80367.

10 Evershed-Martin, *Impossible Theater*, p. xiv; L.O. to Lucette Andrieu, 4/6/68, Add Mss 79899.

11 Chichester to L.O., 3/7/62, Add Mss 80303; M.A. tapes 27; *Observer*, 15/7/62.

12 M.A. tapes 27; Evershed-Martin, *Impossible Theater*, p. xvi; Croall, *Thorndike*, p. 455.

13 *Sunday* and *Financial Times, cit.* J.P., *And That's Not All*, p. 107; M.A. tapes 16.

14 M.A. tapes 16.

15 M.A. tapes 26; Elsom and Tomalin, *National Theater*, pp. 109–10.

16 M.A. tapes 26; L.O. to T.O., 4/10/60, Add Mss 88951/1/2; Clark to L.O., 6/12/60, Add Mss 80366; M.A. tapes 28.

17 Timothy Bateson in *Olivier*, ed. Gourlay, p. 122; L.O. to David Lewin and Lewin to L.O., undated, Add Mss 80303.

18 Evershed-Martin to L.O., 1/2/63, L.O. to Evershed-Martin, 28/5/63, Add Mss 80303.

19 Hall to L.O., 26/9/59, Add Mss 80299; L.O. to Ossia Trilling, 17/2/61, Add Mss 79897; Interview with Peter Hall.

20 Stephen Fay, *Power Play: The Life and Times of Peter Hall* (London: Hodder & Stoughton, 1995), pp. 141–4; Hall to L.O., 30/1/62, L.O. to Hall, undated, Add Mss 80367.

21 Hall, *Olivier at Work*, p. 15.

22 *Daily Mail*, 7/12/62; Add Mss 79830; *Sunday Times*, 12/3/62; Coward, *Letters*, p. 597.

23 Miles, *Serves Me Right*, pp. 5–6 and 8.

24 Interview with D.G.; M.A. tapes 28 and 53; Interview with Sarah Miles.

25 *Daily Express*, 7/8/63; Coward, *Diaries*, p. 519.

26 L.O. diary, Add Mss 79797; Specialist Report of 15/3/63, L.O. to Dr. Dix Perkins, 21/3/63, Add Mss 79867A.

27 Hope to L.O., 29/9/61, Add Mss 80504.

28 N.T.B., 10/10/62, Add Mss 80318; Fay, *Power Play*, pp. 141–2.

29 D.G. tapes, interview with Michael Jayston.

CHAPTER SEVENTEEN

1 L.O. to T.O., 19/8/62, Add Mss 88951/1/2; L.O. to Guthrie, undated, Add Mss 79772; O'Connor, *Richardson*, p. 105; L.O. to T.O., 7/12/63, T.O. papers.

2 L.O. to Cottesloe, 2/8/62, Add Mss 80366; D.G. tapes, interview with Rupert Rhymes.

3 M.A. tapes 7.

4 M.A. tapes 33; Interview with J.P.; D.G. tapes, interview with Jocelyn Herbert.

5 Gaskill, *Olivier at Work*, p. 14; N.T.B., 11/2/63, Add Mss 80318.

6 *On Acting*, p. 29.

7 Bateson in *Olivier*, ed. Gourlay, p. 121; Interview with D.G.; L.O. to Harrison, 23/5/63, Add Mss 80396; Kenneth Williams, *Diaries*, p. 370.

8 Billington, *State of the Nation*, p. 140; Michael Feeney Callan, *Anthony Hopkins: In Darkness and Light* (London: Sidgwick & Jackson, 1993), pp. 96–7; Quentin Falk, *Anthony Hopkins: Too Good to Waste: A Biography* (London: Columbus, 1989), p. 30; N.T.B., 13/5/63, Add Mss 80318.

9 Richardson to L.O., 26/4/61, Add Mss 79777; O'Connor, *Richardson*, p. 150; M.A. tapes 28; L.O. to Richardson, 26/2/67, Add Mss 82045; Interview with Ronald Harwood.

10 Richard Eyre, *Talking Theater: Interviews with Theater People* (London: Nick Hern Books, 2009), p. 6; L.O. to Gielgud, 31/6/64 and 1/10/64, Add Mss 80402.

11 L.O. to Gielgud, 1/10/66, Add Mss 80395; L.O. to Worth, 28/11/67, Add Mss 80402.

12 L.O. to Scofield, 13/5/64 and 30/3/72, Add Mss 80399; Garry O'Connor, *Paul Scofield: The Biography* (London: Sidgwick & Jackson, 2002), p. 245; Interview with Peter Hall.

13 Gaskill, *Sense of Direction*, p. 57; D.G. tapes, interview with Gaskill.

14 Elsom and Tomalin, *National Theater*, p. 197; Stephens, *Knight Errant*, p. 73.

15 Jonathan Miller, *Subsequent Performances* (London: Faber, 1986), p. 91.

16 L.O. to Tynan, 21/8/62, Add Mss 79779.

17 L.O. to Tynan, 31/1/63, Add Mss 87879; Kenneth Tynan, *Letters*, ed. Kathleen Tynan (London: Weidenfeld & Nicolson, 1994), p. 293.

18 Osborne in *Olivier*, ed. Gourlay, p. 152.

19 D.G. tapes, interview with Edward Hardwicke; L.O. to Miss Jepson, 12/6/52, Add Mss 79767; L.O. to Tynan, 12/12/70, Add Mss 89884; Interview with R.O.

20 D.G. tapes, interview with Gaskill.

21 M.A. tapes 41.

CHAPTER EIGHTEEN

1 S.O. to L.O., 29/7/63, Add Mss 79891; M.A. tapes 27; Evershed-Martin to L.O., 28/5/63, Add Mss 80303; Battersby to D. Biart, 9/10/63, Add Mss 80303.

2 Evershed-Martin to L.O., 13/12/63, L.O. to Evershed-Martin, 15/1/65, Add Mss 79891.

3 Stephens, *Knight Errant*, pp. 85–6.

4 M.A. tapes 53; L.O. to Rogers, 1/1/65, D.G. papers.

5 L.O. to Topol, 14/5/69, Add Mss 79781; M.A. tapes 44; L.O. to Regina Berger, 24/3/52, Add Mss 80050.

6 Anna Massey, *Telling Some Tales* (London: Hutchinson, 2006), p. 94; M.A. tapes 12.

7 Fairweather, *Cry God for Larry*, p. 90.

8 Miller to J.P., undated, Add Mss 79875; Interview with Ronald Pickup; M.A. tapes 53.

9 D.G. tapes, interview with Edward Hardwicke; Tynan papers, Add Mss 87806.

10 Jolley to J.P., 11/7/89, Add Mss 79875; Callow, *My Life In Pieces*, p. 46, and Callow, *Being an Actor* (London: Methuen, 1984), p. 108.

11 Stephens, *Knight Errant*, p. 61.

12 M.A. tapes 53; Whitelaw, *Who He?*, pp. 90 and 99.

13 National Theater Liaison Committee, 5/6/73, Add Mss 80358.

14 Pickup to J.P., 15/7/89, Add Ms. 79875; Eyre, *Utopia*, p. 120.

CHAPTER NINETEEN

1 L.O. to Guthrie, 16/7/63, Add Mss 79772.

2 M.A. tapes 56 and 27; Interview with Gaskill.

3 M.A. tapes 27; Coward, *Diaries*, p. 548; O'Toole to L.O., 12/12/67 and 15/4/71, Add Mss 79776.

4 L.O. to Beckett, 10/11/65, Add Mss 87879; L.O. to Pamela Berry, 30/11/67, Add Mss 79766.

5 L.O. to Tynan, 16/5/63, Add Mss 80362.

6 M.A. tapes 32 and 45.

7 *On Acting*, p. 106; Miller and Thorndike in *Olivier*, ed. Gourlay, pp. 193 and 28.

8 Fairweather, *Cry God for Larry*, p. 104; Roy Hills, M.A. tapes 53; Interview with Tamsin Olivier.

9 T.O., *My Father*, p. 247; *Olivier at Work*, p. 76.

10 D.G. tapes, interview with John Mills; Stephens, *Knight Errant*, p. 71; Hayman, *Playback*, p. 163.

11 D.G. tapes, interview with Riggs O'Hara; M.A. tapes 32; Forbes, *That Despicable Race*, p. 299.

12 Michael Coveney, *Maggie Smith: A Bright Particular Star* (London: Gollancz, 1992), pp. 96–7; Interview with D.G.

13 Fry in *Olivier*, ed. Gourlay, pp. 127 and 153; Lewis, *Olivier*, p. 17; Callow, *Being an Actor*, p. 171.

14 L.O. to Julian Blaustein, undated, Add Mss 80499; Hayman, *Playback*, p. 164.

15 *On Acting*, p. 126; M.A. tapes 31; Callan, *Anthony Hopkins*, p. 99.

16 Shellard, *Tynan*, p. 293.

17 M.A. tapes 53.

18 Stephens, *Knight Errant*, p. 74, and see Coveney, *Maggie Smith*, p. 99; Interview with William Gaskill.

19 M.A. tapes 1; Anthony Shaffer, *So What Did You Expect?: A Memoir* (London: Picador, 2001), p. 169.

20 M.A. tapes 53; Coward, *Letters*, pp. 720–1 and *Diaries*, p. 575.

21 Coward, *Diaries*, p. 566, and *Letters*, p. 723.

22 M.A. tapes 54.

23 Hall, *Diaries*, p. 6; N.T.B. Minute 81/65 of 10/12/65, Add Mss 79976; Mortimer, *Olivier at Work*, p. 11; L.O. to David Lewin, 3/2/65, Add Mss 80499A.

24 Memo of 5/10/71, Add Mss 80325.

25 L.O. to Lord Vivian, 11/11/66, Add Mss 79917; Lord Chamberlain's Office to Tynan, 5/5/65, Add Mss 87879; L.O. to Tynan, 10/1/64, Add Mss 80362.

26 Miles, *Serves Me Right*, p. 241; Eyre, *Utopia*, p. 119.

27 Miles to L.O., 29/8/69, L.O. to Anthony Hampton, 5/9/69, L.O. to Miles, 10/10/69, Miles to L.O., 13/10/69, Add Mss 79908.

28 Eyre, *Talking Theater*, p. 50.

29 N.T.B., 19/11/63, Add Mss 80318.

30 L.O. to Plummer, 16/11/65, Add Mss 80398; Ian McKellen to L.O., 22/4/65, Add Mss 80397.

31 N.T.B. Finance Committee, 22/5/63, Add Mss 80318; L.O. to Tynan, 4/3/63, Add Mss 80362.

32 Hall to J.P., 8/12/63, Add Mss 79882; N.T.B., 13/1/64, Add Mss 80319; *Sunday Times*, Atticus column, 16/2/64; Fay, *Power Play*, pp. 162–3.

33 Tynan to L.O., undated and 24/2/65, Add Mss 80362; D.G. tapes, interview with Havelock-Allan.

34 Daubeny to L.O., 15/12/65, L.O. to Daubeny, undated, Add Mss 80367.

35 Trevelyan to L.O., 5/4/65, Add Mss 80420; L.O. to T.O., 17/1/66, Add Mss 88951/1/2; M.A. tapes 60.

36 Whitelaw, *Who He?*, p. 93; *Confessions*, p. 280.

37 L.O. to T.O., 17/1/66, Add Mss 88951/1/2.

CHAPTER TWENTY

1 Interview with T.O.; D.G. tapes, interview with Harris.

2 R.O., *Stone Heart*, p. 81; Interview with J.P.; L.O. to Grimes, 5/3/68, Add Mss 80303; Whitelaw, *Who He?*, p. 25.

3 Drake to J.P., 11/7/89, Add Mss 79874; L.O. to T.O., Dec 1961, Add Mss 88951/1/2.

4 R.O., *Stone Heart*, p. 89; Interview with J.P.

5 M.A. tapes 53; L.O. to T.O., 21/8/66, T.O. papers.

6 L.O. to Richardson, 26/2/67, Add Mss 82045; L.O. to Lewin, 3/2/65, Add Mss 80499A; S.O. to L.O., 29/7/63, Add Mss 79891; Interview with R.O.

7 L.O. to T.O., 12/2/61, Add Mss 88951/1/2; Tarquin Olivier, *So Who's Your Mother?* (Norwich: Michael Russell, 2012), p. 132.

8 L.O. to Beaumont, 25/4/65, D.G. papers; Interview with Mrs. Tovey, H.V. papers.

9 S. M. Whitteridge to L.O., 9/12/66, Add Mss 80619; Spoto, *Olivier*, p. 295; *Confessions*, p. 290; J.E. to T.O., 15/8/67, Add Mss 88951/2/1.

10 L.O. to Chandos, 13/7/67, CHAN 11 4/13 1; D.G. tapes, interview with Irina Tennant; M.A. tapes 34; Fairweather, *Cry God for Larry*, p. 167; Coward, *Diaries*, pp. 651–2.

11 Correspondence in Add Mss 79867A.

12 L.O. to Chandos, 13/7/67, CHAN 11 4/13 1; *Confessions*, p. 293.

13 L.O. to David Fairweather, undated, L.O. to *Sunday Times*, 29/5/69, L.O. to *Chichester Observer*, undated, Add Mss 80594.

14 N.T.B. 10/10/66 and 12/12/66, Add Mss 80321; L.O. to Arnold Weissberger, 16/3/66, Add Mss 79921.

15 D.G. tapes, interview with Charles Kay; M.A. tapes 32; Interview with Ronald Pickup; John Dexter, *The Honorable Beast: A Posthumous Autobiography* (London: Nick Hern Books, 1993), p. 19.

16 L.O. to Dexter, undated draft, Add Mss 80377.

17 M.A. tapes 39; Dexter to L.O., undated, Add Mss 79770.

18 Gaskill in *Olivier*, ed. Gourlay, p. 176; Interview with Gaskill; M.A. tapes 28.

19 Clark to Chandos, 3/8/66, CHAN 11 4/13 1; M.A. tapes 57.

20 *The Diaries of Kenneth Tynan*, ed. John Lahr (London: Bloomsbury, 2001), pp. 45 and 54–5.

21 N.T.B. 6/9/71, L.O. to Rae, 27/9/71, Add Mss 80325.

22 Richard Attenborough, *Entirely Up To You, Darling* (London: Hutchinson, 2008), p. 237; Attenborough to J.P., July 1989, Add Mss 79874.

23 M.A. tapes 38; Lewis, *Olivier*, p. 78.

24 Jacobi to L.O., undated, Add Mss 80396; Bates to L.O., February 1970, L.O. to Adams, 30/5/69, Add Mss 80394.

25 L.O. to Smith, 29/10/69, L.O. to Dunlop, 7/1/70, Add Mss 80402; Hallifax to L.O., 29/9/69, Smith to L.O., 27/1/70, Add Mss 80424.

26 L.O. to Byam Shaw, 22/10/68, Add Mss 80400.

CHAPTER TWENTY-ONE

1 Billington, *Modern Actor*, pp. 56–8; M.A. tapes 26.

2 Interview with Michael Blakemore, and D.G. tapes, interview with Blakemore.

3 Gourlay, *Olivier*, p. 182; L.O. to Lee, 2/11/69, Add Mss 79781.

4 McCartney to Tynan, 24/1/68, Add Mss 87881; Whitelaw, *Who He?*, p. 79; Devine to Tynan. 9/4/64, Add Mss 87878.

5 L.O. to Tynan, 12/4/64, Add Mss 87878.

6 Tynan to L.O., 3/1/66, Add Mss 87880; Harris to Chandos, 26/4/67, CHAN 114/13 1; Tynan to L.O., undated, Add Mss 87880.

7 Interview with J.P.; Tynan, *Tynan*, p. 253; Tynan to L.O., 14/12/66, Add Mss 80362.

8 Tynan, *Letters*, p. 360; M.A. tapes 32; Tynan, *Letters*, p. 398; N.T.B., 24/4/67, Add Mss 80322.

9 Memo of 26/4/67, Add Mss 80432; Tynan to Arden, 2/2/68, Add Mss 87881; L.O. to Tynan, 4/12/68, Add Mss 80363; Churchill to L.O., 23/12/68, Add Mss 80433; *The Times*, 20/1/69.

10 Chandos to L.O., 22/1/69, Add Mss 80433.

11 L.O. to Richardson, 26/2/67, Add Mss 82045; *Olivier at Work*, p. 46; Meyer, *Not Prince Hamlet*, p. 229; Tynan, *Letters*, p. 389.

12 M.A. tapes 31; L.O. to Richardson, 26/2/67, Add Mss 82045; Morley, *Olivier*, p. 152; Richard Findlater, *The Player Kings* (London: Weidenfeld & Nicolson, 1971), p. 232.

13 L.O. to Main, 19/2/68, Add Mss 80499A.

14 D.G. tapes, interview with Jane Lapotaire.

15 D.G. tapes, interviews with Lapotaire and Hardwicke.

16 Gielgud, B.B.C. Radio 4 interview, broadcast 3/6/00; Interview with Frank Dunlop.

17 *Confessions*, p. 287; L.O. to Brook, 21/5/68, Brook to L.O., 8/6/68, L.O. to Brook, 20/6/68, Add Mss 80377.

18 L.O. to Norman Baker, 9/3/70, Add Mss 89884; Stephens, Memo, 24/4/70, Add Mss 80434A; N.T.B. 11/5/70 and 8/6/70, Add Mss 80325; L.O. to Kanin, 9/6/70, and to Coward, 24/6/70, Add Mss 80434A.

19 L.O. to Kanin, 28/9/70 and 29/1/71, Add Mss 80434A; M.A. tapes 32.

20 Interview with Jonathan Miller; M.A. tapes 59 and 16; Miller, *Subsequent Performances*, p. 104; *On Acting*, p. 119.

21 D.G. tapes, interview with Lapotaire; *Confessions*, p. 302; Gielgud, *Letters*, p. 356; Tynan, *Letters*, p. 472.

22 M.A. tapes 57; D.G. tapes, interview with Constance Cummings; Interview with J.P.; Plummer, *In Spite of Myself*, p. 522.

23 D.G. tapes, interview with Cummings; Tynan, *Diaries*, p. 35.

24 Falk, *Hopkins*, p. 64; L.O. to Hopkins, 1/6/71, Add Mss 80396.

25 M.A. tapes 5 and 38; L.O. to Tynan, 10/3/70, Add Mss 89884.

26 L.O. to Tynan, 14/12/71, Add Mss 80363; Lewis, *Olivier*, p. 83.

27 D.G. tapes, interview with L.O.; Wardle, *The Times*, 22/12/71.

28 Tynan to L.O., 9/12/71, Add Mss 80363; D.G. tapes, interview with Adler.

CHAPTER TWENTY-TWO

1 Osborne in *Olivier*, ed. Gourlay, p. 151.

2 J.P., *And That's Not All*, pp. 185–6; N.T.B. 10/2/69, Add Mss 80323.

3 Tynan, *Letters*, p. 503; Richard Eyre, *National Service: Diary of a Decade* (London: Bloomsbury, 2003), p. 27.

4 Tynan, *Letters*, p. 503; L.O. to Tynan, 16/2/72, Add Mss 80363.

5 Chandos to L.O., 10/5/67, CHAN 11 4/13 1; Tynan, *Letters*, pp. 480–1.

6 N.T.B., 7/6/69, Chandos to L.O., 19/6/69, Add Mss 80363.

7 Tynan to L.O., 3/2/72, L.O. to Tynan, 10/3/72, Add Mss 80363; L.O. to Mrs. V. Green, 28/7/70, Add Mss 80363.

8 N.T.B. 13/7/70, Add Mss 80325.

9 L.O. to Evans, 30/10/68, Add Mss 80499A.

10 L.O. to Wilson, 14/5/67, CHAN 11 4/13 1; Wilson to L.O., 18/5/67, Add Mss 79864.

11 *The Richard Burton Diaries*, ed. Chris Williams (London: Yale University Press, 2012), p. 370; M.A. tapes 12; L.O. to various friends, 15/6/70, Add Mss 79864; Interview with J.P.

12 L.O. to Anthony Wagner, 31/7/70, Add Mss 79864.

13 *Confessions*, pp. 360–4; M.A. tapes 12; J.P., *And That's Not All*, p. 203; Interview with J.P.

14 N.T.B. 12/7/71, Add Mss 80325; Fay, *Peter Hall*, p. 214; Interview with J.P.

15 L.O. to Cottesloe, 8/8/66, Add Mss 80366.

16 O'Connor, *Scofield*, p. 257; Interview with J.P.

17 M.A. tapes 37; L.O. to Goodman, 5/2/70, Add Mss 80366.

18 *Richard Burton Diaries*, pp. 459–60; Burton to L.O., undated, Add Mss 79766.

19 M.A. tapes 37.

20 L.O. to Hall, 8/8/66 and 14/9/66, Add Mss 80361.

21 L.O. to Hall, 3/1/68, Hall to L.O., 11/2/68, Add Mss 80368.

22 M.A. tapes 59; L.O. to Shaffer, 16/9/69, Add Mss 87883.

23 M.A. tapes 59.

CHAPTER TWENTY-THREE

1 Callow, *Being an Actor*, p. 88; L.O. to Peter Brook, 29/8/68, Add Mss 80378; Billington, *Modern Actor*, pp. 199–200.

2 *Confessions*, p. 322; L.O. to Gillian Floyd, 11/5/49, Add Mss 79935; Munn, *Lord Larry*, p. 231.

3 Interview with Tom Stoppard.

4 Interview with D.G.; Baxter, *Evening Standard*, 21/1/49.

5 Interview with J.P.; Elsom and Tomalin, *National Theater*, pp. 234–5.

6 Hall, *Diaries*, p. xi; J.P., *And That's Not All*, p. 208.

7 L.O. to Rayne, 5/5/72, and Rayne to L.O., 8/5/72, Add Mss 80365.

8 J.P., *And That's Not All*, p. 209; J.P. to Tynan, 11/10/72, Add Mss 87886.

9 M.A. tapes 43.

10 Hall, *Diaries*, p. 3.

11 Hall, *Diaries*, p. 7; Lipman to L.O., 17/3/73, Add Mss 80401.

12 Kathleen Tynan, *Tynan*, p. 314; Hall, *Diaries*, pp. 7–8; Tynan, *Diaries*, p. 88; N.T.B. 8/5/72, Add Mss 80326.

13 Rayne to L.O., 14/4/72, Add Mss 80365; Hall, *Diaries*, p. 9.

14 Meeting of 25/4/72, Add Mss 80365; Worsley to L.O., 21/12/73, Add Mss 79780; L.O. to Keenan Wynn, 16/2/70, Add Mss 80505.

15 Shaffer, *So What Did You Expect?*, p. 61; Interview with J.P.

16 Shaffer, *So What Did You Expect?*, p. 78; Spoto, *Olivier*, p. 314; *Confessions*, p. 315; Michael Caine, *The Elephant to Hollywood* (London: Hodder & Stoughton, 2010), p. 175.

17 L.O. to Richardson, 3/5/72, and Richardson to L.O., 10/5/72, Add Ms. 79777; Kenneth Geist, *Pictures Will Talk: The Life and Films of Joseph L. Mankiewicz* (New York: Scribner, 1978), p. 378.

18 Caine, *Elephant to Hollywood*, p. 175.

19 L.O. to Pinter, 22/11/72, Add Mss 79777; Interview with J.P.

20 Memo for N.T.B. 12/3/73, Add Mss 80329; Furse to L.O., undated, Add Mss 79771.

21 L.O. to Hall, 1/3/73, Hall to L.O., undated, Add Mss 80361; L.O. to Hall, 6/9/72, Hall to L.O., 12/9/72, Add Mss 80329.

22 L.O. to Rayne, 6/2/73, Rayne to L.O., 20/2/73, Add Mss 80365.

23 J.P. to Dexter, 31/10/72, Add Mss 79882; Tynan, *Diaries*, p. 119.

24 Hall, *Diaries*, pp. 33 and 38.

25 Hall, *Diaries*, p. 71.

26 Hall to L.O., 25/1/74, L.O. to Hall, undated, Add Mss 80361.

27 Hall, *Diaries*, p. 12.

28 Tynan, *Diaries*, p. 119; Simon Callow, *The National: The Theater and its Work 1963–97* (London: Nick Hern Books, 1997), p. 42.

29 M.A. tapes 57; D.G. tapes, interview with Boddington; Tynan, *Diaries*, p. 119.

30 Tynan, *Diaries*, p. 160; Atkins to L.O., 1/3/73, Add Mss 79766; M.A. tapes 57.

31 Grainger, *The Independent*, 18/5/07.

CHAPTER TWENTY-FOUR

1 Hall, *Diaries*, p. 31.

2 Hall, *Diaries*, p. 110.

3 Hall, *Diaries*, pp. 46 and 74; Interview with J.P.

4 Hall, *Diaries*, pp. 75, 233–4 and 243; O'Connor, *Richardson*, p. 206.

5 L.O. to Robert Flemyng, 29/11/77, Add Mss 79910; *Stage and Television Today*, 18/12/77; Andrew Denham and Mark Garnett, *Keith Joseph* (Chesham: Acumen, 2002), p. 268; Interview with J.P.

6 L.O. to *The Times*, 21/5/73; L.O. to Rosemary Winckley, undated, Winckley to L.O., 3/10/74, Add Mss 79792.

7 L.O. to Hall, 4/11/74, Add Mss 80361; M.A. tapes 53; Hall, *Diaries*, p. 150.

8 Gielgud, *Letters*, p. 422; Hall to L.O., 7/10/75, L.O. to Hall, 17/10/75, Add Mss 80361.

9 Hall, *Diaries*, pp. 58, 34 and 40.

10 Eyre, *Talking Theater*, p. 50; Hall to L.O., 17/5/76, L.O. to Hall, 20/5/76, Add Mss 80361; Tynan, *Diaries*, pp. 190 and 384.

11 Hall, *Diaries*, pp. 264 and 266; Tynan, *Diaries*, p. 384.

12 M.A. tapes 3; L.O. to Rayne, 6/9/74, Add Mss 80356; L.O. to Hall, 8/7/75, Add Mss 80361.

13 L.O. to Weidenfeld, 27/2/81, Add Mss 80579; *Confessions*, p. 323; D.G. tapes, interview with Alan Davis.

14 Munn, *Lord Larry*, p. 240; *Confessions*, p. 329; D.G. to Tynan, undated, Add Mss 87804.

15 D.G. tapes, interview with Peter Sallis.

16 D.G. tapes, interview with John Schlesinger.

17 William Goldman, *Adventures in the Screen Trade: A Personal View of Hollywood and Screenwriting* (London: Macdonald, 1984), p. 246.

18 Spoto, *Olivier*, p. 328.

19 L.O. to Cukor, 17/9/75, Add Mss 79768; Munn, *Lord Larry*, p. 242; D.G. tapes, interview with John Schlesinger.

20 Goldman, *Adventures in the Screen Trade*, p. 248; Hall, *Diaries*, p. 274; *On Acting*, p. 225.

21 M.A. tapes 7.

22 Walton, *Letters*, p. 451; L.O. to T.O., 22/10/78, Add Mss 88951/1/2; Tynan, *Diaries*, p. 384; Michael Palin, *Halfway to Hollywood: Diaries 1980–1988* (London: Weidenfeld & Nicolson, 2009), p. 144.

CHAPTER TWENTY-FIVE

1 L.O. to Darleen Rubin, 29/9/79, Add Mss 79867A; *On Acting*, p. 225.

2 Interview with R.O.; Tamsin Olivier to L.O., 4/3/80, Add Mss 79889.

3 Interview with D.G.; J.E. to T.O., 22/3/78, Add Mss 88951/2/1.

4 T.O., *So Who's Your Mother?*, p. 158; L.O. to Hiley, 25/6/79, P.H. papers; *On Acting*, pp. 242–3.

5 L.O. to Drake, 5/10/77, Add Mss 79770.

6 Interviews with J.P. and Laurence Harbottle.

7 M.A. tapes 8; Spoto, *Olivier*, pp. 334–5.

8 Sarah Miles, *Bolt from the Blue* (London: Orion, 1996), pp. 74, 88, 95 and 100.

9 Tynan, *Diaries*, pp. 224–5; Fairbanks to L.O., 25/6/82, Add Mss 79771.

10 Stephens, *Sunday Times*, 18/7/10; Interview with Hugh Whitemore; M.A. tapes 4.

11 M.A. tapes 9.

12 Peck to L.O., 13/8/79, Add Mss 79777; M.A. tapes 5; *Newsweek, cit.* Coleman, *Olivier*, p. 448.

13 M.A. tapes 5 and 20; Croall, *Gielgud*, p. 486; Flemyng to L.O., 5/3/82, Add Mss 79771.

14 Croall, *Gielgud*, pp. 507–8.

15 J.P., *And That's Not All*, p. 245; D.G. tapes, interview with Peter Sallis; D.G. tapes, interview with John Hurt; *Olivier at Work*, p. 8.

16 J.P., *And That's Not All*, p. 245; Plummer, *In Spite of Myself*, p. 599; Interview with George Hall.

17 L.O. to Donald Hall, 8/8/59, Add Mss 79897.

18 Tynan, *Letters*, pp. 591, 622, 625 and 631–2.

19 Kathleen Tynan, *Tynan*, p. 396; Miles, *Serves Me Right*, pp. 114–15. Hall, *Diaries*, p. 425 and 442; Tynan, *Letters*, pp. 631–2; L.O. to John Cottrell, 21/5/79, Add Mss 80590.

20 Hamilton to L.O., Easter 1974, Add Mss 79772; L.O. to J.E., 5/12/74, T.O. papers; Evans to L.O., 28/11/80, Add Mss 80579.

21 Interview with M.A.

22 Interview with M.A.; L.O. to Drake, 2/3/81 and 2/4/81, Add Mss 79770.

23 L.O. to Weidenfeld, 20/4/82 and 30/4/82, Add Mss 80579.

24 Billington, *Observer*, 17/10/82; Pickup to L.O., 6/12/82, Add Mss 79777; T.O., *My Father*, p. 253; Croall, *Gielgud*, p. 518; Rayne, *Sunday Telegraph*, 3/10/82.

25 Raine, *London Review of Books*, 4/2/83; Carey, *Sunday Times*, 17/10/82.

26 Note by Furse, P.H. papers; D.G. tapes, interviews with Mills and Havelock-Allan; Burton, *Diaries*, p. 636; L.O. to Richardson, undated, Add Mss 82045.

27 J.P., *And That's Not All*, p. 269.

CHAPTER TWENTY-SIX

1 D.G. tapes, interview with Mills.

2 Gielgud, *Letters*, p. 418; Sheridan Morley, *Our Theaters in the Eighties* (London: Hodder & Stoughton, 1990), pp. 135–6; Williams, *Diaries*, p. 764.

3 Shirley Luke to Gawn Grainger, 12/7/85, Add Mss 80589.

4 Niven to L.O., 14/4/82, Add Mss 79776; D.G. tapes, interview with Burton.

5 R.O., *Stone Heart*, pp. 3 and 153; *Daily Mirror*, 10/9/83; M.A. tapes 57.

6 Interview with Tom Stoppard; Eyre, *Utopia*, pp. 117–18.

7 Interview with Desmond Biddulph.

8 Interview with D.G.; Sheila Allen to J.P., 16/3/90, Add Mss 79883; Interview with J.P.

9   Piers Paul Read, *Alec Guinness: The Authorized Biography* (London: Simon & Schuster, 2003), pp. 567–8; Guinness to L.O., 11/12/83, Add Mss 79772.

10 Blakelock, *Round the Next Corner*, p. 54; Huggett, *Beaumont*, p. 275; Adrian in *Olivier*, ed. Gourlay, p. 41; L.O. to Hencher, 25/11/63, Add Mss 79935; Interview with R.O.

11 Add Mss 79868; Interview with Ronald Harwood.

12 Interviews with Blakemore and Grainger; Brandreth, *Gielgud*, p. 153.

13 R.O., *Stone Heart*, p. 9; D.G. tapes, interview with Jayston.

14 D.G. tapes, interview with Harris; Dexter, *Honorable Beast*, p. 286.

15 Croall, *Gielgud*, p. 530; Gielgud, *Letters*, p. 473.

Acknowledgments

My first acknowledgment must go to Laurence Olivier's widow, Joan Plowright. Without her support I would have never have undertaken this book. She has been unfailingly helpful, has shown me papers not previously made available to researchers, has not hesitated to point out when she disagrees with my interpretation of events, but has never sought to impose her view. Biographers traditionally shudder when confronted by the widow or widower of their subject; I have only had reason to rejoice in the existence of mine.

Tarquin Olivier, Laurence Olivier's son by his first wife, Jill Esmond, has been similarly helpful. His advice has been invaluable and he has kindly made available to me a highly important cache of papers, particularly rich in letters between his father and mother. Laurence Olivier's three children by Joan Plowright—Richard, Tamsin and Julie Kate—have been equally tolerant of what they must have considered with some gloom, as yet one more book about their father. Richard Olivier's *Shadow of the Stone Heart* provided some perceptive insights into his father's personality and relationship with his children.

Mark Amory interviewed Laurence Olivier for many weeks in preparatory work for Olivier's autobiography. More than fifty hours of these interviews survive on tape and he has most kindly let me listen to them. Day after day I have had Olivier in my study, speaking with sometimes alarming candor about every aspect of his life and career. My biography has been immeasurably enriched as a result.

Derek Granger for a long time worked on what was to be Laurence Olivier's official biography. His personal recollections of Olivier have been of great interest and he has allowed me access to his treasure trove of manuscript material, much of it unavailable elsewhere. Even more important, he has let me listen to the tapes of the interviews that he conducted while working on the book; many of which, for a variety of reason, I would have been unable to repeat.

Hugo Vickers has written by far the most substantial biography of Vivien Leigh. He is a researcher of immense resourcefulness and has accumulated a highly important archive of unpublished material. It is my good fortune that his skill in the accumulation of material is matched by his generosity in sharing it with others.

The late Peter Hiley for many years worked closely with Laurence Olivier. I much wish that I had been in time to speak with him. I am most grateful to his son, Will Hiley, for allowing me to study the important collection of papers that he has inherited.

Michael Reddington, who as a young actor went with the Oliviers to Australasia in 1948, has allowed me to read the letters that he wrote home to his parents during the tour.

Ronald Harwood did me the signal kindness of reading this book in draft so as to pick up the errors and omissions that I feared my lack of theatrical background might have caused. Those that remain are, of course, entirely my responsibility.

Maggie Smith was kind enough to read the many passages in my book in which she featured. Generally she accepted them; though with the caveat that her final relationship with Olivier was more friendly than the record of her many clashes with him might have suggested was the case. Peter O'Toole also read the extracts in which he featured. He considered that they gave "an entirely false account of what actually happened" but did not feel disposed to divulge in what way they differed from his own recollections.

All biographers must owe a debt to those who have worked in the field before them. Nearly every book about Olivier contains at least one nugget of information that I would not have been able to obtain from other sources. The most considerable of previous biographies is that by Terry Coleman. I have benefited signally from his labors.

Archivists and keepers of public papers are nearly always helpful in their advice and generous in the time that they spare researchers. Kathryn Johnson of the British Library has far exceeded what might have been expected of her: her contribution to this book has been of inestimable importance. Gavin Clarke of the National Theater Archive was similarly helpful.

My old friend and publisher, Christopher MacLehose, has been indefatigable in his efforts to improve my text. He is a great editor; if his handwriting was as clear as his mind he would be the perfect one. To him, to his assistant, Paul Engles, and to the copy editor, Nick de Somogyi, my obligation is enormous.

Many others have in one way or another contributed to my work: notably Desmond Biddulph, Michael Blakemore, Roger Braban, Simon Callow, Frank Dunlop, Mary Evans, Suzanne Farrington, Trader Faulkner, Frank Finlay, Patrick Garland, William Gaskill, Gawn Grainger, George Hall, Peter Hall, Laurence Harbottle, Rohan McCullough, Sarah Miles, Jonathan Miller, Ronald Pickup, Tom Stoppard, John Ure, Moray Watson, Hugh Whitemore and Joan Winterkorn. The list is not complete. There has been a sad breakdown in my filing system. I hope that anyone whose name I have omitted will forgive my incompetence.

Index

Abbreviations Used in Index

J.E.	Jill Esmond
J.P.	Joan Plowright
L.O.	Laurence Olivier
N.T.	National Theater
R.S.C.	Royal Shakespeare Company
T.O.	Tarquin Olivier

Picture Credits

PHILIP ZIEGLER was born in 1929 and educated at Eton and Oxford. He was a diplomat before becoming an editorial director at the publishers William Collins. His many books include acclaimed biographies of William IV, Lady Diana Cooper, Lord Mountbatten and Harold Wilson, as well as the classic history of the Black Death.